AF837012

The German Ocean

Studies in the Archaeology of Medieval Europe

Series Editor: Neil Christie, University of Leicester
Founding Editor: John Schofield

This series offers a range of volumes which explore the archaeology of medieval Europe (c. AD 1100 to 1600). Our knowledge of this period has been transformed by the results of excavations (rescue and research), landscape studies, closer analyses of material cultures, and architectural studies, but appreciation of the scale and impact of such new work is arguably limited. This series is a vehicle to generate publications which highlight the evolving archaeological image of territories across Europe, to help show connections, differences and transitions between regions, to question identities and to reveal the qualities of the evidence. From these we will be able to build a more complete, if undoubtedly complex understanding of an emergent Europe and explore cultural, economic and religious ties.

The series is made up of three strands: Territories—This will include studies of modern countries, such as Spain, but also of connected regions such as the North Sea. Great Towns—This examines the archaeology of key towns and cities that shaped kingdoms, trade and religion. Themes—Here, pan-European topics are explored, such as castle building, monastic expressions, rural life, health, pilgrimage, metalworking.

Published

Castles and Landscape: Power, Community and Fortification in Medieval England
O.H. Creighton

Medieval Towns: The Archaeology of British Towns in their European Setting
John Schofield and Alan Vince

London 1100–1600: The Archaeology of a Capital City
John Schofield and Alan Vince

The Archaeology of Medieval Spain, 1100–1500
Magdalena Valor and Avelino Gutiérrez

The Archaeology of Prague and the Medieval Czech Lands, 1100–1600
Jan Klápště

Forthcoming

Medieval Visby and Gotland:
The History and Archaeology of a Baltic Metropolis in its Context
Anders Andrén

The Archaeology of Medieval Sicily: Cultures, Social Structures, Economies
Alessandra Molinari

The Archaeology and Architecture of Monastic Ireland, 1100–1600
Tadhg O'Keeffe

The Archaeology of Stari Bar: The Evolution, Dissolution and Reinvention of an Adriatic Town
Sauro Gelichi

The German Ocean: Medieval Europe around the North Sea

Brian Ayers

equinox

SHEFFIELD UK BRISTOL CT

Published by Equinox Publishing Ltd.

UK: Unit S3, Kelham House, 3 Lancaster Street, Sheffield S3 8AF

USA: ISD, 70 Enterprise Drive, Bristol, CT 06010

www.equinoxpub.com

First published, 2016. First printing in paperback, 2018

ISBN 978-1-904768-49-4 (hardback)
ISBN 978-1-78179-722-8 (paperback)

British Library Cataloguing-in-Publication Data
A catalogue record for this book is available from the British Library.

Library of Congress Cataloging-in-Publication Data

Ayers, Brian.
The German Ocean : Medieval Europe around the North Sea / Brian Ayers.
pages cm. — (Studies in the archaeology of medieval Europe)
Includes bibliographical references and index.
LCCN 2016002900 (print) | LCCN 2016007870 (ebook)
ISBN 9781904768494 (hardback) | ISBN 9781781794401 (e-PDF) | ISBN 9781781794418 (e-epub)
North Sea Region—Antiquities. | Europe, Northern—Antiquities. | North Sea Region—History.
Europe, Northern—History. | Material culture—North Sea Region—History.
Regionalism—North Sea Region—History. | North Sea Region—Commerce—History.
North Sea Region—Economic conditions. | Social archaeology—North Sea Region.
I. Title.
LCC DL46.A94 2016 (print) | LCC DL46 (ebook) | DDC 948/.02—dc23
LC record available at http://lccn.loc.gov/2016002900

Typeset and edited by Queenston Publishing, Hamilton, Ontario, Canada

Printed by Lightning Source Inc. (La Vergne, TN), Lightning Source UK Ltd. (Milton Keynes),
Lightning Source AU Pty. (Scoresby, Victoria)

Dedicated to the memory of my wife

Robina McNeil

1950–2007

A fine archaeologist, a creative artist and a passionate person

‘It is said that all isles and continents ... are so seated, that there is non but that, from some shore of it, another may be discovered ... Every one hath so much relation to some other, that it hath not only use often of the aide of what is next to it, but through that, also of what is out of ken to it’.

John Selden 1584–1654
English jurist and historian

Contents

List of Maps

List of Figures

Acknowledgements

This book explores an extensive region and has only been made possible through the kindness and assistance of many friends and colleagues both in Britain and on the continent. These friends and colleagues have taken me to sites and buildings, provided me with information, discussed discoveries and ideas, argued with passion on occasion, tolerated my lack of understanding on others, and above all shared in a desire to know more about the extraordinary and varied region within which we are privileged to live and work.

My first debt is to John Schofield who asked me to contribute to the Equinox series *The Archaeology of Medieval Europe*. He was kind enough to say that he knew that I could write and so I hope that this much delayed work justifies the faith that he had in me. My second debt is Janet Joyce and Valerie Hall of Equinox Publishing who commissioned the book and have been steadfast in their patience as it moved from delay to delay in preparation. No writer can have had a more supportive publisher and for this I am very grateful. My thanks also go to Neil Christie who took over from John as general editor at a late stage in the preparation of this book and has been both thoughtful and commendably restrained in his comments on my efforts.

When John asked me to write the book, he said that he wanted me to bring the content of the Lübeck colloquia entitled *Stadtarchäologie im Hanseraum* (Urban Archaeology in the Hanseatic Region) to a wider audience. These meetings and their subsequent publications are referred to in the introduction, with the data supplied by them underpinning much that follows. The colloquia were established in 1995 by Manfred Gläser, head of Bereich Archäologie Lübeck, and it has been my great good fortune to attend nine of the ten meetings that have been held. These wide-ranging colloquia have been immensely valuable in broadening my understanding of north European archaeology and have introduced me to colleagues from a dozen countries, many of whom I am lucky enough to now call my friends. I am very grateful to Manfred and to his colleagues, Manfred Schneider and Alfred Falk. These thanks need also to be extended to the Hanseatic City of Lübeck which has generously supported the colloquia financially since their inception. The published results are a splendid example of investment by a public body in wider dissemination of our common European heritage.

My introduction to Manfred Gläser resulted from a recommendation made by David Evans, only one of many kindnesses that Dave has shown to me. He and I have had parallel careers, both of us of working in the cities of Hull and Norwich, he in the former for much of his career, I in the latter for much of mine. Dave's knowledge of the archaeology of Hull and Beverley is unrivalled but he is also something of a polymath, writing extensively on matters such as the overseas trade of Hull and, as importantly, always happy to answer questions and discuss ideas. His contributions to all ten of the Lübeck colloquia are fine examples of the breadth of his interests and I am most grateful to him for all his help towards me.

The list of those who have helped me through discussion, the sending of information, and hospitality is long. I am very grateful indeed to all of the following: David Adams; Betty Arndt; Steven Ashley; Michiel Bartels; Peter Bitter; Alice Cattermole; Pamela Cawthorne; Wendy Childs; David Dobson; Wolfgang Ebert; Anton Ervynck; David Gaimster; Elly Gietema; Tsjeard Gietema; Jenny Glazebrook ; Gitte Hansen; Palle Birk Hansen; Sandy Heslop; Stephen Heywood; Carole Hill; Jesper Hjermind; Richard Hodges; Maurice Hurley; Jakob Kiefer-Olsen; Anna Kowalska; Alice Leftley; Helen Lunnon; Ailsa Mainman; Petter Molaug; Hans Moll; Joachim Müller; Ulrich Müller; Magdalena Naum; Grażyna Nawrolska; Ieve Ose; Tim Pestell; Jerzy Piekalski; Carole Rawcliffe; Marian Rębkowski; Anders Reisnert; Mats Roslund; Paul Richards; Dirk Rieger; Edgar Ring; Erki Russow; Elizabeth Rutledge; Andy Shelley; Hans Skov; Morten Søvsø; Jan Stobbe; Dries Tys; Johan Veeckman; Hubert de Witte; and colleagues at the Lübeck colloquia. I owe a particular debt of thanks to David Stocker who has opened my eyes to much as well as kindly providing me with rich sources of material.

The multinational nature of the above list is a reminder of how very fortunate I am to be a native English speaker and of how generous all the above colleagues are to converse with me in that language. This privilege has helped me greatly. Danish, Dutch, Estonian, Flemish, German, Norwegian, Polish and Swedish friends and colleagues have made this book possible, not least from detailed discussions in English. I am particularly grateful to Dirk Rieger who has most kindly produced the four maps showing the main sites referred to in the text. Without him, therefore, many of the sites mentioned in the text would be difficult to locate.

Betty Arndt and Manfred Schneider cornered me one day in Lübeck and insisted that I become a member of the *Deutsche Gesellschaft für die Archäologie des Mittelalters und der Neuzeit* (DGAMN or the German Society for the Archaeology of the Medieval and Post-Medieval Periods). I did so, joining a small cadre of English members which, at the time, I believe consisted of Dave Evans, David Gaimster and myself. Joining DGAMN was an excellent thing to do, as the annual thematic publications of the society (resulting from its peripatetic meetings held across Germany) have been a rich resource for my research. Commendably, as well as print editions, these volumes are also published freely online, again helping research greatly.

Online access has been afforded to me through the library of the University of East Anglia in Norwich, a facility which is akin to a marvellous gift. The library of the Society of Antiquaries in London has also been of very considerable assistance to me; I am grateful to the librarian, Heather Rowland, to the assistant librarian Adrian James, and to all the staff for their help. In addition, I can now make my way around the basement at the Antiquaries with much more facility as this is where many of the Scandinavian, German, Dutch and Flemish journals and publications are held.

Acknowledgements

The provision of the illustrations in this volume has only been possible through the generosity of many institutions and colleagues. My thanks go to all of them for their help in both giving permission and frequently providing good quality images.

Two friends and colleagues have most generously read through the text and provided me with comments upon it. Andrew Rogerson, with whom I have worked in Norfolk for over 35 years, has saved me from error and over-generalisation as well as providing me with information. Jenny Kermode most kindly brought both her historian's eye to the text and her experience as an editor. I am very grateful to her and Andrew for their time and comments. Obviously the errors, omissions and solecisms which undoubtedly remain are my own.

I have been sustained during the preparation of this book by the affection of both close friends and family. Amongst the former I am truly indebted to Carol Hardman and her late husband John. Their 'open house' whenever I knocked on the door together with their witty and engaging conversation always lifted the spirits. My daughters Emily Havercroft and Megan Ayers seem often to be amused by their father, which is itself a blessing, but they also support me unstintingly in everything that I do and I thank them and love them dearly.

Finally, I owe very great debts of gratitude to two people who are not here to read this. The first is my late friend Richard Hall. He and I first worked together in 1974 in the crypt of Ripon Cathedral and our friendship over the years subsequently was one of the joys of my life. A scholar with a deep knowledge and a keen dry wit, I have very happy memories of long late evening discussions about archaeology over glasses of whisky in his house in York as well as whispered asides as we sat next to one another at Lübeck colloquia. He encouraged me to write this book and discussed its subjects with me at an early stage. I know that I am not alone in missing him both professionally and personally.

My late wife Robina McNeil said 'You can do this' when I told her that I had been offered the opportunity to write a book on the North Sea region. Subsequently, she remained steadfast in her encouragement, supporting me wonderfully with suggestions and ideas. She had an extraordinary ability to foster the capabilities of others. She was a fine archaeologist who spoke and acted with passion, urging both herself, myself and others to engage with projects and to produce work which reached out to a wide audience. I hope that she would have been pleased with the book that has resulted from her confidence in me. I resolved then to dedicate the book to her and I do so now, with continuing love.

MAPS

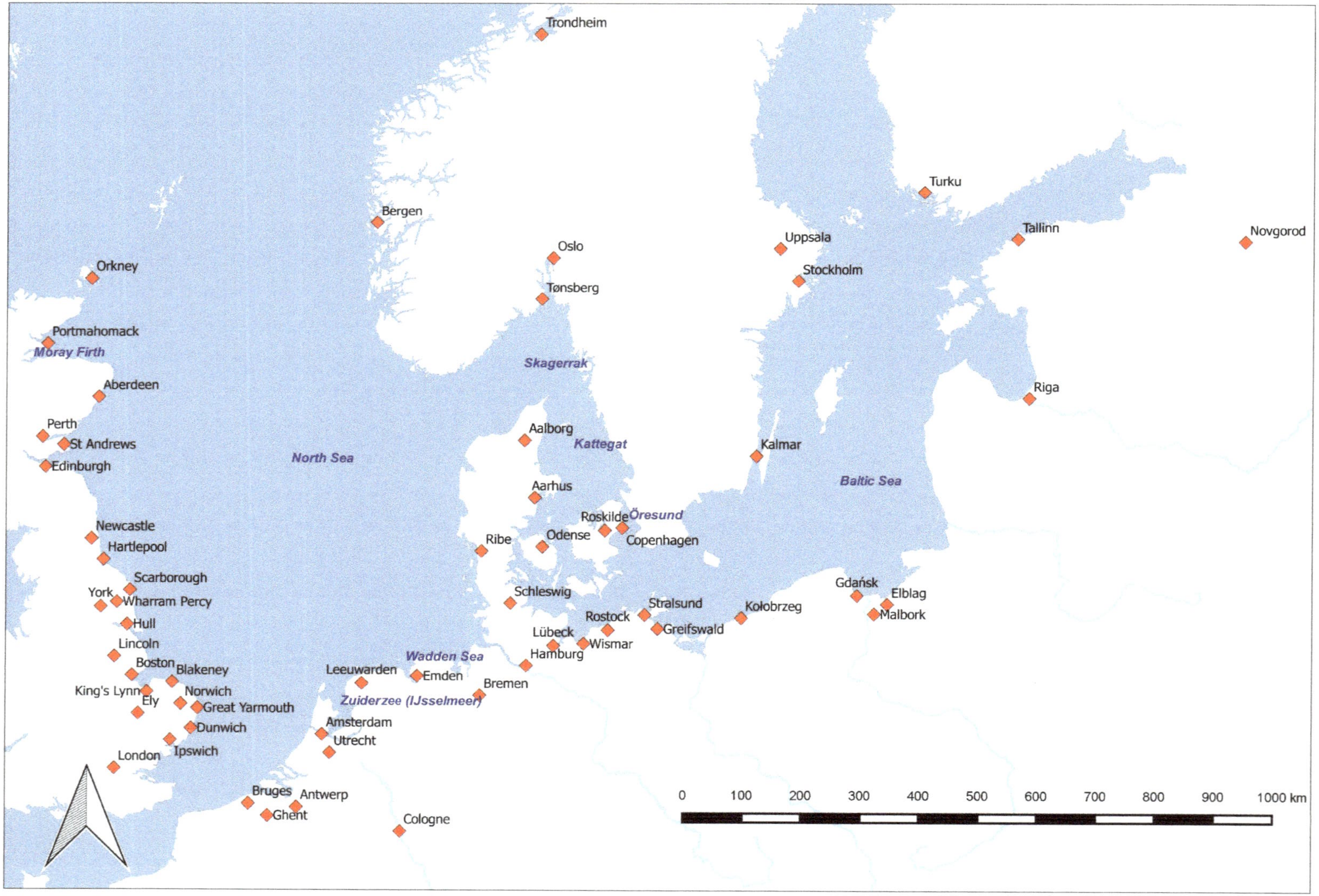

Map 1 Northern Europe showing principal locations mentioned in the text (Dirk Rieger).

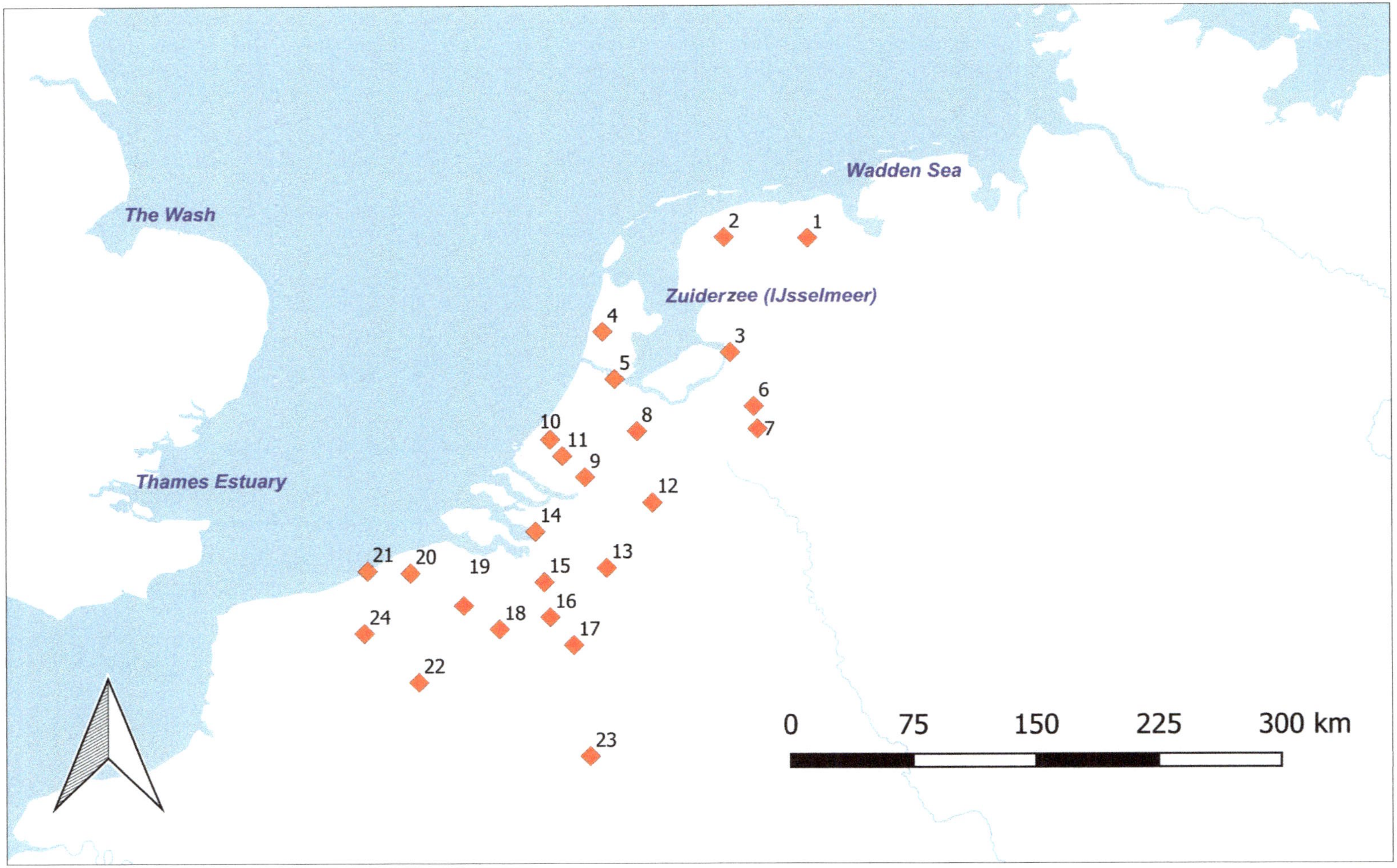

Map 2 The Low Countries showing locations mentioned in the text (Dirk Rieger). 1. Groningen; 2. Leeuwarden; 3. Kampen; 4. Alkmaar; 5. Amsterdam; 6. Deventer; 7. Zutphen; 8. Utrecht; 9. Dordrecht; 10. Delft; 11. Rotterdam; 12. s'Hertogenbosch; 13. Turnhout; 14. Bergen-op-Zoom; 15. Antwerp; 16. Mechelen; 17. Leuven; 18. Aalst; 19. Ghent; 20. Bruges; 21. Walraversijde; 22. Tournai; 23. Dinant; 24. Ypres.

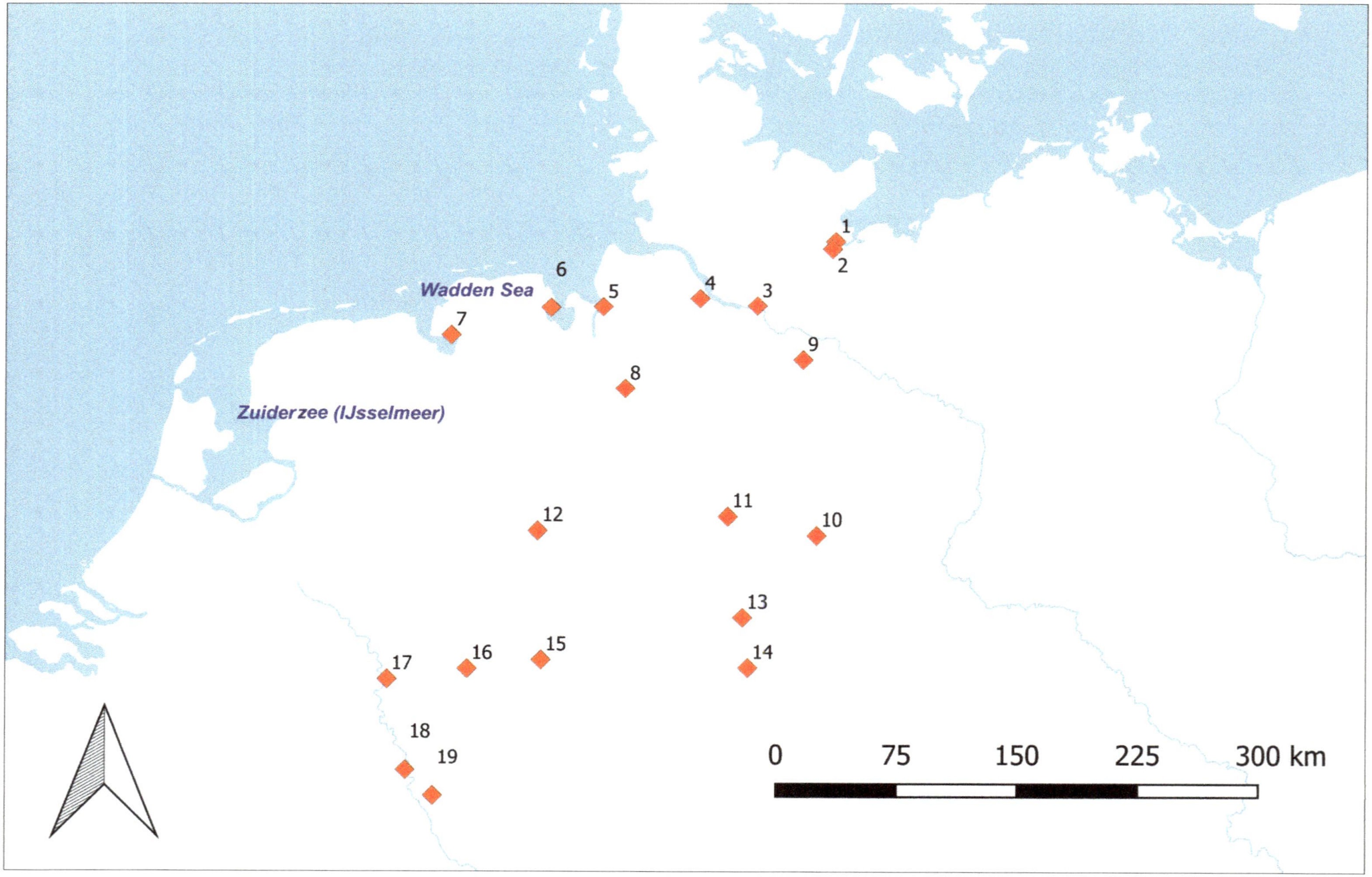

Map 3 North-western Germany showing places mentioned in the text (Dirk Rieger). 1. Alt Lübeck; 2. Lübeck; 3. Hamburg; 4. Stade; 5. Bremerhaven; 6. Wilhelmshaven; 7. Emden; 8. Bremen; 9. Lüneburg; 10. Braunschweig; 11. Hanover; 12. Osnabrück; 13. Einbeck; 14. Göttingen; 15. Soest; 16. Dortmund; 17. Duisburg; 18. Cologne; 19. Siegburg.

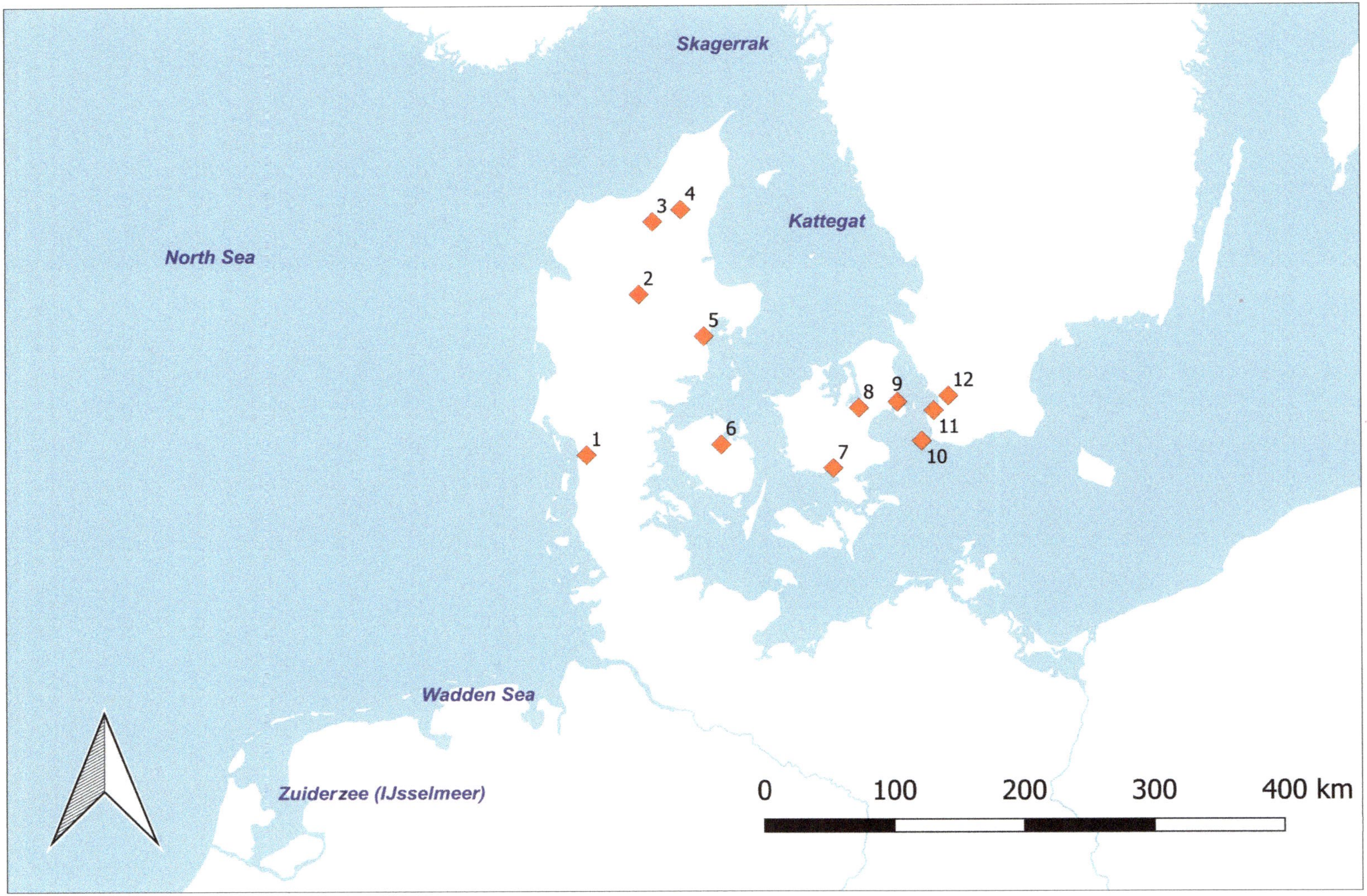

Map 4 Denmark and south-western Sweden showing places mentioned in the text (Dirk Rieger). 1. Ribe; 2. Viborg; 3. Sebbersund; 4. Aalborg; 5. Aarhus; 6. Odense; 7. Naestved; 8. Roskilde; 9. Copenhagen; 10. Falsterbo; 11. Malmö; 12. Lund.

Introduction

This book is not primarily about the North Sea itself but about the North Sea *region* and the medieval communities which inhabited that region. It forms part of the series *The Archaeology of Medieval Europe* and therefore is an archaeological exploration of how those communities and the people within them developed, flourished, sometimes declined, and interacted with one another. Interaction will be a key theme because, in essence, the economic and social structures which can be observed around the North Sea region in the Middle Ages were ones governed by the contact and exchange that was facilitated by the sea. To occupy the littoral of the North Sea was to have access to a potentially large hinterland, one much larger in general than that available to land-locked communities, which were reliant at best on river links to provide ready contact with distant peoples and markets.

The area of the 'German Ocean' of the book's title therefore is taken to mean that large swathe of northern Europe which, for much of the period under consideration, was dominated by German-speaking lands at its centre. The name 'German Ocean' for the North Sea can be evidenced from at least the 15th century, appearing on 'Ptolemy' maps printed in 1477 as *Oceanus Germäic,* and this Germanic appellation continued as the generally common designation until the end of the 19th century, with occasional attempts to use the term 'North Sea' instead. 'It was the First World War that not surprisingly put an end to any British indulgence in the German option. More surprisingly, German cartography fell in line in the 1920s ...'.[1]

The sub-title of this book (Medieval Europe *around* the North Sea) has been chosen deliberately to emphasise the littoral in order to explore the shared hinterland–or hinterlands–made possible by the sea. Access across the sea, of course, was only effected by use of the ship and the concept of 'ship' is a useful one for setting out some of the themes that will follow. In a review of Robert Van de Noort's recent study *North Sea Archaeologies*, Graham Fairclough stated that 'This reviewer cannot help noting ... the irresistible link between "ship" (as "container" for its crew, working together collectively, as they must), the suffix -skip or -skap (*landskap* as the shared territory, "polity" of a community farming, living together collectively, as they must ...) and finally -ship as in township (that socially-constituted building block ...) or fellowship (the place of shared interests)'.[2]

Fairclough is careful to note that his observation is 'despite what etymologists say' but he introduces three concepts pertinent to exploration of the North Sea region: the physical geography within which people lived (landscape or, more generally, the environment), the communities which they created (farms, villages and towns), and the mechanisms of contact (represented by the ship as vessel). Van de Noort himself, in his wide-ranging book, also has thought-provoking observations on concepts drawn from language. In a chapter entitled 'An archaeological theory of the sea' he notes that 'The suffix *-schap* or *-scap* means skill or ability; it survives, for example, in the [Dutch] word *ambachtschap*, or, in its English translation workmanship and craftsmanship, and in the German *Wirtschaft*, meaning economy'.[3]

Thus, to the concepts of environment, community and interaction, the word 'scap' makes it possible to add production and commerce as themes which will be discussed within this volume. These are all areas which, in recent decades, have been subject to archaeological investigation, not simply to uncover and record evidence of practice and products but also, where possible, to establish meaning, an understanding of what the people of the Middle Ages thought about their societies, how these thoughts influenced decision-making, and what of the results of that decision-making can be observed archaeologically. It is a development within medieval archaeology which now has a number of practitioners in various disciplines: landscape studies, buildings' analysis and the study of artefacts to name only three. Work of this kind results in such volumes as Roberta Gilchrist's recent publication entitled *Medieval Life* on 'archaeology and the life course', a book which, as noted by one reviewer, 'could not have been written even ten years ago'.[4]

The methodological approaches needed to be adopted by medieval archaeologists in order to make the shift 'away from economic explanation towards social explanation' have been summarised by Gerrard.[5] Significantly, it is worth noting that an early volume that he identified as containing 'key polemical texts' was primarily devoted to Europe between the Baltic and the Black Sea (although actually published in Britain).[6] Much innovative work is indeed being undertaken by colleagues east of the North Sea and this present volume will seek to capture examples. Scandinavian scholars in particular have a questioning approach to archaeological evidence which is refreshing, if occasionally challenging: a combination of buildings' analysis and documentary evidence, for instance has led to a study charting 'gentrification' of Malmö in the 16th century;[7] the development of a 'capitalist' spirit in 12th-century Denmark has been explored using archaeological material;[8] and, in a paper largely using Scandinavian examples but building from parameters established by Gerrard, an examination of social identity in the Middle Ages is set out.[9]

This thematic approach will therefore form much of the structure of the book which follows. The volume seeks to review recent developments in knowledge and understanding and, within the context of emerging research frameworks, provide a greater appreciation of the potential of future research. It aims to show how the North Sea not only enabled the development of societies, often bound together by common geographical situations and by the trade which access to the sea facilitated, but also provided a focus for the emergence of north-western Europe as a leading economic region. Emphasis is placed upon the developing nature of archaeological research, investigating processes and trends as well as physical structures, buried features and artefacts.

Despite a commonality of experience, however, geography, access to raw materials and political expediency could nevertheless all combine to provide distinctive regional variations. Economies developed more rapidly in some areas than others; local solutions to problems produced urban and rural environments of different aspect; the growth, and sometimes decline, of towns and ports was often dictated by local as much as wider factors. This book therefore explores a 'diverse commonality' while, where possible, examining tangible evidence of a common material culture.

Much of the focus of the text is upon towns and the nature and role of urban communities within the North Sea area. However, towns are necessarily 'parasitic' entities, dependent upon their hinterlands, and therefore they inevitably impacted upon their rural hinterlands. Occasionally that impact could be far-reaching; it has been noted that 'a commercial outlet for the Wealden woods [in Kent and Sussex, southern England] were the fuel-hungry towns of the Low Countries, to which they regularly sent large quantities of billets and other types of firewood via the river Rother and the port of Winchelsea'.[10] The rural topographic impact of other 'fuel-hungry' towns remains evident today in the flooded peat diggings of east Norfolk known as the Broads, their scale exacerbated by the vast quantities of peat used in towns such as Norwich and Great Yarmouth (below, pp. 10 and 49).

This text will therefore argue implicitly that towns were the engines of the medieval economy, driving change and changing themselves in response to economic growth. Such change is frequently visible in dramatic form through the growth of urban infrastructure, the development of urban institutions, the management of a complex society, the impact of diverse trades and industries, and the fostering of commercial opportunities. Archaeological research is singularly well-placed to trace this 'urbanisation' of society, prefiguring developments in the post-medieval and modern periods, through examination of the historic environment both above–and below–ground.

Where possible the following text explores themes and discoveries within a broad chronological framework. The period covered by this volume extends from the beginning of the 12th century to the middle of the 16th century. It is not, however, intended as a further history of the North Sea region, with archaeological evidence illustrating the historical record. Rather, it seeks to demonstrate how archaeological research itself is broadening understanding of the past, answering key questions which hitherto could not be addressed. Increasingly often too, archaeological results, allied to cutting edge scientific techniques and new methodologies, can also identify new areas of research and produce startling new historic evidence.

While key human concerns such as food, clothing, shelter and spiritual nourishment remained constants in the five centuries under consideration, the responses to them in terms of resource acquisition, exploitation, commercial interaction, design innovation, technological development and social context all changed through time (in form, intensity or both), as well as varying from place-to-place. While attempting therefore to maintain a basic chronology, the book also seeks to utilise archaeological data to enhance, and sometimes challenge, traditional narratives by providing evidence for such topics as systemic change and perceptions of resource needs and exploitation. For this reason, the very first chapter, 'The Region in 1100', opens with an assessment of recent archaeo-zoological research on the 'fish event horizon' and its influence on the medieval studies of the region (below, p. 7).

Archaeological work over the last 40 years, on both sides of the North Sea, has produced vast quantities of material, some spectacular (for example the commercial waterfronts located in London, Hull, Dordrecht and other towns),[11] some contributing to art history (such as the painted tombs in the church of Onze-Lieve-Vrouwe, Bruges),[12] much investigating the rural landscape and its contribution to society (as explored by Oosthuizen amongst others),[13] and a great deal increasing understanding of the development of churches, technology, and the potential of human bone[14]–to mention but a few examples.

Interest in the world of the North Sea has grown in recent years. Van de Noort's exploration of its 'archaeologies', covering a vast period of time from 10,000 BC to AD 1500, was published in 2011. The following year a collection of essays on later historical archaeology, entitled *Across the North Sea* and with particular reference to Britain and Denmark in the centuries after 1500, was published.[15] Two years earlier, a major conference had been held at the University of East Anglia entitled 'East Anglia and its North Sea World' (the transactions of which have also now been published).[16] This inter-disciplinary conference took a broad approach to definition of the North Sea World, although at least one contributor felt that continental Europe south of the 'Rhine-Meuse-Scheldt Delta' would be more appropriately included in an English Channel maritime region.[17] However, as Liddiard has noted, 'regions were themselves made up of constituent sub-regions, frequently connected by bodies of water, so there is no difficulty, for example, in the inclusion of the Baltic in such a 'North Sea' World'.[18] This broader concept is one which will be used in this book. An investigation of communities around the North Sea cannot ignore either Flanders or the Baltic. Flemish contact with England has long been visible (for instance with 14th-century brasses in St Margaret, King's Lynn) but evidence for Baltic resources brought to medieval England also continues to grow, be it found in documentary evidence or in analysis of roof timbers which prove to be fashioned from Baltic oak. Similarly, exports from England to the Baltic are known such as rabbit fur sent to Gdànsk (Danzig) and the wider Baltic[19] while an amber signet was probably lost by an Englishwoman called Ada de Bernham visiting the Baltic about 1260 and subsequently recovered in excavation at Steinbecker Straße 26b in Greifswald (she was possibly from Burnham, a port on the north Norfolk coast).[20]

The importance of the Baltic to the North Sea region is further emphasised by the dominance, for much of the period under review in this volume, of the Hanseatic League, a loose confederation of trading communities. The Hanse operated throughout the Baltic Sea and their ships, as well as those of non-hanseatic members, transported both raw materials and goods to and from Baltic ports to those on either side of the North Sea. Indeed the concept of a 'Hanse archaeology' has been discussed recently by Mehler who defines it as having 'both a narrow focus, concerned mainly with analysis of the intercultural exchange between the Hanseatic merchants and their agents (e.g., seamen, crafts-men) and their customers abroad, and a wider focus, which studies the social, economic, and cultural impact these contacts had for both societies'. She differentiates it from hanseatic history on account of the different source materials used and includes the study of 'artifacts, biofacts, architectural remains in towns and rural areas, coastlines and their hinterlands, port facilities, ships, and commercial routes'.[21] This book seeks to cover these areas but also to explore the transmission of ideas, the growth in archaeological understanding of resource exploitation, food production and environmental impact in the past, and physical expressions of social and economic development.

At the head of the Hanseatic League stood the towns of Bremen, Hamburg and, most importantly Lübeck, the 'Queen of the Hansa'. Lübeck is situated at the confluence of the rivers Trave and Wakenitz which connect the city to the Baltic at Travemünde. Now a UNESCO World Heritage Site, Lübeck has also hosted a series of colloquia since 1995 under the heading *Stadtarchäologie im Hanseraum*. The various meetings (on topics such as trade, housing, infrastructure, and industry) have taken a commendably broad view inviting contributions from towns and cities around the North and Baltic Seas and, equally commendably, publishing the transactions with dispatch.[22] These publications, seeking to explore similarities and differences between a range of urban communities, will be drawn upon heavily in the chapters that follow.

The Lübeck initiative is one which is specifically directed at towns and urban archaeology but, across the region, archaeological work and its attendant publication over the last forty years has ensured that records of data collection, settlement appraisals, landscape surveys, artefact analysis, and environmental studies have all contributed to a growing understanding of both urban and rural medieval communities. They do so within a context of rapidly-developing methodologies which seek to explore such matters as settlement hierarchies, environmental impact, and the growth of consumerism. Medieval archaeology is fortunate in having two recently-issued volumes entitled *The Archaeology of Medieval Europe* which summarise the above approaches (and many others).[23] The opening sentence of the volume dedicated to the period of the 12th to 16th centuries is particularly pertinent: 'The purpose of this book is to show what archaeology can do for the understanding of the later Middle Ages'.[24]

This is also the aim of the current work but with two particular foci. Firstly, rather than the whole of 'Roman Catholic Europe' (the focus of the above volumes), the present work seeks to explore a single region (south-to-north from Flanders to Norway and from the Thames Estuary to Iceland; and west-to-east from the Moray Firth to Riga). The southern extent is drawn quite deliberately; to have included Kent, Sussex and on to the port of Southampton in England, as well as the ports and hinterlands of northern France, while often pertinent, would simply have made the book overlong. The volume therefore largely ignores the English Channel. The attempt is made to include reference to most of the significant locations around the North Sea but obviously complete coverage is impossible. Selectivity is essential and has necessarily meant that certain places are favoured over others. The published data from London is extraordinary but already has a volume in this series; much British material is therefore drawn from elsewhere, notably Norwich of the principal medieval urban centres rather than York or Lincoln, reflecting the writer's personal knowledge and experience. Similarly familiarity with Lübeck and friendship with colleagues there means that it receives more coverage than places such as Hamburg and Bremen (although the published data for Lübeck is also of considerably greater quantity).

Secondly, while examining similarities of culture fostered by the exchange that was enabled by the North Sea, it is also necessary to be conscious of the separateness that the sea enforced and the contacts between different cultures that it enabled. Liddiard has helpfully pointed out that '...part of any North Sea identity was bound up in differences, as well as shared affinities'[25] and archaeology is uniquely well-placed to explore such differences and affinities, despite the challenges which can be thrown up by history (such as a known 12th-century appeal in Denmark for fund-raising to purchase English lead for a new roof in Paris).[26] It might be difficult to find physical evidence for similar three-way transactions but archaeological research can and does frequently uncover evidence of two-way transactions while the varied assemblages of material from the pioneering urban excavations in Bergen, Norway, showed the potential complexity of commercial relationships more vividly than any single document: ceramics from England, Germany, the Netherlands, Flanders and France; decorated walrus skulls from Iceland and Greenland; grain from eastern Europe; and boxwood combs from the Mediterranean.[27] It is this rich legacy of interaction and shared experience that this book seeks to uncover.

A note on place-name spelling

The text uses English spellings for place-names and thus has Cologne (not Köln) and Bruges (not Brugge) with one exception–Braunschweig (not Brunswick) as this is now in more common English-usage. Modern Polish spellings are used for towns now in Poland, thus Gdańsk (not Danzig) and Kołobrzeg (not Kolberg) but the German names are given in the text when the town is first mentioned.

King's Lynn was known as Bishop's Lynn before the 16th century but, for ease of reference, is called Lynn or King's Lynn here.

Principal place-names are indicated on four maps preceding this Introduction. Smaller locations when mentioned within the text will be referenced in relation to a larger community (e.g. Wisbech near King's Lynn; Kongemarken near Roskilde).

— 1 —

The Region in 1100

In considering the archaeology of the North Sea region at the beginning of the 12th century, it is instructive to start with a discovery which, while it is the result of recent analysis of recovered archaeological evidence from exclusively terrestrial deposits (specifically from England and Flanders), is also one which emphasises the interplay between land and sea, an important theme of this book. Furthermore, it is a discovery which has produced a dramatic development in the understanding of medieval exploitation of the resources of the North Sea. This analysis additionally suggests strongly that the North Sea world of 1100 was radically different from that of two centuries earlier. The social and economic structures that were coming into being at this period would shape much of the framework of human activity over the next four to five centuries.

The analysis concerns fishbone and draws upon well-dated assemblages recovered from urban sites in locations such as London, Norwich, Great Yarmouth and Antwerp. The results have enabled discussion of a so-called 'fish event horizon' when consumption of marine fish increased rapidly and dramatically. Research focussed upon why this should be so, seeking to identify whether there was an intensification of exploitation of local marine sources or an increase in long-distance trading in fish. The studies discovered that, from the 10th century onward, local stocks were exploited more and more ruthlessly so that, by the late 14th century, long-distance trading had become necessary. Specialists involved noted the specific significance of 'increasing numbers of urban consumers facing the need for new sources of inexpensive and easily preserved protein'.[1]

The growth of towns is a well-known phenomenon in northern Europe between the 10th and 13th centuries. Considerable quantities of ink have been expended on the topic by historians (early and influential works being those of Tait, Pirenne and Ennen;[2] a later one by Reynolds[3]) and by archaeologists.[4] In recent years there has also been an increased emphasis upon the relationships between towns and their surrounding hinterlands.[5] However, while many publications focus upon the topographic changes wrought by individual towns, or upon the economic implications of urban-rural relationships, the importance of the fishbone research is that it identifies *systemic* change as a result of urban development, with considerable and ongoing environmental impact within ecosystems utterly divorced spatially from towns themselves (by the 13th–14th centuries 'more than half of the cod specimens from London are attributed to a source beyond the southern North Sea').[6] Furthermore, it locates initiation of this change at the turn of the last millennium, thus utilising archaeological material to illustrate the consequential context of emerging social and economic pressures.

These pressures were made manifest by alterations to the terrestrial environment on both sides of the North Sea. Partly driven by political developments (the Norman Conquest of England from 1066 onward being a dramatic case in point), there are now sufficient demographic indicators to suggest a sustained growth in the population of northern Europe by the 11th century.[7] Linked to this, environmental change at the North Sea littoral began to have a profound effect upon settlement patterns and especially upon the growth of towns. This change was, until recently, viewed as a marine regression (the 'Saxo-Norman marine regression' in English historiography), but such phases of regression (or of transgression) are now recognised as regionally-determined by such factors as dune formation, the growth of peat and sedimentation patterns.[8] Indeed, sedimentation was directly responsible for the growth of an extensive sand spit which almost blocked the 'Great Estuary' in east Norfolk (the point of outflow for the rivers Bure, Yare and Waveney as well as their tributaries). The creation of the spit enabled the growth of Great Yarmouth from the 11th century onward, a town of only some 70 burgesses in 1086, and thus 70th in the ranking of English towns, but it had risen to fifth place in terms of taxable wealth by the time of the subsidy of 1334.[9]

Great Yarmouth is an early example of the establishment of a coastal port in a previously-inhospitable environment but it was soon followed by other British ports in similar, or estuarine, locations: Boston, although not mentioned in Domesday Book of 1086, is recorded in 1090 in the *Registrum Antiquissimum* of Lincoln cathedral;[10] Hull was in existence by 1203-04 (at least as a point of transhipment if not yet as a town, the lower reaches of the river having two outlets until canalisation into one in the late 12th century seems to have fostered settlement);[11] and Perth probably existed before 1127 (the marginal situation of this Scottish *burgh* being emphasised by 34 recorded floods since 1209).[12] These foundations supplemented earlier towns which were themselves growing: locations such as York, Lincoln, Norwich and, pre-eminently, London from all of which the results of recent excavation illustrate the vibrancy of urban life in the 11th and 12th centuries.[13]

Similar urban development can be observed on the eastern littoral of the North Sea. Archaeological excavation has now identified a 9th-century fortified area in Bruges (or Brugge) in Flanders, a Carolingian initiative which the excavator interprets, together with sporadic finds of Carolingian material elsewhere within the town, as indicative of nascent urban development: several small settlements growing together to form a mercantile entity which was already being fortified in the 12th century.[14] The marginal location of Bruges, however, meant that urban expansion was only achieved by canalisation of the low-lying watery environment between three sand ridges (Figure 1.1).[15] Further north, excavations undertaken in 1973–1976 established that the origins of Ribe in Denmark dated to the 8th century although thereafter there seems to be have been a decline in urban activity in the 10th and most of the 11th centuries until revitalisation after *c.* 1100.[16] Colonisation from the 12th century occupied both banks of the Ribe river and renewed activity was probably also facilitated by damming of the Ribe river (the location of the first dam suggested by changes in plants, excavation-recovered species being linked to raised water levels).[17]

In Norway, pioneering excavation by Asbjørn Herteig after 1955 uncovered both marine deposits and early timber structures upon which the early 12th-century town of Bergen was first constructed. He recorded the subsequent development of timber technologies that enabled the waterfront of the settlement to extend into deeper and deeper water, supporting an array of structures above (below, Chapter 5).[18] Once again, marginal land was being exploited. Herteig's work has been glossed by subsequent excavation; the town was traditionally founded in 1070 by King Olav Kyrre and excavations at Finnegården, south of those undertaken by Herteig, and at other locations have shown that the origins of the settlement can indeed be placed in the 11th century.[19]

Towns such as Bergen, Bruges and Great Yarmouth were therefore able to take advantage of changing environmental conditions in the first century-and-a half after the turn of the first millennium in order to develop spatially. Such urban development would clearly also impact upon natural resources of which the provision of fish is one example. The growth of towns implies the adoption of changing economic and social models. The need to provide large quantities of fish, for instance, is perhaps indicative of a movement towards the carriage and marketing of large quantity but low-value goods. This would

Figure 1.1 15th-century map of Flanders showing the watery environment (Public Library, Bruges: Historic Fund).

have marked a departure from the generally high status, high-value goods observable from excavations in towns of the 8th and 9th centuries, a view perhaps supported by the observation that, prior to the 10th century, 'all ship-wrecks known from the Northern seas belong to all-purpose vessels, designed to carry a large crew and a modest cargo .'..[20] In succeeding centuries, as will be seen, the increased use of specialised vessels enabled the easier distribution of bulk goods (below, p. 130ff.). Furthermore, the marketing of such goods would inevitably impact upon the commercial structure of towns as nodal centres. Environmental, social and technological change therefore was changing the North Sea region.

The North Sea coast

Such change was obviously not confined to urban populations or the providers of resources for urban areas. It also had a profound effect upon the wider landscape. A characteristic of the North Sea, especially the southern North Sea, is that it is bounded by low-lying rural areas. This is most marked on the eastern littoral in Flanders, the Netherlands and the coastline of Germany and, on the western side, by the English counties of East Anglia, Lincolnshire and East Yorkshire. In all areas, the marginal environment means that coastal change remains an active consideration for modern populations. Recent archaeological work, however, has also enabled greater understanding of the impact of such pressures upon medieval populations, the likely human agency involved in precipitating some environmental changes, and the steps taken in order to mitigate the impact of change on marginal lands.

There is particularly good evidence emerging from survey and excavation in the Netherlands. Here, a combined study in north Holland utilising the research of historians, historical geographers, toponymists, geologists and pedologists (as well as archaeologists) has demonstrated that sand dunes effectively sheltered the land from the sea during the first two-thirds of the first millennium. This protection led to the growth of freshwater peat bogs which began to be exploited by drainage in the 8th and 9th centuries. Drainage entailed shrinkage (and, indeed, disappearance) of the peat, lowering the land surface which, linked to increased pressure from the sea (and also, in the 10th century, to climatic change when there are indications of severe drought conditions[21]), intensified coastal erosion. As a result, 'an open and disintegrated coastal region' emerged, enforcing a vigorous response by inhabitants of the region to protect old—and create new—arable and pasture land. The dynamic reclamation process is well-observed in the former peat area of Westfriesland where dikes and drainage systems led, in the 11th and 12th centuries, to the establishment of a series of settlements which themselves fostered expansion southward.[22]

Comparison with the Norfolk fens of eastern England is instructive. Here, as in north Holland, a localised sand ridge of Flandrian deposits against the coast acted to protect land to the south, leading to the growth of a peat bog. Unlike north Holland, however, this peatland (known as *The Smeeth*) was not drained until the early post-medieval period. Settlement grew up in the silt fen of the sandy ridge, a string of villages being established by the turn of the first millennium together with elongated smaller settlements which exploited the silt ridges or *roddens* of former watercourses. These in turn sought enhanced protection, particularly in areas where rivers entered the sea, by the construction of defensive dikes. Examples of dikes, probably originating *c.* 1000, still survive in parishes such as West Walton and Clenchwarton in Norfolk. The West Walton bank was referred to as *fossatum maris* in medieval documentation[23] and its surviving elements consist of short straight and curved lengths, in part apparently enclosing fields rather than the village.[24] The Clenchwarton bank, through which a section has been excavated, revealed phased construction of material recovered from the foreshore and post-dated a marshland drainage ditch which, presumably, had been unprotected.[25]

The Fens were therefore divided into two parts: the southern 'Black Fens' which were covered with undrained peat and essentially used for grazing, the cultivation of hay or the cutting of peat; and the northern 'Silt Fens' where settlement was established, a string of villages occupying the southern edge of The Wash defended by sea banks and echoing in broad terms the distribution pattern of settlements in Westfriesland. These fenland villages were linked to the pasturelands in the peatlands by a series of drove roads, the alignments of which survive within the modern landscape (Figure 1.2).[26]

Marginal coastline environments were not the only locations of increased activity at this period. The river systems which fed into the North Sea, flowing through these low-lying areas, provided both ease of access to hinterlands and opportunities for resource exploitation. The extensive peat digging in the river valleys of east Norfolk, well-documented from the 12th century but probably initiated earlier, not only had a profound local impact (it has been calculated that some 25.5 million cu.m. of peat were removed up to the 14th century) but the peat was also distributed widely within eastern Norfolk and north Suffolk, the two most densely-populated counties of England.[27] Peat-diggings or turbaries also existed in the Fens; work in Cambridgeshire has identified Roman turf-cutting but it is clear from documentary evidence that such activity was also important in the medieval period while other resources such as reeds, rushes, salt and wildfowl would all have found a ready market in the emerging towns of the river valleys.[28] One such was Wisbech, a small port on the river Nene where excavation at Market Mews in 1996 produced 'direct evidence for the use of the stems and leaves of grasses, rushes and sedge for flooring' (from the 14th century).[29]

Human activity therefore was impacting considerably upon the North Sea littoral by the 12th century, through exploitation of the rich soils available; through construction of earthwork sea defences; through drainage and landscape change; and through harnessing of natural resources, be they mineral, botanical or zoological. Much of this activity presumably required investment and controlling authorities. Determining who these were is a difficult proposition using archaeological evidence although, in England, the influence of monasteries was perhaps significant. Everson and Stocker have recently published an exhaustive appraisal of the role of Barlings Abbey, Lincolnshire within the landscape, an inland foundation but one located in the Witham valley with good access to the sea. Significantly, as the Premonstratensian abbey was only founded in 1154, they note that the 'patterning of landscape use'

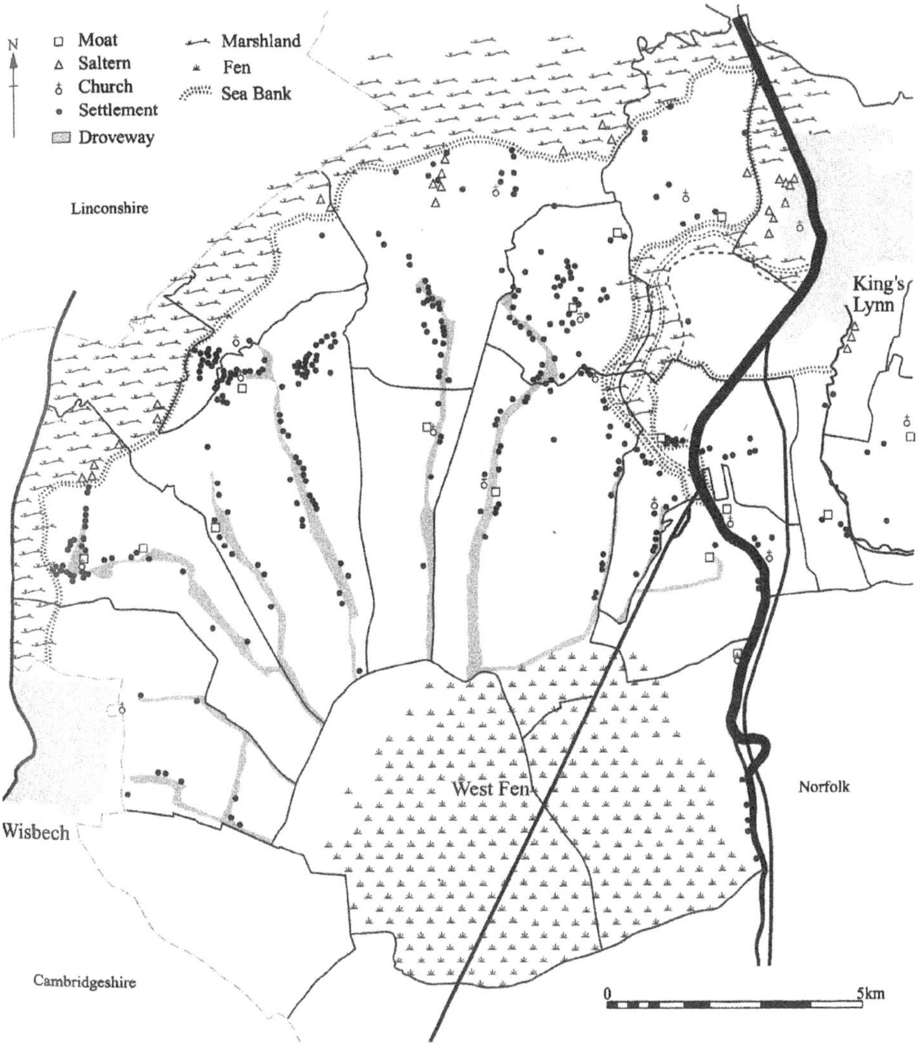

Figure 1.2 Marshland in the Fens of eastern England (Oxford Archaeology East–after Silvester).

probably originated in the 11th century or earlier (the landholding contained a variety of resources such as arable fields, woods, fenland and sheepwalks) (Figure 1.3) but that the monastery appears to have adopted 'a very purposeful progression towards the establishment of a mature estate'.[30]

Barlings (near Lincoln) was situated on an island in the valley, a similar location to an earlier foundation in Norfolk, St Benet's Abbey, traditionally established *c.* 1020 but perhaps even then a re-foundation. Here its island lay off a small peninsula which was protected by an earthwork of unknown date.[31] The monks improved access to their site by construction of a causeway and no doubt effected other improvements on their extensive estates; already in 1046 they held three manors and had 28 dependent churches.[32] To date, the most innovative assessment of the role of such monasteries in early land apportionment in England is that provided by Pestell who, in an interesting book which explores the ideas behind the locational settings of monastic institutions, also asks questions of those institutions associated with marginal, but exploitable, low-lying resources: as well as St Benet at Holm, the abbeys of Crowland, Ramsey, Thorney, Chatteris, Peterborough, St Ives, St Neots and Ely are all discussed. He points out that large 10th-century land endowments following monastic reform in the reign of King

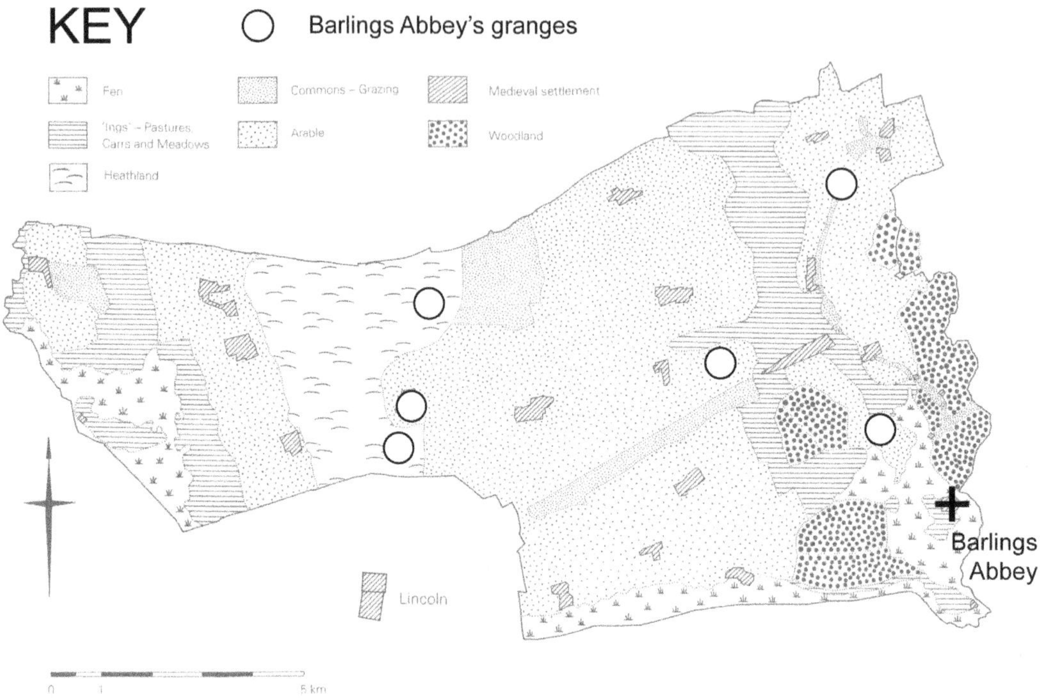

Figure 1.3 Granges and agricultural resources of Barlings Abbey, Lincolnshire (Dave Hopkins and Paul Everson).

Edgar, encouraged 'many of the leading reformers to become land barons, often aggressively acquisitive, leading to much local resentment'.[33]

'Land barons' in England may therefore have been largely ecclesiastical, at least with regard to marginal locations. The situation in the Netherlands, however, appears to have been different. An assessment of documentary resources by Bos suggests land divisions were either effected by the Counts of Holland or, in the area of north Holland, by aristocratic supervision.[34] The methodology of reclamation—known in the Netherlands as *cope*-reclamation—was similar to that which was also adopted in some German marshland areas. Property rights were granted to those undertaking the work, on regular strips of land which could be extended out into the marshes. Despite aristocratic patronage, the system enabled the development of a more egalitarian system of land ownership.[35] Indeed, it could be argued that the seeds of the Dutch Republic in the 17th century were sown in the reclaimed marshlands of the 12th century.

Human occupation of the coastal margins in Friesland (the northern Netherlands and northern Germany) by the 11th century had taken a different course due to differing environmental conditions. Here salt marsh and the gradual natural development of levees forming sandy ridges led to the construction of artificial mounds or *terps* on top of these ridges from around the 3rd or 4th century BC. Archaeological research in the Westergo area has identified *terp* rows; these took advantage of silting within the salt marsh and were configured in such a manner as to suggest a (now lost) funnel-shaped tidal basin. Occupation and development of the mounds continued until about 300 AD after which there was abandonment of the *terps*, re-occupation taking place from about 500 AD following further silting. However, these coastal margins were still only subject to relatively isolated human activity operating from the *terps* until the start of sea bank construction *c.* 1000. Thereafter human agency, notably through improved drainage, impacted more effectively upon the region.[36]

Terps were not simply used as dwelling mounds. A German *terp* at Wurt Hessens outside Wilhelmshaven was excavated between 1939 and 1963 (Figure 1.4). The work uncovered evidence of occupation from the

Figure 1.4 Wurt Hessens, Germany. An excavated terp which included a sheep-washing facility. The parallel wooden structure of rectangular planks facilitated the control of the sheep (photograph reproduced with permission of Lower Saxony Institute for Historical Coastal Research)

7th century through to the 13th century. It also exposed well-preserved timber structures including features interpreted as forming a sheep-washing facility. Four farmsteads were grouped around a central area which contained both a well and a massive wooden tank for holding water. Ethnographic parallels suggest that these and other structures were used for production of high-quality wool.[37]

In Denmark, settlement in the 11th century occupied low sandy moraines called *geest* which lay behind the salt marshes although here too there is evidence of a progression to occasional use of dwelling mounds. The population farmed cattle on the marshes, produced cereal on the *geest,* and fished. Excavation of the site of one such community took place in the 1980s at the village of Vilslev Spang, bordering the Danish stretch of the Wadden Sea. Evidence of fish- and shellfish-exploitation was uncovered as well as a probable cattle shed.[38]

Thus, on the margins of the southern North Sea, considerable topographic change was evident by the beginning of the 12th century. Drainage and protection of low-lying areas was becoming more extensive, exploitation of marginal land was utilising both natural resources and developing areas for agrarian farming, and new towns were being established to supplement older, more inland, settlements. Interestingly, archaeological work is also overturning the older view that much settlement was seasonal and instead now has evidence to show that coastal margins were permanently settled, probably from the 7th or 8th century and certainly by the 11th century.[39] The coastline was dynamic on both sides of the southern North Sea but the volatility was being managed by its human populations. Such was the situation for much of eastern England, Flanders, The Netherlands, the North Sea coast of Germany and that of Denmark.

North of this, however, geography inevitably ensured different responses. Recent archaeological research in Norway, a country where, even today, only some 3% of the land mass is cultivated, has not needed to explore dramatic coastline change. However, such work has been able to modify considerably the received understanding of development of rural medieval settlement. In particular, a more-nuanced view of clustered farmsteads in western Norway, complementing the traditional idea of separate dispersed farmsteads, has led to a revision of concepts concerning development of land usage with an awareness that holdings were often established around a common core. In other words, archaeological research is helping to identify a socio-economic structure which was perhaps less individualistic than hitherto promoted in Scandinavia, and more akin to developments elsewhere in the North Sea region. An archaeological caution has been entered concerning the use of the word 'farm' in Norwegian historiography. This term 'is apt to conceal a wider range of settlement types than traditionally assumed, varying between, as well as within, the different regions of the country'.[40]

Fortifications, control and social organisation

Recognition, particularly in England and the Low Countries, that organisation of tenure could often have a controlling interest from aristocratic, episcopal or other agencies such as monasteries inevitably focuses attention on how that interest was expressed within the environment. An obvious mechanism for effecting such an expression was the construction of a seigneurial fortification, residence or both. Castles, the product of development in France in the 9th century, were well-established in much of northern Europe by 1100. Their deployment in England was largely the result of the Norman Conquest (although earlier sites are now known) and examples survive at the coastal margins, and dominating the edges of wetlands, such as Skipsea in Yorkshire or Wormegay near Lynn in Norfolk. The latter, established around 1086, was constructed on a small island to control a pre-existing causeway across the Fen. Fieldwork has recovered evidence of pre-castle occupation, has established that settlement was re-established east of the castle, and noted that the causewayed road was diverted by the building of this motte-and-bailey structure (Figure 1.5).[41] The former castle at Skipsea (near Scarborough), of similar date to Wormegay, was also sited to control a marshland area, lying at the northern edge of the Holderness coastal marshes although, additionally, it had a role of defending the Holderness coastline against Scandinavian incursion. To this end, it was supported by a wide range of landholdings in the area.[42] The motte at Skipsea stands on an enhanced glacial mound and was surrounded by a mere, probably formed by construction of a dam some 200m north of the motte. It has been suggested that this may have formed an inland harbour (the name *Skipsea* means 'lake navigable by ships') which could also have served the small (failed) borough which was established within the bailey.[43]

Examination of the landholdings in the vicinity of Skipsea castle has been undertaken by Creighton, drawing on both documentary research and field survey. He notes firstly that a significant number of late 11th-century tenants were Flemish, indicating 'that the Norman settlement of the North was part of an expansionist and colonial enterprise'. Redistribution of lands cut across traditional tenures but nevertheless retained a territorial unity. Together with smaller fortifications at Aldborough and Burstwick, the construction of these castles not only reflected 'a systematic appropriation of the more valuable holdings and the management of their associated agricultural resources under new lordship' but also placed key military installations close to pre-Conquest estate centres (held in 1066 by Harold, Ulf and Tostig).[44] Castle-building was a political and economic activity as much as a military one.

Motte-and-bailey castles like Wormegay and Skipsea are also found on the east coast of the North Sea in the Low Countries, generally concentrated around the Rhine and Meuse rivers, although here they date from the beginning of the 12th century. Earlier fortifications are known but have proved difficult to characterise: 'fortified residences' at Aelbrechtsberg and Ridderzaal (The Hague) are currently not known to have had defences.[45] Within Flanders, northward through the Netherlands, and within Germany ringworks of an early date (9th- to 11th-century) exist, the excavated example at Souburg in Zeeland (southern Netherlands) having a highly-organised internal layout.[46] However, much remains to be discovered as to how these sites functioned with regard to their surroundings.

Figure 1.5 Wormegay castle from the air (Norfolk Historic Environment Service).

More is known of other early fortified sites and their relationship to development in the first century after the turn of the millennium, particularly with regard to growing urban centres. Excavations within the tellingly-named *Burg* area of Bruges uncovered parts of a 9th-century earthwork which was replaced in stone in the mid-10th century, when it and a church dedicated to St Donatian formed the nucleus of what became the later medieval city.[47] At Hamburg, an early ringwork was used from the 9th century as a fortified enclosure for the church which became the cathedral at the core of the developing urban centre; the defences were seen in excavations both in 1956 and in 2006.[48] A second ringwork was constructed across the Alster river in about 1060–1070 by Duke Ordulf, it subsequently protecting a mercantile settlement here.[49] A similar, probable 9th-century, ringwork foundation at the confluence of the rivers Schwartau and Trave at Alt Lübeck was extended by the Slavic Obotrite king Henry around 1100 as a princely residence and centre of administration with a suburb of artisans (it was superseded by the late 12th-century foundation of Lübeck itself, some 8km upstream). Excavations at Alt Lübeck as long ago as 1852 recorded the foundations of an early church (it was re-excavated and recorded again in 1949) (Figure 1.6).[50]

Fortifications were not necessarily central to urban foundation but they often enhanced development through centralisation of secular administration. The impact of early Norman castles upon pre-existing towns bordering or close to the east coast of England in the immediate aftermath of the Norman

Figure 1.6 Alt Lübeck showing River Trave and ground-plan of stone church (Betty Arndt).

Conquest of 1066 was profound. Domesday Book of 1086 records destruction to make way for new castles, such as 106 houses or tenements removed in Lincoln and 27 houses in Cambridge.[51] The Domesday record for Norwich is explicit: a total of 98 houses were *in occupatione castelli*.[52] Recent comprehensive excavation of the south bailey of this castle has uncovered some 27 pre-Conquest buildings 'with varying degrees of certainty'. They were timber buildings utilising several forms of construction: sunken-featured or cellared structures; buildings with post in trench; buildings with posts and upright planks.[53] The castle fortifications themselves were also of wood although, by 1100, major stone monuments such as a great *donjon* or keep on the motte, were under construction.[54]

Urban historians during the early part of the 20th century were particularly concerned with castles and their assumed influence: a process of fortification-led urban development known as *incastellamento*. Pirenne adopted a 'generalizing view' of castles forming pre-urban nucleii,[55] while it has been noted recently that the provision of fortified settlements linked to rural colonisation can be seen as part of a similar formation process.[56] Archaeological work, however, is demonstrating that, within towns, matters were more complex. Ghent in Flanders, a growing urban settlement by the early 10th century, was clearly in existence prior to the establishment of a castle[57] but nearby Aalst, founded in the 11th century, may well have flourished initially within the shadow of its fortification. However, urban Aalst had a rural precursor, a manor identified through archaeological research as synonymous with a 9th-century manor belonging to the Abbey of Lobbes and called the *Villa Acost*,[58] an entity which provided the economic and topographic basis upon which the town was established.

Aalst was not alone in growing from such a rural entity. Ypres, subsequently a great cloth-manufacturing city, also originated as a manorial estate, known from Carolingian times and documented as *villa yprensis*.[59] Adriaan Verhulst has advanced the interesting theory that the town which grew from this estate owed its rapid growth in the 11th century to disastrous flooding of the Yser basin in the first half of that century. The flooding created salt marshes on which sheep farms could be established. Ypres, some 2km from the Yser, was connected to it by the river Ieper (subsequently canalised and called the Ieperlee) and the wool could therefore be transported to Ypres easily for processing and manufacture of cloth.[60]

Exploitation of resources

Archaeological evidence for the grazing of animals on salt marshes has come from plant remains recovered in excavations at Schagen in North Holland.[61] Here the material from an early medieval pit revealed animal fodder and dung mixed in with hay. Together with bones from the site, the plant remains indicated both the presence of salt marshes and the husbanding of cattle, sheep and chickens. Threshing seems to have been undertaken on the site and saltwater fish and molluscs were being exploited.

Further south any boost to the development of Ypres caused by saltwater flooding of the Yser basin could only have been sustained in the short-term. Once control was regained over marine inundation, the salt marshes would be removed and the grazing for sheep drastically reduced (documentary evidence for the coastal area north of Bruges suggests that, by 1089, only one parish—Oostkerke—was left with grazing for sheep, 'probably indicating the continued presence of salt marshes' but lost elsewhere due to embankment and drainage[62]). While sheep grazing could obviously continue on pastureland, the continued and increasing prosperity of Ypres needs to be explained by provision of wool from elsewhere. Here Verhulst links embankment of the Yser, necessary for drainage, with improved navigation, facilitating the import of English wool.[63]

The potential for English exports of wool was certainly there by 1100. Domesday Book in 1086 records 46,458 sheep in Norfolk with 37,522 in Suffolk and 46,095 in Essex (in Norfolk alone, therefore, sheep outnumbered all other livestock by a factor of three-to-one).[64] Archaeological study of sheep husbandry is obviously difficult but Williamson has explored the process of 'sheep-corn' husbandry whereby sheep manuring of agrarian fields was fostered by the grazing of sheep on heathland or downland during the day and then by intensive 'folding' of sheep on agrarian land at night. The system ensured development of an open field system as it was necessary for ease of movement of flocks. The system also implied 'communal management of the arable land of a township ... folding could only be carried out if numbers of contiguous strips were cropped, harvested and fallowed in concert'.[65]

While the growing textile industry of Flanders was being supplied by imported wool in 1100, the populations of the growing urban centres themselves also needed to be fed. Considerable research in recent years on both palaeo-environmental data and ecofacts such as animal- and fish-bone has improved understanding of the developing urban/rural relationships necessary for supply and demand. The increase in marine fish consumption has been mentioned already (above, p. 7). Evidence for this enhanced consumption is available from towns on both sides of the North Sea. At Fishergate in Norwich, examination of diatoms suggested the possibility that processing of marine fish or shellfish was taking place in the 11th century.[66] Fishbone evidence from excavation of contemporary Viborg in Denmark (Figure 1.7) indicated that fish was arriving fresh at the town (presumably sourced locally) with both marine and freshwater species being recovered from latrine waste.[67]

Animal bones can also indicate how urban communities were drawing upon the rural environment. Examination of cattle and sheep bones from 10th- to 11th-century deposits in two East Anglian towns—Norwich and Thetford—revealed that animals slaughtered for the Thetford market were more slender than those from Norwich, suggesting that they were sourced from different populations. It is postulated that Norwich, as already a major regional centre, was able to draw upon a wide and diverse hinterland while Thetford may have relied upon the relatively low-quality pasture in its immediate hinterland (largely Breckland, an area of poor soils). However, a note of caution is also entered as a second site in Thetford produced cattle bones that were different, thus suggesting that the town also benefited from a range of sources for its meat. The conclusion is drawn that there is 'a general picture of great complexity ... Systems of supply, such as local production, use of the town hinterland and distant trade would all be adopted, though the emphasis placed on any one of these strategies would vary .'...[68]

An interesting assessment of animal bone from Emden in northern Germany has explored the paleopathology of animal bones. The material dates from the 9th century to the early post-medieval period but the analysis uncovered evidence for a range of conditions which cast light upon husbandry within

Figure 1.7 Excavations at Viborg, Denmark 1981 (Viborg Museum).

an urban environment. As an example, examination of an 11th-century sheep/goat tibia observed nodules around the distal articular which could be interpreted as trauma resulting from close penning of the animal. Cattle bone of a slightly earlier date were seen to have evidence of spavin, the condition often associated with use of cattle for traction.[69] Neither penning of small animals nor traction with larger ones are unexpected activities although the possibility that spavin can also be associated with old age in cattle could also suggest late kill-off rates compared to modern practice.

Much food transportation relied upon preservation and salt production was therefore important. The coastline of the North Sea provided scope for such activity. Domesday Book of 1086 records nearly 1200 *salinas* or salterns in England, in the southern counties of Kent and Sussex (bordering the English Channel) and, further north, in Norfolk and Lincolnshire. Terrington St Clement, on the edge of The Wash in west Norfolk, was recorded as having twelve salt pans in 1086 and field survey has recorded mounds between 0.5m and 2.5m in height over an area of some 50 hectares.[70] Waste dumps from salt-working are visible at Wainfleet Tofts on the Lincolnshire coast while examples of similar but ploughed-out mounds further north in Lincolnshire at Marsh Chapel were photographed from the air in 1953.[71] In this latter location an 11th-century saltern has been excavated at the evocatively-named Burnt Hill where an inlet channel, storage tanks for brine, and briquetage for supporting the salt pans were all uncovered.[72] The remains of mounds here and in the neighbouring parishes of Tetney, North Coates and Grainthorpe are known locally as 'fitties' and all consist of salt-making debris, notably burnt clay and ash.

In the Netherlands and Germany a different technique was used, that of burning saltwater-encrusted peat. Extensive areas of peat digging have been uncovered along the Wadden Sea coast and, to the south, pits excavated on the island of Zuid-Beveland have been found to have originated from peat-extraction, silting up in the 11th or 12th centuries.[73]

The derivation, nature and utilisation of the coastal and rural hinterland resources which were transported into towns can be explored through palaeo-environmental data which survives within many densely-packed urban deposits. In Norwich, for instance, Peter Murphy analysed the cultivated and wild plant assemblages from predominantly 11th- and 12th-century deposits and was able to reconstruct a range of processes leading to their deposition. Crops such as grains were present through kitchen waste and faecal material, floor litter from vegetation such as bracken or heather was recovered, and waste or dispersed evidence from industrial production, such as flax and hemp processing, was observed.[74] Rural sites also produce botanical and faunal information: sites in the Fens at locations such as Terrington St Clement and West Walton provide records of barley, oats, rye, horsebeans, peas, flax brassica, sedge and reed as well as bones of cattle, sheep/goat, pigs, horses, geese and chickens.[75]

The coastal margins of the North Sea were therefore becoming increasingly colonised at the beginning of the 12th century with their resources, and those of the sea itself, increasingly exploited. This exploitation obviously served subsistence communities at the coast and in rural areas but it also fed into developing commercial networks, mainly controlled by emerging urban centres. Numerous sites, both rural and urban, have yielded bones of cattle, sheep and pigs, as well as fishbone, providing obvious indications of protein sources for the population. However, changes in supply as requirements grew can also be observed—in Flanders, for instance, marine fish became more common around 1000, coastal flatfish being replaced by species such as herring. Much of the evidence for this observation derives from work in Ghent, located within a deposit known as the *Zwarte Laag* (black layer' or 'dark earth'). It has been noted that the incidence of herring is 'relatively late' but is paralleled by evidence from England,[76] where, in York, the growth in numbers of marine species coincided with the disappearance of freshwater fish such as shad and grayling, these 'especially sensitive to the pollution of rivers, so it seems that they were driven out of the Ouse by the effluent of York'.[77]

Catching herring implies netting and examples of nets have been recovered from a range of contexts on both sides of the North Sea. A net with a diamond mesh of plied yarn (probably hemp), ideal for herring, was recovered from a building that had burnt down in 11th-century Norwich.[78] A net with a finer mesh but otherwise almost identical is known from Spurriergate in York[79] while further nets are recorded from Lund in Sweden[80] and Haithabu, now in northern Germany.[81] The Norwich discovery was interesting; such nets need to be kept on racks in order to avoid mould and rot. Hazel-wood slats and rods found with the net probably formed part of such a rack. A review of the increasing evidence for other fishing implements—floats, net sinkers, fish hooks and needles amongst them—has been published recently by Ian Riddler.[82]

While the growing urban communities of the North Sea region obviously needed food resources, their economic needs also demanded raw materials which could then be exploited. Animals played a significant role here too: urban deposits from both sides of the North Sea provide plentiful evidence of bone, antler and horn objects, many of which were clearly manufactured in towns. The production of high-quality antler combs and their cases in Anglo-Scandinavian York, for instance, is considered to indicate 'a major industry ... in the hands of professional craftsmen'.[83] However, a note of caution is needed in case the conclusion is too easily drawn that such manufacture was a result of increasing urbanisation. Indeed, there is growing evidence that, rather than innovating such production, towns merely intensified output of products which had hitherto been the work of itinerant craftsmen supplying a dispersed market.[84]

Intensification of resource exploitation is perhaps also visible in activity close to the newly-established towns. Work at the town common of Bymarka, outside Trondheim in Norway, has uncovered a large number of charcoal pits, carbon 14 dating of which centres them on the 12th century (although the activity could have extended over some 300 years). These pits seems to have been producing charcoal for ironworking. Subsequent survey east of the town at Estenstadmarka revealed a further concentration with a similar date range, exciting the observation that the growth of Trondheim was creating a demand for charcoal which, to a considerable extent, was satisfied locally.[85]

The timber used to make the Trondheim charcoal was predominately birch, pine, elm and spruce. Construction of urban buildings could and did use timbers such as pine and, in places such as England, the more common oak. However, the increased demand for building materials as a result of urban expansion will have placed stress on the available resources. While there is documentary evidence for the sourcing of constructional materials in the later medieval period (below p. 75), it is necessary to rely upon archaeological evidence to explore such matters in the 11th and 12th centuries. The lack of surviving timber buildings of these dates is obviously a problem but, in a pioneering study, Damian Goodburn sought to reconstruct timber provision, its usage and the impact upon woodland stocks, by using observed characteristics of timber from Thameside revetments excavated in the city of London. He was able to identify sources which were both wildwood (that is primeval, unmanaged woodland) and coppiced woodland.[86]

It is tempting to suggest that urban expansion by the end of the 11th century was placing stress upon local timber sources and that constructional timber probably needed to be imported from further afield. Currently, however, such a supposition is not supported by the available evidence although there are examples of portable goods being made from imported wood, for instance barrels found at Hedeby near Schleswig on the Jutland peninsula which have been identified as manufactured from timber sourced in southern Germany.[87] Most houses must have been constructed of locally-sourced timber or, on some occasions, of earth itself.[88]

Not all secular buildings were houses of course. The socio-political role of castles has been noted above (p. 14ff.) but castles, and indeed palaces, as residences were also important by the beginning of the 12th century, the former being introduced into England in the the second half of the 11th century, the latter having been present in parts of Germany since the later 9th century.[89] Considerable archaeological work on the study of such structures, and the resources required for their construction, has been undertaken in recent decades, much of it charted by the annual bibliographies produced by John Kenyon for the Castles Studies Group in England (but often covering continental castles as well). Research on early castles has been wide-ranging. Major stone structures of late 11th- and early 12th-century date survive in eastern England and have been subjected to detailed assessment (notably the great keeps or *donjons* at Norwich and Colchester and the White Tower in London).[90] Castle excavations have shed new light upon the form and function of such fortifications in the 11th and 12th centuries [91] while study of the landscape setting of castles has enabled assessments of the wider contextual role played by castles within their environments.[92] The castle at Castle Acre in Norfolk illustrates both the impact of its position upon the landscape (controlling a diverted ancient route, the Peddar's Way) and, through excavation, its changing function from an 11th-century fortified country house to refurbishment as a *donjon* in the troubled 12th century.[93]

Such wide-ranging castle studies are not confined to England. Recent work in Flanders, the Netherlands and Germany is revealing much about the form and role of early castles. As well as Bruges, the Gravensteen castle in Ghent, situated on an island surrounded by the rivers Lys and Lieve, provided a new focus for the pre-existing urban settlement from the 10th century onward. By the 11th century a great stone hall had been constructed and would be supplemented by surrounding walls and towers in the 1100s. In north-western Germany, stone *donjons* were in existence by the 11th century such as the excavated example at Soest.[94] As well as stone fortifications, the lowland landscape of Niedersachsen encouraged the construction of a number of 'ringworks' between the 9th and the 11th centuries, an example being that at Alt Lübeck (above, p. 15). Recent excavation at the 'Heidenwall', a ringwork in Oldenburg (south of Wilhelmshaven), has uncovered remarkable timber lacing of the defensive earthworks. Dendrochronological dates for this construction reveal trees cut in 1032 and 1042 for an episcopal fortification possibly associated with Archbishop Hermann ('eine umstrittene Persönlichkeit'—a controversial personality) whom the chronicler Adam of Bremen states was responsible for starting a perimeter wall around the cathedral precinct in Bremen.[95]

Hermann's work in Bremen was also securing a palatial establishment, the provision of which had regal Carolinginan antecedents in Germany at locations such as Aachen and Paderborn. Study of episcopal palaces has included excavation in the 1980s of that called 'Die lburg', the residence of the bishops of Osnabrück. Stone fortifications dating to the late 11th century were uncovered, a great square tower being enclosed within a perimeter wall.[96] A smaller episcopal establishment was the minor castle of Bishop Bernwald von Hildesheim near the village of Wahrenholz, also in Niedersachsen. An earthwork and timber fortification, it is now ploughed-out and only visible from the air. Recently (2012) it has been surveyed using geophysics, the resulting ringwork data then overlaid on to a plan drawn in 1919 by Carl Schuchhardt after excavations by him from which only brief notes and a small sketch survive. New excavations are now planned to verify the data and establish a context for Schuchhardt's observations.[97]

Within England, an early episcopal palace is that at Norwich. This building was under construction (in stone from the outset) by the mid-1090s and, when complete, was linked physically to the north side of the cathedral church. Still extant if refaced in the 19th century, it retains within it a late 11th-century *donjon*. A recent reassessment of the building by Roberta Gilchrist, as well as considering the fabric and layout of the structure, explores the siting of the palace. She concludes that the first bishop, Herbert de Losinga, 'sought to create an elite landscape', one where the palace, built on a earthwork platform, could provide a commanding presence.[98]

Gilchrist's analysis invites comparison with the positioning of castles, such as that at nearby Castle Acre (above, p. 20) where Liddiard has argued that the approaches to the castle were deliberately manipulated so that the route presented 'a suitably impressive tableau to the visitor'. In a commendable attempt to enter the minds of late 11th-century travellers and their hosts, Liddiard draws comparisons between his landscape observations and Romance literature, arguing that such texts emphasised the importance of viewing a castle from a distance. At Castle Acre visitors would need to pass the priory and the town, negotiating a series of right-angle turns, each revealing an aspect of the landscape before eventually arriving at the castle. Even here the route would require another right-angle turn and an ascent before meeting the lord in his fortified house (subsequently *donjon*) on the castle mound.[99]

An increasing population, coupled with enhanced secular and ecclesiastical centralisation across much of northern Europe by the end of the 11th century, led to investment in the church as well as in architectural statements of lordly power. The growing importance of the church in the North Sea region finds expression in both surviving buildings and in excavated evidence. Study of the fabric of the cathedral in Ribe, Denmark, for instance has shown that this Romanesque structure (construction of which started in the first half of the 12th century under Bishop Thure) contains significant quantities of tufa in its build, a volcanic stone sourced in the Rhineland as well as Tournai limestone. Indeed, archaeological examination of churches of this period is usually necessary in order to establish likely sources of the building materials utilised. It is rare in early documentation—as opposed to later medieval records—to find references to stone sources; an unusual exception is provided by Adam of Bremen, writing in the late 1070s, who refers to the construction of the great church in Bremen by Archbishop Adelbert of Bremen who 'with too precipitate judgement immediately had the city wall ... pulled down, as if it were not at all necessary, and ordered its stones built into the temple [cathedral]'. Adelbert apparently 'often complained only about the lack of clerics and of stone'.[100]

Cannibalisation of earlier buildings was obviously one approach to stone supply and, in those parts of the North Sea province which had Roman antecedents, traces of reused Roman stone, brick and tile can often be located. Good examples are the excavated walls of Thomas of Bayeux's rebuilt York Minster (Thomas was Archbishop from 1070). Here the transept foundations contain many Roman stones and indeed stones with Roman inscriptions. Re-use of later material also occurred as pre-Conquest (that is pre-1066) decorated stones have been located within footings to the nave.[101] Such re-use was not confined to cathedrals. Stocker and Everson have examined churches across Lincolnshire in eastern England and, as well as noting much evidence of re-use during rebuilding of churches between the 10th and 12th centuries, they were also able to define three general patterns of such practice: *casual* 'where the original function of the stone is disregarded in its new use; *functional* re-use where stone was re-used 'for the purpose for which they were originally cut' (such as the tower arch of Alkborough church which has imposts of Roman stone, probably from a Roman arch); and *iconic* re-use, such as the setting of a Roman tomb monument of a seated figure in the west face of the tower at St Peter-at-Gowts in Lincoln,[102] probably to represent Christ or St Peter.[103]

An interesting observation of stone re-use has been noted from Norfolk where a survey has been undertaken of the incidence of Rhineland lava in the rubble walls of parish churches. Such lava is known to have been imported to England both before and after the Norman Conquest of 1066, being the preferred material for fashioning quernstones. Norfolk had some 928 parish churches in the Middle Ages (of which 620 are still in use) with 684 buildings surviving. Survey of all of these found that 425 churches (62%) contained one or more lava fragments within the fabric. However, churches with 10 or more fragments are almost entirely absent from west Norfolk while there is an 'overwhelming preponderance' of churches with 20 or more fragments between the Bure and Yare rivers, both of which flow out eastwards into the North Sea.

Some of the lava fragments are exceptionally large (such as one piece of 365 by 305 by 140mm at Colney church outside Norwich) and may therefore represent parts of imported blocks. Many fragments, however, clearly originated as parts of quernstones and a possible context for re-use (of the smaller fragments) occurs from the 12th century when the use of hand-querns was prohibited in England. Dating the wall fabrics remains problematic but lava can be said to be 'present in wall surfaces ranging in date from the mid to late 11th to the 15th century'. The east Norfolk concentration (Figure 1.8) is remarkable as is the provenance of the stone; it is exclusively Rhenish, no examples of the highest quality French quartzite stones from the Seine basin being observed. The preponderance of finds within east Norfolk is perhaps to be expected; the trade of Great Yarmouth was heavily focussed on the Rhineland whereas that of King's Lynn, in the hinterland of which the number of lava stones is significantly lower, was with the Baltic.

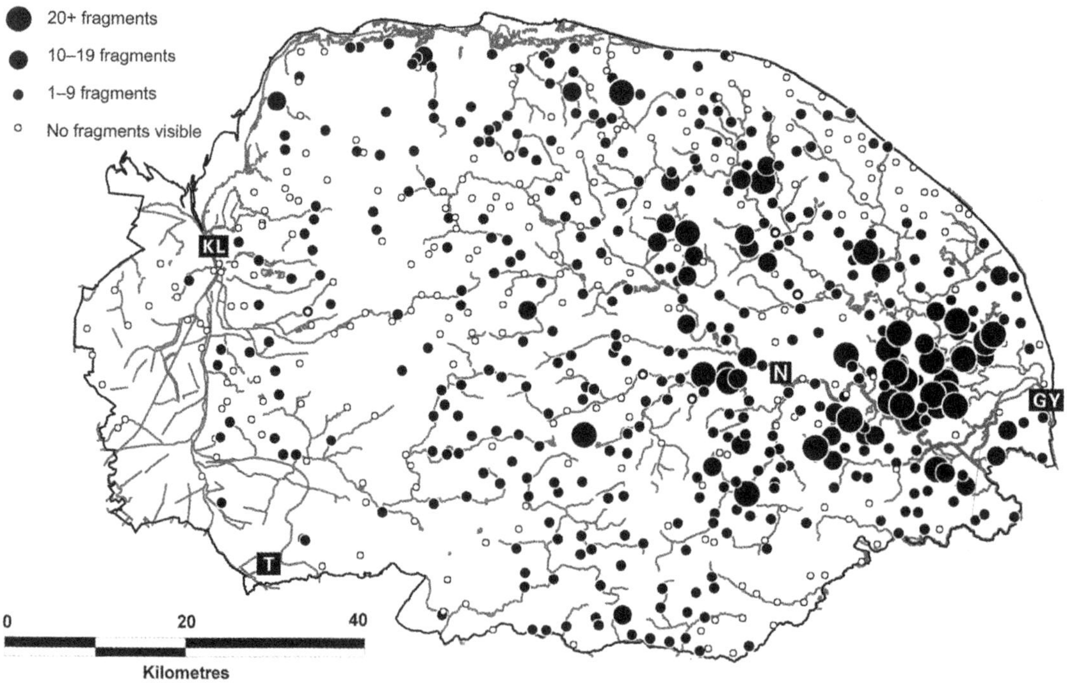

Figure 1.8 The distribution of Rhineland lava stones in Norfolk (Steven Ashley).

The lack of French quartzite stone is the more curious when consideration is given to the construction of Norwich Cathedral. This great institution, founded in the late 11th century, sourced its stone afresh, utilising local flint and mortar as did the 12th-century parish churches of Norfolk. The cathedral's chalk quarries, from which both the lime for mortar and the small flint stones were obtained, remain visible across the River Wensum on what was episcopal land.[104] However, the walls of the cathedral church are faced in limestone, the earliest types used being from Caen in Normandy and Barnack in Northamptonshire (midland England). Transportation of both was facilitated by water, the stone travelling by sea as far as Great Yarmouth, then by river to Norwich and finally via a purpose-built canal to the edge of the building site. The mouth of the canal survives as does a later canal gatehouse (much restored), the canal itself illustrated on 18th-century engravings.

Similarly, water transport facilitated the movement of stone on the continent. The tufa used at Ribe must have been taken down the Rhine to the North Sea and then northward to Denmark. The important sandstone quarries of Obernkirchen provided stone for Minden Cathedral in the mid-11th century (the building was largely destroyed in 1945 and subsequently rebuilt). The Obernkirchen quarries were located only some 13km east of Minden and stone could be easily transported along the River Weser. By the mid-12th century, town walls were being constructed of quarried tufa at Duisburg[105] but elsewhere in stone-poor northern Germany, urban defences generally remained of earth and timber before the introduction of brick in the 13th century. Such stone as was available tended to be *Feldsteine* or field stones, boulders deposited by glaciation.

Exploitation of resources, therefore, whether for food, clothing or shelter, was changing at the start of the 11th century. There was increased pressure upon traditional basic stocks, such as fish or timber, and relatively new exploitation of hard-won resources such as stone. In general terms, the more prestigious the material, the more likely it was to be located within a prestigious environment. Thus stone structures in 1100 were aristocratic or ecclesiastical but the provision of the stone itself would have relied upon more menial labour. It is possible that rare evidence for such labour exploitation was recovered in 1979 when a previously-unknown graveyard, associated with a timber church destroyed by construction of the early Norman castle around 1068, was excavated in Norwich. Analysis of the 11th-century skeletal material found a number of upper-girdle pathologies associated with lifting and labouring strains among the adult males, coupled with vitamin D deficiency. Together, these conditions suggested 'some occupation where individuals, particularly males, were involved in hard physical work whilst excluded from sunlight. One such occupation is, of course, mining'.[106] Medieval flint mines survive in Norwich although, to date, it has not proved possible to assign any to the 11th century.

Population, rising consumption and urban development

The Norwich church and its attendant graveyard were located on the fringes of the 11th-century settlement and were probably representative of a relatively-impoverished population. However, the town within which these people lived and worked was already sizeable (perhaps comprising between 5000 and 10,000 individuals). It was not alone as a growing urban community in the 11th century. Towns on both sides of the North Sea were flourishing by 1100, often with vibrant roles as centres of administration but additionally as developing mercantile hubs. Advances in scientific techniques are now beginning to contribute to a better understanding of the ethnic and social identities of individuals within these towns, as well as within rural communities, through techniques such as stable isotope analysis and DNA analysis.

While the principles behind stable isotope analysis are relatively straightforward (in essence, geographically-distinct strontium and oxygen isotopes are absorbed into the human skeletal structure through ingestation of plants and animals or drinking water respectively, providing a locational 'signature'), the restrictions on effective use of the technique are considerable and have been explored within the pages of *Antiquity*. The authors of a review of results from Britain noted that the work is 'technically difficult, labour intensive and expensive' and that pilot studies were accordingly small-scale in scope.

However, they were able to conclude that identification of first generation immigrants into England from northern Europe and Scandinavia was possible and that, additionally, the impact upon human health could also be examined. 'Combined isotopic and palaeopathological investigation could be a powerful new tool with which to investigate the development and transmission of communicable disease'.[107]

The further role of isotype analysis in identifying changes in diet has assisted study of fish assemblages from major urban areas (above, p. 7) but research is now also indicating how diet sometimes remained stable, despite major environmental change, due to local circumstances and preferences. Thus, at Ridanäs on the island of Gotland in the Baltic Sea, a subsistence fishing economy persisted even though major challenges had to be faced. These challenges consisted of environmental, ideological and socio-economic changes at the end of the Viking Age, including land uplift which closed the settlement's harbour. However, the community nevertheless created new harbour facilities and clearly continued to obtain marine resources. Archaeological recognition of such stability in the face of adversity supports theoretical approaches to understandings of subsistence which focus 'less on simplistic models of economizing activity or mechanistic cost minimization, and more on how the dynamic inter-relationship between cultural, socioeconomic, and environmental variables may contribute to change or stability in a dietary regime'.[108] It can perhaps best be summarised as where there is a will, there is a way.

Elsewhere in Scandinavia, isotope analysis has identified individuals within graveyard assemblages who almost certainly were incomers to the local population. At the trading settlement of Sebbersund in northern Jutland, Denmark three individuals of probable 11th-century date had probably originated in either the northern British Isles or Norway (one was a woman, non- local but buried in a local fashion and thus probably marrying into the community) (Figure 1.9).[109] The use of mitochondrial DNA analysis at another Danish cemetery, Kongemarken near Roskilde on Zealand, identified a further non-local individual dating to about AD 1000 whose immediate ancestors may have originated in the area of the Black Sea. Across the North Sea, in Norwich, similar DNA work located a Romani individual of 10th- to 11th-century date, the earliest recorded instance of such a person in England and one who also perhaps originated from the region of Byzantium.[110] Other recent analysis at Norwich identified two individuals with DNA haplotypes only encountered at that date in Orkney with two more who had haplotypes typical of Norway and the Western Isles. Three out of the four individuals dated to the 10th and 11th centuries, with the fourth being 8th- to 9th-century in date, suggesting continuity migrant flow into the population.[111]

This migration into an urban community, albeit possibly sporadic, would obviously have contributed to a dynamic society. Charting such mobility archaeologically has traditionally been illustrated by the movement of commercial goods, ceramics being the most common commodity to be studied because pottery both survives well (if usually fragmented) and it changes stylistically with a commendable and helpful frequency, thus aiding dating. Ceramic studies within the North Sea region have a long and illustrious pedigree particularly in the UK, stemming from the formative work of Gerald Dunning who, as early as 1933, produced an assessment of imported polychrome wares into England and Scotland and followed this 35 years later with an influential paper on North Sea pottery trade.[112] His work was supplemented by that of John Hurst from the late 1950s onward whose own tribute to Dunning in the latter's *Festschrift* was devoted to imported pottery.[113] (The 1992 *Festschrift* for Hurst was entitled 'Everyday and Exotic Pottery from Europe').[114] More recent British scholars such as Hodges have provided critiques of the uses of material culture, using ceramics and other data to explore economic models.[115]

Continental researchers have also made significant contributions, developing concepts of exchange to broaden understanding of socio-economic developments. Verhoeven has sought to provide a more integrated approach to the complex economics of pottery production and trade, highlighting constraints on production—such as problems accessing clay, fuel and means of transportation—as well as the likely exchange systems.[116] Verhaege has explored the complexity of these trade and exchange systems, summarising a range of problems but also suggesting some general trends, not least the definition of two broad sub-regions identifiable from ceramics—a southern one of southern England, Flanders, parts of northern France and parts of the Netherlands (with influence from France and the Mediterranean),

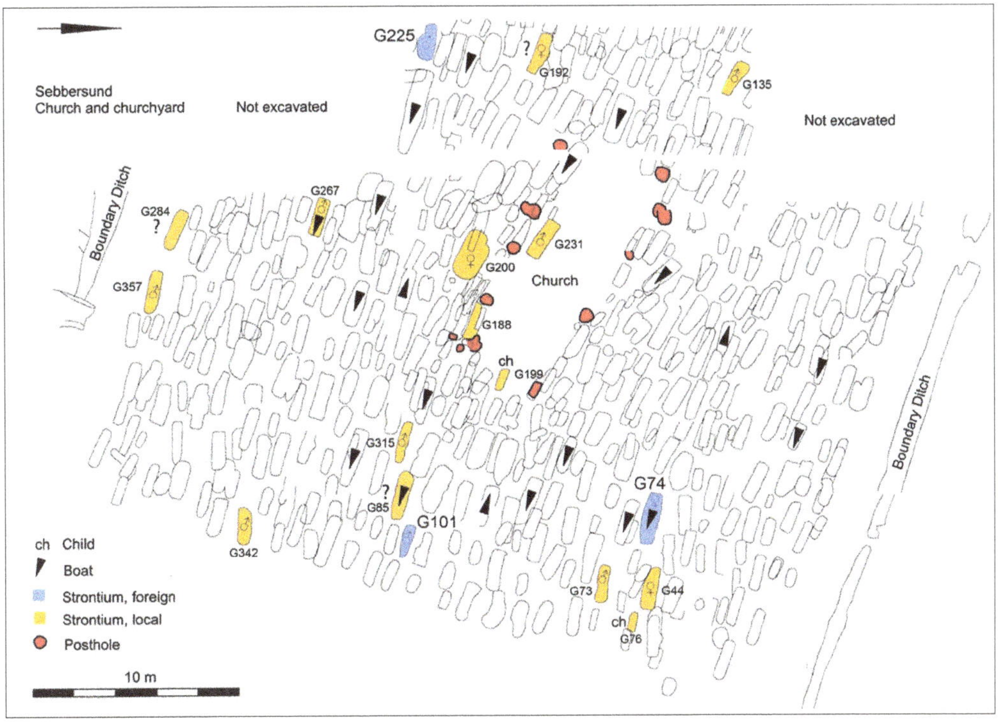

Figure 1.9 Plan of the timber church and graveyard at Sebbersund, Denmark (with permission of T. D. Price from Price *et al.* 2012).

and a northern one extending from Flanders and England to Scandinavia and the Baltic, including Germany.[117] Innovatively, Van Es and Verhers have gone beyond the ceramics themselves and sought to develop a model for the mechanisms of their trade, based upon the capacity of the excavated Skuldelev *knarr* ship.[118] Essentially, these studies are each investigating proto-industrial activities whereby processes were operated around investments in networks and communication within those networks.

All of the above approaches have enhanced understanding of both trans-North Sea trade and of the underlying economic criteria influencing production and consumption, as well as environmental and technological factors behind the acquisition of resources and their utilisation, developments in processes, and mechanisms of trade and exchange. Within England towns clearly played a significant role as producers/consumers and in the distribution of ceramics before 1100—production centres such as Ipswich, Thetford, Norwich, Stamford and Torksey have been identified. The widespread distribution of pottery is confirmed by excavations, particularly of high quality fabrics such as Stamford ware. Additionally, the siting of kilns in towns such as Norwich, immediately outside the boundary ditch of the early 11th-century settlement, suggests strongly that mercantile elements within urban society had controlling interests in the industry. In contrast, continental pottery such as the Rhenish wares of Badorf and the later Pingsdorf types, while traded extensively, had production centres away from towns (such as the Vorgebirge region between Cologne and Bonn) and were probably controlled by ecclesiastical landlords.[119] Urban involvement was almost certainly necessary in order to foster distribution but production may have been subordinated to large institutions.

The probable role of towns in distribution can be surmised from analysis of the ceramics themselves. Recent assessment of assemblages from some 152 locations on both sides of the North Sea involved modelling of associated artefact types between sites. One observation to emerge was the appearance of key locations at the intersections of clusters of activity—such as Canterbury, Lincoln, Norwich, Aarhus and Tiel—places identified as having a high 'betweenness' centrality (Figure 1.10).[120] The study examined

10th-century material, a period when development of some of these towns at least was at a formative stage, so it is possible to conclude that such perceived importance within long-distance trade networks at this date foreshadowed even greater importance by the end of the 11th century.

Trade in pottery is the most visible illustration of contacts across the North Sea. However, other artefacts recovered in excavations can also illuminate cultural contact and include hone stones from Norway imported into England, lava querns (above, p. 22) exported from the Rhineland and, stylistically, Scandinavian designs replicated on antler combs, stonework and brooches in English urban production centres. Imports to continental Europe from the British Isles are, conversely, more difficult to track through archaeological work as much seems to have been in the form of perishable goods—wool and grain to the fore.

With regard to towns, the nodal points of commercial activity, understanding of urban morphology at the end of the 11th century has advanced greatly in the last 40 years through comprehensive archaeological survey and excavation in a large number of locations on both sides of the North Sea. Of particular note are the extensive excavations at Hedeby in northern Germany, a 'green field' site following destruction of the settlement in 1066 and the subsequent development of nearby Schleswig (early excavations were undertaken by Herbert Jankuhn and further, subsequent, work has now appeared both in a series of monographs and summarised by Schietzel); excavations in Bergen in Norway, a town established first in the 11th century but the site of pioneering urban waterfront excavations (above, p. 8 and Chapter 5); the important excavations at the site of the 8th-century and later emporium of Dorestad in the Netherlands; extensive work in London at the waterfront and elsewhere; and wide-ranging work in York, particularly with regard to Anglo-Scandinavian deposits.[121]

Figure 1.10 Graph modelling network of North Sea sites using incidence of artefacts. Sites with less than two artefact types are omitted and affiliations are therefore represented as a network in which links indicate two or more shared artefact types. The relative strength of the links is shown by the shading of the lines, darker lines representing stronger links and, by implication, highlighting key 'betweenness' locations. (Graph drawn by Søren M. Sindbæk using Pajek and reproduced with his permission).

The results of work in these centres, together with other activity such as the excavations in Ribe and Viborg in Denmark,[122] indicate that development of towns within the North Sea region in the period up to 1100 was not a uniform process. A number of factors determined growth: geography, residual urban tradition, economics, and political ambition. Similar factors also contributed to decline or physical relocation of urban centres. With regard to growth, the elements of geography and tradition combined in those areas with a legacy from the Roman empire. Such a legacy did not necessarily simply mean in England (where 14 of the 24 greater medieval towns predated 1066 in origin) [123] and continental Europe as far north as the central Netherlands and the Rhine valley, locations which had residual Roman urban sites. Additionally, parts of northern Germany and southern Scandinavia had certainly experienced interaction with Rome (the extraordinary quantities of Roman material from the Illerup, Denmark site of *c.* 200AD are an example of such contact).[124] Together, this large area of residual Roman influence bounding both sides of the North Sea is now taken to be a 'Middle Zone' of urban development at the end of the first millennium AD with more northern Scandinavia and Germany north of the Rhine and east of the Jutish peninsula as an 'Outer Zone'.[125] The major towns mentioned in the preceding paragraph were all, except Bergen, within the Middle Zone.

Traditionally, the lower Rhine basin and its immediate North Sea/English Channel region has been seen as the commercial heartland of north-western Europe in the centuries leading up to 1100 and beyond. However, Chris Wickham contends that this undervalues longer-distance trade and notes sardonically that the Rhine-Seine-Thames triangle became a focus of attention, 'whether ingenuously or disgenuously', of influential historians whose countries of origin coincided with it. Hodges glosses the point by observing that this is not necessarily the case with regard to influential archaeologists, whose discoveries are indeed seeking to characterise more distant trading activity.[126] However extensive the trade though, commerce was clearly a stimulating factor in urban development. The growth of Ypres has been mentioned above (p. 16) but similarly the substantial flourishing of Bruges, Ghent and Antwerp by the 11th century owed a great deal to commercial activity. Here, however, political ambition also fostered growth; the protection provided by early fortifications at Bruges and Ghent has already been noted. Archaeological work in all of these towns and others has done much to increase understanding of urban development (be it from a single 'core' site outward or by the amalgamation of a number of sites into one urban area) and to characterise the nature of urban settlement, identifying zones of activity in some instances as in 10th- and 11th-century Thetford in eastern England where extensive excavation allows interpretation of localised craft activities such as pottery manufacture.[127]

As well as work on the major towns of this Rhine-Seine-Thames triangle, significant results have been achieved in more distant locations such as Perth in Scotland. Here archaeology has demonstrated that, contrary to previous ideas, medieval society was sufficiently developed by the 11th century for some form of urbanisation to have been initiated. Reassessment of radiocarbon dates using Bayesian modelling has shown that carbonised food remains on the rims of shelly ware pots found in High Street, Perth date from *c.* 1050 rather than a hundred years later as previously thought. Archaeological work therefore is freeing Scottish urban studies from the historical paradigm whereby, hitherto, urban foundation in Perth for instance has been linked to the known designation of its status as a royal burgh in the 1120s. As the researchers note: 'This should not be an enormous surprise, as the view that King David I founded his burghs on "green-field" sites is long outdated'.[128] However, it remains debatable as to how far the earlier evidence represents urbanisation *per se* rather than small riverside settlement, an emergent centre rather than a truly urban one. The earliest phase recorded within the excavations was only capable of being dated to 'pre-1150'; thus, with regard to the characteristic urban 'rigs' or tenement plots of the medieval town, the excavated evidence seems to indicate that their form was indeed dictated by deliberate royal town planning in the 12th century.[129] Accordingly, it must be assumed that occupation of the site of Perth in the 11th century was, at best, 'proto-urban' (and is not necessarily supported by all commentators, at least one of whom has expressed scepticism about the radiocarbon dating[130]).

The probable planned rigs of Perth had parallels elsewhere, often at the level of individual tenements but also in the deliberate planning of entire districts and occasionally the towns themselves.

Early examples of urban planning have been noted for some time (such as the mid 11th-century planned town at Bury St Edmunds in eastern England, an urban settlement fostered by the great Benedictine abbey of Bury)[131] with analytical work on the plan elements of towns being initiated by historical geographers such as Conzen.[132] In recent years his observations and those of others have been subjected to more detailed, theoretically-archaeological, exploration. Lilley, for instance, has considered particular aspects of medieval urban design through an examination of urban form linked to the socio-political changes introduced by the Norman invasion. His chosen towns concern a perceived need for aristocratic control of territorial expansion. He discusses locations drawn from outside the lowland area of the North Sea region but he argues that other sites close to the North Sea, such as the small castle-town of Pleshey in Essex, contain similar urban plans to his examples. In his model, urban 'plan form complexes' enable discussion of the role of urban layout in facilitating early military control, fostering market expansion, and 'providing more formal and regular layouts, sometimes rectilinear in form and sometimes orthogonal ... designed to colonize towns by maximizing the number of urban property holders, and providing them with entrepreneurial opportunities'.[133]

Lilley's examples are mainly concerned with small towns and he admits that there is scope for recognition of his urban plan forms 'within the more complex, composite plans of large medieval urban centres'. Although he discusses English towns he finds that a similar approach to urban morphology discerns similar forms in both France and Germany. The point being made is that it is necessary to go beyond categorisation of plan forms and to use them 'to seek a wider understanding of the intimate dialectic between urban space and medieval society'. This is an urban archaeology which seeks the explore the mentality behind urban development as much as that development itself.

Somewhat more conventionally, careful archaeological study of plot sizes, both from excavated examples and from extant tenement plots fossilised within the old centres of modern towns, suggests re-planning of certain towns in the 11th and 12th centuries. These 'permanent plots' have been observed in the towns of Braunschweig, Osnabrück, Hamburg and Schleswig while, in Cologne, the newly-laid out plots were recorded in Schreinsbücher, medieval directories of land transactions. Development of plots has been particularly well-observed at Echternstraße in Braunschweig where comprehensive excavation has enabled the growth of the old town to be explored through archaeological evidence.[134]

Within urban areas, particular urban forms of building can be observed by 1100. The evidence for the late Viking Age buildings of Coppergate in York, characterised by sunken featured workshops set behind buildings on the street frontage, can be replicated (albeit without the same extraordinary level of preservation) in other towns on the east coast of England such as Ipswich where the number of such cellared-buildings now exceeds fifty; indeed, in Ipswich, 'no other building type is known throughout the 10th and 11th centuries'.[135] On the continent, timber-lined cellars of 11th-century date have been found in Zutphen, Deventer, Göttingen, Soest and Aarhus[136] while, in Sweden, well-preserved footings of ground-level houses have been excavated in Sigtuna. Here 11th-century plots at least 30m long, with as many as five buildings within them, contained log and post-and-plank structures with the houses being heated by central fireplaces.[137] Plot division in 11th-century Oslo was effected by a fence of thin planks called *skigard*.[138]

The growth of towns brought with it a growth in infrastructure. Transport infrastructure was especially important if towns were to maximise their potential as mercantile centres. Riverine and estuarine ports improved dockside facilities through consolidation of the foreshore as seen in excavation at Lincoln, London, Norwich and Schleswig. Both of the last two towns have also produced evidence for boat- or ship-building in the 11th century, or, at least, for boat repair in the form of cradles, pinned to the foreshore with driven stakes.[139] A 10th-century causeway bridge is known from Ravning Enge in Denmark and it is probable that the pile-construction bridge identified at Norwich in 1896 was of similar date. The major construction of a bridge across the Thames in London is now known from archaeological work to date to *c.* 1000 while part of a collapsed 11th-century bridge crossing the River Fleet in London was discovered in 1989. 'Laftwork' or timber caissons filled with stones as supports for a bridge have been located at Brogepollen near Vestvagoy in northern Norway and dated to the 11th or 12th century.[140]

The church

An important element in the development of societies around the North Sea was the church. The role of the church has been characterised as 'the elephant in the room' when considering the economy of the 9th and 10th centuries[141] but the elephant was certainly in plain sight by the end of the 11th century, not least as characterised by the proliferation of parish churches within the larger towns of eastern England. The growing urban communities of London, Norwich, Lincoln and York all had significant numbers of parish churches by the Norman Conquest; a probable 50 or more in London, some 40 in Norwich, 30 in Lincoln and at least 14 in York. The role of these parishes in urban formation is the subject of continuing study by both historians and archaeologists.

Parochial foundation was also very obvious within rural England by the end of the 11th century. In Suffolk some 416 churches (or about 75% of the later medieval total for the county) were recorded in Domesday Book of 1086 while, in Yorkshire, about 390 churches (out of a total of 550 surviving medieval churches) have either fabric or a font that predate 1150.[142] This surviving stone fabric, however, can be misleading with regard to the structure of many churches in the 11th century. John Blair has noted that, of six recent excavations of churches in Essex, five of them had timber phases which were only replaced in stone after the Norman Conquest of 1066. Timber was undoubtedly the principal material used for many English churches until the later 11th century, in urban as well as rural contexts. Evidence for two such urban churches, one never replaced in stone, has now been recovered from Norwich while a third may have had a timber phase on a site adjacent to the excavated church.[143]

Many of these English churches were proprietary churches (that is churches subject to a lordship, either lay or ecclesiastic), known as *Eigenkirchen* in Germany. As in England, such German churches in the 11th century were often constructed of timber. Claus Ahrens has sought to catalogue the numbers of known examples, drawing evidence from surviving buildings, documentary records and excavation. Numerous wooden structures are known from Niedersachsen such as excavated churches at Bunde, Dorum, Etzel, Jever and Middels. The evidence for some of these buildings consisted of large *Feldsteinen* or field stones, essentially forming plinths upon which timber beams for the wooden structures could rest. Some churches were replaced in stone either by or during the 11th century; a good example is the church of Tostedt excavated in 1969.[144] It is probable that many hundreds of similar buildings existed across north-western Germany, as they seem to have done in southern Scandinavia. Lund diocese in Sweden, for example, had some 540 churches in the Middle Ages, although it needs to be remembered that the episcopal diocese had developed into an archepiscopal one after 1104 with an extent across Scandinavia as well as locations as far away the Isle of Man. Nevertheless, it has been noted for Sweden that excavation has revealed a considerable number of 11th-century timber churches subsequently rebuilt in stone, a plausible statement when, in Sigtuna in central Sweden, three of five excavated churches showed evidence for 11th-century wooden structures beneath later stone buildings.[145]

A topographical variation has been observed in Lund itself. Here excavation would suggest that early timber churches, perhaps dating from the end of the 10th century were replaced by stone ones on a slightly different site. This can be seen clearly for the St Trinitas stone church, a large building with its plan now marked out in the paving of Kattesund street, some 30m west of a timber building, also marked out on the same street.[146]

The construction of churches was often the culmination of a process whereby a central place of importance to a community often became a manorial centre or settlement. Just such a process can be seen at the village of Hørning in Jutland, Denmark where excavation in the 1960s uncovered evidence for a late 11th-century timber church (including a well-preserved and celebrated plank with interlace decoration). The excavation discovered that the church had been erected on top of a Viking Age barrow some 30m in diameter, its construction not only a visible indication of the transition in Denmark from

Figure 1.11 Reconstruction of Hørning timber church, Denmark (Brian Ayers).

paganism to Christianity but, as tellingly, the incorporation of an important ritual site as an integral part of a developing community. Research work in the area by the University of Nottingham is seeking to understand the scale, spatial organisation and chronology of this 11th-century community and the neighbouring settlements of Moeskaer, Ammelhede and Stavnsager.[147]

Other excavations of wooden churches have also been informative. At Lisbjerg, north of Aarhus, archaeological investigation established that the first (timber) church, dating to the 11th century, had been created on the site of the main building of a pre-existing Viking Age farmstead. Within, quantities of wall plaster were located, indicating that the church had been decorated in a manner normally associated with stone churches.[148]

It seems likely that communication across the North Sea was responsible for the transmission of stylistic ideas with regard to churches, both in timber and stone. This communication was not necessarily solely from continental Europe to the British Isles but may have been a more complex process. The celebrated stave churches of later medieval Norway have been shown by excavation to have precursors in the mid-11th century, the earliest being that found in Norwich in 1979.[149] This excavated structure, destroyed by construction of the early Norman castle, was very similar in both form and dimensions to the Hørning church but perhaps a generation older. An idea of how both churches may have looked can now be gained at the Moesgård museum outside Aarhus where the Hørning church was reconstructed in 1997 (Figure 1.11).

Stone churches also have trans-North Sea stylistic affinities. While the Romanesque style in general was adopted throughout northern Europe, more localised preferences can be also be observed. Round western towers, for instance, are a feature of 11th- and 12th-century parish churches in Norfolk and, to a lesser extent, Suffolk in eastern England. Over 130 such Norfolk towers still stand with evidence for others continuing to be located (as at the village of Carlton Forehoe in 2013 when drainage works around the later rectangular tower uncovered footings of an earlier round one).[150] Stephen Heywood has made a particular study of such towers and concludes that the majority probably date to 'the period of Norman consolidation (approx. 1070–1140)'. He believes that the 'predilection' for round towers in East Anglia follows the examples set by the two great Anglo-Norman churches of Norwich Cathedral and Bury St Edmunds Abbey. However, he also notes that these two churches sat firmly within a north European tradition whereby round towers were features of notable churches (such as that of St Michael Hildesheim in north Germany) and the fashion was disseminated as far as Denmark, Sweden and Orkney. Isolating the origin of such an architectural form is difficult but, despite 'the earliest single round western towers ...[at] ... Heeslingen near Bremen and Johannisberg near Hersfeld, the number of towers in East Anglia by the third quarter of the twelfth century ... makes East Anglia the most likely source'.[151]

Art-historical and archaeological exploration, therefore, is uncovering a complex interchange of ideas, facilitated by the ease of contact provided by the North Sea at the end of the 11th century. No doubt Norman-French taste stimulated Romanesque stone church architecture in England which, in turn, may have influenced north European buildings but the idea of the great urban church was itself north European. Examples of these churches either still exist, such as the cathedral in Bremen, or have been excavated, as at the church of St Donatian in Bruges. These substantial buildings frequently acted as foci for urban development; Bury St Edmunds (above, p. 28) is an obvious example but, elsewhere in eastern England, the creation of the Benedictine monastery of Ely (and its attendant great church) in 1081 has been argued as the 'stimulus for growth'. This, allied to re-routing of River Ouse-Cam in the early 12th century, led to the establishment of extensive craft industries, including pottery production, and associated commercial distribution thereafter (see also below, p. 65).[152]

Archaeological analysis of these large churches themselves is now revealing unexpected insights. At Lincoln, for instance, it has been argued that the striking *Westwerk* incorporates an early great tower or *donjon* built by Remigius, the first bishop in the late 11th-century.[153] Recent stone-by-stone analysis undertaken by the University of Nottingham has since concluded that the 'phasing of the west front at Lincoln is much more complicated than had been thought, and that the evidence for its design as a secular palace is not at all straightforward'. However, this later work nevertheless concludes that it 'is not the end of the story' with research continuing and incorporating other observations including excavation. The researchers remain aware of Henry of Huntingdon's 12th-century comment that Remigius built his church so that it 'was agreeable to the servants of God and also, as suited the times, invincible to enemies'.[154]

Remaining in Lincolnshire, an assessment of early Norman towers on parish churches of the county concludes that their construction linked back to Remigius and the institution of a new liturgical rite within his diocese. This procedure was particularly apposite for funerary practice, giving 'prominence to the ringing of bells in conjunction with invocations to St Michael, who was to carry the soul from earth to heaven .'.. Within the Lincoln diocese, therefore, the bell-tower became an important adjunct to parish churches. It is argued that these towers 'were the very embodiment of the Anglo-Norman church settlement. They are a very visible expression of the conformity of otherwise unexceptional parish churches .'.. and their attendant populations.[155]

The creation of parish churches also had an impact upon funerary practice itself. Centralisation of community worship led to the consecration of bounded spaces around churches for the burial of the dead. Archaeological investigation of such cemeteries has increased in recent years, seeking topographic, demographic and pathological information although such research is often complicated by long-use of graves and the consequent inter-cutting of burial assemblages. Notwithstanding such problems, useful data has been recovered from cemeteries within the North Sea region. Excavations from London churches provide good examples. Burials can assist understanding of church foundation as at the church of St Bride, now seen to be an 11th-century foundation, the earliest building lying immediately above graves of this date. At the churchyard of St Nicholas Shambles, burial types included those in wooden coffins, graves with pebble floors, graves with stone pillows, graves lined with stone, and stone-lined 'cist' burials. There was also a charcoal burial, a practice of unknown function but paralleled in date by two similar burials at St Mark's church in Lincoln. A particularly poignant burial at St Nicholas Shambles was that of a woman who died in childbirth, the skeletons of both mother and foetus being recorded.[156] Excavations at Barton-upon-Humber in north Lincolnshire established that diversity in burial practice was greatest between 950 and 1150 and included 'the obscure practice of pouring liquid mud into coffins'.[157] Graveyard archaeology also enables investigation of 11th-century pathologies, giving insights into public health around the year 1100 (as at the cemetery of Holy Trinity in Lund, Sweden where the incidence of sufferers from leprosy has been plotted) and of social or gender differentiation (as at the Kongemarken cemetery near Roskilde in Denmark where generally males were buried to the south of the church and females to the north).[158]

Archaeological study of churches and the populations associated with them, particularly assisted by innovative techniques such as isotopic and DNA analysis, is helping to emphasise the interaction of communities across the North Sea at the end of the 12th century. This interaction was clearly part of a continuing tradition but the demonstration both of stylistic affinity in terms of church buildings and of population movement with regard to individuals underlines the importance of the North Sea as a highway which facilitated exchange of ideas and experiences as much as of trade goods and capital. Further, the cultural links now evident in the exploration of early urban centres on both sides of the North Sea, together with parallels in the form of houses, workshops and everyday goods, illustrates the durability of contact despite major political changes in England. Historically, the obvious shift in political priorities towards northern France engendered by the Norman Conquest of England after 1066 has been one supported by the all-too solid materiality of early Anglo-Norman culture—stone castles, great new cathedrals and rebuilt churches in the Romanesque style. Archaeological and art-historical work, however, is now illustrating that such a perceived cultural shift was not as all-embracing or as simple as robust surviving monuments imply. Rather, the increase in Norman French influence was one which supplemented a continuation of traditional trans-North Sea contact, sometimes interacting in interesting ways as has been demonstrated by Heywood's study of churches in eastern England and in northern Germany (above, p. 31).

The evidence of sustained contact provided by archaeological evidence in the broadest sense (excavated features, cultural artefacts, surviving buildings, topographical similarities, population data and environmental change) is perhaps not surprising. 'The economy, stupid' was a phrase coined by James Carville, strategist for Bill Clinton's US presidential campaign in 1992. It was clearly apposite then because Clinton went on to win; the campaign merely spoke 'a truth universally acknowledged', that fostering the economy is important to society. By 1100, the North Sea world, in the form of communities with common challenges of environment and population but also with common aspirations linked to technological and commercial ability, was well-placed to develop a central role as the powerhouse of northern Europe. As with the Clinton campaign, economic needs were key. Archaeological work is now providing evidence of the economic development of coastline communities and their hinterlands at the end of the 11th century. This development was clearly supported by maritime contact even if the importance of that contact was probably not of such intensity that economies were solely dependent upon international trade. Nevertheless, the potential for growth was established and could be built upon. Its impact was profound, growth in the 12th and 13th centuries not only providing much for archaeological enquiry but, as will be seen, creating and enhancing social and economic structures which survive to the present day.

— 2 —

12th- and 13th-Century Consolidation

A developing economy lays the basis for an increased confidence within society in general and within its constituent communities. However, this confidence is not that promoted by aristocratic elites through major structures such as castles. Indeed, it could be argued that where there was a proliferation of castles, as in England during the first half of the 12th century, the phenomenon highlighted a febrile, insecure situation, the reverse of confidence in society. Rather, the display of a broad-based confidence needed to be that engendered by the principal agents of economic well-being, the mercantile class. Stability for these individuals provided the climate for the generation of wealth and, with that, investment in material goods and property. England may have been suffering under the Anarchy until the mid-12th century but elsewhere it is possible to discern an emerging confidence within this mercantile class, particularly as illustrated through surviving or excavated buildings. Archaeological exploration of these, the materials with which they were constructed and the manner in which they were used, has been undertaken increasingly, both through excavation and through analyses of standing structures, over the last 30 years in a large number of settlements, predominantly towns, on both sides of the North Sea.

Mercantile and high status architectural expression

Commercial confidence and investment perhaps has its earliest (and most demonstrative) secular expression in Ghent (Figure 2.1). Here, by the middle of the 12th century, stood over 30 stone houses, mercantile buildings some of which had towers 'that mimicked those of contemporary stone donjons'. Little of these survives although a sense of the stature of such buildings can be gleaned from the early 13th-century elements extant within the Kleine Sikkel fortified merchant's house on Hoogpoort or the more complete—and massive—house erected in the mid-13th century known as the Gerard de Duivelsteen. It has been argued that these buildings represented 'a consciousness of collective identity on the part of that urban elite at least two centuries before historians such as Braudel suggested a similar self-awareness of difference from the rural world for the citizens of medieval towns more generally, especially in the Italian urban republics'.[1]

While the economic capital necessary to enable the creation of such precocious buildings was clearly derived from Ghent's early commercial success, the houses and their builders also benefited from a fortuitous location whereby Tournai or Doornik limestone was readily available for construction. Contemporary Bruges, developing commercially in a similar—and ultimately even more spectacular—manner, was less well-placed for materials and, to date, evidence for the development of such confident architecture there is largely confined to the 13th century with the advent of the widespread application of brick (although the existence of 'large patrician domains' is known in the 12th-century town[2]). In Tournai,

Figure 2.1 13th-century house at the corner of Klein Turkije/Goudenleeuwplein, Ghent (Brian Ayers).

itself, however, two well-preserved stone houses survive on Rue Barre-St-Brice, their style reminiscent of French buildings further south.

Such French influence is also evident in England by the second half of the 12th century, perhaps as an obvious result of the Norman Conquest but probably also in part due to increased mercantile activity and the need for a house type which assisted such activity. France and perhaps Flanders seem to have provided examples; in a review of the origins of English medieval townhouses, Roland Harris has noted that the 'towns of France and possibly much of Europe were dominated by a house type that combined areas for the sale of goods and for domestic use', buildings which he terms the 'ground-level townhouse' (with shops or workshops on the ground-floor and residence above). Unsurprisingly, the type can be found in English towns too and, indeed, Harris goes so far as to state that 'the twelfth-century traveller to both Lincoln and Cluny, for example, might have found a notable consistency in the appearance of the main streets'.[3] He carries on to reassess the famous so-called Jew's House on Steep Hill in Lincoln, demonstrating its hitherto overlooked stylistic affinities with French counterparts. It is tempting to reach the conclusion that a pan-European style, the Romanesque, had evolved a secular architectural tradition that particularly suited increasingly affluent urban merchants.

In England, however, Harris identifies another building type within the Romanesque tradition, the 'split-level' townhouse where a cellar or undercroft lies beneath the retail level. In seeking the origins of this latter form, he has to conclude that the only clear links that he can find are between England and Normandy. Such buildings are evidenced from a number of towns in the English North Sea province (there are examples known from Lincoln, Stamford, King's Lynn, Norwich, Great Yarmouth, Colchester and London) but, pre-1350, split-level buildings can also be found as far west as Gloucester and Exeter.

Harris suggests that the particular urban circumstances of English towns, with a demand for shops in constricted locations, led to a particularly insular solution.[4]

This conclusion could perhaps now be challenged by the results of recent excavations in Lübeck. Work in 1985 on a large Saalgeschoßhaus at Schüsselbuden 6, destroyed by bombing in 1942, has revealed a great cellar beneath an early 13th-century building, itself erected above an earlier three-aisled timber hall. The cellar was of six bays with a groined vault supported by brick pillars and was similar to the still-preserved cellar beneath a neighbouring building at Schüsselbuden 2 (Figure 2.2). Both have been characterised as 'sales cellars' of the early 13th century and may therefore have been a slightly later form of the split-level townhouse.[5]

Whether ground-level or split-level the number of substantial commercial buildings in both England and on the continent was becoming marked by the later 12th century and even more evident in the 13th century. In Lincoln, stone houses of mid 12th to mid 13th-century date in the Lower City, either extant or excavated, have been plotted[6] while in Ghent similar plotting of 11th- and 12th-century stone houses shows a dense pattern, particularly along the main street of Hoogpoort linking an early 'portus' on the Scheldt to the medieval port on the river Leie opposite Gravensteen, the castle of the Counts of Flanders.[7] Elsewhere, as in Bruges, resource acquisition perhaps frustrated early stone building; in Bremen, for instance, three stone buildings built next to the bank of the River Weser were excavated in 2003/2004 and were found to utilise *Feldsteine* from glacial deposits as foundation material.[8] However, the assertion made for such German buildings in 1991 that 'this type of urban building was far more common in the twelfth and thirteenth century than was known until now'[9] continues to remain hard

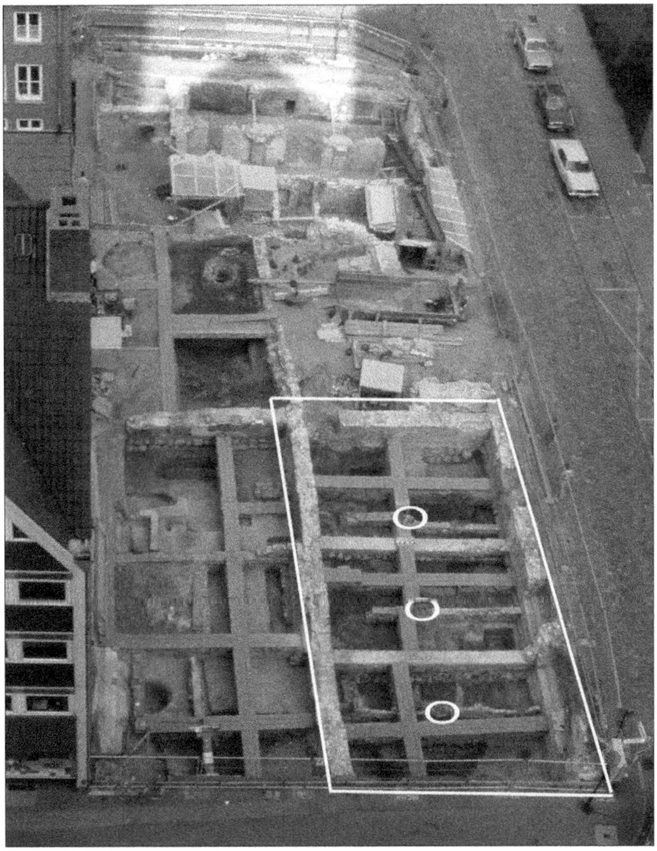

Figure 2.2 Excavation of Saalgeschloßhaus at Schüsselbuden 6, Lübeck in 1985 (Bereich für Archäologie Lübeck).

to prove for the 12th century. The stone buildings in Bremen may date to 1183 if constructed at the same time as the dendrochronologically-dated timber consolidation of the Weser's bank but, in German-dominated Riga at the eastern edge of the Baltic Sea, most stone buildings do not start being constructed until the second half of the 13th century.[10] More commonly in the later 12th century and early 13th century, cases of known early stone construction relate to cellars with buildings of wood above, as demonstrated by a number of excavated examples from Braunschweig.[11]

Another stone building of 13th-century date with a timber structure above is that of Clifton House on Queen Street in King's Lynn. Here a brick-ribbed vaulted cellar lies at right-angles to the street with its long northern side originally adjacent to the Purfleet river where that river met the Great Ouse (subsequent infilling northward has reduced the width of the Purfleet by nearly three-quarters of its original extent). The cellar could be entered from the street where a blocked doorway still exists in the centre of a triple bay, fronting the main two-bayed space divided by stone piers supporting the ribs. The cellar, however, was not the first building on the site because its southern wall is that of an earlier stone building on the same alignment, complete with somewhat confusing but clearly 12th-century architectural elements of a window or other aperture surviving fossilised within the fabric. Here, therefore, there appear to be two phases of a major commercial, and probably domestic, complex occupying a prime site in a growing port.[12]

The relationship of these structures to the port itself can only be suggested in general terms of location given that later structures (16th- and 18th-century in date) now surround and complete the standing complex. The relationship to the quay on the Ouse frontage is therefore unclear as is the case with two other ruinous Norfolk buildings in other ports. The first of these stands in the lost port of Wiveton, adjacent to the site of the quay which lay west of the Glaven estuary. This rectangular flint structure occupied a very similar site to Clifton House; oriented west-to-east, its long northern wall faced towards the sea while its eastern gable fronted the Glaven itself. The building remains overgrown, un-surveyed and un-excavated.[13] Clearly it warrants investigation.

The other remnant has been surveyed and partially excavated. This is the 12th-century cellar in Great Yarmouth known as the Howard Street vaults (Figure 2.3). Again constructed of flint, it has a barrel vault of stone and is located west of Howard Street, its gable end towards the river haven of the port.

Figure 2.3 Vaulted undercroft at Howard Street South, Great Yarmouth (Norfolk Archaeological Unit).

However, it stands at some distance from the haven and its relationship to the port is therefore unclear. Furthermore, the structure is clearly truncated in this direction while it is also cut off from the Howard Street frontage by an inserted range of 15th-century brick vaults, the whole complex now surmounted by a large terrace of 19th-century houses.[14]

Notwithstanding its truncated nature, an interesting aspect of the Howard Street stone vault is that it has been partially infilled. The reason for such infilling is unknown but a similar process took place at Clifton House where the piers supporting the vault are clearly partially buried. The explanation in King's Lynn is that the measure was adopted to counteract flooding, a likely consideration given the location. It should be noted that a further 12th-century cellar, that excavated north of St Martin-at-Palace Plain in Norwich in 1981, suffered from a freshwater flood (silt deposits from the inundation being located together with freshwater mollusca) and that the threshold of the northern doorway was raised in consequence.

Stone buildings were exceptional structures in England and indeed they were probably also relatively uncommon even in places such as Ghent. It was this very exceptionality, however, which marked them out and, in so doing, identified their occupants. One can see this from surviving documentation as evidenced once again by reference to Norwich. Here elements of two 12th-century stone buildings are known to survive (one of them being that mentioned above) but there are textual references not only referring to stone buildings now lost (such as the *domum meum de petra* which was conveyed in a transaction of 1180/1200 by Matilda Persona) but also to individuals identified by their association with stone houses: Simon de Stonhus is recorded on Tombland in the 13th century and John del Stonhus held the adjacent property in 1317. Stone houses were also used as recognition points in abuttals to property deeds as in 1289 when the Abbot of Woburn described land subject to a grant where one boundary ran from the corner of a stone house.[15] Stone buildings were ostentatious status symbols, communicating wealth and commercial power.

Status in buildings could also be communicated by materials other than stone. Nascent commercial power can perhaps be seen in the recently excavated timber buildings from late 12th-century Lübeck. The extensive work undertaken at the *Gründungsviertel* site has uncovered the excellent survival of timber cellars (in one instance to its its full-height complete with doorframe) demonstrating a prodigious use of wood (Figure 2.4) but also enabling a much clearer understanding of the development of the urban building tradition within Lübeck and increasing command of resources. A building revealed at Braunstraße 30 contained a timber cellar measuring 5m by 6m and dated dendrochronologically to 1181; however, its construction was combined with an underpinning of limestone, analysis of which indicated that the stone had been brought from the island of Gotland in the Baltic Sea. A slightly later building dating to around 1200 at Fischstraße 21 incorporated timber, limestone and very early use of brick into a 'three-part complex' which seems likely to have included a tower.[16] The implications of mercantile ostentation, either utilising imported materials or constructing exceptional towers comparable with earlier structures in towns such as Ghent, are obvious.

The extensive use of timber within Ypres in the 13th century is considered so prodigious that the period there has been termed the 'houten eeuws' or the 'wooden century'.[17] Similar widespread evidence for timber in 12th- and early-13th century towns (other examples can be cited from Antwerp, Deventer and Rostock for instance[18]) raises the question of sourcing the necessary wood. Work by Goodburn in London, examining the well-preserved and often reused timbers recovered from Thames waterfront excavations, has been able to demonstrate a change in carpentry technique in the later 12th century when the introduction of the practice of using large saws for the production of planks in turn had an impact upon tree selection as smaller and younger trees could be used. Woodland management could be deduced from the types of timber, the practice of 'coppice-with-standards' (the management of trees both for small wattle work and the like together with larger timbers for boards) becoming the norm in lowland England after the mid 11th-century Norman Conquest. The manner in which raw timber was converted for use could also be explored, whether it had been hewn, sawn or cleft.[19]

Figure 2.4 Excavated timber cellar, Gründungsviertel, Lübeck (Bereich für Archäologie Lübeck).

Construction of ostentatious houses was a form of manipulation of the urban landscape, the buildings designed to serve social and political ends beyond their more quotidian functions as commercial and domestic properties. As such, they served a rising class, primarily that of the merchant but they were not alone in exploiting townscapes. Both the aristocracy and the Crown could, and did, do the same. The impact of their building programmes in England was, of course, most marked in London where, despite massive depredations (notably through the action of the Great Fire of 1666, 19th-century redevelopment and destruction in the Second World War) elements either still remain or can be recovered by excavation.

John Schofield has published a major assessment of medieval London houses with a gazetteer of selected sites. Amongst these is an interesting group of high status buildings in the borough of Southwark, south of the River Thames. Noting that the Archbishop of Canterbury may have had a seat in Southwark before the Norman Conquest, Schofield identifies four other properties of ecclesiastics which were in existence by the middle to late 12th century: the Bishop of Winchester held a house there by 1174 and probably earlier; Merton Priory had a townhouse on Tooley Street *c.* 1150; the Prior of Lewes's Inn on Tooley Street was shown to have a 12th-century rectangular undercroft during building operations in 1832; and the Prior of Christ Church, Canterbury held a townhouse by about 1200. In addition, also on Tooley Street, stood a mid-to-late 12th-century stone building which was recorded in 1829 and probably belonged to the Earl of Warenne.[20]

Little detail is known of the physical structure of these buildings although it is evident from 19th-century engravings that the Warenne house and that of the Prior of Lewes were buildings of some pretension. Warenne's building was set back from the street by about 100m, presumably within its own close, a remnant of which perhaps survived as the yard to the east of the building in 1829 when the house was demolished. Careful setting of an aristocratic—and probable regal—building can be seen in Lincoln with the erroneously named 'John of Gaunt's Palace', now also known as St Mary's Guildhall. This celebrated structure stands on High Street, Wigford, and was built between 1150 and 1170. It is of outstanding architectural quality but is much reduced in size, having lost almost all its first floor save for the north gable wall. Survey and excavation primarily by David Stocker concluded that it was highly likely that it had been constructed originally as the king's house or *hospicium*, a building documented in 1157.[21] Stocker's excavation also revealed that the building did not stand adjacent to High Street (originally the Roman Ermine Street) but projected westward above the east side of the street and thus presented a façade in advance of other structures on the approach to central Lincoln, emphasising its importance. Furthermore, consideration of the remains of embrasures at the base of the first floor walls in the street façade would suggest that the central embrasure, rather than presenting a window as suggested on the reconstructed section within the survey report,[22] instead provided a stand for a regal or similar personage to present himself to the populace.

Merchants and aristocrats on both sides of the North Sea were therefore erecting buildings in towns which, at least in part, served to promote their social status. Such use of architecture was, of course, also present within a rural context. However, in England, while the occasional substantial 12th-century house survives, such as Boothby Pagnell in Lincolnshire, a recent review of seigneurial and elite sites by Creighton and Barry has highlighted the frequent difficulties inherent in both identification and understanding of the meaning of such locations. Two examples from counties bordering the North Sea illustrate such problems. At the famous deserted medieval village of Wharram Percy on the Yorkshire Wolds, the apparent straightforward narrative of an early South Manor subsequently eclipsed by a larger and more complex North Manor proves to be overly-simplistic when subjected to detailed assessment, '... highlighting once again the considerable methodological challenges of unravelling settlement development through archaeology. Extensive excavations of the South Manor did not reveal any evidence for a hall, nor kitchen while the material evidence shows ... no compelling evidence for the presence of a seigneurial household at all'. Similarly, at Goltho in Lincolnshire, a manorial site was 'thoroughly excavated, providing remarkable (and unanticipated) evidence of long-term aristocratic continuity running from the early medieval period until the site's desertion in the thirteenth century'. However, despite two excavation reports, 'fundamental questions remain not only concerning the dating of the manorial site, but the administrative context of the manor within which it lay': the work on the seigneurial precinct a victim of a common failing whereby elite sites have tended to be studied in isolation from the villages and landscape settings around them.[23]

The difficulty of ascertaining true meaning of seigneurial sites within the rural landscape can also be seen with a consideration of the vexed question of moated sites. These monuments, large numbers of which survive within lowland England, Flanders and the Netherlands, seem to have had their origins in the 12th century although their *floruit* was in the 150 years up to 1350. Traditionally viewed as symbolic examples of relatively high status within medieval society, close examination of such sites within the coastal region of Flanders has indicated that here they had 'a much larger social dispersion, often being located around farms in 'a kind of social emulation'. In other words, the comparatively more free Flemish coastal farmers were identifying their distinctive status by adopting a monument type traditionally associated with the aristocracy.

Recognition of this phenomenon, however, led to a new problem; an apparent absence of lordly seigneurial sites within the Flemish coastal zone from which to draw examples to emulate. A solution can now be suggested through interdisciplinary archaeological research. Analysis of the landscape, exploring such aspects as property relationships and site catchment analysis, linked to documentary research, enabled the 'discovery' of large coastal estates associated with the Counts of Flanders. Furthermore, control of these comital estates was undertaken by an aristocratic class of estate officials and knights who seem, by the early 12th century, to have located themselves within moated sites akin to motte-and-bailey structures. The monument type was then 'adopted' amongst lower classes within society although, tellingly, fieldwork indicated that there were fewer such adoptions outside the area of comital estates compared to those areas within them.[24] Archaeological research has thus elucidated a complex social network of status, influence and emulation still visible within the landscape.

The display of power

The expression of status does not necessarily always denote the ability to wield power within society (even though it might originally have been derived through power), status and power being different things. However, the use of architecture and landscape to provide settings for displays of power is being observed increasingly by archaeologists on both sides of the North Sea. In England, Marshall has argued that most high status towers were ordered in such a manner that 'ceremonial function took architectural precedence over domestic provision'; she notes that the latter could be eclipsed by the needs of ceremony and cites the donjon at Hedingham in Essex, eastern England as an example which was probably built specifically to celebrate the elevation of the local magnate as the first earl of Oxford. The structure was thus an immediate expression of power and prestige.[25] In Norway, the location of the archiepiscopal palace in Trondheim, established by the third quarter of the 12th century (initially in timber but rapidly replaced by stone) was situated on the highest point of the Nidaros peninsula, 'a dominating position signifying his [the archbishop's] authority'.[26] Substantial elements of the building remain, designed to work with its landscape.

Displays of power, particularly ecclesiastical power, through architecture can also be seen further south in Norway at Oslo. Here the ruins of the 12th-century St Hallvard's cathedral are extant, located next to the bishop's palace (of timber in the 12th century but rebuilt in stone in the 1200s, elements surviving in the 18th-century Ladegården manor which now occupies the site). This episcopal complex stood towards the northern end of a peninsula bordered by the River Alna to the east and Bjørvika, an inlet from Oslo fjord, to the west. The basilica church occupied high ground above the steep slope to the river, the more gentle westward slope being chosen for the bishop's palace. Both structures lay considerably north of a royal castle, also consisting of timber buildings in the 12th century but soon to be replaced in stone, the fortification being linked to the (stone-built) St Mary's church. Power once again is expressed; it has been noted that 'Church and King, the two poles round which medieval life revolved, found their symbolic counterpart in the twin centres of the city of Oslo'.[27]

John Steane has made a particular study of 'the archaeology of power', exploring secular and ecclesiastical buildings alike. His examination of the Bishop of Winchester's house and precinct in Southwark, London (established by Henry of Blois in the 12th century), for instance, notes that its topographical location provided a 'prestigious setting for royal guests', one dominated by the great hall of 1220–1221 (a gable wall of which, with its large rose window, still survives). However, the hall was surrounded by 'other indications of episcopal power—prisons to punish the transgressors of canon and common law' and exceptionally large gardens, both a kitchen garden and pleasure gardens. The precinct wall separated these amenities from the rest of Southwark, and was itself an expression of power. The similar separation enforced within conventual cathedrals by a stone screen or *pulpitum* dividing those parts of the church for laity from that of the clergy was an equivalent expression of power, the screen enabling control of access to the sacraments as well as providing a place for overt controlling propaganda; the screen in York Minster has a western façade with 'sculptured images of kings—an impressive display of royal and sacerdotal power'.[28]

Provision of new cathedral churches in the 11th and 12th centuries itself gave opportunity for expressions of power. This could, on occasion, be overt as at Lincoln where study of the west front of the great church seems to indicate that it originated as a palatial tower block. The exact form of this block, and its connection or otherwise to the cathedral church, remains under discussion as has been alluded to above (p. 31). Stocker and Everson have published a careful plan which cleverly alludes to either possibility although it seems probable that Stocker's forthcoming book on the building (with Philip Dixon) will argue for a freestanding tower.[29] Shapland, in a recent PhD thesis, sees the Lincoln tower in the tradition of palatial towers constructed in England in the late 11th century: he cites the secular structures of Colchester (c. 1176) the Tower of London (c. 1075-9), Chepstow (c. 1081), Castle Acre (1080s), Norwich (c. 1095) and Canterbury (late 11th century) and argues that, with Lincoln, they were 'statements of royal, ducal or episcopal authority rather than practical residences'.[30] The Bishop of Lincoln, in this case Remigius, was thus using architecture in a similar manner to his secular high-status colleagues.

Palatial towers or other forms of secular architecture therefore could be, and were, used by the higher clergy to promote their power and control but provision of new great churches themselves would also convey similar messages as well as act as agents for social and economic development. An example is the foundation of the cathedral at Lund in Skåne, south-west Sweden (but part of Denmark at the time). This institution was secondary to establishment of the urban settlement itself but was clearly central to the city's subsequent growth in importance. Lund seems to have replaced an earlier extensive trading community identified by archaeological work in recent decades at Uppåkra, some 5km to the south. Uppåkra gradually ceased to be occupied around 990 when Lund itself came into existence,[31] the new settlement seemingly established by the Danish kings to be an administrative centre (there is considerable evidence for early minting of coins, for instance, often employing English coiners as can be gleaned from their coin signatures[32]). However, the city then developed as a diocesan centre, a bishop being in place in the 11th century, and Lund being made the centre of an archbishopric in 1104. The archbishop's seat of Lund Cathedral occupies an imposing site within the city, its earliest extant feature being a large 12th-century crypt. The prelate's jurisdiction was extensive, encompassing Denmark, Sweden, Norway, Iceland, Greenland, the Faroe Islands, the Shetland Isles and the Isle of Man.

Also in Scandinavia, at Uppsala in Sweden, a cathedral was established at Gamla Uppsala, an important Viking Age pagan site where a large cruciform church was subsequently constructed in the mid-12th century following Swedish conversion to Christianity. The building was excavated in part by Sune Lindqvist in the 1920s who argued that post-holes discovered beneath the building were perhaps associated with a pre-existing timber pagan temple. The stone cathedral was devastated by fire in 1204 and thereafter relocated to a new and imposing site some 5km away, the cathedral in Gamla Uppsala being partially demolished and converted to parochial use, a function that it still performs, but that which survives illustrates well the pretensions of the prelate (Figure 2.5). Uppsala cathedral thereafter became the seat of a further archbishopric, albeit one subject to the authority of Lund.

In Trondheim, it has been seen that the archbishop took advantage of the topography to ensure that his palace exuded authority. It can be argued that the locations of the cathedrals of Oslo, Lund and Uppsala were located in a similar manner to transmit a similar intention. A like effect can be seen in 11th- and 12th-century England where the establishment of great Norman cathedral precincts in England, at locations such as Lincoln and Norwich, not only ensured the building of large and impressive cathedral

Figure 2.5 Remains of 12th-century cathedral at Gamla Uppsala (Brian Ayers).

churches but also led to the creation of palatial complexes for the bishops, either involving maximisation of the advantages of existing topography or manipulation of the topography to enhance effects. It was noted above (p. 21) that, at Norwich, archaeological assessment of the low-lying site occupied by the late 11th-century palace donjon suggests that it was situated on a low earthwork platform, designed to raise the structure slightly above its surroundings in order to enhance its visible status. At Lincoln, in contrast, the palace (a completely separate complex to the tower mentioned above) not only sits on top of a great escarpment but practically cascades down the slope, its surviving elements above very substantial undercrofts which terrace out to form platforms upon which the buildings were erected. The engineering involved was prodigious, with massive buttressing to stabilise the structures and even a bridge linking the kitchen to the main complex.[33] The completed building would have dominated the hillside when viewed from the lower city.

The role of archaeology in the study of such monuments is increasingly profound. A good example is that of the castle complex at Castle Acre in Norfolk and especially of the palatial tower there. Work in the 1980s demonstrated that the now demolished structure on top of the motte was far from being a simple tower keep. Rather it proved to be more of a 'country house' (as designated by the excavator), constructed in the 1080s and only converted to that of a tower keep in the 12th century, presumably in response to the changing and volatile political situation in the second quarter of that century. Refashioning in this manner led to the blocking of a ground-floor doorway and thickening of the walls, apparently to support a higher structure (although it remains doubtful whether this newly-fortified building was ever completed).[34]

A characteristic of the 12th century was the emergence of new institutions, be they urban or rural. Within the documentary record, for example, there is a clear, if gradual, increase in distinct independent urban authorities (of 24 greater English towns, 17 received their earliest-known charter in the 12th century[35]). In the countryside, the creation of new ecclesiastical estates under the Cistercian order exemplifies dramatically changes in rural land ownership and usage. Archaeological exploration of the innovation that such developments brought is enhancing understanding of social and economic change from the 12th century onward.

Urban development, organisation and identity

An urban characteristic which became increasingly evident after 1100 was the proliferation of smaller towns and the concomitant growth of the greater towns. In Suffolk, eastern England, the number of towns before 1100 was small although two of them, Bury St Edmunds and Ipswich, became the centres of western and eastern Suffolk respectively in later centuries. Between 1100 and 1350 in contrast, there was an explosion of market foundations, often an indicator of seigneurial ambition following an assessment of commercial potential. Not all such foundations were destined to survive as market towns but many did prosper as small urban centres (places such as Brandon, Framlingham, Hadleigh, Halesworth, Lavenham, Orford, Saxmundham, Southwold and Woodbridge).[36] Elsewhere it has been calculated that, in northern Europe, every decade between *c.* 1240 and 1300 saw some 300 towns being established.[37] As noted above (p. 7) famously historians and archaeologists have debated the question of 'What is a town?" for decades; interesting alternative questions, however, are how far can these embryonic towns be characterised as urban and how rapidly did the larger ones manage to construct a cohesive urban identity? A recent approach to addressing such enquiries has been adopted by Loveluck who, rather than considering the urban product itself, inverts the issue, recognising that central places subsequently understood as towns represented a wide diversity of settlements, often 'with very different archaeological manifestations, varied social fabrics and different relationships with their surrounding hinterlands'. In consequence, urban centres might house a range of functions and thereby understandings of status; he references Douai in northern France where it is possible, for the 11th-century town, to identify 'three distinctive zones of social fabric and activity: secular and religious authority around the comital residence, craft working and commerce in the ports and agriculture, a brewery and a tavern in [the suburb of] Douayeul'.[38]

In some towns, such as Utrecht, it seems clear that such distinctive functions led to the establishment of distinct proto-urban entities which only later coalesced as a single urban unit. At Utrecht, de Groot has illustrated how an early episcopal centre and small associated settlement stood above a bend in the Rhine before AD 1000 (and overlay Roman occupation), supplemented by a probable merchants' quarter to the west (documented in 1007) and perhaps also by further occupation to the south between the Rhine and the River Vecht by 1100. Watercourse changes led to a succession of canals being constructed to enhance the harbour in order to maintain the economics of the growing town but it was only during the 11th century that 'these ingredients constituted the basis from which a genuine urban centre subsequently developed (and which achieved chartered status in 1122).[39] Analysis of later urban growth in Utrecht and the distribution of both surviving houses and excavated examples has enabled Hoekstra to suggest that the majority of house types based upon narrow plots occurred within the older parts of the settlement while those houses set upon a wider frontage were largely located within newly established areas of the city in the 14th and 15th centuries.[40] This observation implies that the distinctiveness of localities would have been very evident topographically to the medieval population even if, by the late Middle Ages, urban wealth (or lack of it) was more randomly distributed within the city.

Douai was a growing town in the 11th century and was clearly already one with a range of communities. It is probable that these communities maintained a sense of individual identity even as the town grew more cohesive as a physical unit, perhaps through broad house plot types as observed in Utrecht. In King's Lynn in the 12th century, the 'newness' and, by implication, secondary status of the 'Newlond' area of the borough (created in the second quarter of the 12th century) may have been emphasised by the continued subordination of the Newlond chapel of St Nicholas to the earlier parish church of St Margaret. St Nicholas was to grow into one of the largest medieval churches in England by the end of the Middle Ages, richly beautified by local merchants, but its status as a subordinate chapel remains to the present day. Topographically, however, it is possible that the degree of apparent planning in the layout of the Newlond area, one where it seems evident that property size was directly related to rental income,[41] may also have subtly implied a local distinctiveness to the inhabitants. Certainly a local pride can be detected; two distinct guilds were dedicated to the Holy Trinity in King's Lynn, one associated with the church of St Margaret and another with the chapel of St Nicholas,[42] a further sense of localism perhaps bordering on paranoia.

King's Lynn also had an identity through its port, the River Ouse forming its entire western boundary. Recent interesting research has explored a nearby urban area, Ely within the Fens, in order to examine how urban identity was expressed in a town which occupied an island site that gradually through drainage became landlocked. Most of this drainage was post-medieval in date but Barrowclough, in a study of the material culture recovered from excavation of medieval sites in Ely and its surrounding area, together with historical information and topographical assessment, argues that it is possible to construct cognitive *mappa* which enable investigation 'at two different scales, on the one hand internally, constructing a perceptual map of the isle from the point of view of its inhabitants, and on the other ... mapping the perception of the islanders' insularity with regard to the region of the Cambridgeshire fens and the world beyond'. His methodology embraces an interpretation of material such as the ceramics and faunal remains recovered from excavations whereby, *inter alia*, it is possible to suggest preferred routes for certain products; while it may seem self-evident that high quality decorative jugs from Scarborough approached the town via the river route from King's Lynn, he can argue that fine red wares from Colchester in Essex almost certainly used a landward route via Cambridge even though a seaward route via King's Lynn was both feasible and probably more practical in terms of ease of carriage. Barrowclough's conclusion from this and other evidence is that cognitive mapping enables appraisal of 'geographical and social factors that created social barriers and corridors .. a human creation, which although influenced by environmental factors [were] not determined by them'.[43] The merchants and townspeople made choices through the mental maps that they themselves constructed of their town and its setting within the landscape.

Elsewhere it can be argued that the construction of urban defences was an act which symbolically emphasised the unity of the enclosed town, hastening its sense of self-identity and separation from the surrounding countryside. Indeed, Creighton and Higham note that the 'city wall features prominently in urban iconography to such an extent that the image of wall and city were often impossible to sever' but they go on to deeper analysis which argues that the creation of urban defences, while they separated urban populations from their rural counterparts, did not necessarily automatically promote a sense of cohesive identity within the town. Indeed, 'the walled enceinte provided a superficial display of unity for communities that could be remarkably fragmented'[44] while the relationship between town and country necessarily needed to remain strong. Towns, being 'landscape elements sustained by the rural economy', had a more complex relationship with their surrounding hinterlands than the apparent simplicity of separation that is implied by a newly-constructed urban defensive system.[45] Indeed, at Ypres, the earliest defences of the 11th century left the artisan quarter outside the fortified area while, at Ghent, 'sparsely inhabited and still partly agrarian' land was incorporated *within* the earliest fortifications (locations such as the Kouter, a field name, and a 'marshy area' called Mere and Paddenhoek).[46]

Such apparently anomalous actions may have been dictated in part by strategic consideration, avoiding unnecessary and vulnerable salients, but it nevertheless suggests a flexible approach to the concepts of 'town' and 'country'. At Haarlem in the Netherlands, for instance, while it is possible that the place-name itself derives from 'Harulaihaima' ('a house on a wooded sandhill'), the earliest town seal of 1299 draws particular attention to both the city gate and the surrounding forest, with wooded branches of this forest bordering the fortification. The forest 'had a key role in the formation of Haarlem's image and reputation'.[47] If such an approach to the surrounding rural landscape was true of the greater towns, many of which were eventually walled, it was surely more true of those smaller towns which had a greater physical association with their rural surroundings.

It is probable, nevertheless, that even as early as the later 12th century, the larger towns were beginning to use their emerging defences as a 'mural ideology' to quote Steane's felicitous phrase. Such promotion of the town as an entity through the medium of its physical boundaries would become more marked in later medieval centuries but the potential of walls to promote the idea of the city as a distinct and even spiritual entity had been evident for some time. It has been suggested that the concept of the ideal city was familiar from antique urban models and that pictorial representations of the heavenly Jerusalem (with twelve gates representing the twelve tribes of Israel) meant that fortified towns would create 'a psychological effect' upon medieval travellers of this heavenly Jerusalem on earth. 'Indeed, when the new town wall of Cologne was erected in the early 13th century, it was deliberately furnished with twelve gates'.[48] Cologne's Rhineland location renders it part of the North Sea world and thus it is perhaps not too fanciful to suggest that when Norwich, in eastern England, fortified its large polyfocal settlement from the mid-13th century onward, the city emulated Cologne and also provided the circuit with twelve gates.[49]

The proliferation of towns on both sides of the North Sea was most manifest in countries such as England, the Low Countries and Germany but was also evident elsewhere. In Denmark, the early towns of Ribe and Aarhus were supplemented in the 12th and 13th centuries by settlements such as Viborg and Naestved, both large by Scandinavian standards and with the former fortified and the latter not (a circumstance commented upon by a German visitor in 1516[50]). Medieval Denmark extended across the Kattegat to Scania in what is now modern Sweden and recent archaeological work has thrown considerable light upon Scanian urban development. The extensive excavations at Uppåkra (above p. 41) south of Lund, have revealed a major centre comprising pre-Christian ritual activity as well as craft-working and a topography dominated by timber buildings set within enclosures. While this large village—perhaps more accurately an early town—may have had a church in the 10th century, it nevertheless lost out to newly-founded Lund. However, its influence was longer-lasting as Lund's medieval topography appears to have been modelled upon that of Uppåkra, the town being characterised by aristocratic enclosures. Early examples of these, their buildings presumably of timber, do not survive but one large, very late medieval brick townhouse still stands on Stora Södergaten. The domicile of a rural aristocratic family, the street frontage building here provided access to an extensive rear yard area where agricultural activity took place and included fishponds (Figure 2.6).

Lund was dominated by its cathedral and accordingly much of its social structure seems to have been particular, aristocratic domains contributing significantly to its urban form although smaller structures are also known. Excavations in the St Clemens quarter of Lund have uncovered 12th-century timber single-cell buildings with larger three-celled structures emerging in the 1200s. Interestingly, these later houses, comprising a central living room flanked by two other rooms, are a type of building 'common in the villages of Skåne from the thirteenth century onwards ... [having] ... exactly the same plan ...'.[51] Indeed, three longhouses are now known from Lund.[52] This observation suggests that, in Danish Sweden at least, the boundary between urban and rural was thin indeed.

Lund was cut off from the coast and depended up nearby Malmö for trade. Here, a port developed from the 13th century, initially to take advantage of the herring trade but with mercantile functions growing rapidly. The town seems to have had a street system which was planned from the outset, the streets being paved with cobbles 'bound with sand and manure'.[53] This feature alone would mark out the settlement as urban and indeed the mercantile aspect of Malmö, much of it heavily influenced by the German Hanse, was made the more obvious with relatively early construction of brick buildings from the end of the 13th century. At the same time, the incidence of imported goods such as red earthenwares

Figure 2.6 Townhouse on Stora Södergaten in Lund (Brian Ayers).

gave status to places such as Malmö, those 'trading ports and urban centres of population on the Baltic littoral [established] by AD 1300, from the Öresund and Scania (Lund, Kalmar) to the trading post of the Hanseatic fur-traders in the Russian pine forest'.[54]

The town of Bergen in Norway illustrates the manner in which different interests combined to ensure the vitality of an urban settlement. Bergen is most famous for its hanseatic settlement of Bryggen ('the wharf'), an area of dense warehousing and other mercantile building located on the north side of the harbour of Vågen, much of it excavated in the late 1950s (see p. 8). However, the town also had royal and ecclesiastical centres, both standing at the mouth of the harbour on a small promontory known as Holmen. It was these institutions which excited the earliest archaeological investigation (from the 1840s)[55] and recent work has established that royal influence probably not only founded the town (around 1070) but was also responsible for laying out the streets and regular tenements.[56] Royal authority took various forms; the construction of a castle (elements of which survive) was an obvious example but a royal mint was also established in Bergen and an excavated runic inscription dating between 1198 and 1248 mentions the name of a mint master: 'Torkjel mint master sends you pepper'. Ecclesiastical authority extended to the establishment of a cathedral, numerous churches and five urban monasteries. However, archaeological research is now sufficiently advanced in Bergen that it also becomes possible to differentiate between areas of the town and, in observing differences such as the provision of drainage, to identify locations which had a topographical characteristic that can be compared to other medieval Norwegian towns such as Trondheim and Oslo. In contrast, archaeological observation of the drains of the German-dominated mercantile Bryggen area of the town suggests an approach which was more regulated.[57] Bergen owed its existence to several imperatives—royal, ecclesiastical and mercantile—but each fostered the urban concept, principally because of the town's role in wealth generation through its port (paralleled in Trondheim where numismatic analysis concludes that 'complex changes were taking place ... involving the consolidation of royal power and the growth of the church ... major driving-forces towards a more commercialised society').[58]

Rural organisation

Petter Molaug has examined the establishment of town plots in Norwegian towns and, in the cases of Bergen, Oslo, Tønsberg and Trondheim, he notes that archaeologically 'there is solid evidence for farming prior to the urban development'.[59] This is a reminder that rural organisation underpinned urban expansion, feeding the towns which necessarily could not feed themselves. The establishment of a systematic feudal system across much of western Europe by the end of the 12th century had an impact upon the way in which rural areas were organised, not least in the relationship of elite sites to their surroundings. The occupants of these sites controlled much of the activity of rural society, be it agrarian, pastoral or spiritual and it is perhaps not surprising therefore that recent research in England has identified close linkage between what has been described as the 'triad' of institutions—the seigneurial manorial site, the parish church and the mill. Indeed, in eastern Yorkshire, some 64 per cent of churches on the southern and eastern Wolds were found to be 'within manorial enclosures or directly opposite manor houses'.[60] The co-terminus of manorial estates with parish boundaries has also been noted.

The correlation of probable manorial locations with churches can be seen too in Essex where moated sites at places such as Aythorpe and High Rodingbury both had churches nearby. The relationship of manor to mill may have been observed at Boreham airfield, also in Essex, where excavation of a site truncated by construction of the airfield uncovered a large rectangular moat, several timber buildings, a granary and an early windmill. This 'sunken-post' mill, the earliest known form in western Europe and probably dating to the early 13th century at Boreham, is likely to have been controlled by the local manor although the excavation report is careful to point out that it is not possible to differentiate between such direct manorial control and that of a facility leased out to a free tenant.[61]

Possible free tenant leasing implies a society which was becoming more economically engaged at lower levels. This is perhaps illustrated by analysis of recent metal-detector finds in eastern England.

Increasingly, lead seal matrices are being discovered, contrasting markedly with the higher quality corpora of bronze matrices assembled hitherto by collectors. These finds are now published annually and it has been observed that the 'variety of metal matrices [is] more truly representative of the range current in medieval times ... These small objects are physical reminders of the well-known 13th-century property market boom, a phenomenon that reached quite low amongst the ranks of the peasantry'.[62] Peasants might not be able to read but they must have been affixing their seals to documents, partaking in a more sophisticated tenurial relationship.

Research by McDonagh in the Yorkshire Wolds has led to the suggestion that groupings of manor and church were often peripheral to their neighbouring village settlements, thereby also exercising control of the villages themselves.[63] However, such topographical positioning of manorial sites to their neighbouring settlements is one which has been discussed recently by Wrathmell. Writing in the context of an assessment of the major longterm excavations at the deserted medieval village site of Wharram Percy (on the Yorkshire Wolds and mentioned above p. 39), he observes that 'it would be easy enough to see the location ... of the North Manor of Wharram Percy, as an expression of lordly dominance over the servile peasantry'. This he characterises as 'modern thinking' and that it was more important in a medieval context to demonstrate 'seisin', that is a rightness to possession of land. In an English context, such a demonstration had an added importance given the great transfers of land subsequent to the Norman Conquest and a consequent need to demonstrate entitlement through 'continuity' expressed 'in a very specific, tenurial sense: the outward sign of a tenant in chief's rightful succession to the lands of his antecessor'. Wrathmell thus concludes that 'the positioning of the North Manor curia is most readily construed as a wish to express seisin of the whole vill, especially when seen by outsiders using route ways into and through the village'. The position of the South Manor, the status of which he does not contest (but see above, p.39), is seen to have fulfilled a similar function with regard to the area of the village known as the West Row tofts.[64] This latter site also has a close relationship to the (now ruined) parish church of St Martin.

Research into the organisational dynamics of rural settlement is obviously not just an English phenomenon. Work in the Netherlands is also exploring the relationship of seigneurial sites, churches and settlements as illustrated by excavations at Geysteren in Limburg province where both the church and the castle have been uncovered although it is lamented that the work has yet to be supported by similar activity within the neighbouring village.[65] Bult argues that the distribution of moated sites from the 12th century onward within Holland can be taken to support the hypothesis that, in return for investment in reclamation of low-lying areas prone to flooding, the Count of Holland 'handed out land and privileges like the provision to build moated sites'. He goes on to point out that certain sites, such as the moat at Huis ten Dorp, appeared 'to play an important role in the parcelling out of the flooded area, which was carried out systematically in plots of 60 rods wide'.[66]

Such seigneural involvement in the development of rural landscapes in the Low Countries is also evident from study of reclamation of salt marshes at Testerep in Flanders where the motivating agency seems to have been St Peter's Abbey in Ghent.[67] More recent work by Tys has also established the relationship between seigneurial sites and the controlling power of the Counts of Flanders but he has made the observation, following the earlier work of Verhaeghe, that the observed 'practice to construct sites with a similar morphology seems to have had mainly residential and ornamental meanings, as a visual reference to the status and position of the nobility'.[68] In other words, as well as positioning their sites, seigneurial individuals developed features such as the moat as a visual expression, both to their own group and to outsiders, of their social status.

Further north, seigneurial influence has also been detected at the farmstead site of Tårnby on the western side of the island of Amager, Denmark, excavated between 1993 and 1994. Here, a late Viking Age settlement (near Copenhagen), apparently dominated by four landholdings grouped around a village green,was transformed in the 12th century to form a large estate. A stone church was built at the same time. The agency behind the transformation process was probably the diocese of Roskilde, the bishop's demesne at Tårnby being documented in 1370 as the greatest of his estates. Topographically, the farmstead changed from one of large holdings to a village of houses situated within tenemented rows,[69] the implication being of a directed top-down change to the rural landscape.

Elsewhere in Scandinavia, the results of excavation on rural sites can suggest social organisation as well as reorganisation of the physical environment. Interesting work at Herresta in Järfälla parish north-west of Stockholm (a location with good links to the Baltic) explored a site which, until the 11th century, appears to have been a relatively-high status farmstead with considerable evidence for horses. It included a separated zone with a small dwelling structure interpreted as housing for a serf. Occupation of this zone ceased around 1200, centuries before abandonment of the rest of the site. It is likely that, as serfdom became obsolete in Sweden at this time, developing social structures may well have been the reason for the removal of this area of activity.[70]

Directed change is known to have occurred within the North Sea region (and elsewhere) subsequent to the establishment of large-scale monastic granges from the 12th century onward. The creation of Cistercian estates, for instance, led to wholesale rural reorganisation with destruction of villages and consequent depopulation.[71] In parts of the north of England, however, it is possible that, prior to the 12th-century arrival of the Cistercians, this process was assisted by the 'harrying of the north' undertaken by William the Conqueror in 1069–70 when extensive areas were laid waste. It has been noted that those parts of Holderness, bordering the North Sea in eastern Yorkshire were only worth some 17% of their pre-1066 value, the disruption no doubt fostering land redistribution. By the mid 12th century, in the lower Hull valley, the abbey of Meaux (founded *c.* 1151) seems to have organised and controlled its large estate through the placing of moated sites. Archaeological survey indicates that many of these were on outcrops of till close to the alluvial river; the moated sites 'can be seen as part of the religious expansionist policy in the region'.[72] Some may have had specialist purposes; excavations at the North Grange moat in the 1930s located a tilery that supplied the abbey while the Fish Holm Barn moated site may have contained a fish house.[73]

While recent archaeological work has become increasingly successful at identifying the remains of such ecclesiastical establishments (and the earthworks of Meaux Abbey are some of the finest in Yorkshire), it still has some distance to go in order to explore the likely disposition of pre-monastic settlement, the form of impact and the likely dislocation of population hinted at in surviving documentation. While clearance of some villages is documented, the issue of wholesale depopulation rather than relocation of populations is a difficult one to resolve. Platt can quote the instance of Rufford Abbey (in Nottinghamshire, some distance from the North Sea) where the Cistercian agricultural system may have been more of 'a programme of resettlement rather than depopulation' (known compensation in cash, land and promises being paid). Archaeologically, however, he can also point to the monastic demesne grange of Rievaulx Abbey at Griff where the 'remains of a peasant settlement, diminutive but well-marked, lie some 300 hundred yards [274m] to the south of the present farm-house, at which there are traces also of some medieval work ... the contemporaneity of grange and settlement earthworks would seem confirmed by their alignments on the ground'.[74] Such observations and others do much to counteract the 'myth' (as Loveluck puts it) of Cistercian monasteries seeking to place themselves in isolated locations, creating 'a Benedictine utopia from the spiritual wildness' exemplified by 'desolate landscapes'. On the contrary, the 'spiritual and economic success of the monastery lay ... in its very interaction with the secular world, and its active acquisition and development of new farming enterprises' which necessarily required local labour.[75]

This success required a commercial outlook, one frequently exhibited at North Sea ports through which a great deal of monastic produce, notably wool, was traded. Waites has detailed the evidence for the role of monasteries of north-eastern Yorkshire in the medieval wool trade, noting land routes, collection centres such as Malton, and shipping ports. Beverley and Hull were two of the most important locations for the export of wool but so too was Clifton on the outskirts of York. There is documentary evidence for Italian merchants sending agents to visit monasteries in order to inspect the wool, checking that it was packed and weighed correctly 'without cocked and black guard, grey scab, clacked and all vile fleeces'. The Italians also reached agreements with Rievaulx Abbey for dispatch of wool to the abbey's house in York for onward shipment via Clifton to Hull.[76] Flemish merchants visited Scarborough where again there is good documentary evidence surviving of their interest although trade here was probably always secondary to the fishing industry with much overseas trade being in foreign ships.[77]

Moorhouse has worked on both documentary evidence and ceramics, exploring both the movement of pottery around England as well as illustrating the commercial linkages between Cistercian houses and major east coast ports.[78] Just as Rievaulx Abbey had a building in York so too a house on Wormgate in Boston (now Fountains Lane) was leased by Fountains Abbey in Yorkshire from one Jordan de Boston in the late 12th century. It had an enclosed court and other buildings and could be used by the abbey at the time of St Botolph's Fair.[79] By 1286, the Cistercians of Sibton, Garendon, Combe and Woburn all held houses next to the river Wensum in Norwich, convenient for the trade through Great Yarmouth.[80]

Landscape change

An attempt to use archaeological practice to understand the impact of monasticism upon the rural landscape has recently been undertaken by the University of Ghent at the Cistercian abbey of Boudelo in the wetlands of Flanders. This site, occupying an area described by the monks of Clairvaux as both *pauper* and *misserimus* ('poor and full of misery'), was investigated using a technique known as electromagnetic induction (EMI) which enables a 'view' of sub-surface features. The generation of an electromagnetic field within the soil deposits created a secondary electromagnetic field, comparison between the two ultimately enabling the adoption of a process of simultaneous mapping of many soil properties. As a result, the residual evidence of a medieval agricultural and water management system could be seen, probably with its origins in the 13th century. It seems likely that the EMI technique will be used increasingly to map complex landscapes.[81]

Just as the Cistercian monasteries established in England sought control over local resources- through land acquisition, selective depopulation and utilisation of local workforces—so too were resources exploited by Cistercian foundations in Flanders such as Boudelo. Here, an important asset was peat, the abbey being endowed with *moorland* for the cutting of *mor* or peat by the Count of Flanders in 1200. It was not alone; St Peter's Abbey in Ghent documented that their *moorland* contained enough peat for a 'perpetual fire'—*sufficiens ad ignem perpetuo*. This is a somewhat ironic statement today as no significant peat deposits survive within coastal Flanders. As a result, it has proved difficult to identify how large the resource was prior to its exploitation and even exactly in which areas it was located. Recent assessment of geoscientific data, historical references and archaeological evidence is now helping to clarify the matter while excavated data includes palynological analysis of peat blocks from the abbey at Ename, the mosses and heathers of which suggest the type of raised bog which may have existed near Kluizen in northern Flanders where the abbey held *moorland*.[82]

Digging for peat obviously had a dramatic impact upon the landscape although it is only in recent decades that this has been noted. Famously, the Norfolk Broads in eastern England were not recognised as flooded peat diggings or turbaries until the 1950s. This recognition was primarily the result of collaborative efforts between geographers and botanists but archaeologists and historians also noted how the peat workings respected the existing landscape. On Barton Broad, for instance, an uncut baulk of peat (now heavily-eroded) was left between two turbaries; It marked the line of the parish boundary between the settlements of Barton Turf and Irstead. Other baulks observable within the same Broad appear to match tithe-award boundaries and may therefore indicate areas of individual ownership of peat extraction (Figure 2.7).[83]

The Norfolk peat-diggings became increasingly prone to flooding as sea level rose from the 12th century onward and ultimately had to be abandoned, resulting in the lakes or Broads known to this day. Similar stress upon resources has been observed on the eastern shore of the North Sea as well where open-water lakes are likewise common in northern Flanders and south Holland.[84] In addition,

Figure 2.7 Air photograph of Barton Broad, Norfolk (Norfolk Historic Environment Service).

examination of the polder area north of Antwerp, *Oosterweel* on the east bank of the River Scheldt, uncovered further consequences of human-engineered landscape change. Drainage here was undertaken in the 11th century, utilising small local rivers. However, this in turn meant oxidisation and compression of the peaty soil and necessitated protection with dykes from the mid-12th century. This remedial action only led to a further fall of ground level through shrinkage, intermittent floods culminating in a major permanent inundation dated from the 1280s to 1340. Reclamation took place thereafter but earlier land parcels had been obscured, except in the southern part of the area where they survived into the 20th century.[85]

Technological innovation obviously assisted rural development. The introduction of the post mill has been mentioned above (p. 46) but a further development improving rural production was that of the wheeled mouldboard plough. Replacing the ancient ard, this plough was able to traverse and break up heavier soils, opening up previously inaccessible areas for agriculture (an example was illustrated in a document entitled *Hortus deliciarum* of 1176/96).[86] As an example of the importance attached to this device, the guild masters of the *herred* or judicial district of Frøs (subsequently Haderslev county and now the county of South Jutland) placed an image of a wheeled plough on the *herred*'s seal of *c.* 1300. Ploughshares of such a plough have been recovered from an earthwork at Gammel Lindholm, also in Denmark.

Ploughs, of course, needed fields within which to be used and the development of field systems has itself become a major area of study over the last three decades, not least in areas bordering the North Sea. That the process was complex can be seen from an excavation at Burnham Market in north Norfolk where 'a complex palimpsest of ditches' revealed probable Romano-British coaxial enclosures which were replaced by narrow strips bounded by ditches, aligned within the enclosures. Finally, the strips themselves were reoriented through ninety degrees, the resultant pattern 'identical to that displayed by [other] coaxial furlong patterns in the area'.[87]

Field types obviously developed in different ways and at different times depending upon factors such as soils, crops and market requirements. A comprehensive review of archaeological and historical approaches to the study of a particularly important and common form within medieval Europe, that of open fields, has been published by Renes. He is especially concerned with the production of grain, noting that the fields 'were Europe's granaries ... [and] reached their climax in the thirteenth and early fourteenth century, in a period of unprecedented population pressure'. As an example, he maps the settlements of the southern part of Limburg province in the Netherlands where it seems likely that early medieval settlement was restricted to stream valleys but settlements on the large plateaus were all established in the 11th and 12th centuries with their attendant field systems.[88]

The provision of grain was a critical factor in the medieval economy and, in some instances, there is evidence for its trade, including across the North Sea. Evidence from Norway where a review of foreign trade and local production has been undertaken, has established that rye was imported into the country, probably from places such as Denmark, while documents record that both wheat and malt were exported to Norway from England. More exotic imports found their way to Bergen as well; evidence for blue and green grapes has been located in 13th-century deposits there.[89]

Another natural resource, and one which needed careful management, was that of woodland. Williamson in particular, in an English context, has examined the evidence for medieval woodland carefully, noting that the relationship between rural settlement and woodland is not a simple one, woodland survival being dependent upon social and environmental factors such as settlement patterns themselves.[90] Exploitation of woodland also varied depending upon whether the wood was grown for timber or coppiced. Evidence for the use of wood within the North Sea region is considerable, ranging from housing to ships, fencing and everyday utensils.

Rural development necessarily led to both the growth of old, and the establishment of new, settlements. Exploration of the former has been undertaken within the coastal plain area of Flanders as a collaborative project between the University of Nottingham (UK) and the Free University of Brussels (Belgium). Four types of archaeological survey technique were used to examine two known but deserted settlement sites in the Leffinge area close to Ostend (Oostende). The total area examined was relatively small at some 7 hectares but both had yielded pottery from the ploughsoil which dated from the 6th/7th century through to the 12th century in one instance ('Oude Werf') and to the 16th century in the other ('Haerdepollems Wal'). The follow-up work comprised geophysical survey (both resistivity and magnetometer), geochemical survey, micro-topographical study and grid-based fieldwalking.

Analysis of the results of the various surveys indicated that the 'Haerdepollems Wal' site was permanently occupied for 1000 years. Ditches and banks of an enclosure were identified with the geochemical and trace element analyses showing midden areas, a farmyard and at least one building (the distribution of phosphates indicating the first two and of calcium the third, probably from line mortar used in the structure; Figure 2.8).[91]

Subsequently, excavation at the 'Oude Werf' site produced archaeozoological material which suggested a concentration on sheep herding, probably for meat rather than wool (given the age range for kill-off of the male sheep). This conclusion amplifies known evidence for historical sources which refer to *marisci* or sheep rearing sites within the coastal marginal areas. It was considered that these were seasonal sites, rearing sheep solely for their wool. However, the archaeological evidence suggests that in actuality the *marisci* were permanent sheep farms within the salt marshes, both wool and meat being produced, certainly from the 10th century onward (from when also dates the *Dode lamstiende* or 'Dead sheep tithe', a tax on slaughtered sheep to compensate for lost wool production). The settlement from the 11th century at the latest was probably part of a larger sheep estate belonging to the Count of Flanders. The rearing of sheep at this Flemish contrasts with the evidence from *terp* sites further north in Friesland where the pasturing of cattle was more the norm.[92]

Parochial organisation

Rural parish formation was possible in a centralised country like England where there were well-established dioceses by the mid 11th century but, elsewhere within the North Sea zone, it took longer.

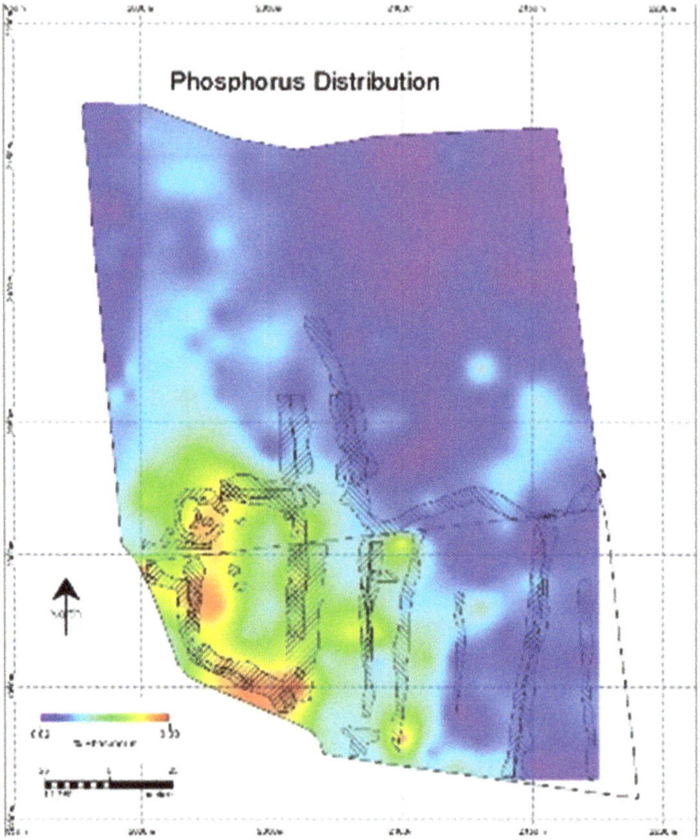

Figure 2.8 Minor element analysis of phosphate concentrations, Wilskerke-Haerdepollemswal (University of Nottingham).

Contested areas for instance, such as Ostholstein where Slavs sought to settle, can be seen to have developed as a result of new German settlement in the 12th century. Parish churches, monastic institutions and important castles within the diocesan boundary of Lübeck illustrate that, by around 1200, Slavic influence was in retreat and the region was being developed as a German province (Figure 2.9). In Denmark it seems likely that parish formation in the 12th century, assisted by the creation of bishoprics, in large part owed a great deal to the introduction of tithe payments (the word used in Scandinavia for 'parish' is *sokn*, thought to be derived from the German *suchen*—to gather).[93] These payments provided a basis for parochial organisation and stone parish churches are known from the early 12th century in Denmark (as at Himmelev near Roskilde, the subject of recent survey and the recording of six 12th-century ship graffiti)[94].

By the 13th century, provision of parochial churches was widespread on both sides of the North Sea with investment reaching even remote locations. At Portmahomack on the Tarbat peninsula in north-east Scotland, the church of St Colman had been established in the late 11th or early 12th century but was significantly enlarged in the 13th century, being lengthened 5m westward and 10m to the east.[95] In urban Trondheim, northern Norway, a small church, probably dedicated to St Gregory and established by the 12th century, was seen by excavation to have been extended around 1300.[96] Further south, a number of excavations within rural English churches similarly show expansion in the 13th century: Asheldham and West Thurrock in Essex being just two examples.[97] However, it is in the emerging towns and cities of the southern North Sea littoral that investment in parish churches and chapels-at-ease is most marked. As an example, in Lynn the parish church of St Margaret, a late 11th-century foundation, had to be supplemented by the chapel-at-ease of St Nicholas, established around 1140 and soon

Figure 2.9 Parish churches, monasteries and important castles in Ostholstein *c.* 1200 (Dirk Meier).

to become one of the largest churches in the east of England (although, as has been seen, never a parish in its own right).[98] In Germany, cities such as Lübeck constructed vast brick buildings for its parish churches of which the supreme example is the Marienkirche of *c.* 1277 onward.[99]

Rural/urban links

It is a truism that all urban settlements are non self-sufficient and can only survive with the importation of resources from their rural hinterlands (and, for much of the medieval period, the importation of people, urban mortality always being greater than that of the countryside[100]). The extent to which this relationship was formalised at an early period has been noted by Loveluck who observes that the linkage of rural estates with urban property was already normal by the 11th century.[101] It was seen above that the development of rural monastic institutions in the 12th century led to the growth of representative buildings and their precincts within towns, notably the greater towns and ports (p. 49). Rural development was also important to urban growth in other ways too: the foundation of Amsterdam would not have been possible but for drainage and reclamation of its low-lying environment in the 12th century. Recent survey, utilising a 'landscape biography study' (defined as 'essentially a survey of surveys, in which landscape history is constructed from layers of existing data that are analysed and presented in a coherent form', that is techniques such as geographical information systems—GIS), has been undertaken of the Amstelland area south of Amsterdam, charting the development of a 'constructed' landscape from a natural one. Here drainage, notably with the digging of a canal between the Amstel river and the Ij river provided the conditions for the growth of a town which, by *c.* 1200, archaeological evidence suggests housed craftspeople such as a blacksmith and a weaver.[102]

Rural contributions to urban resource needs could be more far-reaching than those provided by immediate hinterlands. A research project at the small settlement of Quoygrew on the island of Westray, Orkney produced results which suggested strongly that network links to the southern North Sea from Orkney were profound by the 13th century, engineered through one or more towns in Norway (most probably Bergen). While admitting the difficulty of identifying the actual products exported (and largely discounting such items as cereals, meat and cloth), the zooarchaeological and biomolecular evidence of fish remains does imply a growing trade in stockfish from this period onward.[103] A local boom in fishing and consumption on Orkney in the 11th and 12th centuries seems to have been transformed into a growing export market during the 1200s.

Supplying food to towns was an obvious contribution from the rural environment and economy. However, other major resources were derived from hinterlands such as timber for building. Within the North Sea zone, given the known dramatic increase in population by the 13th century, importation of such material in bulk to western Europe might be expected by that date. However, although Baltic oak is known to have been imported into Flanders from the early 13th century, this is only recorded in documentary evidence; the oldest physical proof in Flanders concerns archaeological finds of herring barrels dating to the 14th century (although a museum display in the Archaeological Museum in Bruges claims that the roof timbers of the St John hospital, variously dated to between 1224 and 1284 by dendrochronology, were Baltic in origin).[104] Elsewhere, the great timbers required for the mid 13th-century roof of Glasgow cathedral, for instance, were sourced from native Scottish oaks.[105] By the beginning of the 14th century imported timber, probably eastern Polish oak, was used in Queen Mary's House in St Andrews[106] and thus, if coastal towns within a relatively well-forested country such as Scotland were beginning to import building timber, more heavily-populated parts of the North Sea world such as England and the Low Countries must have been doing likewise. Indeed, a range of examples of Baltic timber usage from this period onward in England can be cited such as the late 13th-century timber vault of St Albans cathedral in Hertfordshire, the parish chest of Ewerby church, Lincolnshire dated to *c.* 1330, the choir stalls of *c.* 1340 at Ely cathedral, and the boarded walls of a granary of 1409–1425 at Tadlow in Cambridgeshire.[107]

The documentary evidence suggests that such timber was initially imported via Bruges and subsequently Antwerp. The forests of the Baltic lands had a mixture of broad-leaf trees such as oak, ash, elm, lindens and maple. The oak that was exported generally came from slow-grown trees in dense locations which encouraged tall and straight timber and was thus ideal for the production of boards which formed the principal export.

The principal sources of the wood seem to have been the vast forests around the catchment area of the Vistula river in Poland. Export from Poland was co-ordinated through Danzig (modern day Gdańsk) on the Baltic coast. Tree-ring analysis has revealed that boards from the same forest—and occasionally the same tree—could remain in the same shipping 'parcel' from Poland for use at its destination. However, dendro-provenancing the actual forests is proving difficult and generally awaits the completion of tree-ring chronologies for Poland. Exploitation through ports such as Lübeck, Stralsund, Gdánsk and Riga is known but these were obviously transit locations, not production centres. Occasionally provenance can be determined. Imports of Baltic oak to Scotland are particularly evident in the second half of the 15th century (below, p. 139) and, at Angus, painted oak boards within the aisle of Guthrie collegiate church could be shown to have originated within or near the Białowieża forest of eastern Poland.[108]

As well as increasing understanding of resource provenance and exploitation, dendrochronological analysis of structural timber obviously assists study of the development of individual buildings. However, it can also have an impact on the study of towns themselves. It was noted above (p. 27) that archaeological research within Perth now suggests the beginnings of urbanisation in the 11th century (while acknowledging that the more traditional early 12th-century foundation date is that most likely to have seen the initiation of royal-led urban planning). Similarly, at the end of the 12th century, dendrochronological analysis suggests contemporaneous building activity in four Scottish burghs—those of Aberdeen, Glasgow, Inverness and Perth—again indicative of early urban growth. The research is accompanied by the caveat that the ' origin and early development of urban settlements in Scotland is still a subject of some debate and their study is reliant on archaeology to flesh out the burghal charters'.[109] The timbers fossilised within buildings of these burghs nevertheless appear to provide elements of such evidence.

Urban infrastructure

Urban growth in the North Sea region as a whole was little short of spectacular by the 13th century. Some 2500 markets and 300 boroughs existed in England alone while in Germany, as well as some 4000 towns of all sizes by the early 14th century, over 50 towns had a population of at least 5000 people with Köln or Cologne having over 50,000 inhabitants.[110] A clear hierarchy of towns was already evident: within England, London was obviously pre-eminent, followed by such cities as Norwich, York and Lincoln. In the 13th century, however, other English towns grew rapidly in importance notably the North Sea port locations of Newcastle, Hull, Boston, King's Lynn and Great Yarmouth. Similar growth of ports on the other side of the North Sea can also be seen in the 13th century; Lübeck itself, although essentially a 12th century foundation, came to prominence in the 1300s. The historical evidence for these developments is increasingly well-served.[111] Additionally, the quantity of archaeology data continues to grow with much published material from the North Sea region.[112]

Complementary assessment of this growing wealth of historical and archaeological information necessitates an understanding of the relative strengths of each. The results of archaeological excavation will only serve the restricted role of illustration of historical chronologies if such assessment is confined to asking traditional historically-dictated questions of *what?* and *where?*. However, asking more contemporary questions of *how?* and *why?* enables a broader understanding to emerge. As an example, the growth of urban townscapes has become the focus of much archaeological study in recent decades (often drawing upon the expertise of geographers). Aston and Bond published an early work in 1976 summarising approaches to plan elements within medieval towns[113] but, as noted above (p. 28), the field has been expanded in recent years to encompass an archaeological approach to the mentality of urban citizens and the laying out of their urban spaces (as exemplified by Lilley in 2002[114]). These and other works illustrate how urban living, while clearly the result of choices made by individuals and groups in the past, has also left physical expression within the urban environment in the form of streets, tenements and spaces. The relationship of these elements to one another poses questions about urban lifestyle while topographical formation and transformation can often be sequenced through application of stratified archaeological material.

An additional advantage of archaeological study of towns is that it rapidly becomes clear that towns developed at different times for different reasons, with differing impacts and different long-term potential for sustained existence. Successful foundations on the English coast can be cited at Newcastle and Hull, both towns in protected locations upriver from the sea although, in the case of Hull, dangerously low-lying. Archaeological work in both towns, however, has been able to demonstrate that urban foundation was not only complex but built upon unrecorded pre-existing settlement. Evans has summarised the evidence for settlement in the lower Hull valley for instance and it is clear that the 13th-century town known from documentary evidence was not only preceded by hamlets in places such as Drypool, Marfleet and Myton but that such occupation extended back deep into prehistory.[115] At Newcastle, post-Roman pre-urban activity, at least within the area of the quayside, was more limited but it too preceded development of the commercial town, the foot of the steep bank north of the river Tyne being terraced and used in part for pottery manufacture in the 12th century.[116] In both towns, commercial use of the waterfront gained rapidly in importance in the 13th century and both towns flourished.

Towns, whether new or established, faced pressure in the 13th century. The density of urban life was increasing significantly and an oft-quoted example to illustrate the difficulties inherent in such increased density is that of the arrival of mendicant orders from the third decade of the century onward. Seeking establishments within existing urban centres, the friars frequently found themselves on peripheral sites. Norwich in eastern England illustrates the situation: the Dominicans and Franciscans were

Figure 2.10 Excavated culvert in 2015 for cockey or stream at Norwich Augustinian Friary (Brian Ayers).

established in 1226 and were located either on the north bank of the river in the case of the former or on a steep slope, separated from the bulk of the population by the castle, for the latter (the Dominicans were able to move at the beginning of the 14th century to the more central south bank of the River Wensum but were still on marginal riverine land). The Carmelites, also on the north bank away from the city centre, were established in 1256 and the Augustinians, on steeply sloping land above marsh, in 1290.[117]

Excavation at both the Franciscan and the Augustinian sites has provided considerable evidence for the physical manipulation of the local topography in order to enhance the locations of the friaries. The slope upon which the Franciscan establishment stood was rendered more useable by terracing, evidence for revetting of the terraces being seen with the uncovering of parallel battered flint walls.[118] More massive landscaping took place at the site of the Augustinian friary where a steep slope was cut back in order to improve access to the precinct and to win material for levelling of a marshy area next to the river. Additionally, a small tributary to the river was canalised within a brick- and flint-built culvert which was vaulted over. The archaeological work revealed this culvert to be relatively intact (Figure 2.10). A well lined with flint was created within the culvert for drawing clean water which was still crystal clear in 2015, emphasising that the culvert must have been used for water management rather than a mixture of such management and effluent drainage.[119]

Peripheral locations for friaries can be seen in other towns such as Perth and Inverness in Scotland and Aarhus in Denmark. At Perth, the Dominican, Franciscan and Carmelite friars all occupied sites outside the presumed area of the medieval borough.[120] The Dominican friary in Aarhus, established in 1240, took over an existing extramural building. Here a timber church had been established by the late 10th century. This was destroyed by fire around 1050, possibly as a result of a known raid by Harald Hardrada,

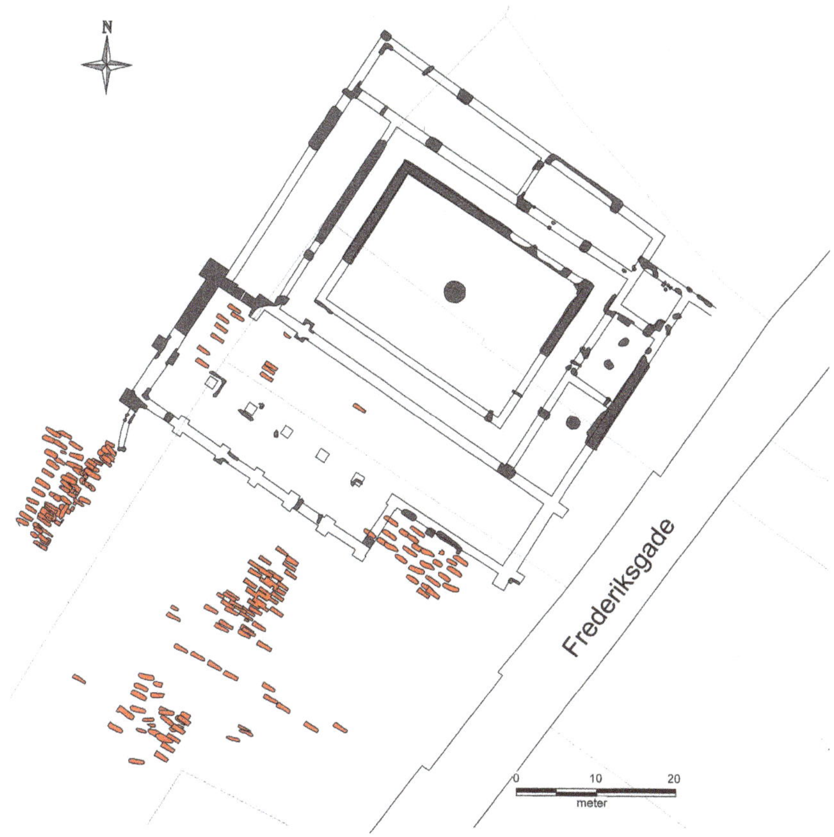

Figure 2.11 Excavation plan of the Carmelite friary in Aarhus (Hans Skov).

and was replaced by a small limestone-vaulted church in about 1070 (Denmark's oldest standing building), itself becoming a crypt soon after for a larger stone building which served as the cathedral (and was re-dedicated as the church of Our Lady—'Vor Frue Kirke'). However, with the arrival of Dominican friars, the building became part of the friary, largely rebuilt in brick *c.* 1260. A cloister was added to the north with a chapter house which is still extant. Similarly, the Aarhus Carmelites, who arrived in 1247, seem also to have taken over an existing site and expanded it. The Carmelite buildings have been destroyed but excavation over a long period of time between 1907 and 1984 has seen recovery of most of the plan of the church and its associated buildings, together with burials (Figure 2.11). Many of the latter seem to precede the establishment of the friary.[121]

One location where the friars appear to have been able to secure more central sites was in Lund, modern Sweden, probably assisted by the 'open plan' of the town (above, p. 44). Here both Franciscans and the Dominicans were able to establish themselves in close proximity to the cathedral, the Franciscans to the west and the Dominicans to the east. Parts of the extensive Franciscan site, which was founded in 1239, have been excavated, including the grave of Archbishop Jacob Erlandsen whose will expressed his wish for interment within the friary. He is recorded as dying suddenly in 1274 while returning from an exile imposed upon him by King Erik V Klipping. Excavation of his skeleton in 1972 revealed an unhealed injury to his cranium as a result of being struck by a crossbow bolt; the archaeological evidence here, therefore, augments the historical texts and suggests strongly that the archbishop was assassinated.[122]

Archaeological work can also illustrate how apparent locational disadvantage was almost certainly converted to an advantage by careful adaptation of the individual sites. Thus, the Norwich Dominicans (on their second site) sought to adjust the layout of their complex so that the preaching nave of the church was directly opposite the main east-to-west thoroughfare in the city; it in turn was fronted by a preaching yard, designed to make use of the hill-slope and thus, like the *cavea* of a Greek theatre, provide an acoustically-privileged asset for the friars and their mission; and the refectory, through which alms of food could be dispensed to the urban poor, was built alongside the side-street frontage. Similarly, the great church of the Carmelites was constructed immediately adjacent to one of the bridges over the Wensum, that carrying the principal road to the bishops' palace, once again in an adjustment to the standard ecclesiastical plan, and here almost certainly providing a statement to highlight known antipathy between the episcopal authorities and the mendicant movement.

Such archaeological observations of the possible meanings conveyed by material culture (in the above instances by the deliberate placing of buildings to be 'read' by the contemporary medieval population) have been characterised by Gilchrist amongst others as 'post-processual' in that they offer 'a social constructivist perspective in challenging scientific claims to unique and objective knowledge'. It is an approach which seeks meaning in material evidence and emphasises the role of agency, by individuals or institutions, 'to reproduce or transform their social contexts'. Within the North Sea region, it is has perhaps been most enthusiastically adopted on 'an Anglo-Scandinavian axis'[123] and indeed such use of theory, particularly in medieval urban studies, can be seen in the work of Carelli and Thomasson.[124] The more mainstream approach, however, remains that of data collection and objective interpretation, frequently characterising urban growth through reference to principal features or processes—thus, the volumes on medieval urban housing, infrastructure, crafts and industries, defences, monasteries and trade produced biennially as a result of urban symposia in Lübeck.[125] However, these publications are also supported by potentially more discursive material, notably with papers which assessed luxury and lifestyle within the hanseatic region.[126] Determining archaeological evidence for luxury proved difficult as it quickly became obvious that appreciation of luxury was subjective depending upon social status, educational attainment, and economic standing and expectation. Theoretical approaches were thus needed, not least to determine *what* to study. Here was a contribution by the North Sea to historiography; archaeological material is necessarily selective in that survival normally dictates selection but seeking to understand the meaning attached to material culture, as exemplified by the concept of

Figure 2.12 Lund—cathedral precinct wall embedded into later library building (Brian Ayers).

Figure 2.13 12th-century brickwork for refectory at Ribe cathedral (Museum of South-West Jutland).

luxury, entailed new forms of selectivity.

Consideration of approaches to material culture in the medieval period raises the question as to how far the development of towns was also leading to a more developed concept of an urban mentality by the 13th century. Expressions of urban distinctiveness are traditionally sought through such administrative and legalistic frameworks as urban charters where definitions of rights, privileges and obligations can be expected. Many towns, particularly smaller ones but also some larger towns only achieving prominence in the 13th century, did not possess such documents (Boston, for example, did not achieve borough status until the 16th century) and yet were themselves clearly becoming independent economic, and presumably, social entities.

This distinctiveness was projected in a number of ways, not least 'mural ideology' as noted above (p. 44). However, technological innovation may well have had an urban aspect on occasion as well. The recent excavation of the Gründungsviertel site in Lübeck, for example, uncovered a precocious use of brick in the construction of a staircase leading to a timber-built cellar at the end of the 12th century.[127] Such urban adoption of brick as a building material was probably led by royal and ecclesiastical promotion of the material: an early use was that *c.* 1165–1182 by Valdemar the Great of Denmark who re-fortified a length of the Danevirke across the Jutland peninsula with a 5m+ high facing of large bricks ('for the protection of the entire realm' according to an inscription on a lead plaque placed in his grave within the church of St Bengt in Ringsted).[128]

The cathedral precinct at Lund, southern Sweden, seems to have been demarcated by a brick wall by the end of the 12th century, some crenellations of which remain fossilised in the east wall of the cathedral library which was subsequently built up against it (Figure 2.12).

In Denmark, work south of Ribe cathedral has uncovered a brick wall, some 2.5m in height which is interpreted as part of the late 12th-century refectory of the monastic community which supported the cathedral (Figure 2.13).[129] The use of brick in such a manner at this period is indeed early although it can now be noted that here 'brick began so suddenly in the middle of the twelfth century that its appearance in archaeological sequences can be used as a chronological marker'.[130] The Ribe bricks were almost certainly produced locally; the cathedral had its own tilery overseen by the monks; a brick inscribed with a graffito of a less-than-happy monk is now displayed at triforium level within the great church (Figure 2.14). Roskilde cathedral was also built of brick from 1170 onward and had its own tileries for

Figure 2.14 Brick with graffito depicting a monk, Ribe (Museum of South-West Jutland).

brick manufacture; that at Bistrup north of Roskilde has been excavated with brick production noted from the 13th century.[131]

Development of infrastructure was also a feature of 13th-century urban life. At Ribe, once again, growth of the town around the cathedral led to linkage with the earlier Viking Age town east of the Ribe river. Massive construction of three dams was undertaken in the 13th century (Overdammen, Mellemdammen and Nederdammen) and provided access between the two zones; they still form the main axial route through the town to this day (Figure 2.15). They also enabled more effective management of the river. Sluices controlled water that was thus available to power the royal mill from about 1250 (it was first documented in 1255) but the dams cut off the early medieval waterfront (next to the original market) from the sea, the medieval port subsequently developing on the opposite side of the river with infilling of the river foreshore. Growth eastward from the cathedral had already led to an increase in the urban area of some seven hectares by about 1200 with further development towards Fiskergade in the 13th century and final establishment of a new waterfront along Skibbroen by the 14th century.

Construction of a dam was a major factor in the growth of Amsterdam. Here the first settlement took place around 1175 and houses were standing on either side of the Amstel river by 1200. The river was dammed about 1265, control of the water thereby assisting further urban development.[132] In Rotterdam, the dam on the Rotte rivulet from which the settlement takes its name, was uncovered by excavation between 1988 and 1992 at Hoogstraat. Dendrochronological analysis of a boat found sealed beneath the dam gave a date of *c.* 1270, construction of the dam clearly post-dating this (and thus later than suggested by documentary sources). Timber sluices for the discharging of water were also located and timber houses had been constructed above.[133] The point to derive from the Ribe, Amsterdam and Rotterdam evidence is that major infrastructure schemes were only possible when an ambitious and prosperous community, such as a dynamic town, was engaged.

Crossing rivers was, of course, also effected by bridges, the most spectacular example within the North Sea region being London bridge, itself a dramatic monument. First constructed in timber in the late 10th century, it was replaced in stone between *c.* 1176 and 1209. Numerous later illustrations survive either showing overviews of the structure, such as the drawing by Wenceslas Hollar in 1647, or details of bridge elements, such as a view through the second arch by E. V. Cooke in 1831 shortly before demolition.[134]

Figure 2.15 The main street of Overdammen, Mellemdammen and Nederdammen in Ribe (Brian Ayers).

Part of the southern bridgehead was uncovered by excavation in 1984, the 12th-century stone piers being constructed above elm piles protected by starlings designed to prevent erosion of the bridge footings.[135] At Newcastle-upon-Tyne a stone bridge of twelve arches was probably also constructed in the later 12th century; like London bridge it was covered with houses and other buildings. This Newcastle bridge stood until it was swept away by floodwater in 1771. One arch still survives in the basement of Watergate Buildings on the north bank of the river.[136] South of Newcastle, Elvet Bridge in Durham was probably constructed in the second half of the 12th century. It continues to stand (although the central section had to be rebuilt after a flood in 1771) with arches extending beneath the streets on both banks of the river. Chantry chapels were added at the upper and lower ends of the bridge in the 13th century (Figures 2.16 and 2.17).

Water not only had to be controlled and bridged in the low-lying towns bordering the North and Baltic Seas but fresh water supplies needed to be provided for the urban population. A public well seems to have existed at the southern end of Store Torv square in Aarhus, Denmark from the 13th century; it was timber-lined, being renewed with a lining of granite a century later.[137] Underground lead pipes for water existed in Bruges by the 1280s.[138] Dendrochronological assessment of timber features excavated in Greifswald, Germany enabled dating of wells to the period between 1252 and 1272 and also illustrated a heavy weighting of infrastructural development to the late 13th century with the construction of timber-lined latrine pits. The evidence from this Baltic town is particularly interesting because it demonstrates how archaeological discovery and research can complement and enhance the historical record.

Figure 2.16 Elvet Bridge, Durham (Brian Ayers).

Figure 2.17 Detail of the arches of Elvert Bridge, Durham (Brian Ayers).

Greifswald in the late 13th century has evidence for a building boom with renewal of street surfaces, reclamation works at the commercial waterfront and the building of a market hall, all most probably linked to greater urban privileges granted by the Pomeranian duke Wartislaw III in 1264.[139] In a similar manner, archaeological work at Uppsala in Sweden can suggest that the provision of timber-lined rubbish pits after about 1270 appears to have been so systematic as to imply organisational direction for its implementation and maintenance.[140] In Lübeck, at a more obviously domestic level, recent excavation of a tenement at the Gründungsviertel site has uncovered a well-preserved 13th-century wooden *Toilettenhaus* complete with two seats side-by-side, one of which was furnished with a step to enable use by a child (Figures 2.18 and 2.19).[141]

Carole Rawcliffe, in her recent book on communal health in late medieval English towns, notes that the removal of rubbish was facilitated by the paving of streets. There is growing archaeological evidence that such paving was becoming increasingly common from the 13th century, the works surely indicating a greater awareness of urban distinctiveness and urban pride. Indeed, Rawcliffe quotes from the Norwich city corporation Assembly Book for 1559 where it was commented that from

> tyme oute of mynde there hathe been a comely and decent order used within this cittye for the paving of the streets ... which thing hath not only bene a great ease and helthefull commodity to the inhabitants of the same, but also a goodly bewtefyng [beautifying] ...[142]

In many towns early paving was undertaken in wood, an example being that found beneath Polstraat in Deventer where at least four successive levels of timber street paving were observed in 1906. Polstraat was lined with stone houses of the greater merchants of Deventer so it is perhaps only to be expected that such members of the urban elite should benefit from early infrastructure improvement. Other streets were covered with gravel as is known from High Street in Perth by the beginning of the 13th century and 'carefully and laboriously constructed, and subsequently well-maintained, [gravel] pathways' have been noted from the cemetery of St John's Hospital in Cambridge.[143] Elsewhere, however, stone-paved streets are also apparent in the 13th century: a crude example is known from Klosterstraße

Figure 2.18 Excavation of Toilettenhaus at the Gründungsviertel, Lübeck (Bereich für Archäologie Lübeck).

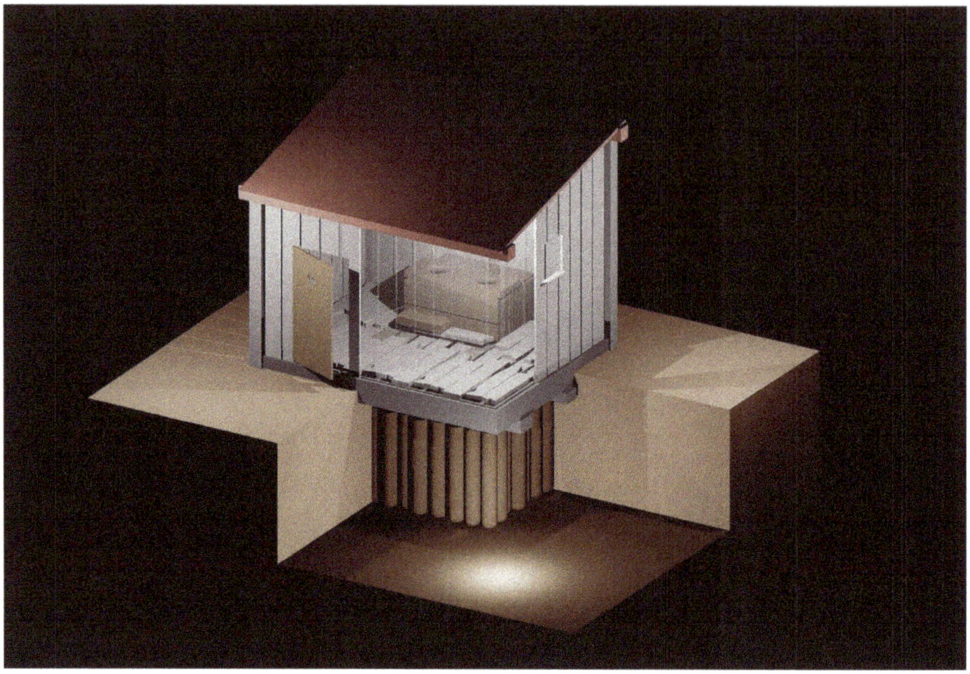

Figure 2.19 Reconstruction of Toilettenhaus , Gründungsviertel, Lübeck (Bereich für Archäologie Lübeck).

in Stade dating to around 1200; a street of stone cobbles constructed about 1270 has been uncovered beneath Martin-Luther-Straße in Greifswald; and a similarly well-paved stone street has been excavated at the lost settlement of Freyenstein (near the hanse town of Brandenburg and destroyed *c.* 1263) where it remains exposed.[144]

Urban connections

Freyenstein lies some 120km inland from the Baltic Sea; this may seem remote but access to the North and Baltic Seas from inland locations such as Göttingen or Brandenburg was not only feasible but practised. Archaeological data also implies that the concept of 'inland' was very different at a period when much transport of goods had to be by water and most vessels were small or, at best, of medium size. As an example, historical and archaeological evidence combine to suggest international trade in the 1200s between Swavesey, very much 'inland' within the Cambridgeshire fenland, and the Low Countries. Excavations at Swavesey have uncovered a 'lode' or or artificial channel leading to a hythe or staithe, perhaps associated with a neighbouring fish-processing site in use from the 12th to 16th centuries. The lode was only 8m wide but ships of Swavesey are documented as being attacked by pirates off the Low Countries in the 13th century.[145] A similar lode is known at Lakenheath in Suffolk, linking a small inland port there to the River Little Ouse and thus to the monastic centre at Ely and the growing international port of Lynn (Lakenheath was recorded as 'Lakingahethe' in 1086 or 'Laking hythe', thus emphasising the wharves of the settlement.[146] Infilled quays and access waterways have also been identified at Isleham on the Cambridgeshire fen-edge and argued to have been in existence by the late 12th century.[147] Vessels of small size must therefore have plied both the east of England's inland waterways and perhaps also the North Sea at this period.

Evidence for such craft is scanty in Britain but several discoveries have been made in Scandinavia and have been linked to the development of both inland and wider commercial trade from the 11th century onward. A 12th-century boat, some 14.5m in length, was discovered in 1922 at Ellingå in north Jutland, Denmark and was similar to a further discovery, also of 12th-century date, found in 1928 in

Halland, Sweden. Both vessels are considered to be coastal craft and, significantly, the Halland ship was not only found in a creek but close to a location called *Gamla Köpstad* which means 'Old Market Town'.[148] However, perhaps the most impressive discovery was that of the Gedesby boat on the island of Falster in southern Denmark in 1988. This well-preserved craft could be dated to the mid-13th century, was some 13m in length, and had a hull lined with wattle work. A thick organic deposit found within the hull was examined for its botanical content, leading to the conclusion that the material was almost certainly cattle dung. 'Prior to being taken on board the cattle drank water from freshwater ponds or lakes and grazed a variety of habitats, arable fields, roadsides and field boundaries, pastures and heaths, shoreline and shore meadows, in a coastal cultural landscape. The evidence suggests that this took place in late summer or early autumn around harvest time'.[149] The wattle lining was also of interest, its presence in the hull presumably helping the cattle to maintain their footing.

The development of inland and coastal vessels along the margins of the North Sea was complemented by deliberate improvement of waterways themselves. An early example is that of the Ouse-Cam river at Ely in the Cambridgeshire fens which had been diverted some 2.5km to its present location by the early 12th century. At Ramsey, the abbey there seems to have created a lode which provided access for vessels bringing materials such as stone to the site by *c.* 1200 and excavation also found evidence for a probable 'wippe' or see-saw crane.[150] A greater work cut a course for the Ouse-Cam (via the 'Ten Mile River') towards Lynn and therefore ensured that products of the Ely pottery industry could reach a broader market. Kiln waste for Ely Ware has been recognised close to the waterfront at Potters Lane, the industry fostered by local clay sources and peat for firing. It has been calculated that the large quantities of broken pottery of Ely Ware fabrics found in Lynn had travelled no more than 400m overland, use of waterways clearly being of paramount importance (Figure 2.20). The trade only declined when, in the 13th century, more local pottery was manufactured on a massive scale at Pott Row, Grimston, close to Lynn.[151] A similar decline in the trade of Stamford ware ceramics—presumably a major contributory factor to cessation of production of that material—was the growth of Boston, cutting off direct contact between Stamford and the North Sea.[152] On the other hand, the trans-shipment of commodities upstream both to and from a port such as Boston might well have been facilitated by small riverside settlements. A collection of ceramics from land at the junction of the River Witham and Barlings Eau at Short Ferry, in Fiskerton parish, Lincolnshire has led to the suggestion that this may mark the site of a small out-port for both imports to and exports from the city of Lincoln.[153]

Ely imported materials as well as exporting pottery; Lakenheath supplied it with about 100,000 peat turves per annum around 1300 while ceramic assemblages from excavations include vessels such as Essex red wares (above, p. 43) and, occasionally but more exotically, Scarborough ware and Saintonge ware, the latter from south-western France and, with the Scarborough material, presumably sourced through Lynn.[154] Rivers gave both Ely and smaller settlements such as Swavesey and Lakenheath access to both their hinterlands and to the sea, fostering their roles as distribution centres locally, enabling wider commercial contacts and, in the larger towns, encouraging specialisation. As an example, the importation of large quantities of animals to feed urban populations necessarily encouraged crafts and industries, exploiting the byproducts of meat provision. Thus bone- and horn-working in the mid-to late-12th century was being practised at High Street, Perth with that part of the street occupied by numbers 75–95 High Street already characterised as a 'horn-working centre'.[155] However, the town's craft industry was not solely devoted to specialist activity; elsewhere on High Street at numbers 80–86 (that is, across the road) evidence was found for a range of crafts with 'no one craft approaching industrial scale'.

Ideas could be exported as well as as products. Technological innovation within pottery production has recently been summarised for the 12th and 13th centuries in Denmark. Here, where only two kiln sites were known before 1983, kilns have now been recorded on Jutland, Funen and Zealand with kiln waste known from a number of other sites. The oldest known kiln-type is that characterised as horizontal with separate firing and kiln chambers (as at Farum Lillevang and Faurholm, both in north-eastern Zealand). At Hellum in Northern Jutland, however, the excavated kiln was of the vertical type with the

Figure 2.20 Ely Ware jug from Cambridge (photo Gwil Owen: © Oxford Archaeology East).

kiln chamber located above the firing chamber. It has been dated to the 12th century and sufficient survived to enable the creation of a reconstruction. It is likely that development of this vertical structure took English kilns as examples, probably from the east of England.[156]

North Sea contact may also explain tile-kiln development in Scotland. Here, excavations at the site of a priory of Cistercian nuns in North Berwick on the coast east of Edinburgh, first undertaken in 1929 and then again in 2011, produced evidence of roof-tile production which could be radiocarbon-dated to the mid-13th century. This is easily the earliest evidence to be recovered for such manufacture in Scotland, the coastal location of the priory perhaps influencing the importation of the technology.[157] Floor-tile production within Scotland seems to have been limited; local manufacture perhaps took place at Melrose (for the abbey) in the late 13th and early 14th centuries but most floor-tiles seem to have either been imported from Northern England or from the continent.[158]

Urban hierarchy

Archaeological data from urban settlements such as Perth is helpful in seeking to understand the developing economic base of towns and the nature of towns themselves. In England it is possible for historians to characterise three main types of town: royal towns which essentially over a period of time acquired self-governing status; *mesne* towns which were boroughs with burgesses but where control of institutions remained within the hands of the local lord; and manorial market towns which were not boroughs but markets where local lords gave consent to market activity.

Royal towns could be large, such as York or Norwich, and archaeologically can be characterised by specialisation: thus, in Norwich, the cloth-finishing trade entailed the employment of dyers, fullers, shearmen and tentermen amongst others[159] while in London evidence of boat and ship-building has been discovered recently. Excavations at Three Quays House near the Tower of London in 2011 uncovered deposits containing a range of ships' timbers including keels, stems, framing timbers and a mast step. The area is one documented as being occupied by shipbuilders at the end of the 13th century and finds included tools such as augers, axes and a pair of clamps (possibly the only example from Britain although there are parallels in Scandinavia suggesting use of similar techniques) as well as two tar barrels.[160]

Mesne boroughs and smaller markets tend to show more diversification amongst their artisan groups. Thus the archaeological material from late 12th- century Perth shows that, although the settlement was emerging as one of the great royal towns of Scotland, it still housed a diverse range of craft industries to meet everyday needs, only gradually evolving into specialist enclaves.[161] There has been a tendency in urban archaeology in recent years to concentrate on the great towns with relatively little work being undertaken in smaller boroughs and markets. This is particularly true of the North Sea world where an interest in trading networks necessarily seeks out the nodal points of trade and explores connections which are more readily evident in such locations (although startling finds can still be made in less obvious places: excavations in the East Yorkshire town of Beverley for example unearthed a 12th-century pewter spoon incised with three fish, each about to take a hook in a manner paralleled by similar, slightly later, finds at Bergen and Oslo—Figure 2.21).[162] However, increasingly both archaeologists and historians have been turning attention to the broader economic picture, examining urban hinterlands, urban hierarchies and local patterns of trade.

To a great extent, much of this process has been led by the documentary record, particularly in England where the survival of manorial and other written material is generally good. There has been recognition of the complexity of the urban framework, the importance of infrastructural development (such as the construction of roads and bridges) to foster internal trade, and the often pivotal role of manorial or religious lords. This historical research results in schemes of urban growth, notably for the period 1100 to 1350, and places considerable emphasis upon factors such as the greater use of standardised weights and measures, the growth of common commercial practices, often underwritten by guilds, and commensurately the development of legal ideas and processes to make these systems effective.

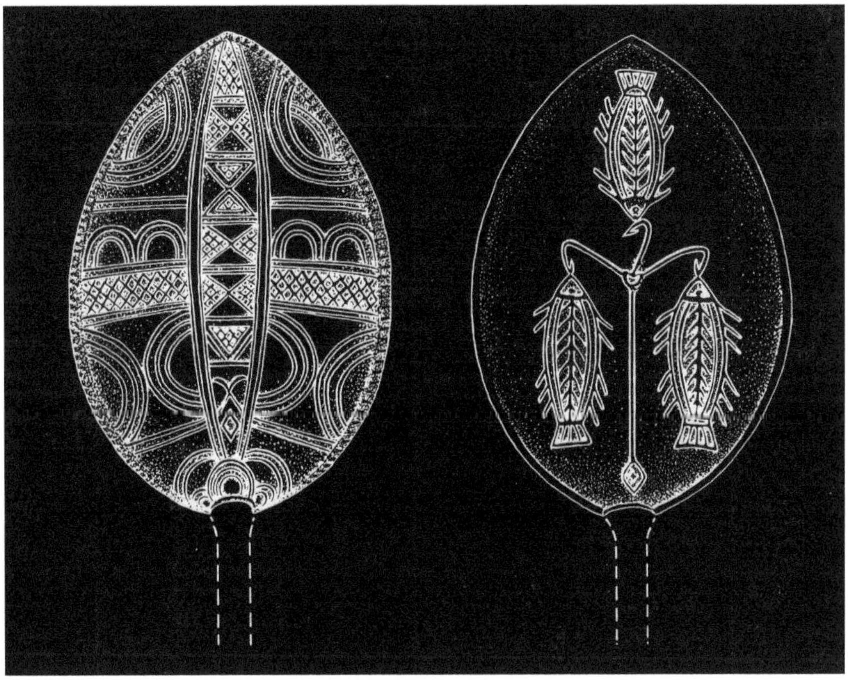

Figure 2.21 Beverley—12th-century incised spoon (Humber Archaeology Partnership).

Archaeological data can contribute to this growing understanding of towns, their hinterlands and networks in a number of ways. An obvious practical contribution is recognition of settlement hierarchy, differentiating small towns from villages. Dyer has reviewed the archaeology of small towns in England, concluding that perhaps the greatest archaeological contribution to such differentiation is that of recognising usage of space that is 'distinctively urban ... high densities of buildings; rows of houses closely packed along street frontages; narrow plots behind the houses; peculiar street patterns including the accommodation of market places in front of church doors, at the convergence of streets, or in deliberately widened main streets'. He extends his criteria and identifies 'benchmarks' of material culture which assist definition of urban character and hierarchal status, exploring social structure through house size and quality as well as artefacts, occupations as indicated by 'structures, implements and debris', hinterlands through pottery distribution and the provision of building materials, and 'civic consciousness' exemplified by public buildings, provision of utilities such as water supply, or refuse disposal and public works such as defences. However caution still needs to be used; as an example, the town of Aalst in Flanders had defences added to it in the 13th century but recent examination of botanical evidence from two sites within the town, that called *'t Haaantje* and another adjacent to the *Grote Markt* suggests that both 'preserved their character of an open landscape at least until the 14th century'.[163] Towns may therefore have grown spatially but it did not necessarily mean that their economies developed at the same time.

Small towns are relevant to the study of the North Sea world because, as Dyer observes, 'imported or manufactured goods ... such as dried cod, dyestuffs or copper alloy dress accessories' were accessed by rural communities through the markets of such towns.[164] While noting that, despite a growth in archaeological investigation of small towns, large towns continue to receive greater attention, he also points out that ports are some of the lesser towns which have also benefitted from considerable research. Notable amongst these is Hartlepool in north-eastern England where a sustained campaign of well-published excavations has resulted in both a clearer understanding of the origins and development of the settlement as well as detailed information on its likely functions. As an example, some 38 ovens have been excavated within medieval Hartlepool, dating from the 13th century onward. Many of these, such those of the 13th-century from south gate, can be characterised as 'external' to the buildings with which they are associated and therefore essentially communal, implying a role within victualing of shipping reaching the harbour.[165]

The use of small ports as distribution centres has also been observed in north-western Germany where a series of occupation sites housing craftsmen and merchants has been identified within the marshland area between the rivers Ems and Weser. Characterised as *Langwurten*, these linear settlements are located on dwelling mounds parallel to tidal inlets. The largest such port was the town of Emden where an apparent rectilinear plan has been shown by excavation to have developed piecemeal from the 9th century onward, with added areas to both the north and the south. Borehole evidence indicates a suitable berthing area for shipping south of Pelzerstraße with subsequent development of a deepened harbour to the east, the 'Delft' or 'Ratsdelft'. Further north, archaeological work in Langwarden was able to identify expansion of the settlement in the 12th and 13th centuries, partly because of the *securi portus* documented in 1307 but probably also because it was associated with a fair, recorded at the same time. Excavation both west and east of the settlement was able to identify the location of the port, to the east of the *Langwurt* mound at the site of a former tidal inlet called the 'Altes Sieltief', recovering imported tufa stone, bricks and ceramics which may have marked the site of the fair as well as that of the wharf.[166]

Increasing environmental pressures

Langwurten settlements were clearly located on marginal land and, towards the end of the 13th century, such situations were becoming increasingly perilous on both sides of the North Sea. Probable climate change plus isostatic movement combined with the shrinkage of drained marshland and peat bogs to threaten coastal and low-lying communities. At some point in the 1200s the North Sea breached the line of Dutch dunes and formed the Zuiderzee.[167] Archaeologically, the impact of the threatened inundation can be seen at Medemblik in the Netherlands where, as early as 1164 and 1170, storm surges had caused widespread flooding, depositing evidence uncovered in excavations within the town. In order to survive, the inhabitants had to restore and raise a defensive bank which became a 'high elongated terp' and was attached to an encircling dyke. Study of the composition of this *terp* has shown that it was constructed of differing elements, suggesting that individual property owners were responsible for maintaining and enhancing those sections adjacent to or within their plots.[168]

Ribe in Denmark is a further example of where the volatility of the coastal zone impacted upon the settlement. The town, always well-placed for North Sea trade, was also favoured by a rich hinterland with grazing for cattle and good fishing grounds. In addition it was a royal town which received much support from the Danish crown, ensuring that its port continued to be used even though nearby ports such as Tønder (subject to the Duke of Schleswig rather than the Danish king) were better situated to take increasingly larger vessels. Ribe nevertheless, despite its dramatic expansion as a result of infrastructural investment and its royal support, was situated on the Ribe Å, a narrow, winding river which became increasingly restricted as the construction of protective banks prevented water ingress. In consequence, the town became isolated from the coast and ultimately declined as a port, retaining only local importance.[169]

At Wisbech in eastern England, recent excavation has recorded a series of flood events, silt deposits sealing occupation levels from the 13th century onward. Work at Market Mews in the heart of the medieval town recorded a thick flood deposit characterised as 'a fine pale brown sandy clay-silt layer 0.25m thick, increasing in depth towards the southern limit of the excavation'.[170] Nevertheless, the town continued to be occupied as did the surrounding area where large numbers sheep grazed on the low-lying land north of Wisbech and a complex network of droveways ensured access to summer pasture at West Fen.[171] Clearly, the income from this rich agricultural area offset the expense of reclamation and recovery following flooding episodes.

Climatic conditions posed a different problem at another English east coast town in that Great Yarmouth suffered severely from windblown sand in the 11th and 12th centuries. Difficult excavations at Fullers Hill within the town in 1973 were able to isolate 12 occasions when sand covered the area, providing horizons between stratified levels of occupation.[172] The situation appears to have stabilised by the 13th century, perhaps aided by the construction of more substantial buildings (a stone house is documented from 1199 and elements of the surviving 'tolhouse' within the borough also date to the 12th century).

A diifferent and probably devastating climatic impact seems to have hit the North Sea region, and most probably the rest of Europe, in 1257/8. A cataclysmic volcanic eruption is now known to have taken place at this time, most probably at Mount Rinjani in Indonesia but perhaps in Mexico or Ecuador. The global impact of this eruption was a stratospheric sulphuric acid aerosol veil or 'dry fog' which blocked sunlight and cooled the earth's surface. Contemporary chroniclers reported heavy rains, with Matthew Paris mentioning 'such unendurable cold ... [which] suspended all cultivation and killed the young of the cattle ... Owing to the scarcity of wheat a very large number of poor people died and dead bodies were found in all directions, swollen and livid, lying by fives and sixes in pigsties, on dunghills, and in the muddy streets'.[173] Recent mass burials, excavated at Spitalfields in London, have been accurately dated by radiocarbon and almost certainly relate to famine victims of this mid-13th century natural disaster.[174]

Medieval communities around the North Sea were therefore threatened by climatic change in the atmosphere but perhaps most noticeably from the sea itself, evident throughout the 13th century. A serious flood is documented as causing severe damage in Perth in 1209, archaeological evidence of 'gap' sites in the town late in the 13th century being interpreted as probable effects of this event.[175] In 1236 Matthew Paris recorded that

> 'there burst forth extraordinary inundations of the sea, and a very strong wind was heard at the same time as unusually great waves of the sea. Especially in places by the sea, the wind tore up

> anchors and deprived the ports of their fleets, drowned a multitude of men, wiped out flocks of sheep and herds of cattle, ripped out trees by their roots, blew down houses and destroyed the beaches'.[176]

In order to sustain occupation within such a potentially volatile environment, communities had to take extraordinary measures. Security could frequently only be found with constant repair and maintenance of protective embankments. At Leeuwarden in the Netherlands, it took construction of the Tjessingadijk to the north of the city around 1280, enhancing defensive banks which originated in the 11th century, to enable urban occupation to expand effectively.[177] Prior to this occupation had been marginal, essentially a village with craft industries supporting an agricultural hinterland. Control of the local environment brought prosperity and development to Leeuwarden as it did to other communities on both sides of the North Sea. Not all such communities, however, would be sustained in the 14th century.

— 3 —

The 14th Century: Increasing Wealth and Increasing Pressures

Contemporary urban foundations which did not survive and flourish in the 14th century include an English example which shared the same estuary as Hull. Ravenser Odd, or Ravensrodd, was a port founded on Spurn Point, a sand and shingle spit at the mouth of the Humber, about 1235. Spurn Point is the result of longshore drift, building up from eroded material and subject to regular inundation, removal by the sea and re-formation. It forms a prominent but very narrow peninsula at the south-eastern corner of Yorkshire and the siting of a new town here was therefore a somewhat perilous enterprise. Despite an importance as a fishing port, particularly for herring, it was not a situation that proved sustainable. The port was destroyed by the sea in the 1360s but its existence even until then was one which clearly startled contemporaries. The late 14th-century chronicle of nearby Meaux Abbey related:

> For that town of Ravenser Odd ... at the extreme limits of Holderness, situated between the waters of the sea and the Humber, lay about a mile or more distant from the mainland. Access to it from early times from Old Ravenser was by means of a sandy road strewn with rounded yellow pebbles ... [and] scarcely a bowshot in width and marvellously withstanding the floodwaters of the sea on its eastern side and the tides of the Humber on its western side.[1]

Ports were extant in similarly precarious positions on the North Sea coast of continental Europe. The most noted was that of Rundholt in North Friesland within the Wadden Sea area. This settlement, perhaps of some 1500 people, appears to have been a port with a significant trade in cattle and salt from the marshlands. It stood south of the present small island of Südfall within an embanked area of marshland, on one or more *terp*-type mounds. It was overwhelmed in a storm surge in 1362 called 'de Grote Mandränke' or the great drowning of people but traces of medieval settlement within the area can still be seen on the islands of Pellworm as well as the peninsula of Nordstrand south of Husum and adjacent mudflats. The tidal river of Norderhever between Pellworm and Nordstrand may be that responsible for the loss of Rundholt.[2] Fragments of buildings from the destroyed port have reportedly been uncovered by fisherman in their nets while archaeological evidence for the probable site was first noted in the 1920s. Stray material was collected, including an ocarina or globular stoneware flute apparently discovered by an English airman, shot down in the area in 1943.[3] Work by Andreas Busch between 1932 and 1956 recorded several farm mounds associated with strip-shaped fields which he linked with the lost settlement of Rundholt.[4] Most recently in 2014, a press release concerning excavation work ahead of a proposed offshore wind farm also suggested the possibility that the town had been located.[5] This is helpful because the nature of the settlement remains unclear; claims that it was a significant port exporting locally-manufactured salt have been countered by arguments that it was little more than a large village within the marshland.

Losses such as Rundholt, however, need to be contrasted with urban success, particularly in the first half of the 14th century. A notable example is the port of Hull itself, growing dramatically at the expense not only of Ravenserodd but also of the nearby port of Hedon. Hull occupies a marginal site at the mouth of the river Hull, the original situation of which has become more clear in recent years following archaeological research. The outflow of the river Hull in the early 13th century had been through a channel known as Sayer Creek or the 'Old Hull' which lay west of the later medieval town. Its course was still visible in the 18th century when the meandering line of the channel was marked on Phillips's plan of 1725. Bore-hole transects have now isolated the channel, the original deep-watercourse being characterised by an absence of organic and peat deposits.[6]

In the late 13th century Hull was acquired by Edward I (1293) and thereafter was renamed Kingston-upon-Hull. The town was subject to a survey so that the king knew exactly what he now owned. This survey survives as do subsequent surveys, notably that for a rental assessment in 1347 when the royal surveyors clearly progressed from house-to-house around the town, identifying the individual properties one-by-one and recording not only their relationships one-to-another but also the width (in feet and inches) of their street frontages. Their remarkable document has enabled the 14th-century property boundaries which they recorded to be located on the 19th-century 1st edition Ordnance Survey map of Hull; in consequence a detailed plan of the city can be drawn for 1347 and, by extension, backwards to 1293 as well as forwards to a later rental return of 1352.[7] In addition it is also possible to plot probable wealth distribution in the port, based upon the rents of the properties (Figure 3.1).

The growth of Hull in the 14th century shows clear signs of having been the result of a planned enterprise. Its neighbouring port of Hedon had been planned too, probably by the counts of Aumale who were lords of Holderness, the name of the low-lying land of east Yorkshire. Assessment of the documentary,

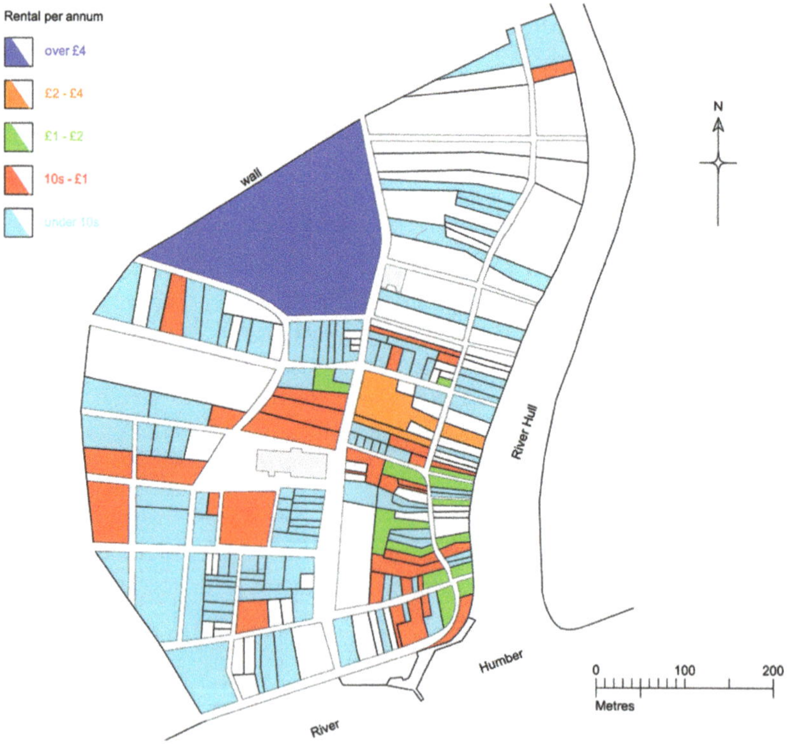

Figure 3.1 Reconstructed tenement map of Hull showing the distribution of wealth in 1347, as indicated by the amount paid in annual rents (Dave Evans; Humber Archaeology Partnership).

cartographic and archaeological evidence for Hedon suggests that the process was undertaken in several stages, starting with a planned hamlet of the late 11th century and progressing to a settlement with urban and port facilities in the early 12th century. It was almost certainly intended as a centre of legal, administrative and commercial activity within Holderness. The town plan was extensive with additions to the south and east later on in the 12th century and contained purpose-built docks. However, progress faltered and, by the middle of the 13th century Hedon was in decline, so much so that, within the 14th century, much of the town's area had become pasture. Excavations seem to underline the port's lack of commercial importance save for a short period in the late 12th and early 13th centuries: only 0.2% of the pottery recovered in 1975–1976 was imported (just 16 vessels) and, although these represented contact with south-western France, the Rhineland and the Low Countries, the excavator acknowledges that they could have reached Hedon via coasting trade from Hull or elsewhere.[8]

Hedon and Ravenserodd were not alone on the east coast of Britain in suffering decline and even extinction. Dunwich on the Suffolk coast was largely lost to the sea by 1384 (the Dominican friars of the town petitioned for land elsewhere in that year because their 'mansion-house is in peril by incursion of the sea, which has destroyed the greater part of Dunwich'[9]) while the small township of Forvie in north-eastern Scotland was inundated by windblown sand in August 1413; only the ruins of the church are still visible here (the modern sand dune is some 30m in height). Across the North Sea, it seems likely that some 50 parishes in Schleswig Holstein, including above-mentioned Rundholt, were lost in a great flood of 1362 (see also above, p. 71).[10] That villages even on *terps* were destroyed is clear. Aerial photography, for instance, has revealed a lost terp mound beneath the water at Altnordstrand, a little to the north-east of the probable site of Rundholt.[11]

Coinage and trade

The Grote Mandränke flood of 1362 devastated a coastline which, along with the rest of Europe, was already suffering from the impact of the Black Death a decade or so earlier. Prior to this epidemic, however, the economic growth visible in late 13th-century urban expansion and rural development continued into the 14th century. Archaeologically, one mechanism for exploring economic development and the fostering of trade around the North Sea, is the study of coinage, either individual finds or those of coin hoards, although its study has to be surrounded by caveats (not least the increasing use of paper credit for long distance trade). Spufford has noted the importance of an adequate money supply for the oiling the wheels of both the urban and rural economies but he also cautions that money usage tended to be seasonal in the countryside and all-year in towns.[12] One might therefore expect urban finds of coins and hoards to be considerable, not least because of the urban role in trade, but against this supposition must be set a further caution noted by Kermode that merchants frequently settled accounts by paying off a supplier with unpaid owed balances, thereby militating against large quantities of coinage.[13] She cites examples from the 15th century but the situation surely obtained earlier as well. Additionally, particularly in the early 14th century, an island state such as England was especially susceptible to infiltration of foreign imitations of its own coinage[14] as evidenced, for example, by the 2012 record of coinage finds in Norfolk where, of 10 foreign coins of late 13th and early 14th-century date, eight were foreign imitations.[15] Calculating the indigenous money supply can therefore be problematic.

Examination of coinage is nevertheless particularly useful for exploration of such issues as state formation and sustainability. Regular coinage was known in Denmark, for instance, from the 11th century but, just as the issuing of coins can illustrate state organisation, so perhaps the debasement of coins, the use of foreign coinage and the hoarding of coins may well be indicators of state decay or even dissolution. It is therefore interesting that Danish minting of coins almost ceased for some years after 1330 (contemporary with the disastrous reign of Christopher II who died in 1332 leaving what was essentially a 'failed state') and hoards found within the country often contain large quantities of foreign issues. A good example is the Kirial hoard, found in two iron cauldrons in 1967 in Djursland, Denmark with some 81,000 German coins (the larger of the two cauldrons has a foundry mark which indicates that it was made in Stralsund in Germany). This hoard was deposited within a year or two of 1365, perhaps in 1368 –69 when there was a war in Jutland involving rebellious nobility and the Danish king. The coins and cauldrons are now in the National Museum of Denmark in Copenhagen.

A slightly earlier hoard of some 12,000 coins was deposited in Aberdeen around 1324. This too used a cauldron as a container and may also indicate a hurried concealment due to military activity. However, it has been noted that both this and the Kirial hoard need not have belonged to a single individual and indeed, it is considered that the Aberdeen hoard, representing a sum of money of only some £50, was 'quite compatible with the fortunes of professional and business men in the town. It is easy to underestimate the wealth of the trade carried on in Aberdeen, and the prosperity of many of the Flemish families established there'.[16] Concealment in this instance therefore may have been an activity by a member or members of a mercantile group, seeking to safeguard assets when state organisation failed.

Coin hoards are also useful for exploring the amount of inter-state dependence. The huge number of German coins in the Kirial hoard indicates that Denmark had to place considerable reliance upon Germany for much of its coinage in the late 14th century just as the slightly earlier Aberdeen hoard, in common with other Scottish finds of the period, is dominated by coins from England (although it is probably best not to assume that coins had straightforward journeys; it is possible that English coins on occasion formed part of the trade from the Low Countries to Scotland). Nevertheless, it has been claimed that, at this period, 'Scottish economic life was entirely dependent on the products of English mints for its money supply',[17] archaeological evidence here supplementing analysis of data such as tax receipts. Aberdeen has been described 'as probably unique in Europe in the number and size of its medieval coin hoards. No fewer than five have been unearthed in the city centre with another two having been uncovered in the Futty area [a fishing suburb to the east]'.[18] Aberdeen's trade was both with its hinterland and overseas, exporting, fish, wool, woolfells and hides, although only a few exotic items have been recovered from the town (such as a fragment of silk and an elephant ivory spindle whorl).[19]

Documentary evidence has long been used to chart individuals engaged in trading activities. Work by Kermode on the merchants of York, Beverley and Hull has identified numerous merchants whose activities took them overseas. Her examples include William Agland of York, mercer, who was resident in Bruges *c.* 1371, John Gisburn, also of York, who was buying wool and hides in Scotland in 1358, and Thomas de Holme of Beverley, resident in Bruges in 1332.[20] Amor has noted similar activity by merchants of Ipswich such as John Bernard who, in the 1390s, imported iron from Spain.[21] Archaeological evidence can also indicate such trading activity. Attention was drawn above (p. 3) to the discovery of a personal signet belonging to Ada de Bernham, probably lost by an Englishwoman in north Germany in the late 13th century. In the following century archaeological discovery of personal seals in Denmark shows a range of merchants, often from the Low Countries, visiting southern Scandinavia. They include individuals such as Egbert of Deventer, Alart van Vechte of Oldenburg and Gerhard of Zeebrugge.

An obvious archaeological approach to trade contacts is to examine residual materials, notably artefacts which survive well such as ceramics. Finds of pottery can be used to explore both bulk and specialist trade activity but caution is needed. Firstly, an absence of traded ceramics does not necessarily mean an absence of trade; Evans has pointed out that the trade of Hull, where excavations have yielded conspicuous quantities of imported pottery vessels, also included trade in perishable goods or consumables with extensive areas such as the Baltic, where the traded material does not survive within the archaeological record. He also summarises documentary references to imports from these regions, such as herrings from Scania. Conversely, though, he notes the minor trading activity of the export by Hull of locally-made ceramics to locations such as north-eastern Scotland and Norway, an activity entirely unrecorded in surviving documentation.[22] His work emphasises the value of assessing as wide a range of sources as possible.

Secondly, and with regard to careful assessment, Verhaeghe has considered the overarching methodological problems associated with consideration of ceramic assemblages. He identifies two broad areas of concern. The first of these he terms 'technical' problems, such as a lack of knowledge with regard to production centres (although he acknowledges that this is improving), methods of quantification and the use of distribution maps. The second group is that of 'interpretative' problems, examples of which he summarises under 'equifinality', that is 'the phenomenon whereby more or less identical and archaeologically detectable patterns may in fact result from a series of totally different actions and/or events in the past'.[23] Again, a comparison of documentary and archaeological sources is helpful: using Hull material once more, he notes (in the 15th century) that the customs accounts mention pottery as cargo in ships from the smaller harbours of Zeeland but that the actual ceramics as recovered by excavation were sourced from locations such as Bruges and Bergen-op-Zoom. In other words 'the actual port of embarkation of the goods is not recorded; neither are any other ports of call on the way to Hull'.[24]

An additional complication is added when one wishes to assess the likely onward distribution, and therefore universality or otherwise of use, of the ceramic vessels themselves. Many imported pots into England seem to have had a limited distribution, often staying within the maritime and estuarine ports themselves or, at most, penetrating upstream on the dendritic river systems but no further. Mechanisms other than trade could distribute ceramics as noted by Moorhouse [25] and Verhaeghe postulates as an example that the discovery of highly-decorated Scarborough ware jugs at the fishing village of Walraversijde in Flanders may have been 'souvenirs, as occasional purchases made on trips to Yorkshire or even as acquisitions resulting from other activities (i.e. piracy)'. A late 13th- or early 14th-century Scarborough ware 'knight jug' fragment located in Lüneburg is interpreted as possibly a trade object but also as a personal belonging of a merchant.[26]

A variety of tangible import and export items can be enumerated by archaeological evidence from a range of locations around the North Sea and the Baltic. Thus imports of building materials such as stone, bricks and tufa have been recorded from Bremen, Ribe, Bruges, London, Lübeck and Norwich while barrels are known from Aarhus, Malmö and Oslo.[27] Indeed, it is possible using such material to locate evidence not only for the importation of timber, either fashioned as barrels or as raw materials for the barrels themselves, but also the likely sources of the timber when it was growing in forests. Research on timbers recovered from the north German towns of Lübeck, Wismar, Rostock, Stralsund and Greifswald indicates origins in northern Sweden and Finland as well as the Baltic States and what is now modern Poland. A wreck discovered in 2011 in southern Norway (the Skjernøysund 3 wreck) was found to contain a cargo of slaked lime in barrels and split oak planks dating to 1393–1394 which were perhaps for wainscotting or the manufacture of barrels. The timber derived from the Vistula hinterland of Poland and was similar to discoveries made in the 'Copper Ship' which sank in the Baltic some 10 years later (below, p 131).[28]

Timbers can survive when buried in the ground, as in the case of barrels used to line wells or cesspits, but other organic materials are more perishable. Cloth imports and exports are known from extensive documentation but examples rarely survive within archaeological contexts (there are exceptions of course; thousands of cloth fragments have been recovered from cesspits in Tartu, Estonia while, exceptionally, a chasuble of silk damask and probably a Chinese import in the early 14th century *via* Genoa, was found in a tomb in the church of Our Lady, Bruges in 1979[29]). More commonly, cloth seals are discovered and can indicate the types of cloth that were traded and their origins. An example is a 14th-century seal for a Brabant cloth from Malines or Mechelen in Flanders found at Swan Lane in London[30] (see also, below p. 173).

Much of the evidence for trade naturally relies upon surviving documentary evidence such as customs accounts for it to be observed. Very occasionally, however, it is possible to glimpse commercial interaction through rare archaeological discoveries: one such find was that of fragments of the account book of a merchant in Copenhagen where the entries were written on to waxed tablets between about 1350 and 1400 (and now preserved in the National Museum in Copenhagen).

'Secondary' indicators of trade—a terminology used by Richard Hall—can be seen in surviving buildings. He cites the hall in York constructed in 1357–1361 for the Fraternity and Gild of Our Lord Jesus Christ and the Blessed Virgin Mary, a structure now better known as the Merchant Adventurers' Hall.

The fraternity had a seal which depicted the Holy Trinity and two sailing ships; 'this iconography indicates the Gild's main economic business-trade'.[31] Other great trading halls were under construction elsewhere in the 13th and 14th centuries. The cloth hall in Bruges, now known as the Belfort, was constructed around 1240 although heavily damaged by fire in 1280 and subsequently rebuilt. It retains two large timber-roofed brick halls either side of a courtyard behind the massive belfry tower overlooking the main market square.The great cloth hall in Ypres dated from 1304 but was destroyed in the First World War and subsequently rebuilt.

Textile trade and industry

Such halls in Flanders were indicative of the power of the cloth trade here. Much of this trade relied upon English wool (above, p. 48) and much of the cloth was either exported to England or northward into Germany, Scandinavia and the Baltic lands. However, the production of cloth was growing in England as well and, by the 14th century, was becoming an exceptionally important part of the national economy. It naturally excited the attention of the state and thus of administrators so the documentary record is rich with accounts of the customs on cloth. However, its production was also accompanied by technological developments, innovations rarely documented and therefore best understood from archaeological evidence.

As an example, weaving itself had been undertaken on a vertical loom for millennia but, in the 11th century, a more advanced horizontal loom was introduced. This innovation was particularly suited to the manufacture of linen and therefore was utilised in East Anglia, a centre of linen production (and from where evidence for the retting of flax for use in linen production is known from locations such as Norwich [32]). However, archaeological evidence in the form of textile fragments suggests that the vertical loom was used in concert with the new horizontal loom to 1400 at least—'the warp-weighted or two-beam loom producing the individual pieces, the treadle loom the long lengths (rolls or bolts) in double or single widths'.[33] Both linen and worsted cloth were manufactured in the east of England, usually in the countryside with specialist cloth finishing taking place in towns. An early example of industrial scale cloth-finishing has been recovered from London where between eight (and probably originally twelve) hearths were recorded at Swan Lane, several of them being associated with deposits of montmorillonite, better-known as fullers' earth. Traces of lanolin from wool indicated that the hearths had been used as part of the cleaning process of cloth ahead of dyeing at this location.[34]

The commercial reach of textiles produced in both Flanders and England is illustrated by exceptional archaeological finds of textile fragments in Poland. Here examination of discoveries primarily made in port towns such as Gdańsk and Elblag has illustrated that imported west European twills in the 13th century were largely superseded by tabbies, also from western Europe, in the 14th century. Similar observations have been made of material located in Novgorod in Russia. The wool within the cloth is often found to have been provided by long- and coarse-wool breeds of sheep such as those from Lincoln and Leicestershire in England. Interestingly, however, much of the high quality imported cloth seems to have stayed within the larger port towns. Analysis of textile fragments found in smaller Polish towns such as Pultusk or Rawa Mazowiecka (north and south-west of Warsaw respectively) revealed locally-manufactured products made from wool of the *wrzośowka* sheep or of the higher quality *Żuławy*-type sheep.[35] Nevertheless, sometimes locally-made cloth from the far reaches of the North Sea world found its way abroad; a fragment of a tabby weave recovered in King's Lynn seems to have been manufactured in Iceland early in the 14th century and perhaps reached Lynn 'as packing material round a consignment of goods from Bergen'.[36]

Attempts have been made to examine the colours of medieval cloth from recovered textile fragments. This is technically difficult, most excavated examples appearing brownish-black but chemical analysis can occasionally reveal traces of pigment. A case study has been made of a collection of textile fragments in Lödöse, a town in southern Sweden north of Gothenberg with good west European trading contacts. It was possible to differentiate between two types of coloured cloth, namely that constructed of fabrics of different colour and that with different colours in the warp and weft of the same fabric. Colours such as red, yellowish-green and black were observed with one cloth fragment in particular being a 2/1-twill in a dark warp and a weft with a very light stripe.[37]

Sourcing dyestuffs was clearly a crucial activity for cloth-finishers. In England, both documentary and archaeological evidence survives for imported and local dyes. The cloth centre of Norwich, for example, signed an agreement with merchants of Corbie in France in 1286 to provide woad for dyeing[38] while late 14th-century evidence survives for the importation of madder with which to make a red dye. This reference is remarkable also for the light that it sheds upon mercantile practice; Ollard Johannson's vessel *Seintmarieshipp of Arnemuth* sailed from Great Yarmouth on 8th December 1388, reached a continental port where she unloaded a cargo of Norwich-owned worsted, cheese and rabbit skins, and was back in Yarmouth on 26th December 'with a shipment including madder, canvas, soap, oil and wax'. A round trip of loading, sailing and unloading in just 18 days in mid-winter.[39]

Excavations within Norwich have recovered a dyeworkers' premises which was established in the 13th century and continued in existence at least until the 15th century. As well as the furnaces, hearths, a water storage pit and drain that were uncovered, the documentary evidence for the site includes the information that it was held by Ranulf, the son of Robert the Blekester (or bleacher, another textile-finishing trade) in the 1200s, passed to Hubert of Framlingham described as a dyer then, in 1298, to Benedict Bert, also a dyer, and eventually was owned in the 14th century by Robert le Weyder (*weyder* deriving from woad).[40] A further well-preserved dyeworks was excavated in the east Yorkshire cloth-producing town of Beverley in 1983–1986. Located in Eastgate, it lay across two tenements and comprised workshops, vats, cisterns, numerous drains, raised hearths or ovens and enclosures for the storage of fuel and dyestuffs. Dyestuffs are documented as being imported into nearby Hull in large quantities and archaeological evidence for dyes was found in residues of madder, woad, weld and bog myrtle. Wool vats of lanolin and adipocere were also recovered. Even uric acid was present in the soil samples, suggesting the use of urine either as a detergent or to assist in dissolving dyes.[41]

A survey of the terms used for coloured textile has been undertaken for Scandinavia, defining marbled, patterned, striped and parti-coloured clothing. It notes the popularity of such clothing in the 13th and 14th centuries and illustrates this by reference to some of the fine surviving wall-paintings in Danish churches (such as those in Skibby and Kirkerup churches on Sealand, both of the first half of the 14th century).[42] In England cloth was designated by colour: burnet (dark brown), plunket (a form of blue), azure (a hue of blue), blue, and green.[43] Some coloured textiles survive such as offcuts of *scarlet* (a term used for brightly-coloured cloth) from Baynard's castle in London or the full length blue-and red tunic of 1242–1243 from Söderköping in Sweden. A tiny fragment of bright pink spun yarn was recovered from the excavations at High Street, Perth where the anaerobic conditions were particularly good for textile preservation. Here some 411 fabrics were found, comprising tabbies, twills, silks, felts and others, and dating from the 12th to the 14th centuries. In addition numbers of cloth working tools were also located, implements such as spindle whorls, pinsetters, needles, combs, shears and linen smoothers, and a tenting hook (for pinning out fulled and dyed cloth to dry on a tenting frame). The assemblage from this Scottish city has enabled a detailed discussion of the suitability of the various fabrics for the manufacture of clothing, the use of clothing to provide a sumptuary code within contemporary medieval society, the qualities of surface finish to the cloth elite dress, and even clothing as means of demonstrating ethnic identity.[44]

Non-textile trading activity

A colloquium held in Lübeck in 1997 sought to explore the commercial activity of towns across northern Europe. It brought together examples from Cork in the far west to Novgorod in the east, and from Bruges in the south to Bergen in the north. The results were published in 1999[45] and included a summary of traceable items, both imports and exports, recorded either in documentary evidence or through archaeological discovery. The list is formidable: foodstuffs and preservatives included salt, honey, grain, beer, fish, meat, wine, exotic fruits and spices; clothing, aside from textiles, linen and wool generally, included furs and hides; the implements and containers enumerated were pottery, barrels, bronze bowls, moulds (for stove tiles), hones, quernstones, soapstone vessels and crucibles; raw materials of wax, hemp, pitch, tar, limestone, coal, iron, lead, boxwood and timber; and finally livestock in the form of cattle and, for recreation, falcons.[46] Bruges in the 14th century was importing tin and cheese from England and taking palfreys (horses) and potash from Denmark, squirrels from Russia (for their fur) and silver from Bohemia.[47]

All of these goods were moved across the North and Baltic Seas from port to port, sometimes attracting custom and therefore becoming visible through administrative records, sometimes only seen in the archaeological record. The list can be augmented of course. Two examples can be mentioned. Bricks are known to have been imported from Flanders to effect works at Norwich castle in the 1260s while miniature copper-alloy bells, manufactured in Nuremberg, had a wide distribution in England between the 13th and 15th centuries; a recently-discovered example of such a bell from Outwell in the Fens is embossed with an heraldic shield which seems to be the arms of Nuremberg (Figure 3.2). The bells were probably used on horse harness but are quite substantial and thus perhaps more likely as elaborate harness for dray horses than for individual mounts. They are certainly too large and heavy to have been used on any kind of personal dress, and probably too small for use in a domestic or ecclesiastical context.[48]

The trade in fur is one which has been explored archaeologically in recent years. Environmentally, it is essentially a northern trade being the product of animals generally found in the cooler climes of northern Europe. Indeed, the point has been made that fur 'cannot be understood as a commodity in isolation. It is derived from a specific group of animals with distinct ecological niches, and therefore its acquisition is closely related to how people exploited particular environments'.[49] It was also a reciprocal trade in that, while much fur was shipped westward from the Baltic so too were commodities such as rabbit pelts (or goods manufactured therefrom such as hats) shipped eastward from farmed warrens in England. Indeed, the English 'indigenization' of the rabbit, as Pluskowski terms the process, was perhaps overlooked in terms of its contribution to the medieval economy before the publication of a seminal paper by Bailey.[50]

Fur itself is a rare survival on archaeological sites although there are exceptions. An early 14th-century leather workshop at the junction of Gierczak Street and Mariacka Street in the now Polish city of

Figure 3.2 Miniature bell with shield, Outwell, Norfolk (Steven Ashley; Norfolk Historic Environment Service).

Kołobrzeg (German Kolberg) located traces of beaver, otter and probably buckskin being converted to leather (as well as hides of cattle and horse). It was postulated that the fur here was intended for use in hats, collars and lining.[51] More common finds are the bones of animals that have been skinned such as the red squirrels whose foot bones were discovered in a 14th-century pit within the precinct of the College of the Vicars Choral of York Minister and which 'are most credibly interpreted as arriving there still attached to semi-prepared skins, and then removed ... during the preparation of the squirrel pelts'.[52]

Exploitation of wild animals for their fur is therefore frequently best seen in residual remains such as bones. Numerous sites around the North and Baltic Seas have indeed produced bones of cats, fox and hares, all betraying cut marks synonymous with skinning. Capture of wild animals required trapping or stunning in a manner which avoided damage to the fur (squirrels were shot with blunt-headed arrows [53]), neither of which are readily visible within the archaeological record. Occasionally the fur trade is depicted in artistic form, such as in the celebrated fragments of the 15th-century Riga merchants' pew in St Nicholas's church, Stralsund. These show Russian fur traders both bearing pelts and wearing fur.

Trapping was also the technique used for snaring rabbits, famously illustrated in the Queen Mary Psalter of 1316–1321 held by the British Library (two women seek to secure rabbits by placing a ferret in one side of a warren and caging rabbits that emerge at the other side[54]). Evidence of the scale of rabbit breeding, however, survives well in eastern England where recent archaeological survey has complemented documentary research and has been able to map extensive warrens on the lighter sandy soils of south-west Norfolk and north-west Suffolk, the Breckland.

Rabbit warrens, or *coneygarths*, in Breckland occupied large areas and were mainly situated on the estates of monasteries and other ecclesiastics although secular families such as the Warennes were also major warren owners. Documentary evidence is scarce before the mid-13th century but thereafter numerous references survive to the establishment and running of rabbit warrens. As examples, manorial accounts for Brandon, a warren owned by the Bishop of Ely, record the sale of rabbits in 1252; at Eriswell, in 1309, the manor was valued following the death of Robert de Tudenham and included 'a small rabbit warren with right of free-warren valued at 1 marc [13s4d or two-thirds of a pound] a year'; a warrener called Ealfred or Galfrido is mentioned at the Bishop of Rochester's warren of Freckenham in 1295; and, *c.* 1370, rabbits are recorded as being culled at the warren of Gooderstone (probably owned by Denny Abbey) and, in 1376, six acres of oats were planted 'in the warren to sustain the coneys [rabbits] there'.[55] Surveys of all of these warrens and others have located earthwork banks marking the perimeters, probable trapping banks, often complex entrances to ensure that rabbits did not escape, and probable 'clapper' areas or constructed warrens within which the rabbits could live. The banks were constructed of turf, originally stood up to two metres in height, with a vertical inner elevation and a sloping outer side. The banks could be as much as ten metres in width and were surmounted either by gorse faggots or planted with gorse which trailed down the vertical face to discourage rabbits from burrowing. Dating of the banks is difficult but the likelihood that they are of medieval origin, even if subsequently repaired (some warrens remained in use into the 20th century), is enhanced by a documentary reference in the Brandon Account Rolls of 1365–1366 which, referring to Wangford, mentions 'making the bank on the east side of the grange and making a hedge on the crest of the same bank ...'.[56]

Some of the enclosures thus fashioned are still remarkably intact such as the banks surviving at Brandon and Eriswell. The lines of many banks are still dominated by gorse, whose vivid yellow flowering in springtime renders the earthworks highly visible (Figure 3.3). Within the warrens, the land was kept free of tree cover to provide visibility for the warrener who occupied a lodge, usually in a location from which most of the warren could be seen. A lodge is recorded at Brandon in 1368, its site known from surface archaeological survey in 1989. Other lodges almost certainly existed by the 14th century but most documentary references date to the 15th century (such as Methwold in 1413; Snarehill by 1482; Bodney 'before 1499'; and Santon repaired in 1499). Remains of two lodges survive: a roofless, two-story flint structure some 7m square at Methwold warren with four windows and a doorway retaining their stone dressings; and Thetford Warren Lodge, another two-storey flint building, larger at 9m square with

Figure 3.3 Gorse hedge above boundary bank to medieval rabbit warren, Breckland (Nicholas Gibbons).

windows at first floor level, slits for light on the ground floor and a defensive door. It also retains a first floor fireplace and garderobe and could perhaps therefore also have been used as a hunting lodge by the warren's owner, the Abbot of Thetford Priory. Like Mildenhall, it probably dates to the mid-15th century but it is first recorded in 1514 (Figure 3.4).[57]

Warrens could be very large, probably around 1000 acres (405 hectares) in the case of locations such as Eriswell and Wangford.[58] Their value lay in their products (a source of meat in winter and a saleable commodity in the pelts) but also in that the keeping of rabbits provided a profitable return on otherwise marginal land for a low cost in labour. The 14th century may have been the height of such direct return for the landowners as later documentary evidence suggests that most warrens were leased out. However, with very few exceptions, the Breckland medieval warrens were unique in England, sometimes breeding specialist rabbits such as those with silver-grey and black fur as at Methwold (which was fashionable as trimming for clothing) or producing large quantities of pelts for export (John Calwer shipped 12,000 rabbit skins to Flanders in 1365).[59] Much fur was exported through the port of King's Lynn (the 1392 roll of William Leche, controller of the subsidy account of charges levied on exports, includes both rabbit skins and 'hoods lined with rabbit fur, worth 13s4d' in a list of goods intended for markets in the Low Countries and the Baltic[60]) but Norwich too become a centre for furriers with thousands of skins being exported from there.[61]

The study of the Breckland rabbit warrens illustrates the impact of medieval commerce upon the environment with large-scale interventions promoting a rural industry that was probably driven by the overseas market. Environmental change can also be seen in Scandinavia, the source for many of the furs—such as sable and marten—which were exported to western Europe although here the change was probably more negative in impact than that in East Anglia. Archaeological work in central Norway has illustrated over-exploitation of fur-bearing species. An excavation at Tøften in Grimsdalen uncovered evidence for a reindeer trapping system of particular intensity in the 11th and 12th centuries. Some 56,000 bone fragments were recovered, of species including mountain fox and red fox, but with the vast majority representing reindeer. However, the system had ceased to be used by the 14th century, no doubt 'because of its devastating effect on the migrating reindeer population'.[62]

Figure 3.4 Thetford warren lodge (Brian Ayers).

Food trading and diet

Furs, as a perishable, organic product are naturally rare within the archaeological record as are foodstuffs, another organic product. However, elements of foodstuffs, such as grain, are frequently recovered through paleao-environmental work on suitable (usually wet and anaerobic) sites and can also indicate both consumption and commercial exchange. An example of the latter was recovered from an excavation undertaken in Norwich in 1979 when hops were recognised in waste deposits adjacent to the river. The hop is not indigenous to Britain and the excavated example is one of the earliest to be recorded in the country, probably a reflection of the situation of Norwich on the east coast, close to the continent.[63] Hops enable beer, rather than ale, to be made and recent work near Deventer has demonstrated how extensive a trade the production of beer could be. Deventer was a medieval town known to have contained a number of breweries which would have needed raw materials, such as hops, from the surrounding countryside. An extensive archaeological project, undertaken in 2002–2004 at Rielerenk-Ost outside Deventer, uncovered a hop field. Distinctive parallel lines of postholes to support hop-poles were found in 2003, dating from the 14th century and remaining in use into the 15th century. The depth of the postholes indicated poles some 5m to 6m in height with the lines of poles orientated in order to ensure maximum exposure to sunlight.[64] It seems clear that production was on an organised, industrial scale, probably supplying hops to a range of breweries (Figure 3.5).

The importance of beer in the North Sea economy should not be overlooked. Recent excavations in Lübeck have uncovered a 12th-century wooden storage cellar containing the remains of hops and cereals which may perhaps indicate domestic brewing[65] but cities such as Hamburg and Bremen were developing an industrial capability and became great centres of beer production. The addition of hops for the making of beer meant that it had an advantage over ale because it would keep and therefore could be traded. Both Bremen and Hamburg became major exporters of beer from the 13th century onward with a third of Hamburg's beer production that was shipped overseas going through Amsterdam (whose own international trade developed in the 14th century, assisted by its right to levy a toll on beer).[66]

Figure 3.5 Plan of excavated medieval hop field near Deventer, The Netherlands (© Archeologie Deventer NL).

The trade in beer probably fostered a similar trade in grain and barley. German production of beer was in the forefront but Dutch production was established by the mid-1320s with considerable export to Flanders following on.[67]

The brewing of beer obviously required access to water supplies and it is therefore unsurprising that documentary references to brewing often indicate a grouping of brewers and breweries within towns (such as Stade in Germany). It is perhaps more surprising that evidence for breweries themselves is so scarce. Einbeck was important for its beer but this is generally only known from documentation (over 600 breweries are recorded here by the 16th century and a staggering 700 a century later). Archaeological evidence is very restricted; 'Mühlen- or Malz-zeichen', that is small 1.5 sq cm metal trade tokens emblazoned with the arms of Einbeck, survive and also doubled as use for the city taxation system.[68] In addition, a substantial beer barrel capable of holding 400 litres was reused as lining of a cesspit in the 15th century.[69] The significant Hamburg trade, together with its associated cooperage, remains to be identified archaeologically. Similarly, there is little archaeological evidence for brewing in Bremen; here, the only reported discovery of a barrel was that located on the wreck of the Bremen cog (below, p. 150), an item thought unlikely to have been of local use but more probably for the importation of tar.[70] Nevertheless, there is evidence of cooperage from other towns such as Rostock, where discarded barrel covers and stave blanks suggest production, and Gdańsk (Danzig) where 46 coopers are known to have been working at the end of the 14th century.[71]

Gdańsk was important as an entrepôt for grain shipments, exports going to Flanders, the Netherlands, Germany and Sweden. Granary Island, a large area of warehousing within the port at Gdańsk, has received considerable archaeological attention and 14th-century samples of grain have been recovered there. With regard to beer specifically, it is known that a quality inspector for hops worked on Granary

Island in the 14th century and, within Gdańsk, fruits of hop 'are found in nearly all backyard deposits dated to ... the Middle Ages'.[72] The ubiquity of hops at this period is also shown from results in Sweden together with sweet gale (*Myrica gale*) which was added to ale prior to the introduction of the hop and continued to be used thereafter. Much beer was imported from Germany but evidence for local Swedish malting as early as the 12th and 13th centuries is suggested for boxlike structures uncovered at Uppsala.[73]

The industrialisation of brewing implicit in the quantities of beer known to have been traded (3,000,000 litres a year to Amsterdam alone in the 1360s from Hamburg[74]) does not necessarily mean that it completely eclipsed domestic brewing. Indeed, it is perhaps possible that such small-scale beer production, as well as producing ale and beer for household consumption, might on occasion be sufficient also to provide modest supplies for consumption elsewhere. In Hull, for instance, excavations in 1977 on Blackfriargate uncovered a series of ovens and hearths, as well as possible drying kilns and 'heated vat emplacements' Figure 3.6). These were located in a large and well-built annex behind a merchant's house, dateable to the period after 1347–1352.[75] It seems likely that the intensity of activity was too great for domestic use alone and it is possible that semi-commercial brewing might have been undertaken, perhaps to supply vessels shipping out of the port. A similar structure with large fireplaces, dating to the 16th century, has been located in Einbeck and may perhaps represent one of the 600 breweries documented there at that time.[76]

Drinking of beer and other liquids was difficult, if not impossible, from porous earthenware vessels but, by the late 13th century, a new type of pottery was becoming available in Germany. The pottery centre of Siegburg in the Rhineland started to produce hard-fired vessels, notably small distinctive jugs called *Jacobakannen,* which rapidly gained a wide distribution. Significant numbers have been found in English cities such as London and Hull but the majority of the early vessels seem to have reached locations in Germany itself, to hanseatic outposts such as Bergen, and to sites around the Baltic. Thus, by the 15th century, Siegburg was the second most common pottery in Bergen with quantities of vessels also reaching Riga in Latvia and Tallinn in Estonia.

Figure 3.6 Heated vat emplacements, Blackfriargate, Hull (Humberside Archaeology Unit).

Siegburg pottery is particularly significant because, as well as the ceramics themselves, good documentary evidence for its production exists enabling assessment at a range of levels: as an 'index of commercial contact; influence on local markets and industry; [and a] medium of cultural exchange'. Allied to this excavation of the main production site has been undertaken. This work (by Bernhardt Beckmann) at the Aulgaße *Scherbenhügel* or 'sherd mountain' in Siegburg took place between 1961 and 1966. Despite '150 years of systematic robbing by antiquities dealers and the local building industry' this deposit still measured 60m long, 30m wide and 5.5m high with the excavations producing over 8000 intact vessels and over two million sherds. Wasters from the 13th to 17th centuries were recovered. The Aulgaße district extended for some 600m with documents suggesting an average of 15 major workshops in the middle of the 16th century.[77] A research project exploring Siegburg pottery within the economic context of the Hanseatic League is currently in progress.[78]

Another notable traded commodity was wine, both from the Rhineland and from south-western France. Evidence for the French wine trade is well-documented (such as for Hull in the 14th and 15th centuries[79]) and is also revealed by ceramics, notably vessels of Saintonge-type ware which are found in the major south and east coast ports of England such as Southampton, London, Great Yarmouth and Hull, although the wine itself, of course, was transported in barrels. Fragments of a medieval wine barrel capable of carrying some 37 litres of wine were found during excavations of Pevensey Castle in southern England.[80] The quantities of wine imported to England were significant; documentary evidence from such records as customs accounts suggesting some 20,000 tuns containing 5 million gallons (about 22,730,500 litres) at the end of the 13th century.[81] While wine was obviously important for church use, the bulk of these imports must have been to satisfy the secular market.

The archaeological problem concerning wine in northern Europe is identifying consumption. Ceramics associated with the wine trade do not necessarily indicate drinking of that wine. While archaeobotanical evidence, such as grape seeds, could be sought on production sites, the wine product itself is obviously absent. Analysis of residues on wine vessels can be problematic but a new technique utilising gas chromatography–mass spectrometry offers a way forward. It has recently been used to assess ceramics associated with the production and consumption of Mediterranean wines. The technique identifies tartaric acid amongst other wine markers such as the acids fumaric and malic. Isolating these latter is important because it is recognised that tartaric acid alone can also be an indicator of fruits other than grapes, such as star fruit or yellow plum.Tartaric acid could additionally indicate grape juice or syrup rather than wine but, when observed with the other acids, it is indicative of the presence of wine or its derivatives.[82] To date the technique does not appear to have been utilised in northern Europe although clearly there is potential for contributing to studies of the use of ceramic vessels, wine consumption and trade.

Importation of wine was essentially that of a luxury commodity and other luxury foodstuffs are now also being identified in palaeo-environmental samples from across northern Europe. Exotic fruits and spices such as figs, walnuts and black pepper have been located as far north as Estonia. While it is tempting to equate such studies with affluence and high social status, interesting research in the German towns of Lübeck, Lüneburg, Braunschweig and Rostock has sought to isolate deposits associated with higher social classes (such as on Alfstraße in Lübeck) and those of craftsmen and others (as on Hunderstraße, Lübeck). The results are slightly surprising: while a spice such as black pepper is only recorded from higher societal contexts, as is the case generally but not exclusively with plums, figs are noted across the spectrum in all towns. The conclusion drawn is that, where possible, 'even members of the lower classes treated themselves to a little bit of luxury'.[83]

Not all scholars share this assessment. Analysis of exotic imports by Livarda led her to conclude that north European medieval consumption of such commodities was restricted to the more affluent sections of society. She sees a direct connection between trade and urban wealth and notes the rarity of exotic discoveries on rural sites.[84] Urban sites certainly produce evidence: figs were located in a 14th-century deposit in Hull (including a tentative identification of fig tissue so a whole fig may have been present in the sample) as were date stones, probably the earliest record of such a fruit in England.[85]

It is likely that the figs arrived via the Low Countries as did other Iberian goods such as Portuguese cork, raisins and oil, all of which are documented.[86]

Livarda backs up her assessment with a range of examples. She notes that *Elettaria cardamomum* (cardomum) has been recorded at very few locations, those sites where it has in Germany, for instance, being a cesspit of a 'higher middle class household' in Johannisstraße, Göttingen and cesspits (the provision of which is 'indicative of high-status consumption') in Turnierstraße and Gördelinerstraße in Braunschweig. Similarly *Nigella saliva* (cumin) and *Oryza saliva* (rice) were recovered from three urban contexts, all with 'an impressive array of exotics and other taxa, indicating affluent inhabitants'.[87] Rice was certainly exotic; it is recorded from Göttingen (the same location as the cardamom), Lübeck, Braunschweig and Freiburg but was clearly not in common use. Interestingly, the discoveries of exotic fruits suggest an Asian rather than an African connection for sources and thus probably hints at trade with the Muslim world, presumably through Italy and Spain, rather than access to Africa via early Atlantic trading.

The general exploitation of fish around the North Sea has already been noted (above, Chapter 1). One aspect of this exploitation was a large trade in air-dried cod or stockfish. This product, despite its unappetising nature, was an important source of protein for the growing populations of both urban and rural settlements in northern Europe. Much of the trade was controlled by ships of the Hanse, centring on Bergen in western Norway where fish were landed and either dried or salted before being shipped onward to market. Fish remains of cod treated in this manner can be identified by the lack of skull bones in the fishbone assemblages recovered on excavations; the heads were removed ahead of drying while fresh fish sold at market obviously retained their heads.

Large quantities of stockfish were imported into England, notably through the port of King's Lynn where King Street, one of the two principal quayside streets of the town, was known as 'Stockfish Row'. Margery Kempe, the most famous medieval woman known from Lynn, conveys contemporary understanding of stockfish when she reports God speaking to her with a metaphor: 'Daughter, you are obedient to my will, and cleave as fast to me as the skin of a stockfish sticks to a man's hand when it is boiled'.[88]

Cod was not the only fish supplied to populations around the North Sea. Fishbone recovered from excavations can indicate the variety of fish consumed but can also suggest the likely environments within which they were caught. Thus, in a report on a large assemblage of fishbone from Norwich for instance, Alison Locker was able to suggest the likelihood that the examples of fresh cod were caught from a winter inshore fishery. She also identified remains of numerous marine fish such as flounder, plaice, sole, gurnard and haddock. Herring was the most numerous species, forming between 31% and 43% of the assemblage depending on the period.[89] Somewhat surprisingly for a city site about 32 kilometres from the sea, the percentages of freshwater fish were small (4%) but this may well have been due to problems of pollution as seen at York (above, p. 19). The quantities of fish imported to the city could on occasion be substantial; Norwich Cathedral Priory bought 15 lasts of herring in 1327–1328 or, with 12,000 herring in each last, about 180,000 fish. It has been calculated that this would have rendered some 53.4 million kcal a year or the equivalent of about 2258 kcal per monk each day if each monk ate eight fish.[90]

In Flanders, Van Neer and Ervynck have undertaken assessments of fishbone from excavations in Ghent. They too found marine fish throughout the medieval deposits but with a trend from flatfish through species such as cod to herring. Combining their study with the results of analysis of material from coastal villages of Heist, Nieuwe Yde and Walraversijde, they were able to conclude that there was a northward shift in fishing practice at this time. Most of the plaice identified is likely to have been sourced from Flemish coastal waters but large cod from Antwerp and Ghent were probably the result of northern catches. Otolith analysis of growth patterns, undertaken in the hope of identifying fishing grounds (fish growth being more rapid in southern waters) proved problematic but nevertheless revealed a seasonal exploitation pattern with fishing for haddock in winter and plaice being taken in early spring and summer.[91]

The excavation of the fishing village of Walraversijde in Flanders contributed data to the above assessment but other scientific work on recovered material from the settlement was also revealing. Stable isotope carbon and nitrogen analysis was undertaken on the collagen of animal bones from the village as well as from inland sites in Aalst and Bruges. The results indicated that animals such as pigs were being fed a considerable quantity of fish at Walraversijde (where fish processing is known to have taken place) but unsurprisingly this was not the case at the more inland locations. However, analysis of bulk soil samples from these three places (together with evidence from Namur) revealed information that was more startling. Isotopic markers indicate that the diet of the various populations was a mixture of plant, herbivore and animal products but with very little fish. This held true for Walraversijde as well as the inland sites, leading to the conclusion that 'the main staple in medieval diet was bread; vegetables and meat or fish were added'.[92]

The lack of fish in the diet of a coastal community as at Walraversijde is both paralleled and contrasted by results from five sites in northern England (Hartlepool, Newcastle, Scarborough, Wharram Percy and York) and a recently-published example from Scotland. All of the English locations had good access to the coast, two of them, Hartlepool and Scarborough being coastal ports and a third, Newcastle, easily accessible upstream on the River Tyne. Isotopic analysis of skeletons was undertaken on a variety of groups (a monastic assemblage and a lay group from York; a village at Wharram Percy; friaries at Hartlepool and Newcastle; and a lay cemetery in Scarborough) although it was considered that all the individuals examined were lay people except those from the York monastic site (a Gilbertine priory). Inhabitants of Newcastle and Hartlepool seem to have had a good input of marine resources in their diet and at both Wharram Percy and the lay cemetery in York there was also evidence of some fish consumption but not to a great extent (the diet at Wharram might have included as much freshwater fish as marine fish).

The most interesting results were those from Scarborough and the monastic cemetery in York. At the former the consumption of marine resources was considerably lower than at Hartlepool and Newcastle, the quantities observed being 'statistically significant, so they reflect real differences at the population level, not chance findings'. The York group, as well as showing high levels of marine consumption consistent with a monastic diet, was also sampled from individuals who had a markedly lower rate of dental caries than the lay group from the same site (marine foods not contributing to cariogenic problems). The actual fish products recovered at the York priory indicated a substantial proportion of herring.[93]

Dietary preferences therefore do not necessarily seem to have depended solely upon access to resources. The relatively low consumption of fish by the lay population from York is unlikely to have been due to economic circumstances; the sampled individuals were from burials within the priory church of the Gilbertine priory and were thus likely to have represented the more affluent members of society. Similarly, in Scarborough, the population may have been less wealthy but it had much greater access to marine resources. The non-consumption of fish may therefore represent choice, presumably enabled by reasonable economic circumstances. Within this context, the recent results from Portmahomack in north-eastern Scotland are interesting. Isotopic analysis here, together with study of faunal remains, suggest a late medieval dietary dependence upon terrestrial plant and animal resources augmented by fish. Local environmental and husbandry factors beyond proximity to the sea seem to have been influences here with probable increased manuring as well as grazing on salt marshes.[94] Portmahomack was a much smaller community than that at Scarborough and a more mixed diet may therefore reflect a greater dependence upon resources generated locally.

The implied complexity of determinants influencing dietary consumption is emphasised by consideration of further evidence from burials located on Orkney. Here, as at Portmahomack, individuals of various dates were assessed and a marked decline in fish consumption was noted for the later medieval period. Possible reasons for changes observed from the Viking Age through to the 15th century include such factors as ethnicity, gender (women seem to have consumed less fish than men), fasting practices, population change, trade and environmental causes. Concerning the last of these, a decline in readily-available fish resources due to climate change after the 14th century cannot be discounted although much more evidence is needed before firm conclusions can be drawn.[95] To the above potential causes could perhaps be added political instability, trade in the later 14th and 15th centuries being disrupted by both war and piracy and no doubt contributing to a less buoyant fishing economy.

It is likely that trade in stockfish was part of the Orcadian economy as evidence for 'semi-specialised fish-processing middens' has been recovered in northern Scotland (a dried fish production site is known from Knowe of Skea in Orkney for example). As such, it would form only one of the sources for cod exported southward to England and north-western Europe. Once again isotopic evidence is proving remarkably adept at suggesting the extent of trade. Cod from the northern North Sea or Arctic Norway was being sourced as early as the 11th century and results from Wharram Percy in Yorkshire in the 13th and 14th centuries show that the dried cod reaching this village on the Yorkshire Wolds included arctic examples as well as a fish probably caught in the Kattegat off Denmark.[96] The scientific evidence complements well the known documentary sources which record English involvement in the fish trade of the arctic north from the 14th century, a mixture of salted fish (salted by the English fishermen aboard ship) and dried fish (by the saltless Icelanders). The importance of the trade is emphasised by a poetic extract of 1436:

> Of Yseland to wryte is lytill need
> Save of stokfische ...[97]

Apart from cod, the other great traded fish around the North Sea was herring. An annual focus of activity from about 1250 was at the south-western corner of Sweden where a large herring fair was centred on the settlements of Skanör and Falsterbo (see below, p. 174).[98] Hanseatic merchants trading at Skanör have left their marks on the outer face of the 14th-century oak door to the parish church there.[99] The area involved in trading at the fair was some 16 square kilometres but, within this space, had to be accommodated traders from cities such as Lübeck, Hamburg, Bremen, Rostock and Danzig, each with their retinues and goods. In addition, space had to be found for salting and packing the herring. Fish was also smoked; a smoke-house measuring some 4m by 4m in size was excavated in the village of Skegrie in 2007. Quantities of herring and cod bones were found together with very small lead tax stamps (the largest only measures 12mm by 12mm) which had been issued by the bailiff of the Danish king as proof of tax paid.[100] A further, slightly later and larger, building was uncovered further north in 2010 in Örja village (Figure 3.7). Again a tax stamp (or 'toll chip') was found. Analysis of both the sites and their rich osteological and archaeobotanical material has enabled detailed discussion of how the houses functioned and suggests the possibility that the smoking activities, being clearly greater than necessary for the sustainability of single households, 'may indicate the movement of those involved in such production from the status of peasant farmers to that of industrial entrepreneurs'.[101] Such supposition of an increasingly organised network serving the herring industry is supported by evidence for the handling of fish beyond the immediate Falsterbo area; Örja lies some way north while clay-lined pits interpreted as seasonal excavations associated with the herring trade have also been located in places such as Copenhagen and Malmö. These latter perhaps indicate 'transit sites' where temporary bases were established for the sorting and drying of fish.[102]

Isotopic analysis is clearly providing new and interesting information about both the trade in marine resources and consumption by populations around the North Sea in the Middle Ages. However, such work is also being complemented by other analytical approaches. An interesting study of skeletal material from a medieval cemetery at Ahlgade 15–17, Holbæk, in Denmark has sought to provide information about subtle variations in individual diet by exploring dental microwear, dental macrowear, and oral pathologies, combining this work with isotopic analysis. The latter detected consumption in the group based upon a mixture of terrestrial and marine foodstuffs although with a greater variation of diet amongst men. Dental microwear and macrowear analyses suggested some plausible pathologies based upon diet, notably the erosive impact of dental abrasion from grit in cereals. Probable behavioural differences between men and women were also observed with microwear on the teeth of men showing markedly more fine scratches and puncture pits on the occlusal surface than in women. However, it was clear that this was not a result of dietary difference, despite the greater variety of food consumed by men, but more likely to be occupationally-related, such as craftsmen holding nails between their teeth (which also contributed to tooth loss).[103]

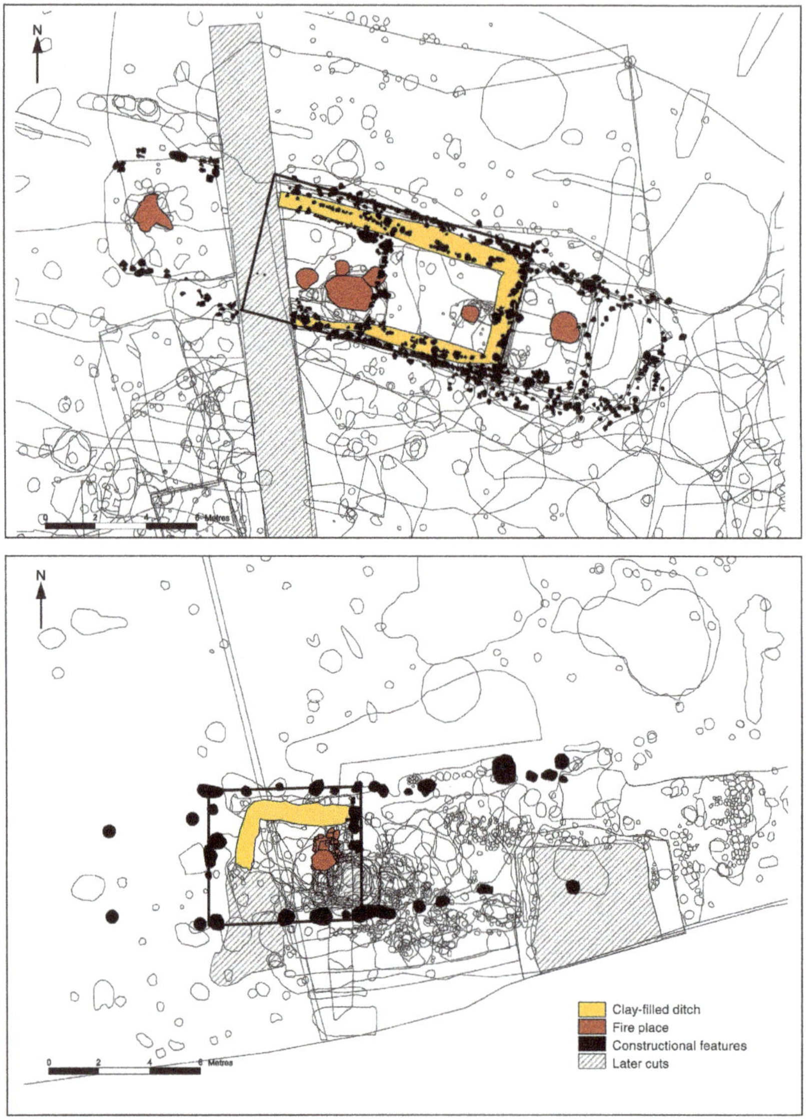

Figure 3.7 Smoke-houses at Örja and Skegrie, southern Sweden (after Bolander 2014).

The examined skeletal material spanned the 14th century with burials from before and after the Black Death of 1348/49. Interestingly the study did not find any change in dietary habits, mirroring work undertaken by Yoder who, examining skeletal material from three Danish sites on Jutland (Øm Kloster, St. Mikkel,Viborg and Ribe) concluded that while there was some regional patterning of a general medieval diet of terrestrial animals and plants plus both freshwater and marine fish, there were no perceptible temporal differences. This is an observation contrary to expectations raised by consideration of historical sources which imply that, following the Black Death, there was a greater concentration upon the rearing of stock such as cattle and pigs at the expense of cereal production. Yoder suggests that either a change in the agricultural system took place, rather than one of diet, or that there was 'an isotopically invisible change in diet, for example a change in food preparation and food type within the larger food categories (barley to wheat, cheese to meat etc.)'.[104]

Dietary information, notably using isotopes to complement more traditional archaeological approaches to faunal and fish remains as well as palaeo-botanical material, is now available for a number of sites and for a range of population types around the North Sea. As examples a monastic community has been explored at Dunes, Koksijde in Flanders while two different groups were examined from northern England: a rural medieval hospital at Brompton Bridge in North Yorkshire and a mass grave of casualties from the Battle of Towton, also in Yorkshire, in 1461. The Koksijde material indicated most protein was obtained from terrestrial animals although there was marine intake as well (the monastery was located at the coast) and thus produced similar results to the Danish samples.[105] Similarly, both the English groups indicated a lack of significant plant consumption but were high in terrestrial animal consumption supplemented by fish resources. Examination of faunal material recovered suggests that the sampled individuals ate a mixture of terrestrial, freshwater (possibly eel) and marine protein. The researchers conclude optimistically that 'it is appealing to interpret [the results] as a consequence of the fasting regulations imposed by the church, which proscribed the consumption of meat for nearly half the days of the year. Stable isotope data could therefore illustrate the enormous impact of religious dietary rules on the wider population'.[106]

Finally, analysis of faunal assemblages has the potential to suggest particular approaches to food resource acquisition. Work at the neighbouring towns of Lund and Malmö in southern Sweden is informative here with early deposits at Lund (11th century onward) suggesting that its open form of urban settlement (above, p. 44) encouraged exploitation of locally-produced resources (there is good evidence for the slaughter of animals for instance). This is in marked contrast to Malmö which seems to have imported most of its foodstuffs, meat arriving ready-slaughtered presumably in the form of salted and dried products, as implied by the lack of skulls and other diagnostic material in the animal bone assemblages. Later in the Middle Ages, Lund too appears to have imported more and produced less.[107]

The Black Death and its impact

The consumption of food obviously had a bearing upon the health of individuals. Rawcliffe has recently dealt comprehensively with the erroneous notion that medieval food was frequently highly-spiced to hide its rank and rancid nature as well as citing the numerous steps taken by medieval authorities against purveyors of unwholesome meat.[108] However, such legislative and administrative action was powerless in the face of bubonic plaque which, in the late 1340s, ravaged the North Sea region as it did the rest of Europe. Archaeological evidence for the devastating impact of this disease has been located both in the British Isles and on the continent.

The most compelling material is presented by those locations where the numbers of deaths were the greatest, namely urban areas. The most densely-populated city in England in the 14th century, as now, was London and it is known from documentary evidence that two supplementary graveyards were established in 1348/1349 in order to accommodate the drastic increase in mortality. These were located at West Smithfield or Charterhouse and at East Smithfield. Much of the latter was excavated in 1986–1988 with the recovery of 759 skeletons.[109] In 2013, a further group of burials was uncovered in Charterhouse Square, close to Farringdon station, by archaeologists working in advance of the Crossrail project (Figure 3.8). These recently-discovered skeletons were presumably part of the West Smithfield cemetery and consisted of 13 men and women in two rows, without coffins but with shroud pins. There was also associated 14th-century pottery and a layout paralleled by the East Smithfield cemetery and thus itself suggestive of plague burial.

Radiocarbon-14 dating of the Charterhouse burials confirms that some of the skeletons relate to the plague of 1348/49 although others seem to have been interred during a later outbreak in the 1430s. DNA analysis of the teeth of the individuals founds traces of the *Yersinia pestis* bacterium which is linked to both pneumonic and bubonic plague.[110] These results are very interesting in the light of recent detailed DNA research which has been carried out on the East Smithfield burials located in the 1980s. Techniques previously unavailable have allowed isolation of the genomic sequence for the *Yersinia pestis*

Figure 3.8 Black Death victims, London (Museum of London Archaeology).

pathogen. The research showed that this pathogen was a causative agent of the Black Death, a conclusion supported by the absence of the pathogen from earlier burials sampled. The deadly pathogen seems to have been a variant of *Yersinia pestis*, one which may no longer exist.[111]

Within the North Sea region, it is likely that Black Death victims were also unearthed at the cemetery of the Heiligen-Geist Hospital in Lübeck (some 696 individuals were recovered, in mass burial pits of five or six layers deep)[112] but, to date, the only attempt at similar DNA research to that undertaken in London seems to have been conducted in the Netherlands. Here an interesting project on a large-scale uncovered over 750 skeletons at St Catherine's church in Eindhoven. It was hoped to identify DNA from 75% of these individuals and, in so doing, seek to isolate a genetic variant which is known to increase resistance to HIV in modern populations. It is possible that the same variant may have helped resistance to plague in the 14th century. The variant is known as the CCR5D32 allele (alternative forms of a gene arising through mutation) and its isolation within a medieval group could assist gene therapy and thereby the development of new drugs to combat AIDS.[113] Published results are awaited.

The importance of the bioarchaeological approach to studies of the Black Death and successor attacks of the plague is indisputable. For example, work on burials from within the church of St Mary Graces in London, founded in 1350, may shed light on the plague outbreak of 1361.[114] A recent summary by DeWitte notes that it is only since 2009 that published results have confirmed the role of the *Yersinia pestis* pathogen in spreading the disease and she contends that future research is vital for an understanding of plague virulence, host-pathogen interactions and for disease that might manifest itself in the future. She argues that establishing the human context through archaeological work will provide demographic data as well as molecular information, thus enabling 'a disentanglement of the factors that affected medieval health and demography—that is, a determination of whether it was the biological effects of plague or the social and economic consequences of the epidemic that primarily shaped demographic and health patterns in the surviving population'.[115] The application of such research to future understanding of how disease impacts on factors such as age and genetic resistance is clear. The work has a particularly urgency given the number of emerging, often virulent, diseases in the modern world.

The provision of special areas of burial in London was necessitated by the unprecedented levels of mortality generated by the Black Death. Other special provision can be seen in the creation of mortuary chapels. These seem to have originated in Germany in the 1160s and such mortuary or charnel chapels are also known from the later 12th century in London. A surviving chapel in the cathedral close at Norwich, located adjacent to the lay cemetery in the medieval monastic enclosure, dates from 1316 and contains circular windows or *occuli* to light its undercroft. Display of bones here was 'an effort to prompt intercessory prayer ... The chapel served as a giant reliquary into which visitors could peer to view the bones of their ancestors'.[116] It was constructed at approximately the same time as the excavated chapel and cemetery of St Mary Spital in London (the chapel was probably built between 1310 and 1325). Interestingly, however, archaeological research does not tend to support the claim of historians that charnel was regularly exhumed from cemeteries and placed in such chapels in order to make space for later burials. Rather, the evidence would suggest that such removal was the result of accidental disturbance and thus much more of an *ad hoc* process.[117] Chapels themselves were not that common although they existed adjacent to cemeteries of the larger parish churches in some medieval towns bordering the North Sea such as Great Yarmouth and King's Lynn. Roadworks in Lynn in 2014 uncovered parts of the chapel constructed there about 1400.

A problem in studying the impact of the Black Death (and indeed of successive plague outbreaks) is that the evidence, both historical and archaeological, is primarily urban. From an archaeological perspective, it was only in urban areas that the concentrated numbers of people and associated number of deaths necessitated the provision of special cemeteries such as East Smithfield and thereby recognition. In rural areas, plague victims were buried in parish cemeteries and, because plague left no traces on the skeleton, are thus indistinguishable from other burials. Comparative osteoarchaeological studies can reveal interesting differences between inhabitants of rural and urban locations (such as asymmetrical development of the *humeri* or upper arm bones of urban males which is not exhibited by urban females implying a gender differentiation of activity compared to the upper body patterns exhibited by men and women alike in rural skeletal assemblages which suggests both sexes engaged in hard physical labour).[118] However, without a prohibitively expensive programme of DNA analysis of rural burials, isolating cases of plague will remain extremely difficult.

One area where the impact of the Black Death is traditionally said to have left a mark upon the rural landscape is in the prevalence of deserted medieval villages. Popular sentiment frequently characterises settlement loss as due to plague but the erroneous nature of this view was recognised as early as 1954 when Maurice Beresford published his groundbreaking book on the lost villages of England. He had literally broken ground in 1950 with trenching—uninformed as he recognised being an economic historian rather than an archaeologist—at the deserted village site of Wharram Percy in Yorkshire; he was rescued by an eminent archaeologist, John Hurst, and together they developed the longest-running research project in English rural archaeology. Beresford remarked that 'the plague has been given too much credit for destruction of villages, and many sheep-enclosures passed by unnoticed as long as the Black Death could be invoked as an explanation'.[119]

Beresford noted that rural settlement loss was a feature of medieval life in England, generated by a range of causes not least, in the context of the North Sea, the agency of the sea. It was also not solely an English phenomenon. For instance, deserted villages have been explored and mapped in Schleswig Holstein where parish formation, consolidating the area as German territory (above p. 52), seems to have come to a halt by 1300, with numerous villages deserted by 1350. By no means were all of these desertions attributable to the Black Death. Some villages, such as Adelby and Hemstrup-Laibüll had gone at the end of the 13th century, their continued use proving uneconomic; others declined and became deserted in the second half of the 14th century. Interestingly, the effects of this process could be seen in a programme of pollen analysis where a decline in settlements coincided with an increase in woodland.[120]

Economic change is also seen behind rural settlement loss in the Waterland region of the Netherlands. Often such loss was associated with a change in activity, particularly a move from agricultural work to trade, shipping and industry. Bos has noted that many 'lost' villages actually moved site, towards traffic routes of road and water.[121] Movement of villages has also been observed in a landscape survey conducted by Wade-Martins in the Launditch Hundred of Norfolk. He noted 'a lack of stability of settlement sites throughout the whole history of the post-Roman period' and a gradual retreat from areas of marginal land by the beginning of the 14th century. The eventual impact on Launditch with its heavy soils was a 40% loss of village sites.[122]

Wade-Martins observed that climatic deterioration was often cited as a major factor in the long-term decline of rural settlement in northern Europe. Recent research has sought to establish a temperature series for Norfolk in the period 1256 to 1431, using manorial records, especially the accounts of Norwich Cathedral Priory which survive particularly well (the priory was directly managing its estates from around 1250 and the earliest accounts survive for 1255–1256). The slightly complicated methodology seeks out grain harvest dates and calibrates the resulting series using a linear regression transfer function to known 18th- and 19th-century data. The results indicate a deterioration of climate over the period 1256 to 1341 with prolonged winters delaying the growing season.[123] Longer winters characterised the 'Little Ice Age' of the later Middle Ages and early post-medieval period, the impact of poorer weather most likely being felt on the more difficult soils, helping to accelerate retreat from marginal land.

Changing temperatures had an impact upon marine resources as well as terrestrial ones. It is known that plankton-eating herring 'are highly sensitive to water temperature and chemistry, which affect the adult schools directly, their larvae, and the plankton on which they feed. Herring-like fish everywhere are thus subject to sudden and catastrophic population crashes resulting in failures of the fishery' as happened in the North Sea off East Anglia between 1360 and 1380. A similar collapse overtook the Øresund fishery early in the 15th century.[124]

The later 14th century

The complex nature of societal changes in late medieval northern Europe is highlighted in a recent paper by Schreg. He provides a useful assessment of factors and potential interactions influencing the 'late medieval crisis', illustrating how the impact of the Black Death was one contributor, albeit a highly significant and catastrophic contributor, to the changes which were gradually taking place. He presents a twofold argument. Firstly, he recognises that observed factors—such as land-use, clearance, erosion and inundation (associated with landscapes) or environmental considerations such as hydrology, soil and biodiversity—are important in terms of individual studies. However, he also seeks a more-developed theoretical approach which combines both observed archaeological phenomena with new understandings concerning medieval economics, human ecology and environmental history.[125]

Schreg is not alone in seeking a wider, more inclusive approach to understanding. An appraisal of seigneurial and elite sites within the rural landscape has recently demonstrated the importance of avoiding a traditional site-based approach, whereby lordly establishments such as castles and manor houses are studied in isolation, to one which roots such examination within the landscape as a whole. It was noted above (p. 46) how, within the English North Sea zone, appraising the inter-relationship of church, manor and mill is frequently important if an understanding of settlement operational function through time is to be elucidated successfully. The point is made forcefully by Creighton and Barry's assessment when they illustrate two parts of southern Lincolnshire bordering The Wash; different approaches to lordship led to different landscape settlement patterns with presumed implications for societal organisation.[126] Consideration of the surrounding landscape also enhances understanding of major adjacent monuments; Spynie Palace, for instance, residence of the Bishops of Moray (Figure 3.9), once stood at the side of an 8km long (5 miles) sea loch bordering the North Sea, a loch now almost entirely lost through silting and subsequent drainage (its 17th-century form is depicted in the Bleau Atlas of Scotland of 1654).[127] A *toun* or township was associated with the palace. Alexander Bur, the bishop between 1362 and 1397 issued a 'protestation' concerning his fishing rights via the township which illustrates the links between his establishment and the local settlement: he asserted that for over a century 'the Bishops of Moray ... had and were accustomed to have the fishers of sea fish living in the town of Spynie with their wives and families, sailing from Spynie out to sea and bringing back their boats (*batellas*) with fish through the same port'. Archaeological research has identified the road linking the palace and the township with surface finds indicating the likely extent of occupation.[128]

The contribution of an understanding of the development of the landscape as a whole, together with exploration of trends within contemporary society, is also illustrated by work on Flemish and other coastal communities prone to flooding. Among others factors, it can be demonstrated that property ownership of marginal lands adjacent to the North Sea changed markedly from the late 13th century onward with a tendency for small property-owners to lose control of the land to larger, often institutional or aristocratic, landowners. As a result, the 'entitlement' of the occupants of the coastal areas to

Figure 3.9 Ruins of Spynie Palace (Brian Ayers).

flood protection underwent a transformation as control of flood prevention became more susceptible to influences such as market forces, the redeployment of labour to other more short-term but financially advantageous tasks such as drainage, or lack of investment by absentee landlords. In consequence, it can be concluded that flood disasters in the later Middle Ages were as much endogenous disasters, that is rooted in human agency, as natural disaster, due either to changing climatic conditions or, in the aftermath of the Black Death, population decline with associated lack of effective action.[129]

Tim Soens produced the above conclusions after working with the concept of entitlement theory for which Amartya Sen won the Nobel Prize in Economic Sciences in 1998. His application of this theory to consideration of the protection of North Sea marginal land in the medieval period is thus an instructive example of how archaeological approaches and practice can develop. At a more local level, a well-structured archaeological research project such as that undertaken at Walraversijde provides a useful illustration of medieval land tenure change in the face of volatile environmental circumstances. This coastal village, excavated since 1992 and now in part reconstructed, was a replacement settlement for an earlier village destroyed in 1394 by a severe storm (the Saint Vincentius' Day flood). The storm realigned the dune system of the coast, necessitating the creation of a new village behind the realignment. This was effected on a planned layout covering some 10 hectares with over a hundred houses on 'small, almost urban plots'. The extraordinary investment suggested by such an undertaking (which must have been implemented almost immediately after the inundation as Walraversijde is documented as protected by a new dike in 1399) implies an organising authority. Indeed, assessment of known land ownership reveals a concentration in the hands of just four individuals by the middle of the 15th century.[130] The economic pressures not only meant that small landowners were expropriated but it also probably led to changed occupational status, former peasant farmers becoming waged labourers or fishermen.

Unsurprisingly there is evidence of coastal change from both sides of the North Sea. As noted above (p. 71ff.), entire towns and villages were lost to the sea but more gradual, sustained pressure could also bring about substantial alterations to coastal and estuarine geography with lasting consequences for neighbouring communities. A good example is that of the Glaven river which flows into the North Sea between the medieval ports of Blakeney, Wiveton and Cley-next-the-Sea on the north Norfolk coast. Here a 'cast' or shingle bank, created by erosion of the Cromer moraine, started progressively to block the river's estuary from at least the 13th century. The port settlements of Wiveton and Cley both appear to have developed in a linear fashion northward, in part no doubt seeking to maintain access to a usable haven. Cley church is a kilometre from the modern village centre, itself a similar distance from the sea. The emerging difficulties of navigation led to the construction of seamarks of which one survives, a small turret or 'lighthouse' of 13th-century date on Blakeney church. It is considered that the 'light had doubtless to be read in conjunction with another in the west tower thus providing an approach line from the east-north-east'.[131] A further possible seamark was the so-called 'Blakeney Chapel', the ruins of which stand on Blakeney Eye, a raised mound within the sea marsh. Recorded on a map of 1586, the ruins of this structure survive and have been excavated, the results suggesting domestic and agricultural use.

Commercial contacts

The Glaven estuary is no more, its former haven now also sealed off from the sea by a dike which carries the modern coast road. Nevertheless, sufficient relict topography survives on both banks within Wiveton and Cley villages to illustrate long tenement plots running back from quayside roads, the intervening haven area now a range of low-lying, and frequently wet, fields of pasture. Recent test-pit excavations, undertaken as part of a community archaeology project within the gardens of houses, has revealed a range of ceramics which suggest a floruit of activity until about 1400 with contraction thereafter. The ruins of a 13th-century vaulted stone building stand close to the lost haven in Wiveton and may represent a merchant's house or warehouse (above, p. 36). Interestingly, one excavation close to the former shoreline produced German and Dutch pottery sherds of the 16th century which suggest a wharf in that location associated with a small commercial revival at that time.[132]

The former importance of the Glaven estuary and therefore of these north coast ports is also visible in the still extant parish churches. Blakeney church is dedicated to St Nicholas, the patron saint of sailors, and it, together with the churches at Wiveton, Cley and Salthouse, the four settlements that were the ports of the haven, has been shown by an important survey of medieval graffiti to be covered with incised images of ships. The focus of these images tends to be in one location; thus, at Blakeney, they are grouped on the eastern pier of the south arcade, facing the side aisle altar and opposite an empty image niche. The supposition must be that the images of ships are a form of prayer, incised either to seek protection on a voyage or to give thanks for safe delivery.[133]

The continued impact of trade across the North Sea is illustrated by the development of churches such as St Margaret in Cley, a building begun under the celebrated master mason William Ramsey in the early 14th century but eventually completed half a century after the Black Death. Work was clearly interrupted by the plague and indeed Ramsey and his son both died as a result of the pestilence. Other great churches in the east of England received investment at this time. The port of Boston in Lincolnshire, which had suffered some economic decline in the early 14th century, revived after the Black Death with wool and cloth exports important as was the importation of woad for cloth-producing centres such as inland Coventry. A merchant called Walter Pescod imported alum and madder into Boston in 1387 and is recorded trading in wool in 1395. He died in 1398 and is commemorated by his surviving, if damaged, brass in the church of St Botolph. This very fine and opulent brass was commissioned from a London workshop and depicts Pescod in a tunic and gown, the latter decorated with a pea-pod (or Peascod) device, the imagery arranged to form a 'W' and thus, in a pun, referencing his name.[134]

Funerary brasses were also imported from Flanders. In King's Lynn, brass memorials to two 14th-century merchants and their wives, Adam de Walsoken (who died in 1349 with his wife Margaret) and Robert Braunche (who died in 1364 with his two wives Letitia and Margaret), are spectacular examples of Flemish brasses imported into England (Figure 3.10).These very large commemorative statements (the Walsoken brass is 3m in length and 1.73m wide) are of exceptionally high artistic quality, the principal figures located within canopies and their images supported by scenes such as a peacock feast on the Braunche brass. A further similar Flemish brass to Alan Fleming, a merchant of Newark who died in 1361, is extant in the church of St Mary Magdalene in that town (Newark, on the river Trent, was an inland port from the North Sea). Many others must be lost, such as two known from Lynn (to Robert Attelath who died in 1376 and his wife Joan, and to William de Bittering who died in 1369 and his wife Juliana) and that to one Robert Taylor in Cley church (from which a fragment of canopy was reversed and reused for a brass memorial in 1570).[135]

The Flemish production centre was Tournai and brasses from there are known to have been distributed to Germany, Poland, Sweden, Norway and Denmark as well as to England. Some 14 such brasses, for instance, are known from Lübeck although only three survived by 1884 and, of these, one was damaged and one destroyed in air raids in 1942. The brass to Bruno Warendorp in the Marienkirche depicts him in civilian dress although he was also a military commander and seems to have died at the siege of Helsingborg in Denmark in 1369 (the brass is now suggested as of local manufacture—below, p. 97). Further east in Germany, a brass to Albert Hövener (died 1358) survives in St Nicholas church, Stralsund. This well-preserved and decorative memorial also contains his merchant's mark but, in common with the Lübeck examples, depicts him alone without his wife. This is in contrast to the King's Lynn examples. Only in Toruń (now Poland and formally Thorn) is there a continental example of a Tournai brass to a merchant and his wife. This commemorates Johann von Soest (died 1361) accompanied by his wife Margaret. He himself was probably a merchant from the west, trading within this Baltic city.[136]

Slightly earlier memorials imported from Tournai were large marble ledger slabs which were exported from Flanders to Boston and elsewhere in eastern England as well as to Scotland (where a ledger slab commemorating William Bell, bishop of St Andrews between 1332 and 1342, survives). Some 19 such ledger slabs predating 1350 have been located at St Botolph's church in Boston with others now lost (Figure 3.11). Although unlikely to be in their original locations, analysis of wear patterns suggests that

Figure 3.10 Sepulchral brass of Robert Braunche and his two wives , King's Lynn (drawn by John Sell Cotman, Yale Center for British Art / Wikimedia Commons).

they were originally set within areas of heavy footfall. It is considered likely that most of them commemorated Boston merchants but that some may have been memorials to hanseatic merchants who died in Boston (such a hanseatic burial is known from London in 1403 when Godfried van Kessel stated in his will that he wished to be buried *corm stacione mercatorum Alemannie* ('before the station of the German merchants') in All Hallows church. The Boston slabs contained merchants' marks as well as incised portrayals of the commemorated individuals, with white marble or gilded brass. Together the 'quickly growing clusters of slabs would have become of increasing importance to the merchants as manifesting a communal entity of remembrance. They were becoming bound together in death as in life, but bound by a communion of trade rather than family: commerce rather than inheritance'.[137]

Figure 3.11 Interior of St Botolph, Boston (Creative Commons Attribution 2.0 Generic License).

A recent study suggests that, by the mid 14th century, brasses were being produced more locally, notably in Lübeck which was itself the centre of distribution for high status memorials. The brasses to Bruno Warendorp in the Marienkirche and that to Bishop Bertram Cremen (who died in 1377) in Lübeck cathedral both show a 'devaluation in figural representation ... reflected in contemporary Lübeck sculpture and painting' and are set into a hard crystalline limestone that was imported from Gotland. The brasses follow German design principles already a common feature of inscribed grave slabs found in 'phenomenal numbers' across northern Europe from Lübeck to Tallinn in the late 13th century and throughout the 14th century.[138]

Analysis of objects that were more portable also shows continental European influences on English artefacts in the 14th century. The celebrated Macclesfield Psalter, dating to the 1330s, for instance seems to have been illustrated by artists associated with both the royal court and the Dominican Friaries in Norwich and Cambridge. However, the work of these artists seems to exemplify a 'vigorous exchange between local, metropolitan and continental trends in fourteenth-century East Anglia'.[139] This bilateral influence can also be seen in such objects as the Ormesby (Norfolk) and St Omer (northern France) psalters of the late 1320s/early 1330s (Figure 3.12). Both of these were connected with Norwich but included Italianate elements and represented a style which 'spread to Flemish manuscripts and thence to Cologne and other parts of Germany, France, and even Austria'. Norwich, as well as being a production centre for manuscripts and increasingly for brasses which themselves drew on Flemish traditions, was also a city with numerous goldsmiths. The earliest recorded goldsmith was Henry de Trith de Brabant in 1306, probably of northern French origin while Edmund Lamberd was probably Flemish (documented in 1312/1313). Their artistic products are lost but a contemporary was one Guillaume of Nourriche (or William of Norwich) who was working as a sculptor in Paris in 1319–1324. Two statues of apostles carved by him survive in the Musée de Cluny in that city.[140]

The incidence of trans-North sea contact can also be seen in more modest artefacts than high quality manuscripts, gold-work or sculpture. Grimston ware pottery for instance, a product of kilns at Pott

Figure 3.12 Detail from the Ormesby Psalter (Web Gallery of Art / Wikimedia Commons).

Row, Grimston near King's Lynn, has been found at Bergen, Borgund, Kabelvag, Oslo, Skien, Stavanger, Tønsberg, Tromsø, Trondheim and Veoy in Norway. Most of the vessels discovered date to the 13th century rather than the 14th century although 14th-century short-beard face jugs have been found in Bergen (and also in Bruges and Aberdeen). The Bergen material is almost entirely confined to the period 1225–1350 (the so-called 'highly-decorated' period of Grimston ware manufacture) with a steep decline thereafter. The Norwegian exports left England through King's Lynn, destined primarily for Bergen itself although a small amount also went to Trondheim. The quantities were considerable: a century and a quarter of exports accounts for nearly 18% of all pottery in Bergen between *c.* 1100 and 1700 (compared to Siegburg wares at 11% and Scarborough wares at 8%)'.The vast quantities of ... Grimston Wares found in Norway ... are the result of organised direct bulk shipping, while the occasional vessels found along the eastern coast of England, the North Sea coast and Scotland represent casual trade'.[141]

Other English exported pottery included Hedingham ware, a 12th- to 14th-century product of north Essex in the east of England (decorated rim glazed fine ware and grey-fired coarse wares). A recent survey has charted and discussed its distribution in England, noting that this largely extended across East

Figure 3.13 Painted tomb in Onze-Lieve-Vrouwekerk, Bruges (Musea Brugge).

Anglia, with a significant incidence at coastal locations as well, but it is also reported from Bergen.[142] Scarborough ware face jugs have been found in Norway at Bergen with the fabric also recorded from Tønsberg and Trondheim.[143] A jar of Humberware was recovered from excavations in the northern part of Lödöse, Sweden, in 1964.[144]

Some specialised English industrial products in the 14th century were therefore sought after in parts of continental Europe (and the growing importance of English cloth as an export needs to be remembered) but this should not be overstated. 'In almost every manufacturing skill the men of the Low Countries led the way, in beer-brewing using hops, in cloth weaving and dyeing, in the manufacture of brass and latten [an alloy of copper and zinc, used to make memorial brasses], in techniques of oil-painting, in shipbuilding, brick-making, the manufacture of spectacles and surgical implements and in surveying, hydraulics and map making'.[145] As an example of this broad cultural supremacy, awareness of the quality of painting in Flanders has recently been enhanced by discoveries uncovered by archaeological excavation in Antwerp and notably in Bruges. Here, in the Onze-Lieve-Vrouwekerk or the Church of Our Lady, plastered brick tombs have been exposed, decorated internally with painted depictions of the Crucifixion, the Virgin and Child, saints such as St James and censing angels (Figure 3.13). The earliest dates from 1295 with the greatest number in the first half of the 14th century although examples continue into the first quarter of the 15th century.[146] Such discoveries occur elsewhere in the Low Countries; excavations beneath the side aisle of the Franciscan friary church in Dordrecht uncovered a painted crucifixion of around 1375.[147]

Trans-North Sea influences: Brick manufacture and utilisation, exotic stone and sand

It is nevertheless salutary to reflect upon development on both sides of the North Sea and how influences could clearly flow back and forth. Thus, while Flemish memorial brasses were imported to King's Lynn so 14th-century panel paintings from the Dominican Friary in Thetford, Norfolk (and now in the Musée de Cluny in Paris) can be shown to be' stylistically independent of artistic currents on the Continent' and 'a harbinger of the fashion for *pastiglia* grounds seen in German, Bohemian and Netherlandish ... work after 1350'.[148] At a more basic level of human experience, that of brick technology, it has already been noted how usage was promoted across and around the North Sea with brick architecture reaching Ribe in Denmark before the end of the 12th century (above, p. 59). England was a slow adopter of brick although there were occasional relatively early exceptions; a relatively-unknown example is the very early use of brick to form internal quoins in the first phase *c.* 1216 of the priory at Beeston Regis in north Norfolk (immediately adjacent to the North Sea). Large and rectangular, with hues of yellow and pink, the bricks may have been imported; they were perhaps considered a poor substitute for stone because they were only employed in areas where they would be covered with plaster.[149]

A later but still early use of brick is that visible in the choir, transepts and lower stages of the tower of Holy Trinity, Hull. These areas are examples of monumental brickwork, construction probably beginning about 1300. At least one secular building in Hull, its gaol (apparently a four-storey tower, perhaps of *c.* 1310 and almost certainly by 1333/34), was being erected around the same time, no doubt utilising bricks from the earliest recorded brickyard in the country.[150] Furthermore, excavation at High Street, Hull has revealed a brick building of the early 14th century which seems to have combined both commercial and domestic accommodation. This structure, on the 'Ousefleet property', not only contained highly skilled brickwork, including ground level relieving arches, but examination suggests that it was clearly influenced by developments on the continent, notably in the Low Countries with parallels cited from Schniedam and Delft.[151]

Hull was thus a precocious English user of brick, reflecting the paucity of local stone sources although, in contrast to the Ousefleet property, its 14th-century houses normally tended to have limestone sill walls, the limestone being imported from near Brough on the edge of the Yorkshire Wolds. It is indicative of the wealth of Hull that one house on Blanket Row even seems to have had limestone walls to first floor level.[152] Nevertheless, the use of brick was becoming more and more evident, with excavations revealing details of structural techniques, such as the 'interrupted sill' where short limestone pillars supported vertical posts into which were jointed horizontal sill beams resting upon brick sillwalls. The technique was noted on the 'Wytelard property' on Blackfriargate, Hull in a phase which could be closely-dated to the mid 14th century. At the time of the excavation it was the only recorded use of this constructional methodology in the region.[153]

The early use of brick in Hull emphasises the importance of the town's east coast location, its citizens open to continental European influences. A defensive wall of brick was probably begun here in the 1320s and was strengthened in the 1340s and 1430s. It eventually enclosed the port on three sides with the River Hull to the east and is depicted well on Wenceslas Hollar's 'bird's eye view' illustration of the port in 1640 (Figure 3.14). Comprising some 30 towers and contained an estimated 4.7 million bricks, the fortifications formed 'the largest brick-built structure [in England] since the Roman period'.[154] A number of excavations have taken place on these defences, highlighting constructional techniques and also identifying remains of three of the four principal gateways. The Myton Gate was briefly exposed in 1976, on a road development site when an hour was made available for archaeological recording one lunchtime; it was possible to see that the brick gateway had contained an arched carriageway some 4m wide.[155] More controlled excavation was possible in 1986 at the Beverley Gate where the foundations and lower courses of a single-tower brick gateway dating to the late 14th century were seen both to enclose an earlier timber gateway and to project in front of the town wall itself.[156] Happily, these remains have been left exposed to public view, the monument being an important location in English history as it is where Sir John Hotham, the governor of Hull, refused Charles I entry to the town in 1642, the first overt act of the 17th-century English Civil War.

The early use of brick in England remains an area exciting much research. A recent publication contained numerous papers exploring the introduction of brick with Andrews examining the influence and importation of Low Countries products, together with the almost haphazard manner in which

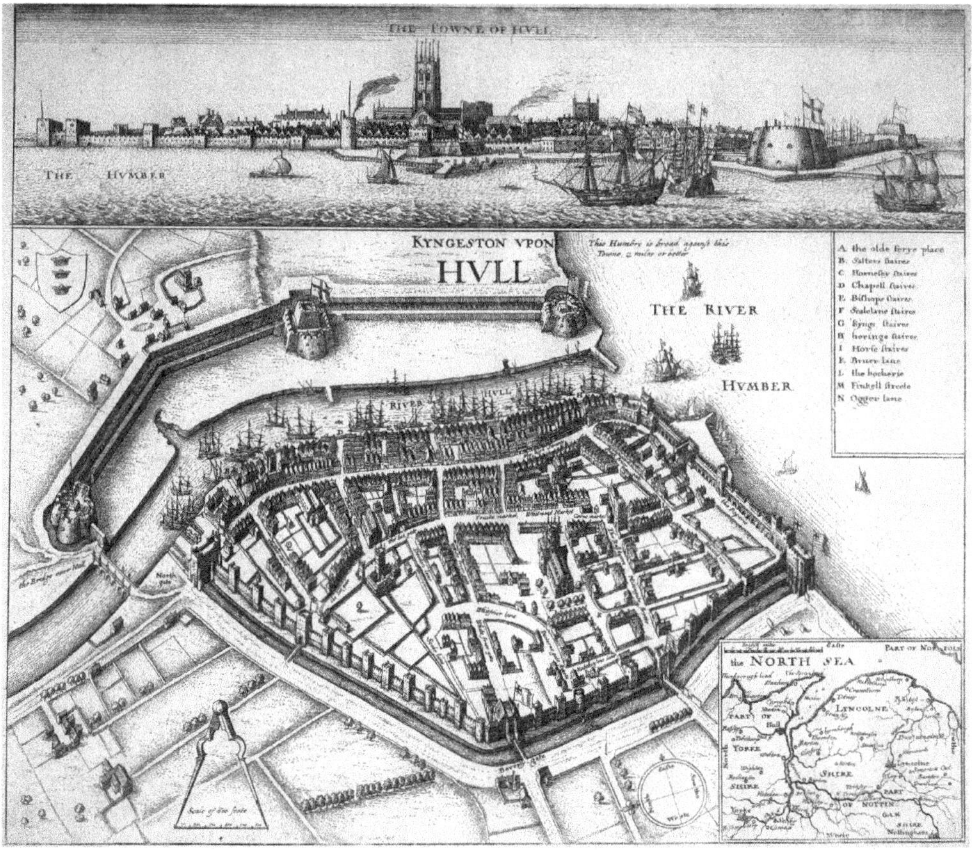

Figure 3.14 Hull in 1640 by Wenceslas Hollar (University of Toronto Wenceslas Hollar Digital Collection / Wikimedia Commons).

the technology was developed in 14th-century England. He notes localised use in Boston and Lincoln together with known production of bricks for the still extant free-standing Cow Tower in Norwich in 1398/1399 (the bricks here were used to face a tower of flint construction; the defensive walls of Norwich elsewhere contain earlier bricks too, used as vaulting and for door surrounds in towers dating to the 1340s).[157] However, in at least eight churches, one house and seven excavations in Essex, instances of imported 14th-century Low Countries bricks have been recorded. This influence continued into the 15th century where it has been observed that the high quality of the brickwork at Darby Tower in Maldon, also in Essex, would only have been possible had it at least been 'directed if not executed by a Low Countries bricklayer'.[158]

Early brickwork in the east of England is clearly indicative of continental influence as were other early features such as artillery provision in urban defensive systems. Gun-loops dating to the 1340s exist within the city walls of Norwich where the Cow Tower, mentioned above, is an early example in England of an artillery bastion, positioned to defend a bend in the River Wensum, strengthening an area which otherwise had only the river itself and a timber fence as effective defences.[159] Great Yarmouth is a town where study of early brickwork needs to be undertaken; the town stands in a county with poor local building stone except for flint and yet the hinterland of Yarmouth was devoid even of that. In consequence its citizens were forced to adopt brick construction early as can be seen in much of the surviving town wall, building of which started in 1285.[160] The adoption of brick was almost certainly influenced at least in part by links to the continent.

Another striking instance of continental contact is readily visible in King's Lynn where surviving stretches of the town wall contain an estimated 55,000 constituent rocks and other material. Analysis of the rocks showed that about 3000 clasts (fragments of geological material) were alien to the region of King's Lynn and indeed, with a few exceptions, had a provenance in the Baltic. Several specimens are of igneous and metamorphic rock and originated from the Balto-Scandian basement complex or Baltic Shield. Many others are rounded cobbles of basaltic, porphyritic and metamorphic rock which can be expected with Balto-Scandian examples. It seems very probable that the material was imported as ballast, collected from Baltic beaches. Further analysis was able to discount southern Denmark and Poland as sources for the rocks and to isolate beaches of the western Estonian archipelago as the primary source. Interestingly, there appears to have been significant trade between King's Lynn and the Estonian island of Saaremaa in the 14th century.[161]

Similar use of ballast stone has been observed in Flanders where recent research on the churches of Our Lady at Damme and St Quinten at Oostkerke has identified well-rounded stones of glacial erratic origin (20 types in the case of the Damme church). The southern Baltic is thought to be the most likely source of these stones. Large numbers of exotic stones have also been located at Hoeke, a location which stands out as a trading site. It is known that hanseatic merchants established both a hospital and a church here around 1280, probably with a trading colony exploiting the port's location as a trans-shipment site for goods going on upstream to Bruges. Identified stones include Larvikite from the Oslo area of Norway, red and brown Ostsee quartz porphyries from Aland, Sweden, Kalmarsund sandstone from Sweden and bryozoan-bearing flints from Danish chalk cliffs.[162]

It is possible that Flemish sand was taken back to the Baltic on occasion, also as ballast. Wulperhoek and two other locations are known to have been permitted as sand extraction sites in Flanders. Paleontological analysis of medieval ballast sand used for land reclamation at Lohberg 14 in the 14th-century port at Wismar on the Baltic coast, notably studying sub-fossils within the deposit, indicates an origin for the sand as a North Sea intertidal sand flat. The quantity uncovered was estimated at between 20 and 30 cubic metres, equivalent to between 40 and 60 tons of sand. The excavated deposit may therefore reflect the ballast of a single cog. It was certainly loaded in one location as it was a pure deposit without mixing.[163]

Reverting to defences, brickwork within urban fortifications is much more obvious on the continent than in Britain. At Zutphen in the Netherlands, for instance, substantial remains of the Berkelpoort or watergate, constructed after 1312, survive astride the River Berkel, linking the Old and New Towns of the settlement. The walls of Zutphen at this period were also heightened in brick, helped by extensive brick protection from kilns around the city. The New Town had nine brick towers of which the remains of one, the Schullen Tower, were exposed and recorded in a sewer trench in 2006. Collapse of the southern wall of Zutphen around 1340 led to comprehensive rebuilding in the mid-14th century, the results of which survive as 'one of the most beautiful city views in the Netherlands'.[164]

Zutphen apparently also used bricks for its houses in the 14th century but the quantities of bricks needed for construction of town walls should not be underestimated. In Hull, the output of the municipal brickworks is calculated to have been about 100,000 bricks *per annum*. In consequence, the fact that defensive works started in the 1320s were only completed in 1406 may be more a matter of logistical possibility than intermittent financial exigency. The provision of nearly 5 million bricks for the town walls alone was a major commitment for the brickyard.

The hesitant use of brick in England can be contrasted with the country's clearly confident implementation of tile manufacture (it is perhaps telling that early documentary references to bricks in England mention 'wall-tiles'). A 'tile factory' which operated between *c.* 1275–1285 and 1325–1335 has been excavated in Essex [165] and English tiles seem to have influenced continental developments.[166] In Denmark, a tilery has been excavated at Bistrup north of Roskilde. This seems to have been in operation from the beginning of the 13th century to the middle of the 15th century, providing an estimated 20,000 to 30,000 tiles in each firing. It supplied the cathedral at Roskilde as well as many of the churches and houses of the vicinity. An example of a floriate or daisy-wheel floor tile on display in the cathedral museum in Roskilde bears a superficial similarity to English 'Westminster-style' tiles.

Brick building in the Low Countries, as in Germany and elsewhere, was generally much more assured than in England. In Ghent, major structures such as the church of the Carmelites, were built between 1320 and 1330 as, also in the 14th century, were the Kapel van de Wolwevers (the Chapel of the Wool Weavers), the belfry and the 'shiphouse' located at the current Butter Market (known in the Middle Ages as Plaestre and also the site of assembly rooms for the aldermen and the location of the crossbowmens' guild; it was the centre of political and economic power in Ghent, expressed through architecture).[167] In Oudenaarde brick buildings were even older; the north wall of the Cistercian Abbey of Maagdendale dates to the second half of the 13th century as does the south wall of a merchant's house located at Hoogstraat 7 while the belfry at Kortrijk and the octagonal tower at Lendelede are examples from the early 14th century.[168] Remarkable 'narrow-fronted' buildings of 14th-century date survive on Lijnmarkt in Utrecht where the rear gables were extended towards the canal (the Oude Gracht). However, construction on the canal side wharf itself was not permitted and the houses, which survive, were therefore built with arches to support their gable walls.[169] Even more extraordinary were the two towers erected either side of the Yser river in 1284 by Count Guy de Dampierre. The larger of these was of brick and was only demolished as late as 1914 by retreating allied troops to stop it being used by the German army. Its footings were excavated in 1996[170] and it may have been one of the earliest lighthouses in Europe. Another early example, also of brick, is the still extant Neuwerk watchtower at the mouth of the River Elbe dating from *c.* 1310.

'Hanseatic' culture

Commerce and administration were reflected in the construction of brick buildings. The distinctive brick façades of houses in towns such as Lübeck and Lüneburg are sometimes viewed as characteristic of hanseatic culture, these locations being centres of the Hanseatic League. Public buildings in northern Germany similarly adopted brick as both a structural and a display material. The Rathaus or town hall in Lübeck is an early 14th-century brick building, slightly later in date than that of the dramatically-gabled Rathaus in Stralsund (Figure 3.15). By the late 14th century, England was catching up and, in Boston, St Mary's Guildhall was constructed of brick around 1390 although both its scale and its exterior façade are much more modest in aspiration (Figure 3.16). The late 14th-century date is a recent re-calculation for a hall which previously had been thought to have been built in the mid 15th century. Dendrochronological dating of crown-post roof trusses and tie beams now suggests *c.* 1385–1390 for the timber with luminescence dating of the bricks suggesting a date range of 1390–1395. The hall belonged to a religious fraternity called the St Mary's Guild which received a royal licence of incorporation in 1392; the organisation 'offered members a useful means of combining spiritual concerns with secular activities'. The guild 'seems to have attracted a socially diverse range of male and female members, particularly merchants, prominent landowners, customs officials and mayors of the staple ...'.[171] The building itself provided flexible space which could be used for storage, examination of goods and possibly sale as well.

Boston was not the only town to provide structures that fostered mercantile activity. In Hull, the corporation had built a weigh-house on the quay next to the River Hull by 1365, rebuilding or extending it in 1389.[172] A 16th-century plan survives showing the structure as arranged around a courtyard or 'quadrant' with an entrance from High Street to the west and wharves to the east. A crane, balance and 'jibbets' were located on the wharves. The street range at least was apparently colonnaded to enable the 'merchants to walk dry' and, in this respect, appears to mirror the provision shown on a celebrated portrayal of hanseatic merchants at the port of Hamburg in the late 15th century[173] (and now preserved in the Staatsarchiv, Hamburg). The wharves were separated by a projection of the main building which housed the Customs House in a four-storey tower.

A Custom House was also established in London in 1382 by John Churchman, 'newly built for the quiet of the merchants ... To serve for the tronage of wools in the Port of London' (a 'tron' was a weighing

Figure 3.15 Rathaus, Stralsund (Wiki Loves Monuments 2014 / Wikimedia Commons).

machine). A chamber and latrine were added in 1383 together with a solar over the counting house. Excavations in 1973 revealed chalk and ragstone foundations with 1.5m long piles and indicated that the building was 24m by 10m in size, aligned along the river. It too was arcaded as was the hanseatic Steelyard upsteam, this latter being observed by excavation in 1989. Interestingly, Geoffrey Chaucer was Controller of Customs between 1374 and 1386 so he must have overseen the move to the new building. A wooden drain from the latrine was also discovered in 1973 and the excavators delighted in claiming that this had been used by Chaucer.[174]

It seems very likely that the weigh-house/customs house complex in Hull was largely a brick structure. In Germany, Rieger has explored the use of brick in the mixed domestic/commercial buildings of Lübeck, noting how the selective use of bricks for certain features, such as staircases, within timber buildings of the late 12th century had already given way to wholly brick structures by the mid 13th century.[175] Such *Dielenhäuser* (below, p. 116), constructed at right-angles to the street, were also built in Deventer in the Netherlands in the 14th century. Deventer suffered a devastating fire in 1334 and thereafter brick houses were encouraged by the city corporation (which, in an early example of 'grant-aid', subsidised roof tiles). One such post-1334 house has been surveyed at Polstraat 14; it measures 14m by 7m with walls two bricks thick.[176] Brick houses seem to have begun to be built in Sweden from the end of the 14th century. Some 14 small brick structures have been recorded in Malmö of which the earliest (where only the cellar survives but a good later inventory helps reconstruction of the likely height and interior) measured only 6.5m by 4.5m. The cellar was unvaulted but probably had two storeys above and has been interpreted as a small warehouse.[177] As noted above, in England, apart from some buildings in east coast ports such as Boston and Hull, brick remained unusual as a major structural material but was being used increasingly for such features as window and door surrounds, staircases and vaults by the end of the 14th century. The grand squared-and-knapped flint-faced house now known as the Bridewell in Norwich dates from around 1380

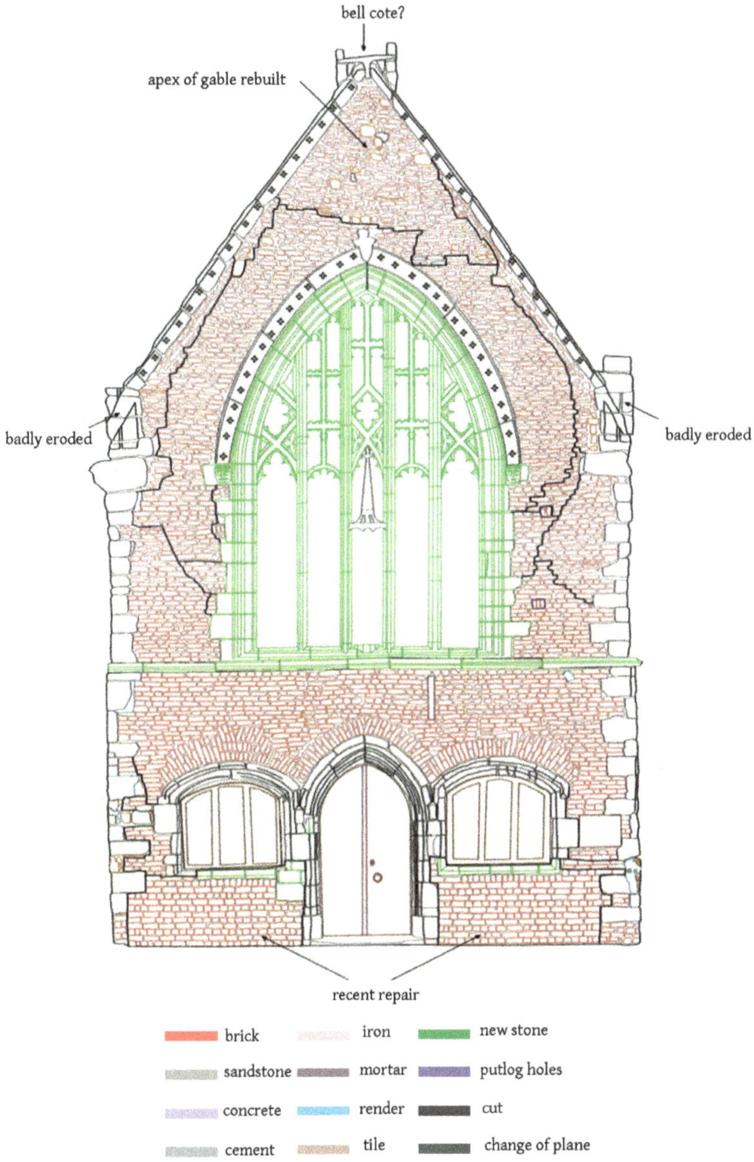

Figure 3.16 Survey of west external elevation of Boston Guildhall (FAS Heritage).

and has a suite of brick-vaulted undercrofts, the walls of the cellars also enhanced by brick wall-arches.[178] On the exterior of the building, the invisible magnificence of this vaulted interior is suggested to the observer by a stringcourse of brick running the length of the building.

It can be argued that the gradual development of brick architecture around the North Sea is an example of *Kulterträger*, the carriage of hanseatic style to those locations with which it was associated. A further example of such transmitted culture (or 'copycat consumerism'?) is that of the medieval hypocaust or heating system. Although not as well known as the much earlier Roman examples, such hypocausts have been recorded across the North Sea world. In Tallinn, alone, at least 52 are known from extant medieval buildings standing there, 26 of them in houses within the Lower Town.[179] Similar systems can be found in Germany, Lithuania, Denmark, Sweden and Finland, their spread across the region considered to be largely 14th-century in date. Subfloor heating dating to 1305/1320 was discovered in a Dielenhaus at Koberg 2 in Lübeck, beneath the *Stube*, a warm residential room on the ground-floor.[180] A good German example is that of the Rathaus or Town Hall in the hanseatic town of Göttingen. Probably remodelled from 1369, the main hall incorporates underfloor heating, powered from a furnace in the cellar. The flue shafts for the hot air survive.[181] Other examples survive in the town halls of Uelzen, Lübeck and Lüneburg.

The idea of a hanseatic 'cultural signature' is one explored by Gaimster whose most recent work on the subject examined its impact on the North Sea and Baltic regions, primarily (although not exclusively) utilising the evidence of ceramics. He notes the early importance of fragile Low Countries redwares in the Baltic and how, to overcome the problems of transportation, such wares were produced locally using similar clays, probably by migrating potters. In the southern Baltic, 'suitable clays were ubiquitous and could be fired through the oxidising process to emulate the red earthenware jugs and cooking utensils ... so familiar to the urban populations of the North Sea littoral'.[182]

These highly-decorated lead-glazed vessels were originally made on the coasts of Flanders and the Netherlands in the 13th century. They were distributed northward although Verhaeghe has noted that they rarely seem to have reached inland centres.[183] Local Baltic production fostered by their friability is now archaeologically proven from several manufacturing locations: on the Danish islands of Funen and Zealand; on the coast of Scania in southern Sweden; and along the German Mecklenburg coast. The pottery made at these sites is 'typologically and technologically indistinguishable' from the wares produced in the Low Countries 'which suggests the movement of western European workshops into the southern Baltic region ... Trace element analysis of excavated urban deposits is helping to assign medieval traded redwares to their manufacturing sources, creating a platform for reconstructing local pottery supply networks'.[184]

Redwares were gradually eclipsed in the marketplace by stonewares in the later medieval period. These, unlike the earlier fabric, were more robust and could therefore travel long distances. Their importance is clear from Kolberg (Kołobrzeg in modern Poland) where, by the late 14th century onward, one in five vessels found in excavations was from Siegburg in the Rhineland. Overall, nearly 40% of ceramic vessels recovered in the town were imports with 71% of these being Siegburg stonewares.[185] 'With its technologically superior body, which is impervious to liquids, stainless and odour free, stoneware revolutionised many domestic activities from washing up to preserving food' and can be regarded as a 'type-fossil of mercantile ... urban culture'.

This pattern of German ceramic dominance is repeated elsewhere; in Elblag (also modern Poland), Siegburg vessels accounted for about 80% of the pottery assemblage located near the cellars of the cloth hall.[186] At Kalmar in Sweden, drainage of the harbour in 1932–1934 enabled the recovery of a vast assemblage of pottery vessels, many of which were intact or almost intact (and presumably were generally vessels representing loss during trans-shipment in the harbour). Of the 14th- to 15th-century ceramics, 68% per cent were Siegburg vessels. Imports to Kalmar were no doubt assisted by the large resident German population there in the later Middle Ages (one-third of the known family names of Kalmar in the late 14th century were German) [187] but the overall pattern of ceramic finds in the Baltic region nevertheless illustrates a cultural supremacy, whereby robust and fashionable products were driven into diverse markets by efficient systems of manufacture and distribution.

Despite this seeming cultural dominance, Gaimster is nevertheless careful to observe that some areas illustrate resistance. Novgorod in particular, shows a marked differentiation between the ceramics used in the German enclave and the highly-decorated wooden vessels clearly preferred in Russian-occupied parts of the city. It suggests a mutual desire to express individual cultural identity, a theme also explored by Mehler in the northern North Sea and Atlantic region. She too observes that it is possible to identify hanseatic contact through culturally-obvious hanseatic-linked artefacts such as ceramics but she notes in addition that such cultural contact can be seen through objects such as Norwegian whetstones which are not diagnostically hanseatic but were probably reaching Nordic locations through the medium of hanseatic traders. However, she goes on to argue that it is important to differentiate between the societal value of objects and their other values, be they economic or functional. 'Nordic societies assimilated some aspects of Hanse culture by accommodating rather than simply accepting it'.[188] Hanseatic culture needs to be viewed as a contributor to a distinctive Nordic culture, rather than an imposition upon it.

The church

A distinctive, pan-European activity in the Middle Ages concerned religious practice, the church itself being an international institution and one with key elements of lay church practice, such as the veneration of particular saints or sacred sites through pilgrimage, transcending national boundaries. Physical expression of pilgrimage is seen in the archaeological record with finds of pilgrim badges, small souvenirs of base metal acquired—and subsequently lost—by visitors to shrines. As an example, a study of pilgrim badges of the shrine of Our Lady of 's-Hertogenbosch in the Netherlands, while showing that most pilgrims to the shrine appear to have originated from the area of modern-day Belgium and the Netherlands, also noted the discovery in London of a badge from the shrine. Additionally, the geographical spread of non-'s-Hertogenbosch badges (found in that town) has both locally-regional examples from southern Brabant, Flanders and the Rhine-Moselle area as well as badges from Spain, England, France, Switzerland and eastern Germany.[189]

In eastern England, a recent interesting find has been that of a mould fragment for a large 14th-century pilgrim badge for the shrine of Our Lady at Walsingham in Norfolk (Figure 3.17). However, the discovery was not made at Walsingham but in the regional capital, Norwich, presumably the site of the manufacture of such souvenirs. Close inspection of the mould suggests that the craftsman or workshop responsible also made badges associated with the Canterbury shrine of St Thomas Becket. The implications of this observation are that, rather than pilgrim badge production being an entirely localised activity, manufacturing centres such as Norwich were generating products for a wider national market, exploiting opportunities where they presented themselves in a manner more akin to an understanding of the modern economy.[190]

The Walsingham pilgrim badge mould produced an intact badge that was found in 1899 near London Bridge. It is possible to assume therefore that the badge was made in Norwich, purchased in Walsingham and lost in London. The unlucky pilgrim probably travelled to and from the shrine largely by water, progressing from the Thames to one of the north Norfolk ports such as Blakeney or King's Lynn where it is known that many pilgrims landed en route to Walsingham. Excavations at Baker's Lane, King's Lynn next to the Purfleet in 1968–1969 uncovered remains of 14th-century timber revetting, in two phases of alder and oak, consolidating the margin of the Purfleet stream (following 'the same pattern as the Dutch dyke towns'). The Purfleet was probably the disembarkation point for pilgrims to the shrine.[191]

Pilgrimage earlier in the Middle Ages had tended to be directed towards the major sites of Christendom such as Rome and Jerusalem. By the 14th century, however, the numerous shrines of western Europe were also attracting pilgrims. The most famous shrine was that of Santiago de Compostela in northern Spain and souvenirs in the form of shells pierced with holes (for a thong so that the shell could be hung around the neck; the shell is the symbol of St James) have been located in a number of north-west European locations. Examples are displayed in the Danish National Museum for instance and pierced shells have been excavated from graves in both Aberdeen and York. The York example was from the grave of a woman, the shell probably originally contained in a small bag suspended from the waist and with the species of shell in this instance being *Pecten jacobaeus* of Mediterranean origin.[192] Pilgrimage souvenirs and symbols of pilgrimage in the Baltic region of Germany include Santiago shells from Greifswald, St James illustrated as a pilgrim on a wall-painting in the church of St Margaret Gelwitz, a rosary of intricately-carved jet pearls found during excavations at the market place in Wismar (and also linked to Santiago), and a pilgrim badge of French origin depicting the Virgin and Child.[193] In Bremen, on the Weser river, pilgrim badges have been recovered from the shrine of St Léonard-de-Noblat which

Figure 3.17 Fragment of pilgrim badge mould, Norwich (Norfolk Archaeological Unit).

lay east of Limoges in France as well as badges of three-linked circles representing the three allegedly bloodstained hosts from the more-local shrine at Bad Wilsnack.[194]

Pilgrim badges from the Cologne shrine of the Magi are known from London and Denmark amongst other locations. Scandinavia is notable for the number of graves which contain pilgrimage souvenirs. A survey published in 1980 detailed 41 Scandinavian graves where such items had been located (and no doubt the total is now higher) and was able both to explore the range of cult sites visited and the duration of the popularity of such imagery. Burial with a pilgrim souvenir was most common prior to 1300 with a marked decline—and indeed abandonment in some places—of the practice after 1400. The shrines represented obviously included Santiago but also Vadstena in Sweden, Trondheim and Aachen. One burial of *c.* 1300 from Helsingborg in Sweden was that of a pilgrim interred with ten pilgrim souvenirs; this person had been to Rome, Lucca, Bari, Tours, Rocamadour and four other locations.[195]

Some 17 of the burials included in the Scandinavian survey undertaken in 1980 were from monasteries, friaries and hospitals. However, in all the countries bordering the North Sea, the impact of the 16th-century Reformation meant the removal, in nearly every case, of monastic institutions. This means that, for the North Sea world, the parish church remains the most self-evident architectural statement of medieval Christianity. For long the preserve of art historians, archaeological investigation of churches has

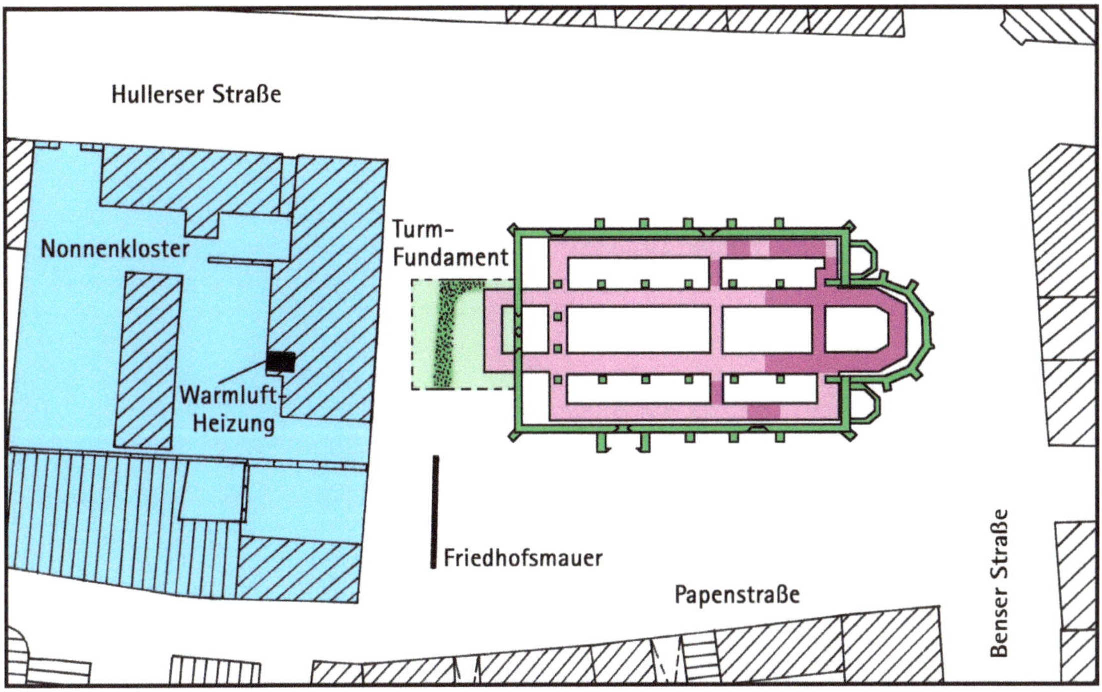

Figure 3.18 Recovered plan of the Neustädter Kirche in Einbeck (drawing: Pit Becker, Einbeck).

become increasingly common over the last three or four decades. Earlier research frequently took the form of excavation following damage or destruction in the Second World War. Thus, St Bride's church in London was excavated by W. F. Grimes between 1952 and 1954, fortunately as a research excavation and thus providing 'a landmark in the development of London's archaeology ... of great significance in the development of medieval archaeology in general ... one of the first parish churches in England to be excavated in plan ... using modern archaeological techniques ...'.[196] The work, with subsequent survey work by the Museum of London between 1992 and 1995, revealed the church sequence, extending it back over a century before the earliest known documentary reference with a well as its primary focus.

Other work on war-damaged churches includes the excavation of St Benedict in Norwich, gutted in 1942 and subsequently demolished except for its iconic round tower (probably because of a perceived surfeit of churches within Norwich which still retains some 30 such structures within the city walls).[197] In Germany, the Jakobikirche in Rostock, also severely damaged in 1942, was likewise demolished in the late 1950s (probably as a result of being in the DDR). Excavation, however, has recovered the plan and details of the building such as a painted tomb.[198] In Bremen, excavation beneath the nave of the cathedral, the roof of which had collapsed due to war damage, revealed a series of earlier church buildings.[199]

Some excavations of urban churches concerned buildings demolished in the past, such as St Helen-on-the Walls in York which was comprehensively excavated and, like St Bride's, extending back its known history by at least a hundred years[200] or the Neustädter Kirche in Einbeck of which only elements could be seen during trenching with other information being recovered from historic illustrations and cartography (Figure 3.18).[201] The graveyard was also excavated at St Helen's, York as was much of that of the church of St Margaret *in combusto* ('in the burnt area'), demolished in Norwich in the mid-15th century. This church was also known as St Margaret *ubi sepeliunter suspensi* ('where those who are hanged are buried') and the excavation revealed numerous individuals who had clearly been executed, buried with their hands behind their backs, often face-down, in groups, occasionally reversed west-to-east, and probably fully clothed rather than stripped as many pins for holding clothing together were also found.[202]

Rural churches have also been the subject of archaeological work, both standing examples, as undertaken by Rodwell at the Essex churches of Asheldham and Hadstock in the east of England[203] and ruined examples, notably at the church of St Martin, Wharram Percy in Yorkshire.[204] Work at the latter led to consolidation of the ruined fabric and a recent reassessment of the building sequence.[205] Detailed archaeological assessment of standing fabric in Norfolk is also advancing understanding through study of medieval graffiti. A spectacular discovery at Binham appears to have located a scratched design for the great west window of the church, additional information for an important architectural feature (of 13th-century date) thought to be the earliest example, following Reims in France, of Gothic 'bar' tracery in England.[206]

Links between churches in Britain and on the continent have already been seen in the monuments that were imported to churches such as St Botolph, Boston in Lincolnshire (above, p. 95). However, architectural assessment of churches on the east coast of Scotland would suggest a strong link between the development of ecclesiastical style there and that of the Low Countries. The evidence is perhaps most compelling for the 15th century but is also visible earlier, at the cathedral in Aberdeen. Here the freestone crossing piers are considered unique in Scotland with parallels in the Netherlands.[207] Aberdeen had a thriving trade with the Low Countries and even a 14th-century bishop who may have been a canon in Bruges so it seems very likely that Dutch and Flemish influence was considerable.

The role of the church in assisting understanding of landscape development in the Middle Ages is one which has been reviewed in England by Morris [208] and briefly in the Netherlands by Stoepker.[209] Work on monasteries and their associated estates has proved particularly fruitful in advancing understanding on both sides of the North Sea. The role of Flemish monasteries in coastal management in Flanders has already been noted (above, p. 49). In Lincolnshire, analysis of the landscape by Stocker and Everson has shown how monasteries of the Witham Valley (Barlings, Kirkstead, Stixwould and others) have revealed a complex medieval network for the management of resources such as those of fishing, water fowling and woodland. This network was sufficiently effective to survive the Reformation.[210] The research stimulates thought with regard to other lowland riverine landscapes; the Nar valley in west Norfolk, for example, contains a monastic string of pearls with houses at Castle Acre, West Acre, Pentney, Blackborough, Marham, Shouldham and Wormegay. Only limited archaeological assessment to date has been undertaken for the lower valley area within which the last five of these lie but it was possible to conclude that 'Responsibility for the utilisation and maintenance of the fen must have fallen largely on these religious houses. It is not unreasonable ... to assume that they played a large part in canalising the River Nar in its present form .. they were able to exploit the resources offered by the fen: reeds and rushes, peat (turf) and the pasture for summer grazing'.[211]

Castle Acre priory is one of two monastic ruins in Norfolk which retain good (and rare) examples of 14th-century medieval wall-paintings. The other is within tomb canopies in the south wall of the nave of the Franciscan friary in Great Yarmouth. Analysis of these paintings has revealed not only exceptionally high quality of workmanship and expensive use of materials (such as azurite at Great Yarmouth and gilding and vermillion at both locations), it has also enabled an assessment of likely influences.[212] These seem to be English with the possibility of Norwich as the workshop centre. Excavation at the Franciscan friary in that city uncovered a medieval painter's palette fashioned out of an oyster shell and of early 14th-century date. It too contained trace of azurite and vermillion.[213] Sourcing the costly material of azurite, however, necessitated acquisition overseas; the early source was the mine at Chessy-Les-Mines in the Rhône region of France. It is a form of copper carbonate, gives a greenish blue and was a favourite colour in northern Europe.[214]

Fashions in colour changed in the Middle Ages with violet and black being coveted for clothing by the end of the 14th century. Archaeological research is now able to identify residual colour from textile fragments with the use of chromatography and spectrophotometry on material from London. The use of vivid colour may have been largely restricted to urban areas with their more affluent populations.[215] The evidence for mercantile trading in beautifully-coloured cloth becomes more obvious in the 15th century with information known from both sides of the North Sea.

— 4 —

The 15th Century: Towards Greater Sophistication

Coloured cloth was only one aspect of an increasing sophistication in the 15th century, witnessed by the evolution of a more complex world of ideas, a development of institutions and a flowering of art. The role of women within society is also more visible and, as with other disciplines, the need for a more gender-aware approach to the study of women is now being addressed, belatedly, by archaeology. The work of Roberta Gilchrist is particularly pertinent here. After initially concentrating upon religious women in East Anglia, she subsequently broadened her approach to one that sought to explore the role of gender archaeology as a concept, examining archaeological approaches to 'gender ... revealed as a metaphor for relations between men and women: gender is an expression of social practice and beliefs about sexual difference'.[1] This theoretical approach is complemented by her most recent work which provides an accessible study of the human medieval 'life course' through consideration of archaeological material and contexts while nevertheless still counselling that it remains important to 'avoid reducing the social complexities of gender to simply making male and female activities 'visible' in the archaeological record'.[2] Archaeological gender studies are now a focus of research within the North Sea region.

Women

One approach to understanding the role of women through the examination of material culture is to explore forces and beliefs that were important to women. Obvious female concerns are frequently those of conception of children and safe delivery of babies. Work by Carole Hill has explored how such concerns were expressed within the city of Norwich, identifying thereby spaces which were important to women. She has observed that St Anne, the mother of the Virgin Mary, was associated with conception and pregnancy and that, despite later iconoclasm, images of her still survive such as that in the 15th-century painted glass in the church of St Peter Mancroft. Similarly, St Margaret, the patron saint of women in labour, is also depicted in the Mancroft glass, a panel painting from the church of St Michael-at-Plea, a wall painting within Norwich cathedral, a bench end and a sculptural boss in the church of St Helen Bishopgate, on the stem of the font in St James Pockthorpe, and illustrated in the north porch spandrel of St Margaret Westwick. Such ubiquitous display suggests strongly how important this saint was to women in the city.[3]

The above examples within parish churches do not, of course, suggest gendered separation within the buildings. However, they do imply that certain locations within churches could—and frequently did—have important meaning for women in particular. In consequence, the identification of such spaces contributes an important reminder that women were integrated members of medieval society, not excluded or unnecessarily separated but with social and spiritual needs which could be met within society as a whole.

Specific gender separation did exist, notably within religious communities. Monastic institutions especially for women are obviously known from both sides of the North Sea, many locations being visible with surviving buildings (as at Lüneburg) or locatable through buried archaeology (as at Alkmaar in the Netherlands where there were three convents for women, the *Oude Hof*, the *Jonge Hof* and the *Middelhof*).[4] However, even such separated institutions did not necessarily mean a divorce from society; the great nunnery at Carrow, immediately outside the city wall of Norwich, not only operated local quarries but also owned property and churches within the city.

A particular form of religious activity specific to women was that characterised by beguinages, communities of women who were often spinsters or widows with their own discrete and disposable income. Frequently described as an urban movement halfway between the monastic and lay ways of life, the *Mulieres religiosae* originated *c.* 1200 in the diocese of Liège with most successor foundations in regions to the north and south dating to the 13th century. Following condemnation by the Pope in 1311, the institutions disappeared in northern France but were protected in the Low Countries. While, in consequence, these survivors tended to lose autonomy, their enclosures became strengthened with walls, thereby enhancing local distinctiveness. Sites existed—and in some case continue to exist—in locations such as Leuven, Mechelen, Ghent, Bruges, Leiden, Haarlem, Turnhout, Dendermonde, Diest, Brussels, Courtrai and Tongeren. Usually erected on marginal land some of these institutions began outside the urban area but, as the adjacent towns grew, became incorporated within them. Examples are Bruges, Brussels and Leuven, the last established in marshland which had to be drained. Others were never integrated into towns as at Bergen-op-Zoom, Liège where topographical factors militated against such inclusion, and Sint-Truiden which remained outside the town until the 19th century.

Morphologically, beguinages can be divided into two types—'street-beguinage' as at Leuven and 'courtyard-beguinage' as at Bruges, Turnhout or Diksmuide. The only excavation of medieval structures to date, at Schiedam near Rotterdam, has revealed individual timber-built houses for the beguines of either single- or double-room form with a fireplace. The 'great Mistress' of a beguinage is known to have had a house located close to the gatehouse and church. The churches normally formed their own distinct parishes thus enhancing spiritual as well as material and social control by the beguines themselves although priests would have had to be male. Indeed, the Beguine movement is asserted to have been 'created by women and for women—and not affiliated with, or supervised by, a male order'.[5] Their churches can generally be characterised as displaying 'architectural poverty' and it is instructive in the surviving examples to compare their architecture with prestige churches such as St Nicholas in Ghent.[6]

Decoration of the churches, however, where it survives, seems to have consisted mainly of female iconography such as the wise virgins at Leuven. A remarkable series of paintings, probably dating to the first decade of the 16th century, exists at Sint-Truiden in the eastern part of the nave. There is considerable focus on the Virgin with scenes such as the Annunciation, Visitation, Birth of Christ, Death of Mary and finally her heavenly Coronation. This series is supported by one depicting a range of female saints including St Ursula, St Elizabeth of Hungary, St Agatha, St Cecilia and St Mary Magdalen.[7]

The income of the beguines was often derived from work with textiles, such as bleaching, and laundries are frequently mentioned in documentation. Some 41 institutions survived the Reformation in the Low Countries, some being maintained into the 20th century. Those that still exist contain little visible medieval fabric, much rebuilding taking place, notably in the 16th and 17th centuries.

Beguinages appear to have been a phenomenon of the Low Countries but there is a tantalising suggestion that the concept, if not a copy of its execution, may have crossed the North Sea. In Norwich, there are 15th-century documentary references to two groups of women living in community in a manner akin to nuns but not linked to any known female monastic order. One of these groups lived in a house in St Laurence's parish previously owned by John Asger of whom only two individuals are known: either that John Asger who was a merchant of Bruges and mayor of Norwich in 1436; or his son John Asger who was born in Zeeland but became a citizen of Norwich. The possibility exists therefore that the community of women living here in the house from at least 1442 had' a tenuous link with the Low Countries, the heart of the beguine movement'.[8]

Figure 4.1 Norwich, Britons Arms, a possible 15th-century *beguinage* (Brian Ayers).

A third group of women was recorded in the 18th century (without a reference unfortunately) as living in a house in a corner of the churchyard of St Peter Hungate. This early 15th-century building still stands, a thatched structure with a doorway at first floor level on a sloping site, giving direct access to the churchyard and thus to the north door in the west end of the nave of the church (Figure 4.1). Buildings analysis suggests that, as constructed, the house consisted of a number of rooms on three self-contained floors, accessed by an external stair to the east, implying occupation by a community.[9]

Identifying roles for women in the archaeological record is difficult save when they occupy distinctive locations such as beguinages. Further such locations include anchorholds, places where women could follow a solitary life. Anchoresses were particularly common in Norfolk where some 42 different sites are recorded from the diocese of Norwich, the majority in the 15th century although the earliest example dates to the 11th century.[10] Occasional material remains survive such as the squint and blocked entrance to a demolished anchorhold against the north wall of the choir of the Dominican friary in Norwich.

Secular activity is more difficult to ascertain. It was noted above that dental analysis can on occasion differentiate occupations undertaken by the different sexes (p. 87) and skeletal material can also differentiate some urban females from those living in rural areas (p. 91). Female graves are, of course, common, sometimes strikingly and tragically so such as with the women who died in childbirth and were buried with stillborn neonates in the cemeteries of Hull's Augustinian friary, that of the Hospitaller preceptory of St John of Jerusalem in London, and that of the Carmelites in Aarhus.[11] The social status of certain women can be inferred from their burial location: a number of women were excavated from the walkway of the cloister of the Franciscan friary in Aalborg, Denmark, for instance [12]; this favourable position must have been reserved for individuals who were patrons or benefactors of the friary and therefore likely to be ranking members of society.

Children

A further important group within medieval society, also until recently not studied sufficiently, is that of children. As with examination of the role of women this is now changing. The remains of children can obviously be observed directly through skeletal material but their contribution to both the urban and rural economy, implied from documentary sources, is often difficult to see in the archaeological record. Toys survive for very young children. There are excellent examples of toys made of wood, bark, clay, amber, tin and pewter, dating from the 11th to the 15th centuries, from Gdańsk for instance.[13] However, as it is known that children as young as seven years could be considered as contributors to the economy, it would also be useful to determine archaeological evidence for this.

One area where it has been suggested that work by children can be seen is that concerning ceramics. A recent review by Mellor notes how it is possible to observe marks such as thumbprints on pottery vessels which, even allowing for shrinkage as clay dries, must have been made by children. Such involvement of minors (by modern consideration) has been identified on Siegburg stoneware dating from the 13th to the 15th centuries in Germany, in handprints from vessels at Wrenthorpe in Yorkshire where modern experimentation suggests that children were engaged in applying handles to jugs during manufacture, and on Grimston ware from East Anglia, the decoration of face jugs perhaps benefitting 'from a child's nimble fingers'.[14] Children probably turned half-dried bricks during the brick manufacture process in Malmö; impressions of children's hands and feet have been found on medieval bricks recovered from the city.[15]

Advancing techniques of palaeopathology are providing increasing evidence for stresses related to children and occasionally, when linked with other data, suggesting occupational activity. Examples of poor diet and vitamin deficiency in children are common amongst urban assemblages as at Norwich for instance where, in the cemetery of St Margaret *in combusto*, an impoverished parish abandoned in the mid 15th century, iron deficiency in childhood probably accounted for the condition called *cribra orbitalia* (pitting of the orbits of the skull) which was observed in 36 individuals.[16] Elsewhere in the same city, examination of burials from the Franciscan friary found a preponderance of subadults in an assemblage of 136 individuals with more than 40% of adults also dying before the age of 30. The Norwich friary was an internationally renowned *studium* so it is possible that this location was reserved for students (and probably women as well because some 16% of the adults were female).[17]

Recent research in Britain has explored the prevalence of skeletal disease in medieval children, collating data of 4,626 individuals from 95 sites. Analysis of the information was interpreted with consideration of ecological, social, economic and environmental conditions. Historical information indicated that 'childhood' probably persisted until about the age of 11 but that, from six years old, children 'began entering and interacting with the adult world' and gender differentiation of tasks became more marked. Occupational tasks would become formalised around the age of 12 although the palaeopathological results imply that contrary to 'previous interpretations that suggested the medieval child was thrust mercilessly into the adult world at a young age, these data indicate not only a sustained period of juvenility, but also a period of transition rather than an abrupt move into adulthood'. It was only with the onset of the Reformation in the 16th century, together with its profound social changes, that a pronounced negative impact upon children in the form of increased evidence of skeletal stress could be seen.[18] This interesting observation clearly cries out for similar research across the North Sea.

A perceived problem with studying children in the past is that they do not conform to social norms but are essentially anarchic, erupting into urban and rural spaces in unpredictable ways. An interesting essay by Sarah Smith, however, suggests that the manner in which spaces are organised can enable a greater understanding of the impact of medieval society upon children. She draws upon both historical geography and sociology to consider children within likely power relationships in rural medieval society. Her work examines the case of the 'North Manor' area at Wharram Percy in North Yorkshire where expansion of the complex removed earlier peasant tofts, and argues that this would have impacted upon 'children's very strong association ... between the home and feelings of safety due ... to the fact of the home's private, enclosed space'. Smith points out that families are of primary importance in the socialisation of children and that the destruction of such a place of safety by manorial lords would necessarily have an impact upon the children involved (indeed, this expression of power would have had 'strong effects on the types of cultural knowledge that is imparted to children'). The Wharram Percy example, therefore, emphasises the importance of archaeologists considering 'spatial reorganisation of medieval settlements, particularly domestic structures, in terms of their effect on medieval children'.[19]

Smith is also of interest when she considers observed settlement organisation and the inculcation of gender roles. Exploring tofts and crofts excavated at Wawne in eastern Yorkshire, she notes that in the 'Type C' house, the crofts themselves behind the houses were not delineated by boundaries. This would encourage socialisation between those largely charged with control of such areas (a 'taskspace' identified by Smith and others as predominantly female). Assuming that gendered roles are acquired through imitative action, girls thus socialising with their mothers within a largely female environment would acquire a more pronounced sense of gender identity within a social group than the more 'muted' sense gained within settlements where boundaries inhibited such contact and thereby necessarily emphasised the family group.[20]

More traditional archaeological studies of the world of children draw upon diagnostically identifiable artefacts associated with them. However, with the exception of toys and occasional discoveries of items of clothing and shoes, such objects are comparatively rare although commemoration in church memorials of children from the more affluent levels of society can indicate familial relationships and even suggest emotional ties. Other than these, medieval depictions of children tend to be admonitory such as the mid 15th-century wall painting from Tuse church on Zeeland, Denmark which shows a schoolmaster supervising his pupils with a birch.[21] In Norwich the imagery on a cathedral misericord is worse, with a child bent over the knee of a schoolmaster who is thrashing his bare buttocks. Four other boys studiously read their books.[22] These are adult views of children, not the evidence of children themselves. Such evidence is always going to be scarce but recognition of this scarcity is itself a positive step forward because it acknowledges that the absence of archaeological data for medieval children obviously does not mean that the children themselves were absent but were actually integral members of society and probably not treated very differently to adults, adding to their 'invisibility'. Identifying them and their roles more closely, therefore, will require new methodological approaches.

Housing

The context of rural housing was alluded to above when considering children in a peasant community in Yorkshire. With regard to urban housing there has been considerable research in recent years as a result of the number of excavations undertaken within urban areas ahead of modern redevelopment. Such work has resulted in a plethora of excavation reports for buildings now lost but is also increasingly augmented by assessments of standing buildings. Domestic houses of 15th-century date necessarily survive in greater numbers than those of earlier centuries although a problem with standing structures is that almost all of the survivors represent the homes of the more affluent classes within medieval society rather than the poorest members of that society. Thus, excavation of the houses of the urban poor is particularly valuable—and can be startling. Atkin reviewed clay-built structures and discovered that not only were they necessarily small but that they were frequently unheated.[23] He found that their use persisted in Norwich well into the 15th century with one such single-storeyed building, constructed with posts encased in clay, only having a loft inserted *c.* 1450, probably at around the time that a central hearth was also created (Figure 4.2).

Such persistence of an impoverished urban building type seems to have occurred more rarely across the North Sea. The results presented at a colloquium held in Lübeck in 1999 on housing suggested that buildings constructed with timbers in post-holes or on padstones did not generally continue beyond the 14th century and were frequently being replaced by more substantial houses in the 13th century. Only in Zutphen was a post-built 14th-century house recorded and, as has been seen (above, p. 102), this town

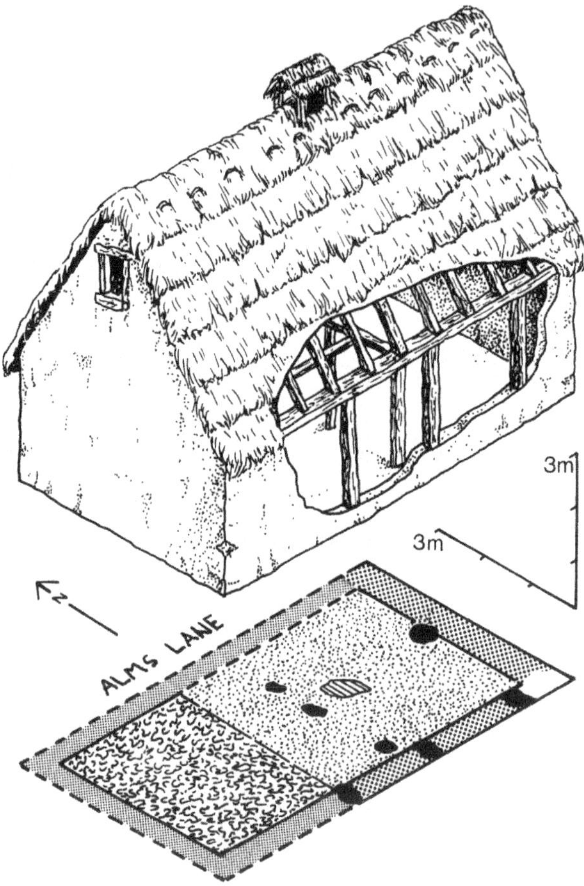

Figure 4.2 Reconstruction of excavated clay-walled house, Norwich *c.* 1450 (Norwich Survey).

too was generally upgrading its housing stock at that time. However other work, particularly in smaller towns, notes that the tradition of simple timber construction lasted into the 15th century; excavations adjacent to the market place in the small town of Heide in Schleswig Holstein have recovered a hall house with two very narrow aisles of this date, built above post-holes (it was only replaced in the mid-16th century) (Figure 4.3).[24] In larger towns, however, brick-built structures occurred earlier. Timber houses in the Hessenburg area of Nijmegen were rebuilt in brick in the 14th century (and were occupied by a beguinage in the early 15th century)[25]. *Dielenhäuser,* large brick-built structures with a lofty ground-floor hall (below, p. 170) were known in Lübeck from the mid 13th century, Lüneburg at the beginning of the 14th century and, at the same time, in Deventer, Greifswald, Rostock, Uelzen and Zutphen. They were extant within Stade by the 15th century and, further east, in Gdánsk.

Cellars were common beneath *Dielenhäuser.*[26] Numerous examples of late medieval date have been recorded in Bremen[27] while others remain on Oude Gracht in Utrecht. Here archaeological buildings' analysis has recorded a range of patrician buildings, 'large, sturdy brick houses' where, in some instances, the commercial front part of the house was constructed in brick and the rear, familial, part of timber-frame.[28] At Alkmaar, also in the Netherlands, fire destruction in 1972 of two late medieval and early post-medieval buildings on Langestraat was followed by archaeological excavation, some limited building recording of walls that survived the fire, and documentary study. This work revealed that Langestraat 113 also had a brick-built frontage above a vaulted cellar. Its neighbour at 115/117, brick

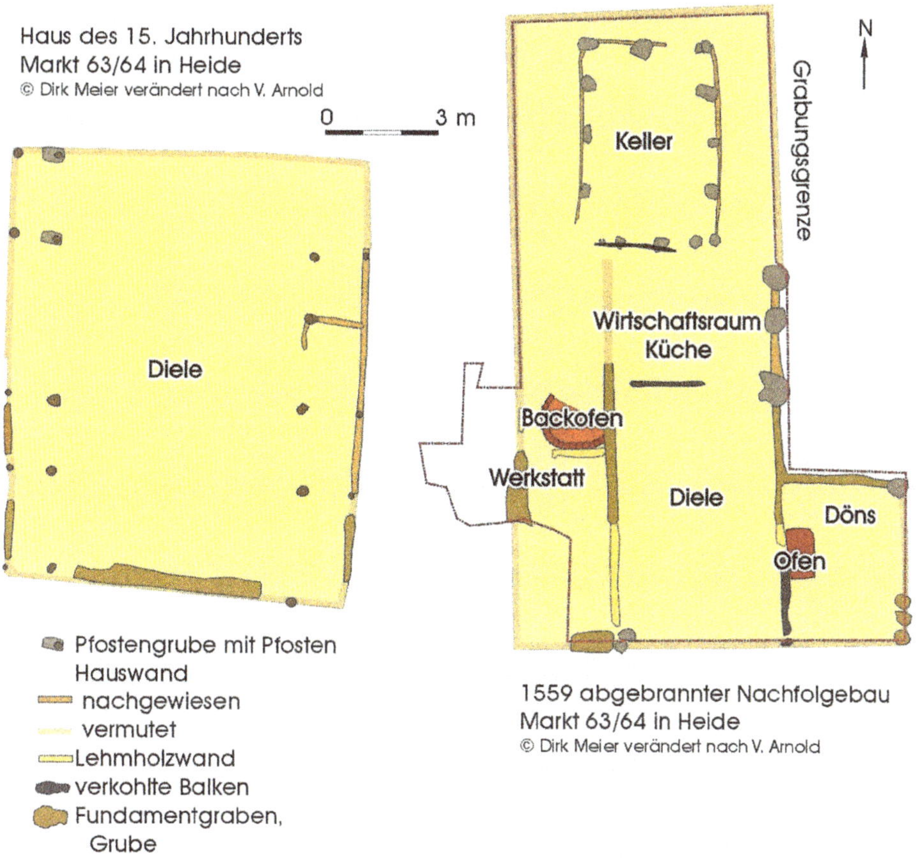

Figure 4.3 Heide—plan of excavated 15th-century house with its 16th-century replacement (Dirk Meier).

with timber to the rear, appears to have been occupied by relatively impoverished inhabitants until 1425 when the house was extended and, by the first half of the 16th century, became associated with a cesspit containing rich finds of decorated Cologne stoneware, southern Netherlandish majolica plates and Spanish lustreware.[29]

Excavations at 's-Hertogenbosch have shown that brick-built houses with cellars stood around the marketplace from the 13th and 14th centuries. Initially the cellars were sealed in timber but brick vaults were added subsequently. The houses were constructed on sandy ridges above steep slopes towards a rivulet, the cellars effectively forming a platform for the houses above.[30] A similar disposition of cellared brick buildings has been noted at Groningen where, unsurprisingly, the majority of large vaulted examples occur in the commercially important areas around the marketplace and at the waterfront.[31] In England, such association of undercrofts and mercantile use can be seen even in very small centres such as the village of Worstead in Norfolk. This village gave its name to the woollen cloth which formed the basis of much of the late medieval economy of East Anglia and a 15th-century ribbed brick-vaulted undercroft still survives beneath St Andrew's Cottage here, with access stairs from the exterior on the market place at Church Plain.[32]

At Norwich, the construction of brick-vaulted undercrofts beneath merchants' houses began in the late 14th century, becoming common in the 1400s, especially on the south bank of the River Wensum where the sloping ground favoured the building of such structures to provide flat platforms. A survey undertaken in the late 1970s and early 1980s showed that these fireproof cellars were both groined and barrel-vaulted, often with access staircases surviving. Non-domestic undercrofts were accessed from the exterior, facilitating separate occupation and perhaps enhancing rental possibilities. Some 54 such undercrofts are known to survive with 34 more having been destroyed.[33] Some at least were for public use; the vaults of the White Swan Inn, lamentably destroyed in 1961, were clearly an extension of the tavern above although, contrary to a previously published summary, the plastered brick wall recorded during demolition and decorated with a charging horseman on a frieze panel with a blue border and a diaper of red rosettes and pale blue birds, was part of the buttery of the superstructure, not the vaulted undercroft.[34]

It might be expected that ports susceptible to flooding in low-lying marshy areas would lack such cellared structures. This indeed seems to have been the case in Hull but elsewhere undercrofts could provide a platform within poor ground for the house above. This probably accounts for the early Clifton House undercroft in King's Lynn which stands on an infilled area of the River Ouse foreshore (above, p. 36) and also for the Howard Street undercroft in Great Yarmouth, now well away from the haven on South Quay but nevertheless providing a secure platform above the sand spit upon which the town sits. At Newcastle several undercrofts survive, notably The Cooperage on the landward side of The Close and this building, together with those at Milbank House and Surtees House, must have provided storage for goods unloaded at the neighbouring quayside. All seem to date from around 1400.[35] No doubt they were used on occasion for the storage of wine, as were undercrofts in London such as that of Gerard's (Gisor's) Hall in Basing Lane (probably constructed by a wine merchant). This London example, however, in common with most other known examples there, was built earlier (in *c.* 1290) and few of the known surviving London examples of vaulted structures can be dated to the 15th century. Instead, new London cellars seemed generally to have been covered by wooden ceilings, emphasising a probable exclusive use for storage.[36]

Few of the houses above the Norwich undercrofts were constructed of stone or brick. Indeed most were of timber and themselves therefore vulnerable to fire. In consequence, many 15th-century vaulted undercrofts are known to survive beneath later buildings, as on Elm Hill where all the celebrated timber-framed structures (save one, the isolated Britons Arms—see above, p. 113) are 16th- and 17th-century in date following a disastrous fire in 1507. Many nevertheless contain earlier cellars. Other victims of the same extensive fire were houses to the west on Pottergate but here the cellars were ceiled in timber and the contents of the destroyed buildings collapsed into them. Excavation in 1974 uncovered the well-preserved contents of late medieval kitchens as well as finds such as fragments of German stove-tiles and part of a terracotta plaque decorated with the image of St John the Baptist. Such discoveries within a house of the likely middling sort of urban society indicate an aspirant culture with good continental links.[37] Moreover, the *variety* of kitchen equipment recovered, if not the quality, was considered by the excavators to be 'on a par with a nobleman's well-to-do household of the period' (the comparison was with documentary evidence from an inventory of goods in the kitchens of Sir Roger Wodehouse at the manorial site of Kimberley, Norfolk).[38]

In urban England, therefore, timber-framing persisted although increasingly producing buildings of greater technological sophistication. It can be argued that the use of timber increased the flexibility of buildings and that changes in fashion and use also encouraged construction in wood. Anthony Quiney suggests that the early stone house, still largely extant at 29–32 King Street, King's Lynn, was given a new frontage in the 15th century 'fashionably recast in timber so as to include shops'.[39] The White Swan Inn in Norwich, mentioned above, was rebuilt about 1404 and included external decorative wooden brackets. One of these survives, the bracket enhanced by the sculptured figure of a young man in a closely-fitted buttoned garment and with a low-slung belt.[40] Timber-framed urban houses could be elaborate constructions; Little Hall, Lavenham in Suffolk, almost certainly an affluent clothier's house of perhaps 1390, has been described as 'ostentatious', its jettied cross-wing enhanced by herringbone timber bracing.

Within rural contexts as well, the increasing sophistication of timber-framing was illustrated forty years ago by Cecil Hewett who, working on buildings in Essex, demonstrated the innovative approaches to carpentry which buildings required by the later Middle Ages. One building alone, that known as Rookwood Hall and dating to *c.* 1440, has a complex series of timber joints used to effect both its wall construction and that of its roof.[41] Elsewhere in the east of England, Letheringham Lodge in Suffolk has recently been dated by dendrochronology to 1472–75. A curious structure, again moated but situated within a very small moat, it is a square building jettied on all four sides with decorated corner posts. It probably served as a form of banqueting house within a park, parallels for which seem to be continental. Edward Martin has pointed out the similarity of the structure in terms of its location and general decorative design to that of small moated buildings in Flanders.[42]

Rookwood and Letheringham were buildings from the upper strata of society, illustrating a flamboyant use of timber as a building material but one which nevertheless perhaps betrays an innate conservatism in England despite influences surrounding usage from mainland Europe. Peasant buildings, where the occupants probably had less opportunity for innovation, were similarly conservative as can be seen from the results of archaeological excavation. Work at Wharram Percy and the nearby deserted village site of Cowlam on the Yorkshire Wolds have both uncovered evidence for late medieval structures which were essentially cruck-built houses with roofs of thatch.[43] The contrast with the rural environment of the Low Countries is marked as can be seen from the large-scale excavations undertaken at Walraversijde. Here, the rebuilding necessitated by storm realignment of the dune system (above, p. 94) was undertaken in brick, resulting in substantial structures (now reconstructed using information from archaeological excavations). The houses were erected in rows either parallel with or at right-angles to the coastline. In further contrast to Wharram Percy or Cowlam, there was little space around the buildings which occupied almost urban-like property strips. Indeed, the density of inhabitants suggested from both archaeological and documentary sources for Flemish fishing communities such as Walraversijde has been characterised as reflecting an urban environment. The walls of the houses were plastered on the interior, with the plasterwork sometimes being decorated. Occasional evidence of glass windows was also located. Roofs seem to have been thatched, floors were of brick or clay, and heat was provided by burning wood or peat. Outside surface areas were generally of stone although these were linked to the houses by brick pavements.[44]

It is clear that the built environment of a fishing community such as Walraversijde was markedly different to that of a contemporary village on the Yorkshire Wolds. However several factors need to be considered when exploring the different approaches to such rural housing. Firstly there is that of availability of materials; timber was almost certainly easier to obtain in northern England, even on the Yorkshire Wolds, than in the Flemish coastal region. Secondly, investment in Flanders is likely to have been more 'top-down' than in England; the rebuilt 15th-century Walraversijde is known to have been controlled by a small number of individuals (above, p. 94). Thirdly, the economic nature of Walraversijde needs to be considered. While the community was obviously engaged in typical rural activities such as peat digging, agriculture and the breeding of stock, the predominant activity concerned fishing and, in particular, the processing of fish. The evidence suggests a small quasi-industrial complex where fish were prepared for onward sale. Plaice were certainly being processed as shown by examination of a dense concentration of flatfish remains where the heads, tails and stomach contents of some 130 plaice were recognised, the edible part of the fish presumably sold on for consumption elsewhere. In addition, small rectangular structures interpreted as smoke-ovens were recovered, the capacity of which would ensure over-production if merely intended for consumption by a single household. Indeed, it was noted above (p. 86) that the evidence of isotopes from Walraversijde indicated that fish consumption within the community itself was actually very low.[45] The impression is one of onward sale of the fish resource with profit being ploughed back into the housing stock of the village.

Economic activity

Interpretation of archaeological discoveries at Walraversijde enables further insights into economic activity at this celebrated site. Numerous barrels, frequently reused as linings of wells and cesspits, were recovered and, through dendro-provenancing, have been established as made of Baltic timber (nearly all from the Gdánsk region), imported to Flanders between 1380 and 1430 within hanseatic vessels. It is considered that the barrels probably carried herring to the port of Sluis where repacking following shrinkage and brine evaporation created a surplus of containers which were then re-used locally. The known collapse of the hanseatic herring trade to Flanders after 1430 coincides with a lack of re-used barrels from the excavation.[46]

As well as timber artefacts, study of ceramics from a range of coastal or near coastal sites in Flanders has revealed interesting contacts between the region and the Mediterranean in the 15th century. The sites examined vary themselves in type: from the great entrepôt of Bruges, through the smaller ports of Damme and Sluis, to the fishing settlement of Walraversijde. Finds of Spanish Malagan or Andalusian, Valencian and Sevilla majolica have been recorded together with two fragments of a possible Tuscan bowl from Italy. While careful to point out that 'these Mediterranean imports clearly do not represent a major item within the households ..'. it is noted that 'they are a recurrent phenomenon' at both coastal sites and also, but perhaps to a slightly lesser extent, at inland sites.[47] Indeed, the admittedly speculative analysis (due to the lack of comparanda) suggests that while the Spanish majolica wares penetrated inland to locations such as Bruges, indicating high status consumption here, finds of this exotic pottery were reasonably significant at the coast. Sherds located at the coast were not necessarily the result of transshipment breakage. It is suggested that, just as majolica at affluent urban sites might be indicative of conspicuous consumption, so too the incidence of these ceramics at settlements such Walraversijde may demonstrate that individuals here had sufficient means to own—and perhaps even display—quality vessels. Such treatment seems to be mirrored at Flemish monastic sites as well where observations from excavations suggest that, on average, Valencian majolica was only thrown away some 50 to 75 years after it has been manufactured, implying that it was not put to daily use but treated with care.[48]

Late medieval fishing communities along the Flemish coast, therefore, seem to have existed within a commercial framework, partly at least in contact with international trading networks, whereby the acquisition and processing of fish employed relatively dense numbers of people who profited by feeding into a market which helped to provision populous Low Countries urban settlements such as Bruges, Ghent and Antwerp. Control appears to have been exercised by a small number of oligarchs who would obviously take profit but were probably also ploughing some of that profit back into the village environment in order to ensure an efficient and effective workforce for a reliable product. As ever, form followed function assisted by the benefit of ready access to a wide range of markets. In contrast, at Wharram Percy in northern England, the function was more local. Walraversijde could boast majolica from Spain, ceramics from England, the Rhineland and southern France, amber and wood from the Baltic, and whetstones from Scandinavia. Despite the justified claim that in the late Middle Ages 'the inhabitants of Wharram can be seen in constant contact with the outside world',[49] that world was more circumscribed than that of their Flemish counterparts. Lava hand-querns from the Rhineland and Norwegian whetstones plus, in one case, German stoneware by about 1500, cannot be compared favourably with access to Mediterranean ceramics and interaction with hanseatic traders.

Archaeological research is increasingly developing an understanding of economic development in northern Europe, particularly through the study of tradable goods and of the relationship of manufacture to that trade. Stove tiles are a good example of this. Use of these tiles probably originated in southern Germany in the 13th century but became widely adopted in northern Europe by the 15th century, lead-glazed interconnecting earthenware tiles being used to create the walls of enclosed stoves and to assist radiation of heat. However, such stove tiles were difficult to transport being very fragile. In order to help distribution, therefore, the solution was either to export the technological expertise for their manufacture (through travelling specialists) or to trade in moulds for stove tile manufacture.

Fabric analysis suggests that most stove tiles in the Baltic region were manufactured locally. Excavations of late15th-century sites on Fischergrube in Lübeck and on Pläterstraße in Rostock have revealed stove tile moulds and wasters, including matrix-identical moulds for a religious sequence of the *Charity of St Martin.*[50] Further work in Greifswald in north Germany and Malmö in southern Sweden where links between stove tile design have been observed, imply a range of 'satellite workshops' exploiting sea-links to develop trade in such tiles in the immediate pre-Reformation period through the movement of craftspeople and moulds.[51]

It is interesting to compare the widespread evidence for the adoption of enclosed stove technology in continental northern Europe with its clearly slow, almost grudging, adoption in the British Isles. Excavation is beginning to recover fragmentary examples of tiles from locations such as London, Norwich and Edinburgh, all either ports on the east coast or cities with ease of access to the North Sea and therefore well-placed for imports. Examples such as a late 15th-century fragment from Norwich seem to be of continental manufacture and thus it is possible that the technology and the skills associated with it were not exported to Britain. Such export to places like Tallinn and Riga may well have been facilitated by the essential German character of settlement there, in contrast to the very controlled manner with which any German visitors to England were compelled to accept. It is important to recall that, even in a port such as King's Lynn with its well-documented and extensive trade with the Baltic, German merchants only obtained their own warehouse as late as 1475 following hanseatic success in war against England and the provisions of the 1474 Treaty of Utrecht.[52]

In the previous chapter (above, p. 106) it was noted how David Gaimster characterised the spread of red earthenwares as a form of 'cultural signature'. Similarly, he observes that the spread of stove tiles acts as a 'key comparative measure of long-distance trade together with cultural and technological transfer'. Stove tiles are thus a 'Hansa type-fossil', another 'cultural signature' within northern Europe (and the Baltic in particular).[53] However, this conclusion is disputed by Atzbach who points out that if one regards the Hansa 'as a more or less organised cooperation between trading towns and there [sic] most important families ... A specific expression of its explicit urban and civil culture might be expected in its stove tiles, which could be represented e.g. by the series of the coats of arms of Hanseatic towns or the depiction of the cog as symbol and basis of the Hansa's common wealth'. However, tile stoves were not used to convey this sort of imagery or iconography even though hanseatic production of them is known.[54]

Atzbach notes that the actual iconography displayed on tiles is of scenes such as the Birth of Christ, the Adoration of the Magi, the Virgin and Child with St Anne and the like. He therefore considers the distribution of stove tiles to have been one fostered by imitation rather than conscious and deliberate cultural transfer. In truth, the exact impetus behind the geographical spread is impossible to know but it is likely to have been a mixture of commercial marketing, imitative adoption, awareness of a superior technological product, and fashion. Whatever the impetus, as noted above archaeological evidence is now clearly showing production of tiles in diverse locations in a similar manner to that noted for the production and trade of red earthenwares.

Industrial output in portable artefacts was frequently concentrated in the towns of northern Europe. A review published as a result of one of the Lübeck colloquia on urban archaeology in the hanseatic region provides much detailed information of a range of craft activities. Viborg in Denmark alone in the 15th century housed tailors, shoemakers, weavers, furriers, metal-workers of many types (cutlers, coppersmiths, swordmakers and pewterers for instance), glaziers and coopers with archaeological evidence for woodworking and brickmaking. The town probably also produced bells in the late 14th and 15th century, a corpus of 11 surviving bells cast by one Nicolaus with inscriptions so closely matching that the letters appear to be all from the same mould.[55] In Norwich both documentary and archaeological evidence combine to provide a good understanding of an extensive manufacture and trade in bells (as well as other artefacts such as the manufacture of metal cauldrons in the same locations). Much of the bell-founding of the city was in the hands of the Brasyer family from the first half of the 15th century and they may have been responsible for the bell-founding pit located in 1989 in the churchyard of St John Timberhill.[56] Further bell-founding waste has also been recovered nearby off Ber Street while, in the late 15th century, an exceptionally well-preserved bell casting pit was excavated at the Franciscan

Figure 4.4 Norwich, excavation at Mountergate with layer of sheep and goat horn cores and excavator Frances Green (Brian Ayers).

Friary. This contained the remains of a ring-shaped pedestal of brick and roof tile which supported a loam mould and the carbonised remains of a post for pivoting the wooden template which shaped the bell.[57] Archaeo-magnetic dating of the feature enabling dating to between 1490 and 1525, suggesting that either Richard Brasyer the younger (who died in 1513) or his former apprentice, John Aleyn, was the bell-founder concerned.[58]

The Brasyers were a wealthy dynasty, much of this wealth probably the result of their manufacturing business. They chose St Anne's chapel in the large church of St Stephen for their chantry around 1435 and much of the north aisle of the church was subsequently covered with representations of their family arms.[59] Other mercantile families used the parish churches in a similar manner. Robert Toppes, a rich cloth merchant who become both mayor of Norwich and a member of parliament, gave an extensive scheme of window glass to the church of St Peter Mancroft in the mid-15th century. Much of this survives and includes detailing of the fabrics worn by figures such as the Virgin and St Elizabeth (the latter wears a richly-decorated front-laced maternity dress, the former an ermine-lined mantle). The cloth depicted is not only luxurious but was perhaps also advertising the quality of the wares that Toppes himself marketed.[60]

The trade in cloth remained as important in the 15th century as it had been earlier, particularly between England and the Low Countries, the two major centres of manufacture, but also with regard to onward distribution. The importance of luxury cloth, made with English fine hair wools, has recently been discussed by Munro; he highlights in particular the production in Ghent and Mechelen in Flanders and Essex in England.[61] Wholesale marketing of cloth took place in key locations such as London or Bruges, in the latter city of which the Cloth Hall still stands. Retail distribution was frequently handled by German merchants often operating from Lübeck and it was probably through such merchants that Low Countries (or possibly English) fabrics dyed with madder reached Finland, remnants of which were recovered from excavation of late 14th- and 15th-century deposits in Turku in 1998.[62]

Archaeological evidence for cloth-finishing within towns is known from at least the 12th century onwards, with evidence summarised above (p. 76). Other specialist urban production can also be explored archaeologically. Tanning, for instance, is either documented or known from excavation in Beverley, Hull, London, Norwich, Bruges, Braunschweig, Einbeck, Göttingen, Greifswald, Hamburg, Lübeck, Lüneburg, Rostock, Soest, Stade, Stralsund, Gdánsk, Elblag (Elbing), Kołobrzeg (Kolberg), Turku, Malmö, Bergen, Oslo, Aarhus and Viborg among the towns represented at the Lübeck *Stadtarchäologie* colloquia. Discoveries include tanners' tools from Stade and a possible tanners' vat of wood from Turku.[63] Tanning was obviously a common activity, producing leather, a clear necessity, but it also produced vellum from calf, sheep and goat skins. Excavation in 2015 at Mountergate in Norwich, uncovered great quantities of sheep or goat horncores suggesting significant production of vellum. The site was not only conveniently located next to the river for a water supply but also lay between the Augustinian and Franciscan friaries and close to the Benedictine priory, all consumers of vellum for manuscripts (Figure 4.4).[64]

Other high quality production concerned that of painted glass. The two greatest centres for this in England were York and Norwich. Both cities retain glass within some of their buildings—at York, most famously in the Minister and the church of All Saints, North Street; in Norwich, pre-eminently in the church of St Peter Mancroft but also in locations such as St Peter Hungate and the Guildhall. Excavations have also produced glass; work at Blake Street, York uncovered some 500 fragments of painted glass on a site close to the painters' guild church of St Helen;[65] in Norwich, painted glass has been recovered at the sites of the Franciscan and Carmelite friaries, late 14th-century glass from the latter quite probably from a window known to have been donated by John of Gaunt.[66]

Some of the 15th-century Norwich glass shows clear continental influences and not all of it was produced for church buildings. Secular production is also known. The townhouse of Sir John Fastolf in Norwich contained 15th-century painted glass until the 18th century[67] and fragments of secular painted glass showing schemes such as the months of the year survive, either reset into church windows or in museums, as at the Burrell Collection in Glasgow. The documentary evidence for Norwich glaziers in the 15th and early 16th centuries is particularly good and includes one female glazier, Helen Mundeford, who died in 1458, and was the wife of William Mundeford who seems to have been a Dutch glazier working in the city (below, p. 136).[68] In York, a specialised but perhaps non-local secular urban industry is hinted at in the Nine Orders of Angels window of *c.* 1410 at All Saints, North Street, where a man is depicted wearing a pair of spectacles, one of the earliest such images (Figure 4.5). A pair of spectacle frames similar in form and manufactured from bone was found at the Thames waterfront site of Trig Lane in London in 1974–1975. The discovery was made within a deposit dated to about 1440, the style of the frames suggesting manufacture in the Low Countries. Fifteenth-century documentation lists considerable numbers of spectacles imported into England from the continent.[69]

The urban economy and investment in infrastructure

The development of high-quality products such as painted glass was obviously associated with buildings within which it could be set. The Norwich glass was exported widely to its hinterland so that much that survives, albeit fragmentary, can still be seen in rural parish churches. Within the city, however, the glass was associated with an extraordinary 15th-century ecclesiastical building boom whereby practically every surviving church within the city (and some 48 were standing in the 1400s from a total of about 60 parish churches in the 13th century) was subject to refurbishment. This necessarily meant investment from the urban elite, an investment which points to a buoyant urban economy, not always reflected elsewhere. Alan Dyer has noted that, for English towns after 1377 and through the 15th century, urban centres such as Bristol, Beverley, Coventry, Lincoln, Winchester and York lost population (and taxable wealth) while other centres such as Norwich and Exeter grew. He suggests several reasons for this, from geographic influence on industrial production to increasing isolation from water-borne commerce while Kermode notes how cities such as Norwich were able to specialise successfully in cloth while other towns could exploit 'extremely localised activities' as in Great Yarmouth where 'maisemakers'

Figure 4.5 York, All Saints—detail of painted glass showing donor wearing spectacles (Brian Ayers).

produced boxes for the lucrative herring trade. Dyer also links urban problems to ones in the countryside, noting that the hinterlands of towns were clearly influential partners in economic activity.[70]

The physical impact of economic growth in cities such as Norwich is manifest through clear investment in major structures, notably its churches. One could argue that the lack of large-scale investment in the churches of York at the same period was symptomatic of a lack of similar growth. Care needs to be taken with this assessment because the state of all the pre-Reformation churches in Norwich is not known; following 16th-century losses, only 36 parish churches were left standing and it is reasonable to assume that these may well have represented those with the most economic as well as demographic support. The church of St Margaret *in combusto* (above, p. 109), for example, was probably never popular being used for the burial of executed prisoners.[71] It had closed by about 1450. Nevertheless, a buoyant 15th-century economy elsewhere in Norwich can be seen in its new Guildhall of 1406 onwards, a new Market Cross in 1411 (a two-storied structure with a chapel on the first floor, demolished in the 18th century), and construction of city watermills across the river (operational in 1430 and illustrated on a drawing of *c*. 1540).[72]

How far is such buoyancy visible in the towns and cities of north-western continental Europe at the same time? The evidence is mixed. Bruges, for example, remains dominated by a range of extraordinary medieval buildings of which the *Lakenhalle* or Cloth Hall and its belfry is both the most obvious and is early—work probably started on this structure around 1240. Another prestigious 13th-century building was the Water Hall, a covered hall for goods from river craft on the Markt, built between 1284 and 1294 and demolished in 1787. However, numerous substantial structures were still being erected well into the 15th century, despite the fact that it is clear that silting of the city's connection to the sea was progressively worsening; as late as 1478 the German hanseatic merchants rebuilt their property in Bruges as a large house with a tower known as the Oosterlingenhuis (or 'Easterlings House').[73] This brick structure, with attractive blind arcading, remains standing although shorn of its tower.

The material fabric of Ghent too seems to show mixed messages. The city lost much of its cloth trade in the 15th century but nevertheless appears to have maintained a vibrant economy, maximising its role as a regional centre through use of the rivers Leie and Scheldt until the continued rise of Antwerp effectively ended its prosperity. In consequence, the construction of major buildings in the 15th century provides material evidence of ongoing investment: the Butchers' Hall (*Vleeshalle*) was begun in 1407 and completed in 1419 (Figures 4.6 and 4.7); the Cloth Hall (*Lakenhalle* as in Bruges) dates from 1425–1445; and the core of the present Town Hall (*Stadhuis*) dates from 1482–1484. Building work also continued in English towns suffering a similar 'decline'. Boston in Lincolnshire is widely seen as suffering a considerable drop in economic activity in the 15th century but its great church of St Botolph was dramatically improved with the construction of its colossal tower during the 1400s, a project which is perhaps at least partially explained by the use and funding of much of the church by wealthy guilds (Figure 4.8).[74]

One aspect of urban fabric where 15th-century investment can be seen is that of continued and developing use of trading places and residences for alien merchants in the major towns and ports of northern Europe. As noted in a recent review by Jansen, such locations were primarily for German merchants of the Hanse, operating in places such as London, Bruges, Bergen and Novgorod, at their celebrated hanseatic *Kontore*, but also having 'factories' or *Stahlhöfen* in other ports.[75] As mentioned above (p. 121) the *Stahlhof* warehouse in King's Lynn, the only such to survive in Britain, was acquired as late as 1475. As far as can be judged from analysis of the fabric, it was unlikely to have been a purpose-built structure but more probably an adaptation of a pre-existing merchant house complex, one where domestic occupation existed side-by-side with commercial storage. The standing structure consists of two parallel ranges, one timber-framed and the other of brick, at right-angles to the river, and with an early 16th-century cross-range at the street frontage (Figure 4.9). A further cross-range may also have existed at the river end. The southern warehouse range is two storeys in height, the brick northern range is three storeys and was devoid of windows in its northern (external) wall.[76] The building clearly provided security against both theft and fire.

The hanseatic warehouse wings at Lynn appear never to have been sub-divided internally, suggesting that they were primarily used for storage of bulk goods. This is in contrast to the London *Kontor* (known

Figure 4.6 Ghent—Butchers' meat hall of 1402–1419 (Brian Ayers).

Figure 4.7 Ghent—Butchers' meat hall of 1402–1419: detail of the roof (Brian Ayers).

as the Steelyard, an anglicisation of *Stahlhof*), a complex which seems to have reached its maximum size about 1475 and where a plan of *c.* 1598 shows the buildings here to have been divided into numerous small rooms or stalls. The appearance of the site can be seen on Hollar's panorama of London of 1647.[77]

Most of the hanseatic residences seem to have been gated communities enabling control by the Hanse of contact between their merchants and the indigenous population as well as protective storage for goods. Surviving physical evidence is scarce across northern Europe although documentary evidence can help towards an understanding of their organisation (such evidence is particularly good for Novgorod). It is also clear that reciprocal arrangements for alien merchants operating in hanseatic ports and cities were much less common. Only in Gdańsk is there clear evidence of a building used by merchants, that of the *Artushof*, where a great hall of the St George's guild was eventually also opened to aliens (such as the English from about 1492). However, this was not a *Kontor* or a *Stahlhof*, more a meeting hall and alien merchants were therefore not as privileged as Germans were elsewhere. The *Artushof* named, somewhat extraordinarily, after King Arthur and the Knights of the Round Table was perhaps itself an English import. It was much remodelled in the 16th century and severely damaged in 1945 but still stands, east of the Town Hall on the Long Market in Gdańsk. English activity there is commemorated in the opening of a bawdy 16th-century tale:

> '... it fortuned in the worthy Cytye of Danswyke that two yonge marchauntes went walkyng together to warde a place called artus gardyn, whych stoode in the market place...'[78]

As has long been recognised therefore, the economic decline often perceived in later medieval towns is a moveable feast, perhaps best summarised by the title of Salter and Higgins's 2000 paper ('What is urban decline: desolation, decay and destruction, or an opportunity?').[79] Archaeology is beginning to provide the sort of evidence that can contribute to the debate, as illustrated by work in 's-Hertogenbosch in the Netherlands. Here analysis of two 15th-century pottery kilns, excavated in 1984 and 1995, combined with documentary sources, explored how two such polluting industries could survive—and apparently thrive at least for a while—in the centre of a densely-occupied town when such industrial activity elsewhere was increasingly being undertaken in rural areas (documents show how widespread

Figure 4.8 Boston showing the River Witham and the tower of St Botolph's church (Brian Ayers).

Figure 4.9 King's Lynn—courtyard of Hanseatic warehouse (Brian Ayers).

such rural activity was in the region of s'Hertogenbosch, presumably in competition with the urban industry). The range of products from the urban kilns, some of which (such as stove tiles and candle-makers' troughs) it was considered were made-to-order items, led to the conclusion that the potters were successfully targeting their market in a manner 'fully directed at and integrated in the urban economy'.[80] In 's-Hertogenbosch, at least, the town was therefore able to retain earlier industrial functions through specialisation of manufacture which might otherwise have been lost to rural locations. This small example of turning a late medieval economic weakness to advantage was no doubt played out in a range of urban activities across the North Sea zone, underlining the complex problem of achieving an understanding of overall stability, growth or 'decline'.

The work in s'Hertogenbosch can be seen as an example of archaeologists more broadly responding to Astill's exhortation to consider 'the productive capabilities and [the] reproductive efficiency' of later medieval towns. He especially emphasised the bio-archaeological possibilities for research and the potential for archaeology to contribute to 'underlying structural change'. His use of this phrase is interesting as he finds the concept 'difficult to reconcile with an idea of late-medieval decline'.[81] Indeed, examination of material culture as an archaeologist tempts one to consider that the word 'decline' is too often used as a synonym for 'change'. Later medieval society was changing, in both towns and the countryside, as a result of environmental factors, such as climate change, demographic decline in the aftermath of the Black Death and other epidemics, economic transitions, and developing technologies. Archaeological examination of data relating to such a varied set of indicators could well impact upon an understanding of societal transformation.

The 'decline' of major towns in the 15th century clearly had an impact upon a wider community than the town itself. Small towns and villages in the hinterland of Bruges, for instance, along the slowly-silting sea channel called the Zwin, certainly suffered with some settlements becoming deserted. Archaeological work is now investigating these settlements, concentrating on places such as Hoeke, Monnikerede, Michem, Koolkerke and Bonem and using a combination of traditional and new survey techniques. At Monnikerede the application of LiDAR technology is generating information on the geomorphology of the area as well as the micro-topography of this outport of Bruges which is now arable farmland (its fields contain much medieval pottery recovered through fieldwalking). Work at the similar outport of Hoeke, which shrank to a hamlet, its commercial area reverting to arable, has also yielded quantities of material from field survey. This 'Zwinproject' is coordinated by the University of Ghent and has three key aims: determining the location, morphology and quality of preservation of the lost Zwin ports; undertaking cross-disciplinary study of landscape evolution in the area; and developing and evaluating an integrated methodology for the study of such landscapes.[82] It is an example of the application of a range of archaeological techniques to the exploration of an historical problem.

The work of the Zwinproject is utilising increasingly sophisticated survey approaches and similar development of theoretical approaches to recovered material, such as the analysis of rubbish deposits and their disposal, is a further mechanism whereby archaeology can itself turn its own perceived weakness (after all, excavations just find bits of rubbish, don't they?) into an interpretative strength. Not only can archaeological material provide basic information on urban diet and certain fragmentary aspects of material culture, its study ought to enable a better understanding of broad changes in cultural values. Analysis of rubbish disposal can lead to interesting conclusions. In Deventer, Thomas Spitzers has observed that 15th-century pits contain high concentrations of household waste such as pottery and food remains but 'little or no muck'. He suggests that the cess material ('decayable organic waste') was separated off for use as garden compost[83] although it could presumably also have been collected for hinterland night-soiling. Detailed work on earlier manure deposits in Scandinavia has enabled Larsson in Lund to suggest 'a profound change' in waste disposal from one dictated by a 'relocated agrarian' existence to the development of an urban approach to waste, clearly dictated at household level rather than imposed top-down.[84]

Archaeological data, or the lack of it, can be also assessed alongside documentary research. In Hull, for instance, there is a documented introduction of organised rubbish collection in the 15th century for disposal outside the town. This coincides with a decline in rubbish found in late medieval deposits in Hull.[85] Similarly, outside many towns, rubbish material was spread on fields as night-soil; metal-detector surveys of such locations can yield surprising quantities of artefacts which enhance understanding both of urban waste disposal and of rural society. As an example of the latter, survey within the Black Isle, on the north side of the Moray Firth of Scotland's east coast, has recovered book clasps from Fortrose (which may not be surprising given that the settlement had a monastic community) together with a range of 14th- and 15th-century strap ends, buckles and belt mounts, a group of objects which it is considered 'tallies well with that recovered from London and Amsterdam'.[86] Rural and semi-rural northern Scottish communities in the late Middle Ages are thus revealed to have been in good contact with mainstream developments elsewhere in the North Sea world.

Inclusion in mainstream development is more easily viewed in Norwich where, by investing in its built environment, the city was clearly not doing so in ignorance of initiatives elsewhere. Its position close to the North Sea meant that it was highly susceptible to influences from the continent, many of which are becoming more obvious through recent research. The Cow Tower for instance (above, p. 101) was constructed in 1399 as an artillery tower in the meadows of the Great Hospital. It is the earliest freestanding such tower in England and clearly draws upon continental prototypes, in this instance probably French examples.[87] It was seen above (p. 112) that the city in the 15th century may have been importing ideas of female piety from the Low Countries, exemplified by the known female community living in the building known as the Britons Arms on Elm Hill. The city was also sourcing materials from the continent. Recent dendrochronological work on the roof of that building has shown that the timbers are of Baltic oak and date to the first decade of the 15th century.

Defensive works had long been a characteristic of urban investment in infrastructure. Considerable numbers of town walls were erected from the 12th century onward, particularly in the Low Countries and Germany although, interestingly, rarely in Denmark. Ribe, for instance, was defended by water with its canalised river and moats backed by a 7.5m wide earthen rampart and supplemented from the late 13th century by brick-built gates. Protection of the town from seaborne attack was provided, however, by the castle of Riberhus (now surviving as an earthwork) in a similar manner to the probable purpose of Husvolden castle at Nestved, a town which was otherwise undefended. Viborg had a defensive ditch and rampart, both probably dating from the 12th century but was never walled, like Ribe simply being provided by brick gates in the later Middle Ages.[88] Copenhagen was eventually fortified with a wall but recent excavations suggest that completion of the circuit was perhaps a very late medieval construction indeed, possibly as late as the beginning of the 16th century. There is documentary evidence for walls and palisades at the end of the 13th century and excavation at Kongens Nytorv in 1996 uncovered a rampart with a wall above this measuring between 1.4 and 1.8m wide. More recent excavations in 2010–2011, also at Kongens Nytorv, uncovered footings of a structure interpreted as the medieval Østerport (East or Baltic Gate).[89] However, traces of a wall elsewhere have proved elusive although documentary sources mention seven brick towers erected between 1501 and 1536. Some of these are known, such as the Hanetårnet (Cock Tower) which was examined in 1874 prior to demolition and the Jarmers Tårn (Jaromar's tower), found in 1884 and the only part of the later medieval fortifications currently visible.[90] Excavation in 2009 at Dokøen or Dock Island in the city uncovered a further defensive arrangement; three ships laden with stones and apparently scuttled to block the harbour. The sinkings may have occurred in 1428 when between 34 and 48 ships and boats were sunk, documentary sources mentioning stone-filling of the vessels.[91]

Further south, refurbishment of existing defences can be seen in several locations. At Lübeck the city wall close to the Wakenitz river was renewed in brick between 1468 and 1472; it still stands to a height of several metres (Figure 4.10). The defences at Deventer in the Netherlands were improved by the construction of a large brick tower, the Noordenbergtoren, from 1487. This remarkable building some 20m in diameter stood in front of the town wall to which it was connected by a corridor protected by flanking walls. The tower was largely built of brick and was designed as an artillery platform; although pulled

Figure 4.10 Lübeck—brick city wall of 1468–1472 (Brian Ayers).

down in 1773, excavations has been able to recover its basic plan and also to suggest a reconstruction, complete with machicolation which was known to be of Namur limestone because fragments of this were located at the base of the tower.

A further contribution of archaeology to an understanding of the development of urban defences has been identified at Wismar on the German Baltic coast. This hanseatic port has a funnel-like entrance via the *Wismarbucht* or Wismar Sound where, because of wind pressure, water levels can fluctuate and produce strong currents. These in turn led to the formation of channels up to 9m deep, benefiting the port. Here underwater survey within the entrance to the harbour has located a piled barrage, consisting of piles some 40cm in diameter set about 1m apart in two sections of 90m and 200m in length and dated dendrochronologically to 1427–1429. A piled area, some 25m by 15m and dated to 1468, existed in the area of the main channel. Boards were also located suggesting that the barrage was capable of being walked upon. It seems likely therefore that it formed an integral part of Wismar's defences. In 1999, sonar survey detected a 16m long clinker-built hull lying in soft sediment immediately in front of the barrage on the eastern side of the harbour entrance. Dendrochronological examination of this find dated it to 1486 while burnt timbers within its cargo implied that the ship may have been sailed against the barrage in an attempt to destroy the defences.[92]

Shipping and other craft

Investment in towns required income which was largely provided by trade. Shipping was of central importance therefore in the North Sea/Baltic Sea world and its study has become an increasingly important aspect of archaeological work in recent decades. The waters north of Germany and Poland are archaeologically rich with sunken medieval vessels and several 15th-century craft have been discovered in recent years. One such discovery was made in the bay of Gdynia (north of Gdánsk), the wreck of a ship probably constructed locally in the late 14th century and which sank between *c.* 1405 and 1408. This vessel contained a cargo of copper ingots, iron bars, barrel staves and wainscot boards (and is now known as the 'Copper Ship' although it is also referenced as the Gdańsk W5 wreck). At least 226 ingots have been recovered (in excavations between 1972 and 1981 and more recently in 2011 and 2012). Barrels on the ship contained a range of merchants' marks, one of which is identical to that stamped into a surviving account book of a known Prussian merchant, Johann Pilge, who traded in copper between Gdańsk and Bruges at the turn of the 15th century.[93] Analysis of the cargo and the recovered containers suggests a mixed load drawn from a variety of sources which was repacked in Gdańsk prior to the vessel leaving on its last journey. Pilge was based in Konigsburg; the cargo was drawn from locations such as Slovakia (the copper and perhaps the iron), Sweden (an alternative source for the iron), Podolia or Ruthenia (wax in the barrels), Gdańsk's hinterland (oak boards) and possibly the Neman basin (also for oak boards); the intended destination of the ship was perhaps Flanders or another west European port. The successful excavation of the Copper Ship wreck highlights the interconnectedness of trade in the late Middle Ages.[94]

Further south, Bremen in Germany, location of the celebrated discovery of the 14th-century 'Bremen cog' (below, p. 150), continues to be a city where discoveries of wrecks, or parts of wrecks, are made. Three 15th-century examples have been found in recent years. The 'Teerhof-Schiff' was uncovered close to the bank of the Weser in 1978; the 'Becks-Schiff' slightly further from the river and dating to *c.* 1444, in 1989; and the 'Beluga-Schiff', near to the 1978 discovery, in 2007. This last, a clinker-built vessel, only had some eight levels of planking or strakes surviving plus part of its keel and stem but nevertheless it provided some excellent details. The planks were radially-cleft from very high quality oak which was almost entirely free of knots. Two sources of timber could be identified by dendro-provencing: a group felled in the late 14th-century in the Baltic region; and a group of local provenance dating to the second quarter of the 15th century. The second set of timbers was probably used for repairing the vessel before she was eventually scrapped, all its internal frames being removed. These frames may have been salvaged for reuse but strakes were perhaps used for stabilisation of the river bank within the area of the *Teerhof*, the medieval shipyard of Bremen (only some 20m from the earlier 'Teerhof-Schiff' find).[95]

The importance of the 15th-century Bremen wrecks is that they not only demonstrate the hanseatic connections of the city through seagoing craft such as the 'Beluga-Schiff' but also reflect transhipment between river vessels and their seagoing counterparts. Thus the *c.* 3.7m bow section of the 'Becks-Schiff' represents a river barge and, while probably built around 1444, also appears to have been repaired *c.* 1489.[96] It contained various elements which were interesting from a shipbuilding perspective, including an L-shaped chine girder to strengthen the sharp angle between the side and bottom of the craft. The wreck was located in a subsidiary channel of the Weser but coarse deposits of river bedding found within the vessel imply that there was a considerable current within this channel at the time of loss.[97]

Ships and boats were obviously used for activities other than trade. Fishing, already referenced on several occasions above, entailed utilisation of a range of vessels by the 15th century. Documentary references for those sailing from ports on the North Sea have been summarised by Hutchinson—craft-types with names such as 'batellae', 'cobles', 'farcosts' and 'doggers', these last used for the Icelandic fish trade. She also notes the excavation of two wrecks of 15th-century fishing boats. One of these was found in London at Blackfriars (the Blackfriars III boat) and sank in the second half of the century; finds from the craft included over 2000 fishing net weights. A Dutch *waterschip*, also of the 15th-century, was recovered from the Ijsselmeerpolders in 1978 (site MZ22). This vessel contained a remarkable feature called a 'bun' which was 'a fish-well compartment sealed from the rest of the vessel by heavy bulkheads, with holes in the hull planking to allow sea-water to flow through and thus keep the fish alive'.[98] The provision of fresh fish is also made evident by large casks dating to *c.* 1490 which were excavated next to the waterfront in Hull, the international nature of trade again being observed when dendro-provencing of the oak for the casks demonstrated that it was of Baltic origin (Figure 4.11).[99]

Not all fish would have been landed at major ports of course; small harbours abounded on both sides of the North Sea, leaving ephemeral evidence although this can be detected. At Flamborough on the east coast of Yorkshire, harbour construction is known in 1400–1401 when Robert Constable bequeathed the large sum of £40 for the maintenance of a 'kay' (quay) in the sea. This was probably at South Landing, Flamborough where three concentrations of unworked boulders have been recorded, suggesting a structure where these infilled a now-lost timber frame. A similar construction seems to have existed at

Figure 4.11 Casks of Baltic timber, Hull *c.* 1490 (Bill Marsden: Humber Archaeology Partnership).

Filey on the same coast where a 28m long concentration of boulders—known as Old Quay Rocks—has been recorded and is interpreted as the stone core of a pier.[100] Similar landing places are currently being sought off Funen (Fyn) in Denmark, physical survey by kayak being supplemented with existing recorded data, investigation of early mapping and the use of LiDAR . An innovative approach of this project is seeking to date concentrations of boulders through optical stimulated luminescence (OSL) dating of the sands sealed beneath them.[101]

The technological details recovered from the Bremen discoveries did not include any evidence of carvel-built vessels, that is edge-to-edge planking rather than overlapping clinker-type construction. Carvel, a more advanced form of shipbuilding, was well-known in the Mediterranean by the 15th century with ships also being built in a similar manner in both Portugal and the Basque region. That the technique was not adopted exclusively, however, is shown by the Newport Ship of *c.* 1450, the best-preserved 15th-century ship to be discovered to date (in South Wales in 2002); it seems likely that this vessel was constructed in the Basque area but was nevertheless clinker-built. Late medieval ships with carvel timbers remain largely unknown in northern waters despite documentary evidence suggesting construction of such a vessel in Suffolk in the 1460s.[102] However, a 1990 discovery in Nämdöfjärd in the Stockholm archipelago of a small carvel-built vessel dating to the first half of the 16th century suggests that it is only a matter of time before other wrecks are located, enabling greater understanding of the adoption of this more sophisticated technology. This Swedish wreck was initially suggested as being a royal ship known as *The Swan*, one documented as being lost in 1524. However, archaeological work determined that this was not the case (the swan became a duck according to the archaeologist) with detailed analysis ultimately suggesting that the vessel was a northern-built 'carrack derivative' known locally as a 'Kravel', that is one based upon Mediterranean ship design but whose timbers seem to have been sourced in Poland. She carried guns although these were found stowed in the hold rather than deployed.[103]

Church investment

Commerce, as fostered by shipping, was also closely linked to the church. In Bruges, the centre of hanseatic activity was the Carmelite Friary where the German merchants used both the church and the refectory for meetings with elections of alderman of the Hanse also taking place. The location was sufficiently important for the 1474 Treaty of Utrecht between England and the Hanse to be kept there locked in a wooden chest.[104] Pine chests dating to the 15th century, no doubt of similar form to the examples in Bruges, still exist in a number of churches in the east of England. A detailed study of these chests has determined that they were almost certainly all made in a single location, probably Gdańsk. They are constructed of Baltic timber to a standard design and perhaps had an original function as packaging for the transport of goods before an ultimate use either for the safeguarding of administrative documents or household effects. Examples from England include a chest now in the church at Mendlesham in Suffolk which is strikingly similar to a chest in St Leonard's church, Zoutleeuw in Belgium.[105] Their provenance and distribution suggests a strong link to hanseatic commerce and is yet another indicator of trans-North Sea trade.

The Bruges Carmelite friary had been founded in 1264 outside the eastern city defences. It was 'sold as national goods under the French government in 1796' and demolished.[106] Any physical evidence of hanseatic activity is thus lost but the profit of trading activity, hanseatic and other such as French, Italian and Spanish, is nevertheless visible across religious establishments in northern Europe. Just as trade fostered technological innovation and encouraged the growth of mercantile complexes, so the wealth generated was also invested in church buildings and institutions. The evidence for considerable 15th-century expenditure on religious buildings of all types is increasingly clear from both archaeological and art-historical investigation.

Archaeological work on urban friaries is a useful indicator of such investment. Most friaries within the North Sea world were either demolished or adapted to alternative use during and after the Reformation of the 16th century. In Britain, nearly all were destroyed, materials being sold off for use in other structures. A rare survival is the church of the Dominicans in Norwich which, together with claustral buildings, was acquired by the city for use as a common hall in 1540. Similar examples of both destruction and reuse can be cited from the Netherlands, Germany and Scandinavia. As examples, the Franciscan friary in Göttingen, the *Barfüßer*, was demolished in 1820 although the potential for future archaeological work is demonstrated by finds from a friary cesspit which were recovered in 1890 (and include wooden book covers with leather bindings), while the Dominican friary church has survived intact and is now used as a library by Göttingen university.[107]

The friars—whether Dominican, Franciscan, Carmelite or Augustinian—were international orders with international contacts. This extended to resources and it is clear from archaeological work around the North Sea that commodities such as timber were often sourced from afar by the friars for use on their sites. While many buildings have been lost, it is still possible to recover evidence for trans-North Sea trade from excavated sites. A good example is the Augustinian friary at Hull where work on the cemetery uncovered 43 burials housed within well-preserved wooden coffins (Figure 4.12). Analysis of these coffins showed that they were all constructed of fast-grown Baltic oak. Dateable by dendrochronology to the 14th century (the majority between 1327 and 1362) it was notable that such interment had fallen out of fashion by the 15th century. All of the individuals from this later period were buried in shrouds alone. At least three of the dead were immigrants, isotopic analysis revealing that they were all from the Baltic Sea region including one young woman from southern Sweden.[108] Similar movements of people has been observed from anthropological analysis of burials from the cathedral cloister in Riga where skeletons indicate individuals from both northern Germany and Scandinavia.[109]

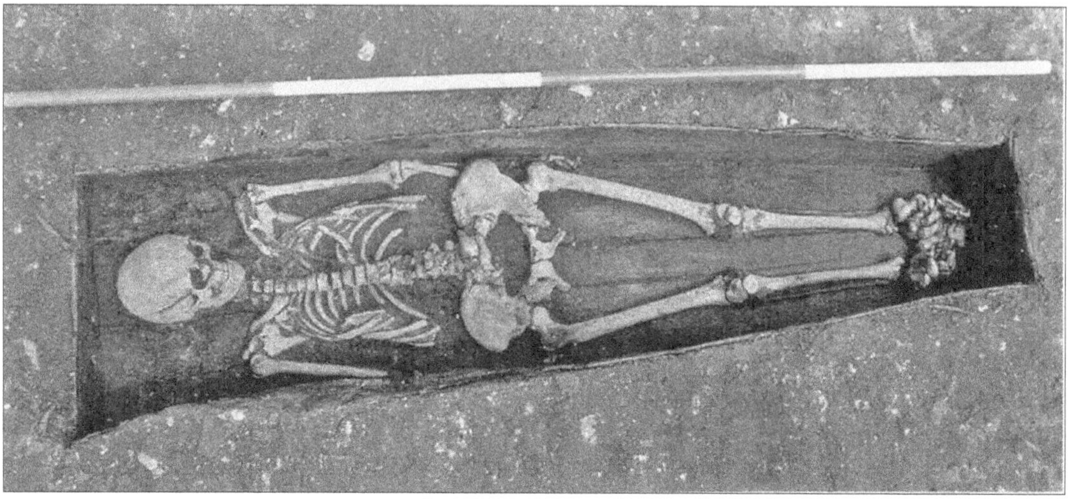

Figure 4.12 Hull, Augustinian friary coffin made of Baltic oak (Humber Archaeology Partnership).

The isotopic data from individuals in the Hull cemetery has been used recently to test an hypothesis with regard to the transmission of treponematosis or treponemal disease. The bacterial genus *Treponema* is evident in four infectious diseases: pinta, yaws, endemic and venereal syphilis of which all but the first have the potential to impact upon the skeleton. Analysis of isotopic data from twelve of the Hull cases sought to isolate whether these individuals were non-local in order to assist studies of the mobility of disease. Samples were taken for strontium and oxygen isotope examination from six diseased and six control (that is non-diseased) individuals. The results indicated that four people had non-local origins with two of them having changes in the bone which might relate to infection from probable treponematosis. The study therefore demonstrated that there is potential for using the technique to explore the mobility of disease although it calls for work on larger groups in future.[110]

The friars were frequently popular within the urban communities within which they were situated and the laity therefore often sought burial amongst the religious. Startling evidence for this was found in the Hull cemetery where, most unusually and as a result of the anaerobic conditions prevailing in the low-lying port, fragments of clothing were discovered, individuals being buried in 'Sunday best' attire, woollen garments such as full-length gowns and even male underclothes. Rare complete examples of decorated female leather girdles were also located.[111] These people were almost certainly buried with burial rites equivalent to those performed for the friars; a document survives relating to the Franciscan friary in Norwich in 1433 when one of the lay benefactors, Thomas Bate, was issued with a letter of confraternity which promised him and his children 'that when your deaths ... shall be shewed in our provincial chapter, there shall be done for you ... that which hath been used to be performed for our friars, and the friends and benefactors of our order deceased ..'.[112] Excavations at the Franciscan friary of Aalborg in Denmark uncovered a grave of a member of the laity accompanied by his personal seal; the nobleman Oluf Mortensen of the Seefeld family, who lived between 1437–1477 was buried in the choir, his skeleton showing a man some 1.78m in height and aged between 25 and 39, thus corresponding well with known documentary references to him.[113]

The sheer variety of monastic provision in towns of the North and Baltic Seas region has been highlighted by recent publication of a volume in the Lübeck *Stadtarchäologie im Hanseraum* series devoted to *Klöster*.[114] Detailing Benedictine monasteries, friaries, hospitals, beguinages and colleges, one surprising point to emerge is how late establishment of new precincts could be. A good example is Alkmaar (above, p. 112) in the Netherlands where the earliest institution dates from 1394 with the creation of 'a residence ... designated for widows and virgins from Alkmaar' as a Dominican initiative although it was under

Franciscan rule by 1428. It was dedicated to St Catherine and became known as the *Oude Hof*. A *Jonge Hof* dedicated to St Mary had been established by 1415 with a third convent in existence by 1430 (and known as the *Middelhof*). A friary for men, Franciscan, was only founded in 1448. All of these institutions are lost but while excavations at the Franciscan friary in 2009–2010 'rendered only incomprehensible parts of foundations' more has been recovered from the *Middlehof* where substantial footings were exposed in 2000 at Canadaplein and, at the same site two years earlier, artefacts included a white earthenware plaque painted in red and gold representing a female saint (its inscription read '*ora pro nobis beata Katherina*'—'pray for us blessed Catherine). Extensive rich wall paintings are known from the *Jonge Hof* where scenes depicting Christ with the globe in his hand, the Nativity and the Last Judgement were uncovered in 1861, drawn and then lost in 1881 when the wall was demolished.[115]

Another monastic foundation of late date is that of the Bridgettine abbey at Maribo on Lolland in Denmark. Founded around 1400 it effectively gave its name to a new town as Maribo means 'the place where Mary lives' (Marian dedications were a feature of Bridgettine monasteries). Construction of the institution was probably underway by 1413 as a double foundation for both monks and nuns. The church survives although all other buildings are lost. A reconstruction has been attempted based upon early drawings and excavated evidence. It depicts the great brick church flanked by two cloisters, reflecting its status as a double monastery.[116] Brick was used extensively across northern Europe, some magnificent buildings still surviving such as the Burgkloster in Lübeck which has been subject to detailed archaeological survey and partial excavation.[117] Lübeck, in common with other towns, was also home to almshouses, the 'Dornes Courtyard' almshouse being founded in 1458. its front range still standing (Figure 4.13).

Figure 4.13 Dornes Courtyard almshouse, Lübeck of 1458 (Brian Ayers).

An interesting aspect of monastic institutions was their role in technological innovation. Form followed function as so often and thus certain improvements were clearly designed to assist religious activities. In Hull, excavation of the choir of the Augustinian friary church uncovered a brick-lined acoustic passage which ran beneath the friars' stalls in order to amplify the sound.[118] Work in Norwich in 2015 also uncovered the choir of the Augustinian friary there and it too seems to have been furnished with an acoustic passage beneath its stalls.[119] David Evans, the excavator of the Hull friary church, points out that similarly 'the medieval author Vitruvius described how placing hollow pottery jars within such passages would improve the acoustics of the building'. Intact examples of such jars have been located at Roskilde Cathedral in Denmark (Figure 4.14).

As noted above (p. 56) the recent Norwich excavation also revealed the steps taken by the friars to ensure their wellbeing. A small stream (known locally as a *cockey*) crossed the site and was culverted as part of the development of the friary. Its discovery complements earlier work on the Franciscan friary in the same city when a complex of drains, debouching into a large covered culvert, was uncovered.[120] Elsewhere comfort could be seen at the Franciscan friary in Wismar where parts of a warm air heating system were found[121] and at the Dominican friary in Visby where remains of a hypocaust have been revealed.[122]

As well as innovators, monasteries and friaries were patrons of craftsmen and artists. Wall-paintings dating to the 14th century were discovered at the Franciscan friary in Great Yarmouth following exposure after bomb damage in the Second World War. They decorate tomb recesses, probably of wealthy lay benefactors, and depict figures including a female saint and perhaps a donor. Comparison has been made with similar wall-paintings surviving at the church of Little Wenham in Suffolk, both examples utilising a distinctive green/blue pigment which is characteristic of later medieval East Anglian painting.[123] In Lübeck, paintings dating between 1460 and 1510 decorate the extant ceiling of the Franciscan friary sacristy (Figure 4.15). In Denmark, where very many more wall-paintings survive than in England, both the cathedrals of Aarhus and Roskilde retain many late medieval images as do parish churches. Aarhus cathedral alone has some 220 square metres of paintings. The wealth of survival is such that individual schools of painting can be identified, such as the 'Kongsted Workshop' of around 1425 and the 'Isefiord Workshop' of 1460–1480. Even the names of individual painters are known on occasion: Morten the Painter decorated several churches in south-west Zealand in the early 15th century, signing a Last Supper scene in Gerlev church 'Martinus malere bene fecit' (Morten the Painter did this well) in 1409.[124] Perhaps emphasising the role of the friaries within wider society, St Dominic and St Francis of Assisi, both founders of mendicant orders, are illustrated together on a wall painting of 1522 in Skive church, Francis holding up his hands to display the stigmata.

Just as painters moved from friary-to-friary and church-to-church as commissions were received, so did other artists. Art historians are increasingly tracking the movements of craftspeople through documentation, sometimes linking individuals to material survivals. Thus David King has established that a 15th-century Dutch glazier, 'William Duchman glasier' subsequently known as William Mounford , from Utrecht moved to the east of England in the 1430s. He thereafter become responsible for the production of surviving glass in locations such as St Peter Mancroft, Norwich as well as Martham, Pulham St Mary, Thurton and Warham St Mary churches, all in Norfolk. He perhaps also travelled to Lincoln and produced glass for the bishop's palace there. His wife, Helen, was probably English and she too was a glazier.[125]

As with glass, so with the architecture within which windows were housed. The communication of ideas across the North Sea in the 15th century has been investigated by Richard Fawcett, comparing the stylistic choices of ecclesiastical buildings in Scotland with examples from the Low Countries. A particularly influential church seems to have been that of the Dominicans in Flemish Bruges which, like the Carmelite friary in that city (above, p. 133), has been destroyed although considerable detail is known from Marcus Gheeraert's celebrated map of 1562 and from 18th-century engravings. The west front of this church may well have inspired the surviving dramatic west front of Haddington church in Scotland along with influences from other buildings such as St Salvator cathedral in Bruges and

Figure 4.14 Roskilde cathedral—acoustic jar (Brian Ayers).

Figure 4.15 Painted ceiling in sacristry of Franciscan friary, Lübeck (Brian Ayers).

St Lebuinus church in Deventer (Netherlands). Similarly, the great tower of St Mary's church, Dundee can be considered a Scottish interpretation of designs pioneered in the Netherlands, such as the towers of Utrecht cathedral and the churches of Amerongen and Culemborg.[126]

Study of architectural interdependence can be extended to explore inter-relationships between monastic institutions and their host cities. An English example is Norwich where the 15th-century cathedral priory mason John Antell worked on city parish churches such as St George Colegate and St Michael Coslany. Here also the design of the 15th-century Erpingham Gate at the cathedral priory may perhaps have been linked to the St Peter Mancroft church workshop[127] and Fawcett has argued that the mouldings of the dark entry to the cloister are 'precisely repeated' in the porch of St Laurence's church in the city.[128] Sandy Heslop has suggested that the distinctive octagonal tower of St James's church was derived from that at the Blackfriars and quite possibly also from the Carmelite church which adjoined the parish graveyard.[129] Additionally, Jon Finch has pointed out stylistic cross-referencing between parish churches in the city, such as the rebuilding of St Gregory at the end of the 15th century which drew upon the recently-completed work at St Peter Mancroft.[130] An interdisciplinary project of archaeologists, art historians and architectural historians is currently exploring the interdependent relationship between city, community, and architecture within the city where 30 medieval parish churches still stand.[131]

Furnishings of churches also show the transmission of stylistic ideas through artefacts. Altarpieces are good examples, numbers of which survive across northern Europe. Many were made and painted in Lübeck, notably those of the great master Berndt Notke. The altarpiece in Aarhus cathedral, donated by the bishop in 1479, is by Notke and bears the inscription *Bernardus fecit me*. He also made the altarpiece of 1483 in the church of the Holy Ghost in Tallinn (Estonia) and was responsible for a *Danse Macabre* painting in the St Nicholas church there (a further such painting in the Marienkirche in Lübeck was destroyed by bombing in 1942). A later master, Claus Berg and also of Lübeck, made a great altarpiece for the Franciscan church in Odense about 1517–1522 (it is now housed in Odense cathedral).[132]

High quality artistic design and workmanship was not confined to continental workshops. In England alabaster, a hydrous calcium sulphate, was quarried at locations such as Tutbury in Staffordshire or Chellaston near Nottingham. The material was especially good for fine carving but needed to be worked soon after extraction from the ground. Accordingly workshops grew up in Nottingham and its region, producing a range of artefacts such as altarpieces, sculptures and tomb panels. As well as distribution within England, numerous alabaster examples from the Nottingham workshops are known elsewhere in Europe including an early 15th-century pietà now in the Musée de Cluny in Paris,[133] an altarpiece including figures of St Michael and St George in Borbjerg church, Jutland in Denmark, a further 15th-century altarpiece at the church in Þingeyrar in Iceland, and a slightly earlier head of St John the Baptist in the church of that dedication in Dortmund.[134] Documentary references help to chart the trade; as an example, Cornelius de Grave's ship, the *Mary of Hull*, set sail from that port on 20th May 1465 with a cargo that included 'ii tables de alabastre' and on 10th November the following year Robert Thornton's *Trenyte of Hull* contained 'iij tables de alabastre. Study of surviving examples on the continent show that English alabasters complemented the export market for altarpieces from the Low Countries and Germany but very few penetrated these production areas themselves.[135]

Churches of all types required fittings such as bells, production of which has been mentioned above (p. 121). Particular furnishings were lecterns and monumental memorial brasses. Both were made of a specialist metal called latten, an alloy of copper, tin, lead and zinc, the latter material giving a bright golden colour to the object. With regard to the latten plates themselves, these were probably imported, at least until the 16th century, probably via the Low Countries from production sites in Germany.[136] Monumental brasses survive in Bruges and other locations in the Low Countries but they and other continental examples are far outnumbered by the survivals in England. Latoners were certainly working in locations such as London, Norwich and York.[137]

Aside from memorial brasses, the most spectacular example of brass work is that of the lectern. By the 15th century, lecterns either in the shape of a pelican or an eagle were common in eastern England.

Figure 4.16 15th-century brass eagle lectern, Norwich (Brian Ayers).

The pelican motif was considered suitable for a lectern holding the gospel because the pelican was thought to feed it young with its own blood; the eagle, as well as being the symbol of St John the Evangelist was apparently favoured through reference to the 17th Psalm 'He did fly upon the wings of the wind', taking the gospel to the four corners of the earth (Figure 4.16).[138] Again, examples are known from the Low Countries with manufacture there centred on Dinant (and export of other brass goods to England becoming known as 'Dinanderie'[139]), but the particular group of lecterns in the east of England suggests centres of manufacture in East Anglia, probably in Norwich, Lynn and Bury St Edmunds.[140]

The construction and fitting out of religious institutions clearly called upon a wide range of material sources and skills. Archaeologically, one of the clearest ways of demonstrating resource acquisition is through dendro-provencing of timber. It has already been seen how the use of Baltic timber for the coffins of the Augustinian friary in Hull obviously reflected the town's considerable trade links with the ports of the Baltic Sea (p. 133). Further north, Scotland's strong ties with Norway are shown by the use of early 16th-century timbers in the Great Hall of Edinburgh Castle. Dendrochronological and dendro-provencing of timbers from the hammer beam roof there gave a probable construction date of 1509 to 1510 although it seems that the trees themselves were felled between 1505 and 1510. The spread of dates implies the stockpiling of the wood while the lack of matching between the timbers also suggests that they were drawn from a number of locations within 'the source area' of Norway.[141] This very late medieval use of Scandinavian timber in Edinburgh was clearly part of a tradition of resource acquisition which began at the beginning of the 15th century in Scotland: examples of Scandinavian oak in locations close to the North Sea have been found in the roof of Guthrie Aisle (the surviving element of a collegiate church northwest of the port of Arbroath) and as reused material in a townhouse in Brechin while 'Estland boards', good quality panels from the Baltic, were used for ceiling panels at Guthrie and for carved panels now in Perth Museum.[142]

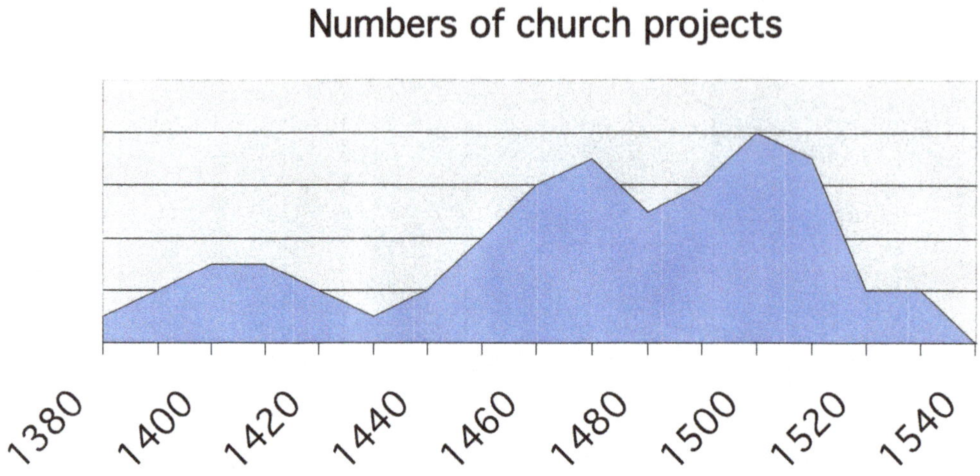

Figure 4.17 Church building campaigns documented for late medieval Norwich (Sandy Heslop).

The quantity of resources needed could be enormous as implied by the evidence of testamentary bequests to church construction. In Norfolk, work by Cattermole and Cotton has explored a body of wills surviving from the period 1370 to 1550 in order to find documentary references to church building, supplementing the information with data from churchwardens' accounts, cathedral account rolls and inscriptions. Their staggering achievement summarises work for churches across Norfolk but the entries for Norwich have been tabulated by Sandy Heslop. He calculates that, of the 30 surviving parish churches in Norwich, more than 80% of them were undergoing major works in the 'long 15th century', that is between *c.* 1380 and *c.* 1540 (major works meaning extending the length of the footprint of the building, constructing aisles or transepts). There was a peak of activity in the city between *c.* 1480 and *c.* 1520, often using substantial sums of money such as £20 bequeathed in 1499 to 'ledyng of the new chauncell' at St Laurence (Figure 4.17).[143] The implications for the quantities of stone needed, the bricks and tiles that had to be burnt, the timber felled, the lead sought, the glass fired and painted, are colossal. The numbers of works in hand at one time also imply a substantial local workforce of skilled and unskilled labour (and no doubt meant equally substantial disruption). A challenge for archaeologists is to characterise how such resources were acquired, marshalled and utilised as well as to explore the impact of such widespread constructional activity upon the community.

Archaeologists can also ask other questions of data relating to the church and its interaction with wider society. It has been argued that such issues as the 'economic impact of monastic institutions can be assessed both from their probable disruptive and negative influence when planted within existing communities ... to more positive indicators such as estimates of food consumption ... the range of sources exploited and thereby the range of producers benefiting'.[144] The relationship of urban institutions to their rural hinterlands is of interest here. While numerous reports now exist citing data from archaeological excavations, addressing issues such as diet (through food waste remains) or use of natural resources (archaeobotanical evidence of rushes used for flooring coverings is an example), there is almost certainly scope for archaeological exploration of rural estates known to be linked to urban monastic institutions. Such work could not only examine how much 'urban culture' found its way through artefact distribution to the rural areas but also how far assessment of the productive capacity of rural estates matched, complemented and commented upon known documentary evidence of rural supply. Historians have done much in recent years to explore the mechanisms and organisation of supply; archaeologists have the potential to augment this work with quantitative analysis of actual production.[145]

Social topography and social meaning

An area where considerable advances in understanding are now being made involves buildings, their contents and environs. Traditional study of buildings, their rear yards and their artefacts is complemented by techniques which not only examine constructional and technological innovation, use of resources and waste disposal, but also seek to explore an apparent greater social sophistication in the late medieval period. Archaeologists are utilising theoretical frameworks to address questions of spatial and social organisation, considering past locations in terms of status, functions, control of access and permeability. This form of 'contextual archaeology' builds upon the work of spatial analysts such as Hillier and Hanson although not unquestioningly; Johnson, for instance, has criticised the approach, placing greater emphasis upon evidence for action rather than systems. He cautions that the study of buildings of a past society could lead to the perception that 'the layout and form ... will ... misrepresent the real nature of exploitative relationships in that society'.[146] Giles, however, has argued that it is necessary for archaeologists to engage with an approach which takes the archaeological record as one which 'is seen to encode past cultural and ideological meanings which can be read or recorded by the archaeologist through an analysis of associations and differences between it and other aspects of material culture produced within the same cultural context'. Archaeology as a discipline can thereby shake off the perception of some historians that it is merely providing a 'passive' mirror to the past but rather 'through a critical examination and engagement with [textual sources] ... the ... use of material culture to reproduce, negotiate or contest dominant social and political discourses becomes apparent'.[147]

Giles undertook an archaeological examination of the surviving guildhalls of York, producing a work which detailed the buildings but also sought to explain the meaning attached to certain spaces within them from the perspective of their late medieval occupants. McNeil fostered the idea of awareness of spatial planning, arguing that it was fundamental to an understanding of the dynamics of buildings as well as to their development.[148] In London, John Schofield has undertaken interesting assessments of London houses, exploring their likely use by a range of groups through access analysis. He was able to identify commercial, domestic, storage and service areas with the aid of this technique.[149] His examples were drawn from detailed surveys of houses undertaken by Ralph Treswell between 1607 and 1614 but it is likely that the buildings incorporated much late medieval material and retained traditional patterns of use. Application of the approach to a mercantile complex of 1427 in Norwich meant that control of access from a single location within the main building to the various public, semi-public and private spaces of the property could be suggested.[150]

Contextual archaeology is also taking place across the North Sea. In Sweden, archaeological survey of Ny Lödöse, a small urban foundation of the second half of the 15th century, has identified regulated gaps between properties and a basic plot layout within those properties (consisting of street frontage shops, chamber/storage rooms, a main heated room and finally a workshop). To one side lay a courtyard and a stable/barn and vegetable patch/waste area. Some 16 plots were excavated between 2012 and 2015 and nearly all of them had the same layout, with access to the shops from the street and from the courtyard to the other buildings.[151]

Also in Sweden, Thomasson has explored the use of a 16th-century town-house using both spatial analysis as well as examination of changes to its fabric. He argues that it can be understood by the use of space which he was able to assess despite the fact that only elements of the structure now exist within a museum context in Lund, rather than standing in Malmö which is where it was built (below, p. 194).[152] In Germany, the Deutschen Gesellschaft für die Archäologie des Mittelalters und der Neuzeit (DGAMN) has recently devoted an entire volume of its journal to 'Archaeological Context and Social Interpretation'. Papers relating to communities with access to the North Sea include work on cesspits in Lüneburg where the social status of family groups using the facilities could be suggested;[153] an assessment, focussed in part on Greifswald, by an historian of such approaches, offering a critique of both archaeological and historical use of data, particularly with regard to understanding social stratification and mobility, and concluding that only by a combined understanding of source materials can progress be made;[154]

this theme was taken up by a third paper, on the site of a monastic complex in Duisburg, subsequently converted to post-medieval university use, where it was clear that, without the documentary evidence, it was perfectly possible for archaeological interpretation to have gone astray, particularly with regard to changing functional use;[155] and a rural settlement paper, divorced from buildings but, again using interpretative approaches, examined evidence for the use of horses, concluding that high-quality animals were not necessarily reserved exclusively for the nobility.[156]

Returning to England, Chris King has undertaken interesting research upon the surviving medieval halls of Norwich. These were all buildings of the mercantile elite, occupying substantial complexes and, as above, King builds upon traditional approaches of architectural and archaeological appraisal by exploring social identities and relationships as expressed through the fabric and form of the houses. He argues that 'the complex structural development of domestic buildings [is] evidence for ongoing acts of 'appropriation', in which the urban elite adopted architectural forms from aristocratic, religious and civic buildings, and re-used older medieval structures, as a form of cultural capital to negotiate and maintain both communal and individual social identities and political authority'.[157] He argues that this 'appropriation' was necessary for a newly-wealthy urban elite which had a relatively fragile power base which they wished to bolster. Their houses were spaces where, along with their investment in local churches, members of the mercantile class could display 'their public honour and domestic virtues ... thus constituting themselves as an integrated governing elite in the earthly city below and the heavenly city above'.

This interpretation links with historical evidence for factionalism within the 15th-century city. Medieval Norwich had over 60 craft guilds and 50 religious confraternities but, unlike London for instance, the guilds did not possess their own communal halls. In consequence social activities such as feasting and political activities such as elections could be circumscribed with cabals allegedly using private houses to conduct business in private. This was the basis of a complaint in 1414 when it was alleged that the 'commons' of the city had been prevented from free elections because business had been 'diverted away from the public worsted seld into ... private houses'.[158]

Portable objects in the later Middle Ages

King was able to undertake his research in Norwich because of the survival of an unusually large number of late medieval domestic halls in the city. Increasingly, however, archaeologists on both sides of the North Sea are looking critically at material culture, whether it is large-scale as in architecture or small-scale as in ceramics or textiles in order to extract meaning, social, political or symbolic, from these inanimate artefacts. As an example, a recently-published paper has provided a thorough appraisal of gloves in the later medieval and post-medieval period, drawing on evidence for types, uses and meanings of gloves, mittens and gauntlets. Amongst much intriguing detail concerning materials (woollen, leather, textile or even metal), glove types (working, hawking , sporting, bishops', nobility's and royal gloves) and social rituals, the symbolic nature of gloves is explored, including the provision of late medieval badges in the shape of gloves (these known from London, Nieuwlande in the Netherlands and Ypres in Flanders and are interpreted as likely to represent St Thomas Becket, murdered as archbishop and thus wearing his gloves at the time—an interesting insight into medieval mentality).[159] Examples of finds of gloves themselves are drawn from locations as diverse as London, Aalst, Amsterdam, Groningen, Sluis, Rotterdam, Utrecht and especially Dordrecht (at least six leather gloves from the site of a leather workshop). Gloves mattered within the civic sphere as well; 16th-century portraiture often depicts sitters holding gloves, signifying both freeman status and market authority.[160]

Ongoing artefact research elsewhere on slightly earlier material is examining medieval anthropomorphic pottery, particularly the Grimston ware bearded face jugs exported from the east of England to the continent. Kelly Green has noted that decoration of tableware is almost exclusively masculine and she is exploring this gendered approach to ceramics as well as expressions of social identity through ceramics within the contexts of urbanism, commerce and community.[161] Ceramics, as has been noted above, are also useful artefacts for the study of contact across the North Sea. The durability of pottery, albeit usually fragmented, ensures much material for study. Considerable quantities of ink have been expended upon investigative methodologies and the care with which conclusions should be drawn; the apparent simplicity, for instance, of the situation in Norway where it seems that no indigenous pottery production existed until the 16th century is nevertheless immediately complicated by concentrations of that imported pottery within coastal regions. Were these ceramics being used by local populations, are they evidence for émigré communities or did the ceramics serve all aspects of medieval Scandinavian society?

One such concentration occurs at Kalmar in south-eastern Sweden where large quantities of imported German ceramics have been recovered (above, p. 106). This material has been examined, together with documentary evidence, by Naum in order to explore both the late medieval German diaspora but also the concept of translocality whereby there is an interplay of presence and absence. She accepts the difficulty of separating German from Swedish households for those sites in Kalmar where excavations have taken place (although she is assisted somewhat by the 15th-century Kalmar 'Town Book' which lists households with the names of residents). Rather, she is seeking to demonstrate 'microcosms of familiarity' where 'furnishings constituted collages of well-known textures representing landscapes of homesteads the migrants parted with upon arrival in Kalmar and mirroring self-perception and identities'. Examining those locations where Germans were documented and which have been excavated, she noted that the high percentage of German, Low Countries and French tablewares encountered were comparable with German sites such as Greifswald and Rostock.[162] Ceramics therefore, along with less tangible survivals such as letters, gifts or 'economic remittance', probably played a significant rather than tangential role in helping to provide a familiar cultural framework for a German community located away from home.

The influence of portable objects has been traced to the remnants of a late medieval timber building surviving in Scarborough on the east coast of England. Here a public house, constructed in 1898–99, called the Newcastle Packet incorporated one side of the structure which was demolished in order to provide the site. This had been a jettied building, originally with dragon beams to help carry the upper floors, the end of these diagonal beams being covered by corner posts. The posts were decorated with figures, one such decoration still being extant. It depicts a woman with a basket of loaves or fish on its north-west face and a male figure with a jar of beer on the south-west face, a large carved head between the two. The figures resemble closely those on a humorous engraving from Frankfurt *c.* 1480 in a print that was signed by the print-maker as 'bxg'. The design was redrawn *c.* 1520 by Hans Schäufelein for a set of playing cards. The image was almost certainly used as a template by the wood-carver when creating the Scarborough post although it is impossible to tell if the carving is from 1480 or 1520. The suggestion has been made that the carver or carvers may have been Flemish; Scarborough had many contacts with Flanders, Flemish wood-carvers were working in York in the 15th century (David Dam and James or Jacob Dam, probably from Damme near Bruges) and buildings with distinctive paired brackets in York share characteristics with the surviving structure in Scarborough.[163]

A 'bxg' figure depicting a woman in a wheelbarrow is carved on to a misericord now in Bishop Tunstall's chapel in Durham Castle.[164] Prints signed by 'bxg' were used to inform the design of misericords at Ripon Cathedral, probably between 1489 (the date on a misericord) and 1494 (the date carved on a bench-end). The same scene of a woman in a wheelbarrow can also be found on a wooden bench-end in Baden-Baden and on the town hall of Wroclaw (Breslau).[165] Carved figures on buildings are more common in Germany and the Low Countries; an example is the much-altered *Junkernschänke* at Barfüßerstraße, a richly-decorated house in Göttingen. The core of this building dates to the mid-15th century although the figures are later, probably from the middle of the 16th century.

The influence of the wide distribution of prints can be seen in other buildings and portable artefacts. The 1496 wall paintings in Bellinge church, Denmark have been shown to be based upon designs in a book of prints entitled *Biblia Pauperum*; a Rhenish clay mould of 15th-century date found in Scotland was based on a print of 1450–60 and English alabaster panels now in Portugal include print designs, one of these also from the *Biblia Pauperum*.[166] Such contact with the Iberian peninsula was probably undertaken through London or Southampton rather than via the east coast ports of England but ceramics from Spain nevertheless have been occasional finds in places such as Hull where Merida-type vessels and 15th-century Valencian bowls have been located.[167] Venetian glass in the form of an occasional bowl or goblet has been found in York.[168] However, such discoveries pale next to the evidence from Bruges. Here fine Spanish lustreware from Andalusia and especially Valencia 'occurs in small but consistent quantities' as well as Isabela-polychrome from Seville and Paterna-blue ware. A particularly fine bowl of mature Valencian lustreware was discovered on Oosterlingenplaats in 1986. Not all the imports were luxury pottery; a large group of jug-amphorae sherds of Mediterranean courseware has been uncovered on a 15th-century site in Bruges where a Spanish coin of Enrique III was also found.[169]

Portable objects also enable consideration of everyday use of resources such as salt. The domestic use of salt and indeed its social importance has been illustrated recently by the discovery of a medieval saltcellar in excavations at Odense. Work here in 2013 uncovered a small hexagonal vessel of 14th- to early 15th-century date decorated with images of the Fall (figures of Adam and Eve are embossed on the interior base) and the Agnus Dei (which graces the exterior base). This combination of imagery was associated with baptism but the container also has seven incised *bomæker*, similar to merchants' marks and perhaps representing members of a guild who were entitled to use the saltcellar.[170]

One of the most startling, and also the most informatively striking, of portable artefacts to be recovered archaeologically was a wax tablet book, found in a well at Schrangen in Lübeck in 1975. This remarkable object dates to the late 15th century and consists of five wooden waxed tablets, with texts inscribed by a stylus still visible. The property of a merchant, his book seems to list transactions with named individuals. While some of the names can read, insufficient text survives to identify the nature of the transactions save for one tantalising but apparently incomplete entry: '*Item dene er 1 c vorkofte*'. The rest is illegible and does not give an indication of the traded goods. Nevertheless, it illustrates well the developing bureaucracy that commerce demanded of its citizens in order that effective management was achieved.[171]

Commerce and environmental impact

Two of the named individuals in the Lübeck wax tablets (Hans van Hagen and Hinrich Wedekinc) seem to have been butchers and, living in the 1460s to 1480s, would almost certainly have been providing imported meat for their customers. A recent assessment of the growth in meat demand in the 15th century suggests that live drives of some 10,000 head of cattle *per annum* were taking place over a distance of 900km from Hungary to Germany in 1400 with these numbers growing to some 85,000 by 1500. Similar, smaller drives moved from Scotland towards London and from Scandinavia to the Low Countries. The environmental impact not only of such movements but also of the cattle themselves upon supplies of pasture must have been great. A challenge for archaeology concerns its ability to contribute to understanding of such increased demand, the effect of such a changing human footprint upon ecology, and the effect upon human populations themselves. 'More now ate what they had never seen alive'.[172]

Increasing the food supply through increased breeding of livestock was clearly one way in which the North European environment was stressed. Another was through over-exploitation of resources. A good example is peat, particularly in the Low Countries where the necessity for drainage ensured the shrinking of peat and the danger of flood inundation as also happened in eastern England where peat extraction pits were flooded (above, p. 49). However, other major environmental changes can be observed on both sides of the North Sea through examination of the generally low-lying terrain. Lewin has reviewed the environmental impact of medieval development on lowlands, exploring catchment areas, river channels and floodplains. He examined deliberate human action such as the construction of embankments, bridges, mills and riverside buildings, as well as features which obstructed flow such as dams and weirs. He also considered unplanned action such as soil erosion through increased run-off from drainage of fields. The interplay between human interventions and fluvial flow meant that 'medieval rivers and floodplains become inadvertently self-modified as intentional [human] development proceeded'.[173] This self modification could have disastrous impacts through such events as severe flooding.

More direct modification of the environment was occasionally associated with technological innovation, seeking to overcome unfortunate circumstances. As examples, at Blankenheim in the Rhineland, a canal was excavated in 1468 to provide water to the castle. However, although the spring was situated only 1km from the castle, it proved necessary both to cross a valley and to tunnel through part of the hillside using a pressure system of connecting wooden water pipes which were laid on the floor of the tunnel. The 150m long tunnel survives and the site of the well house was excavated in 1997 and subsequently reconstructed.[174]

Less visible modifications but ones nevertheless with considerable impact have been explored in the Baltic region. Palaeoenvironmental analytical techniques were used to assess landscape change between the 13th and 15th centuries in the district of Malbork castle, centre for the Teutonic knights and the opening of the eastern Baltic through the 'Prussian Crusade'. Utilising radiocarbon-dated pollen sequences principally extracted from boreholes, complemented by zooarchaeological, dendro-provenancing and documentary data, the research notes 'a fundamental change in the nature of the vegetation landscape and land-use of Malbork, from one dominated by deciduous woodland ... to an increasingly open landscape with evidence for intensive cultivation of cereals, particularly rye, with pastureland and heathland'. Documents and the evidence of faunal woodland animals suggest nevertheless that management of residual woodland was probably also taking place. The growth of trade is seen as a factor in the change process, encouraging deforestation and the imposition of farming.[175]

Archaeological work within the Baltic Sea zone is also shedding new light on details of trade in plants. In terms of export, flax and hemp are documented as being major items of commerce for Gdánsk with both commodities being brought from the Polish hinterland but also from places further afield such as Lithuania. Within the local area, place-name evidence indicates the source of supply being in the Kashubian Lakeland while pollen analysis of sediments within the lakes indicates the retting of hemp from the medieval period onward. Flax seeds decay easily but excavated evidence within rear yards in towns such as Gdánsk and Elblag has recorded the presence of flax weeds such as *Spergula maxima* and *Camalina saliva* (which latter has the splendid English name 'gold of pleasure').[176] In the Netherlands, environmental pressure is evident from changes to agricultural practice as an increasing reliance on the needs of a city such as Amsterdam skewed rural production to mercantile needs (such as hemp for ropes) in the 14th and 15th centuries.[177]

Imports to the Baltic Sea ports included such items as black pepper, fairly commonly observed in deposits from the beginning of the 15th century onward, nutmeg, saffron and gooseberry. The trade in pepper was largely conducted via the Netherlands until the later 15th century when Gdánsk established direct contact with Portugal. The Netherlands was also becoming the major supplier of herring to the Baltic in the 15th century. The famous Scanian herring fishery (above, p. 87) had collapsed around 1410 to 1420, possibly as a result of climate change with cooling of sea temperatures but following pressure from over-exploitation. The loss of such inshore fisheries led the Dutch to move to harvesting of offshore herring populations in the 15th century, capturing extensive markets in the process. Environmental change within the Low Countries themselves had an unexpected side-effect; pressure on fish stocks may have been slightly offset by the growth in the numbers of eels within the Rhine delta due to the development of shallow lakes creating 'turbid, fertile and accessible habitats [which] supported large and lucrative commercial fisheries for eel' as a result of peat digging, drainage and river diversion.[178] This 'reorientation of the rural economy' together with increased investment in developing hydraulic technologies (the wind-powered drainage mill of the early 15th century) ensured that 'the low-lying parts of the Netherlands did not turn into one big swimming pool and merge with the North Sea'.[179]

The extent of freshwater peat digging within the Low Countries remains difficult to assess due to the complete loss of peatlands within the modern environment. However, new techniques, realising that results were slow to arrive both from geoscientific studies utilising present-day hydrological and soil conditions and from historical studies, have discovered that combining 'soil data, elevation data (DEM or digital elevation mapping) and historical data on land use, field names, field systems and infrastructure ...

not only allows for locating peat extraction with a higher degree of accuracy but also identifies new locations, where peat exploitation had previously been considered improbable'. As a result, on two known monastic estates at Moerbeke and Wachtebeke in northern Flanders and where quantifiable archival data is available from the 15th century, it became possible to isolate areas of peat digging, as well as those locations where peat extraction did not take place, the moorland being converted to arable soil.[180]

The constant need to combat the risk of flooding led to the harnessing of wind-powered technology for pumping water in the 15th century in the Netherlands.[181] These wind pumps augmented earlier solutions for water management whereby water was contained and channelled by dams and dykes to sluices which relied upon water pressure of drainage water to open at low tide. One impact of improved drainage, however, was the lowering of ground levels which could cause problems for buildings. The Manor of Kostverloren some 5km south of Amsterdam was one such. The name means 'lost earnings' or perhaps 'money down the drain'. The manor house needed constant repairs, some of which were painted by Jacob van Ruisdael in about 1600. His picture shows wooden piles, which support the brick superstructure, exposed above water level.[182]

Environmental pressure in the Low Countries, often driven by institutional estates such as monasteries, may have removed peat very rapidly but, as has been seen, it could mean that certain species such as eels were fostered by new water-filled areas. Eels clearly helped to feed the large urban populations of the late medieval Low Countries but they were also exported; English custom accounts and Dutch documents both illustrate such trans-North Sea trade. It is also important to remember that intellectual as well as commercial contacts were fostered across the North Sea. 'Archaeological' discoveries of such contact continue to be made. As an example, recent examination of the plea role of the court of Common Pleas has explored the ornament and imagery on the headings of the main records of the court. These included a picture of two men fighting within the initial letter 'P' of the roll dating to the Hilary term 1467. The nearest direct comparison is that with the Basle Alphabet Book of 1464, the provenance of which is French, Flemish or Netherlandish. Transmission of the imagery to an English legal record so rapidly is considered 'surprising' but understandable given that it was likely that such woodcut alphabet books 'were carried about as part of a travelling scribe or entrepreneur's materials in full expectation of a ready market for them.[183] Entrepreneurs or merchants are the subject of the next chapter.

— 5 —

Merchants and their Impact

In September 1340, a merchant died in Boston, Lincolnshire on the east coast of England and was buried in the church of the Greyfriars. His grave cover survives (it is now located in the church of St Botolph), depicting the deceased in his gown, hands held in prayer, beneath an architectural canopy. The inscription around the edge of the memorial stone reads:

> *Hic iacet Wissel(m)vs d(i)ct(u)s Smalenbvrgh, civis et mercator Monasteriensis, qvi obiit feria sexta post nativitatem beate Marie virginis anno domini M CCC XL. Anima eivs reqviescat in pace, amen.*[1]

> [Here lies Wissel called Smalenburgh, citizen and merchant of Münster, who died AD 1340 on 15 September. May his soul rest in peace. Amen].

Wissel Smalenburgh is not the only foreign merchant known to have been operating in England. Numerous other examples are recorded in documents throughout much of the Middle Ages. Slightly earlier contemporaries of Smalenburgh include Pieter le Mouner, woad merchant of Amiens in France who settled in Norfolk in 1287, bought a house and died about 1300 as 'a citizen of Norwich'[2], the Florentine Society of the Bardi who acquired a house in Lombard Street, London in 1318[3] and Nicholas le Fleming who was mayor of York several times between 1311 and 1319.[4] Heinrich Knieval was probably also a hanseatic merchant living in, or at least, visiting Boston in the early 14th century; his seal ring was found in South End (close to the likely site of the hanseatic *steelyard*) in 2002. While the Florentines of London had clearly travelled from a location some distance from the North Sea, the numbers of Flemings and Germans in particular is noticeable, indicative of a thriving and sustained trade which utilised the sea and river ports of the east coast of England.

Trade, of course, is a two-way process and, if Flemish and German merchants were settling in England, there is also clear evidence that the English themselves were located on the continent. Bruges in Flanders had a community of English merchants with their own weigh-house on the street still known today as *Engelsestraat* (Figure 5.1)[5] while the trade in grain (and probably wine) with Bordeaux was so important to Hull that three Hull men—Thomas de Sereby, Richard Upsale and Henry Taverner—were described as citizens of Bordeaux in 1347.[6] Merchants of York held property in Calais, reflecting the importance of the wool trade there, with others having interests in the Low Countries (such as John de Helmesley of York who wished to be buried in Dordrecht in 1383[7]).

However, it is not just documentary evidence or inscriptions that provide evidence of the importance of the North Sea to medieval trade and commerce. Archaeological evidence is becoming increasingly important for developing understanding of the workings of the medieval economy around the

Figure 5.1 Engelsestraat, Bruges (Brian Ayers).

North Sea littoral (and indeed further afield). An indicator can be seen in the type of stone used to make Smalenburg's memorial in Boston. There is no good local stone for such a purpose in south-east Lincolnshire and the raw material necessarily had to be imported. Transportation of a heavy stone nearly two metres in length was more easily achieved by water and no doubt Smalenburg's colleagues made use of their continental contacts when they procured a hard blue-grey limestone from the region of the River Maas.[8] The seal of Ada of Burnham, found in Greifswald (above, p. 74), was made of amber, almost certainly imported from the Baltic although, as she may well have originated from Norfolk, the amber could have been recovered from her local beach where fragments wash up to this day.[9] Amber-working itself was undertaken both on the continent and in England, a workshop for the production of amber beads being uncovered in London in 1972.[10]

Identifying such personal connections with overseas contacts through material evidence is not common but locating wider social groups and their commercial context through both surviving elements within the historic environment and recovered archaeological evidence is more straightforward. A good example of the interplay of both remains very visible in present-day Bruges. The street-name Engelsestraat has already been mentioned (used by Scots as well as English merchants) but other surviving street-names include Oosterlingenplein where the Easterlings or members of the German *Hansa* had their offices (parts of the structure survive and, in 2002, were still used by an international trading company), Spanjaardstraat where a house built by Francisco de la Torre in the early 16th century continues to stand, and Biskajersplein where the Biscayans' lodge of similar date stood. 'De Schottenplaats', around the corner from Englesestraat, contained two houses used by the Scots between 1470 and 1498 but the area is now called Sint-Maartensplein.

Bruges, as indicated by the presence of English, Scots, Germans and Spaniards, was a cosmopolitan trading city and other buildings illustrating this are either extant or are known to have existed. The Saaihalle on Vlamingstraat was built in 1399 for Genoese merchants; opposite, at Academiestraat 1, is the Florentine lodge, a building in use by these Italian merchants from 1420 at the latest but with a 14th-century roof; nearby is the Hof Bladelin owned by the Medici family of Florence from 1466; the former Venetian lodge once stood at Vlamingstraat 37-39; the site of the Lucchese lodge is now occupied by the

Hotel Lucca on Naaldenstraat; the Portuguese lodge was in Ridderstraat; and the Castilians' lodge was, unsurprisingly, on Spanjaardstraat.[11]

The development of discreet locations to house foreign merchants may have given such merchants security in an alien environment but it was also a useful control mechanism for the host city. Bruges was not alone in ensuring the provision of accommodation for foreign merchants which was readily identifiable. The merchants of the Hansa established premises in the major ports with which they traded—notably Novgorod in Russia, Bergen in Norway, London in England and, of course, Bruges in Flanders—while, on a much smaller scale, cities such as Norwich in East Anglia had a hostel where 'stranger' merchants were housed when visiting the city. This was a building erected at public expense on the north side of the Market Place, opposite the tollhouse (and subsequent Guildhall). It occupied part of the same block of property used for the Cloth Seld, another city-owned development built in 1384 wherein the quality and sale of the all-important worsted cloth of the city was monitored.[12] Even if formal lodgings were not provided, alien communities often clustered together for security (the settlement of the *Doche* or Dutch in Southwark being an example) or, in England from 1439, were required to lodge with an English host so that any business could be reported.[13]

Medieval mercantile life, however, has also provided the urban environment of Bruges with a monument of much greater European significance than the individual houses of foreign merchants. The gathering of so many individuals and mercantile companies from across Europe not only necessitated the accommodation of merchants but also the development of banking and exchange facilities. At Vlamingstraat 13, the Van der Beurse family of Bruges owned an inn from the 13th century which was used by foreign merchants and which still stands (Figure 5.2). An exchange market developed in the square in front of the building (which, restored, also still stands) and became known as the 'beurs', a name it retains (Beursplein). Commerce appropriated the term with 'bourse' coming to mean mercantile exchange. The *Byrsa Brugensis* was depicted by Sandarus in 1641 in a volume entitled 'Flandria Illustrata'; the Genoese *Domus Genuensium* and the Florentine *Domus Florentinorum* were also both marked.[14]

The North Sea economy and the development of shipping

The importance of medieval Bruges stemmed directly from its location on the North Sea coast, able to command both transnational shipping routes and a complex of land-routes to the European hinterland. Its spectacular growth dated from the 13th century when, together with much of Europe, it benefited from a commercial revolution. The relative political stability of the time combined with improvements in agriculture, developing technologies and growing populations to foster both rural and urban societies, with a concomitant positive effect upon trade and commerce. The importance of Italian merchants to Bruges (and indeed to locations such as London where an Italian community was based in the north-eastern part of the city),[15] was not only due to their banking skills but also to the fact that they dominated one part of 'a triangle of land-routes, between a Bruges-focused Netherlands, a Florence-based Tuscany and the Bohemian silver mines'.[16] This was economic, land-based *realpolitik* but the real key to the success of Bruges was that its access to the sea enabled it to act as an *entrepôt* for raw materials from the north and west as well as for the distribution of finished goods, be they textiles from late medieval England or wine and ceramics from Germany.

Bruges could not operate in an economic vacuum and its access to the sea was therefore only as good as its trading contacts and its mechanisms for undertaking that trade. Foremost amongst these mechanisms was the development of mercantile shipping from the 12th century onward. Earlier trans-North Sea vessels were essentially shallow-draught, single-masted ships, capable of swift movement and deep penetration up estuarine and riverine valleys but limited in their abilities to carry cargo. An example is the ship known as Skuldelev 1, built about 1030 in western Norway and recovered by excavation at Skuldelev fjord in Denmark in 1962 (and now displayed in Roskilde). It was an ocean-going trader known as a *knaar* capable of carrying about 24 tons of cargo.[17] More recent finds, such as the Hedeby 3 ship, built in 1025 and located in 1981[18] or the Roskilde 5 ship, constructed in 1108 and discovered in 1997[19]

Figure 5.2 House of the van der Beurse family on Beursplein, Bruges (Brian Ayers).

show that larger craft of the Nordic tradition could also carry around 60 tons. However, further south, slower and deeper ships were being developed by the end of the 11th century, vessels capable of carrying between 100 and 200 tons and probably in general use by 1200. Characterised by an almost flat flush-planked bottom, steep clinker-built sides and vertical stem- and stern-post (the latter of which would assist the implementation of a stern rudder on later vessels), such a ship (known as a *kogge* or cog) seems to be represented on the town seal of Lübeck in 1226.[20]

An example of a probable cog was excavated in Riga harbour, Latvia in 1939, an inopportune period for recovering such a vessel which was then badly damaged in the Second World War. Fragmentary elements survive within the Museum of Riga History and Navigation (Figure 5.3). A better-preserved wreck was that dating from 1380 and recovered following exposure by dredging operations in the River Weser near Bremen in 1962.[21] This vessel seems to have been under construction in Bremen when, nearly complete, it broke free and drifted downstream until it came to rest on a mudbank and could not be recovered. As a result of tipping on to its side, the starboard half of the ship is in an exceptional state of preservation, from keel almost to the rail. The vessel is now displayed in the Deutsches Schiffartsmuseum in Bremerhaven and has also been reconstructed. Recently, in 2000 and 2002, two further cogs were uncovered during dredging operations for the construction of the Deurganckdock at Doel, Antwerp, the vessel from 2000 being the better-preserved. It lay upside down in a silted-up channel which was once linked to the River Scheldt. Dendrochronological analysis of this ship dates its likely construction to 1325/1326.[22] A research project is currently underway at the Flanders Hydraulics Research (Waterbouwkundig Laboratorium) in Antwerp.

Figure 5.3 Remains of a cog excavated in Riga harbour in 1939, now housed in the Maritime Museum, Riga (Brian Ayers).

Even more recently, a virtually-intact cog was found ahead of dredging operations in the River Ijssel at Kampen in the Netherlands in 2011. Its preservation has been assisted by both freshwater and its depth (over 4m). Underwater archaeological investigation has shown that the vessel did not carry a cargo and was almost certainly sunk deliberately in order to influence the flow of the river. This hypothesis has added weight because, as well as the cog, a barge and a punter (a small flat-bottomed boat) were found in the same location. Dendrochonological work of the timbers has given a date of the first half of the 15th century for the cog with wood apparently being derived from different places. These timbers may indicate repairs to the ship prior to scuttling but clearly more work needs to be done. Currently it is felt that the three sunken vessels are an example of medieval river management, a somewhat ironic conclusion given that the discovery results from modern action to improve the river. A further irony is that the cog was found close to the dock where a reconstructed cog is berthed. Lifting of the vessel in 2014 was postponed but will proceed in the near future.[23]

The importance of cogs to long-distance trade is evident not only from the cargo volumes apparent from the study of the above discoveries but also from town seals (the Lübeck example is not the only town seal with a ship—among numerous others across northern Europe are the seals of Stralsund in Germany dating from 1267 and the 1350 seal of Elblag in Poland while the first Common Seal of Ipswich, dating to 1200, appears to show a cog with the earliest known representation of a rudder with the blade aft of the rudder-post). Occasional other images appear to illustrate cogs as well, such as the graffito from St Jørgensbjerg church, Roskilde in Denmark [24] as do references in documentary evidence. According to entries in the Bremen records, not only did Herbord of Bremen transport goods in his cog in 1224 but several other merchants were also active that year in cogs in England.[25] The great advantage of the vessel for these men was that its capacity lowered costs. The ship type was not used exclusively; shorter hauls utilised a range of range of vessels such as the *buss* in Scandinavian waters [26] and, by the 14th century at the latest, the keel in England. The cog seems to have been essentially a German vessel, possibly developing either after or in tandem with a deep-water trading ship known as a *hulc* or hulk (but archaeological examples of this latter ship remain unknown). A brick located in mid-15th century deposits at Brinkum , Lower Saxony, seems to depict a *hulc*, and some towns appear to have a *hulc* on their seals, as on the 13th-century seal of New Shoreham in Sussex.[27] However, ' ... many now refute that such a distinctive [*hulc*] tradition ever existed'.[28]

Developing commercial infrastructure requirements

The impact of deep-draughted vessels like the cog, however, was greater than their cargo-carrying capacity. While this facility undoubtedly did much to stimulate trade, the physical effects upon the ports of northern Europe were also profound. Unlike the smaller, Scandinavian-type vessels which could sail up rivers and unload over the side on to beaches, the deeper draught of the cog meant that berthing against a wharf became a necessity. In consequence, not only did ports need to develop harbour-side structures which were appropriate but, on occasion, the entire location of a port became obsolete and was superseded.

Such a transition was not occasioned by shipping technology alone. Increasingly after 1100, marginal estuarine land was becoming occupied by settlements which grew rapidly as ports. Good examples can be found on the east coast of England. The port of Lynn on The Wash was not mentioned in the Domesday Survey of 1086 but, in large part due to sponsorship by the bishop of Norwich, it grew rapidly in the early 12th century, so much so that an entire new suburb, the 'New Londe', had to be laid out in the 1140s.[29] Another Norfolk port, Great Yarmouth, was mentioned in Domesday although in 1066 it had contained a mere 70 burgesses (compared to nearby Norwich with 1320)[30] yet, again assisted by the bishop, it developed quickly and, by 1334, was assessed in the Lay Subsidy of that year as the seventh wealthiest town in England (after London, Bristol, York, Newcastle-upon-Tyne, Boston and Norwich).[31] Boston in Lincolnshire was another town not mentioned in Domesday but its standing in 1334 had already been prefigured by its contribution to King John's 'fifteenth' of 1203–1204 when it was assessed as second only to London in terms of the value of its trade while Hull in Yorkshire, another post-Domesday foundation, ranked sixth.[32]

The development of these ports was, to some extent, undertaken at the expense of older riverine ports. Places such as York and Norwich retained their commercial pre-eminence but, increasingly, shipping became confined to river traffic with transhipment taking place in the relevant estuarine port (in these cases Hull and Great Yarmouth). Similarly, Boston served Lincoln while Lynn, at the end of a Fenland river system which reached into six east English counties controlled trade to such centres as Cambridge and Bedford. The decline in commercial activity in Lincoln can perhaps be seen in its relative standing between the fifteenth of 1203–4 and the subsidy of 1334; it fell from third in the rankings to ninth.

All of the above estuarine ports, in common with counterparts across the North Sea such as Antwerp on the Scheldt, Hamburg on the Elbe or Dordrecht on the Oude Maas, had deep water anchorages which favoured ships such as the cog. Other ports, notably London, were able to develop such anchorages from pre-existing locations. In all cases, however, the need to provide both shelter for and access to larger shipping led to the deployment of innovative technologies. Exploration and assessment of both port facilities and their associated technologies, resource acquisition and use have formed major archaeological contributions to studies of commerce over the last 40 years. Excavation alone has revealed considerable numbers of wharfside revetments and other features, ranging in date from the early medieval to the post-medieval, so much so that a sub-discipline of waterfront archaeology has led to a series of specialist conferences (Figure 5.4).[33]

One of the earliest such excavations also uncovered some of the earliest waterfront structures. Following a disastrous fire in 1955 which destroyed a large part of the predominantly 17th-century hanseatic area of *Bryggen* in Bergen, Norway, work by Asbjørn Herteig revealed a complex of wharves starting in the early 1100s and continuing to be developed through to the mid-13th century. Initially resting

Figure 5.4 Cover image of the Proceedings of 5th International Conference on Waterfront Archaeology.

on the beach, structures after 1198 were extended into deeper water, necessitating a robust substructure. Relatively simple half-lap technology was utilised together with driven piles to create wharves in front of houses and warehouses on the northern shore of Vågen, the harbour of Bergen.[34]

Herteig's work was a forerunner of similar projects in many north European towns. In England, the first such excavation was undertaken by Helen Clarke (née Parker) within the courtyard of Thoresby College, King's Lynn in 1964. While constrained both in the size and the depth of excavation, she was able to identify a north-to-south aligned revetment constructed of oak posts and planks which retained the bank of the River Ouse.[35] This pioneering work was followed between 1969 and 1971 by work in Dordrecht in the Netherlands where revetments of mid-13th century date and later were uncovered[36] and, in 1978, by excavations in Hull where three phases of revetment construction were located including a 14th-century structure, dateable to 1323±9 by dendrochronology, and standing to its full height of 3.47m.[37] By far the most comprehensive work, however, was undertaken on the Thames waterfront in London.

The density of urban redevelopment in London in the 1970s and subsequently has enabled a range of excavations to be conducted adjacent to the River Thames, principally on the City side of the river (that is, the north bank) but also in Southwark. The frequently waterlogged deposits provide anaerobic conditions within which organic material such as timber rapidly reaches an equilibrium with the surrounding material and decay is arrested. In consequence, excellent preservation (Figure 5.5) is added to the benefits of excavating in deep locations where, due to a tendency to seek deeper and deeper water for anchorages, early deposits become sealed by later levels rather than being denuded by intrusive features such as cellars and massive foundations. The resulting discoveries have not only revolutionised understanding of

Figure 5.5 London, late 12th-century front-braced revetment (Museum of London Archaeology).

the development of one of Europe's principal ports but also provided a mass of information on building technologies, relative chronologies, material resource management and other topics.

An overview of the development of the port has recently been provided by Milne within which he summarises harbour construction.[38] However, more detailed consideration is necessarily given in both the interim and final reports of excavations which could be extensive; the site at Trig Lane, excavated between 1974 and 1976, uncovered some 380 square metres while Billingsgate Lorry Park extended to 500 square metres. The Trig Lane work encompassed six periods of waterfront development, from the mid-13th century to *c.* 1440.[39] Excavated features ranged from a late 13th-century front-braced revetment with rear tie-backs, through a mid 14th-century back-braced structure similar to the Hull example, to a complex back-braced revetment complete with a base for a possible water-tank. Analysis of this last structure indicated that the elaborate sequence of construction would have necessitated considerable forward planning, utilising detailed drawings in order to prefabricate the timbers off-site for later erection at the foreshore.

At Billingsgate, earlier features than those located at Trig Lane were uncovered. A possible public jetty of *c.* 1000 was replaced in the mid 11th century by consolidated foreshore banks, consisting of clay and timber fragments which were not only divided into plots but also lay either side of an inlet and probably formed the area of St Botolph's wharf. During the course of the 12th century the inlet, which linked the river to Botolph Lane and Thames Street, was narrowed and ultimately infilled, enabling development of the wharf as a location for civic entry to the city as well as the collection of customs.[40]

While the range of work in London remains unparalleled in any other north European town, excavation has now revealed embanking and the construction of waterfront revetments across the North Sea region. At Trondheim in Norway, work at Kjøpmannsgaten on the west bank of the River Nid uncovered consolidation of the river bank as an (unexcavated) waterfront was extended into deeper water in a process interpreted as associated with the advent of larger vessels.[41] A similar progression was seen at Warmoesstraat 98/Beursstraat 32 in Amsterdam in 1966–1967.[42] A well-illustrated example of the process was observed in excavation at Langenstraße 68 in Bremen where gradual infilling of the west bank of the river Weser began around 1200.[43] In Lübeck, excavations at Alfstraße 36/38 discovered two phases of 12th- and 13th-century timber structures which provided facilities for deep-water vessels.[44] However, Lübeck as a port was too successful for its site; more land was needed and, in the early 13th century, a decision was taken to extend the harbour into the southern part of the east bank of the River Trave, a decision which entailed massive investment over a prolonged period of time.

Topographical impact of commerce

The natural geography of the site of Lübeck, located on a constrained promontory between the Rivers Trave and Wakenitz, was strong but the potential for expansion of both the harbour and the town was limited. The Wakenitz was only suitable for small vessels and larger craft therefore had to use the River Trave. Geologically, the land fell away from the promontory to the Trave in such a manner that there were only three points where a commercial waterfront was possible: in the south adjacent to the cathedral; in the north adjacent to the early castle; and approximately in the centre below the site of the Marienkirche and the Markt. The non-uniform slopes of the hill to both the east and the west created embayments of low-lying land which were unsuitable for urban development. Therefore, any improvement to the commercial port, plus expansion of the urban area, needed an imaginative solution.

South of the Markt, beyond the principal crossing point of the Trave and adjacent to the river lay water meadows at the foot of St Peter's Hill, occupying an area of some 13 hectares. Prone to flooding, particularly in winter, this area would require filling to a depth of between three and five metres in order to provide an appropriate platform for housing and, at its western edge, an extension of the waterfront facilities. Excavations in 1978 at Große Petersgrube and Dankwartsgrube, undertaken with some difficulty due to the depth of deposits and standing buildings, revealed that a deliberate policy of land reclamation was indeed undertaken, probably between 1210 and 1250. Not only were substantial quantities of material tipped into the site, but any tendency of this material to subside or slide was inhibited by the careful placing of horizontal timbers at intervals throughout the deposit (Figure 5.6).[45] A similar massive programme of reclamation is also suspected on the north-western side of the promontory, facing the Wakenitz, but this remains to be tested by excavation.

The consequence of this extraordinary reclamation initiative was that the town increased considerably in size and the port itself could also develop, becoming an international port downstream of the crossing and an inland port upstream. The work at Große Petersgrube (Figure 5.7) is an excellent example of archaeology increasing understanding of urban growth, isolating a major undertaking which was not visible through study of the available documentation. With the benefit of hindsight, the local place-name evidence is probably also of assistance: it is thought that the drying-out process for the meadows, embanked prior to infilling, was assisted by drainage channels or 'Grube', the word now fossilised in the streets of Beckergrube, Fischergrube, Engelsgrube, Effengrube and, of course, Petersgrube.[46]

Lübeck was not the only town where such a co-ordinated municipal approach to urban expansion can be seen. Archaeological work in both Hamburg and Stade suggests similar action in these locations as well. Both towns were founded on *geest* sites, elevated areas above the marshy levels of the River Elbe. Both also sought to expand in the later 12th and early 13th centuries. At Stade, it is calculated that deposition of some 258,000 cubic metres of material was needed to infill part of the marsh, increasing the size of the town by some 12 hectares (from 21 to 33 hectares in extent). This material was held in place by a timber 'box' construction similar to that seen in Lübeck and from which dendrochronological dates of 1235 or 1236 were obtained.

In Hamburg, excavations took place in 1988–1989 on the Reichenstraßeninsel within the Nickolaifleet waterway (south of the *Hammaburg* ringwork—above, p. 15). The work located an extensive mound some

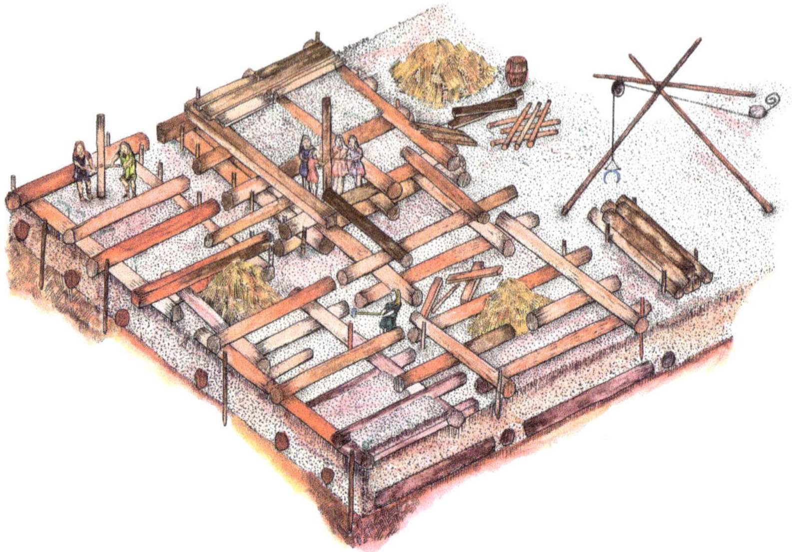

Figure 5.6 Reconstruction of boxlike infilling, Große Petersgrube, Lübeck (Bereich für Archäologie Lübeck).

Figure 5.7 Große Petersgrube, Lübeck (Brian Ayers).

2m to 2.5m thick consisting of clay, manure and household waste. This deposit, divided into a series of dam-like plots with parallel drainage ditches and with each plot some 5 to 8 metres in width and some 70 metres in length, also contained box structures to assist stability of the infill. Connecting this excavated evidence to an assumption that similar infilling took place on both sides of the Nikolaifleet, it is possible to envisage an enlargement of Hamburg within a period of 60 years from an area encompassing some 15 hectares to one covering about 80 hectares, a staggering fivefold increase. Assuming also an average height of 2 metres for the infilling, the development of such new urban land entailed the dumping of about 850,000 cubic metres of material. Unsurprisingly, it has been concluded that the work was undertaken 'with the substantial participation of the city council' ('mit wesentlicher Mitwirkung durch den Rat der Stadt').[47]

While these massive infillings at Lübeck, Stade and Hamburg were thus demonstrably deliberate acts, similar infilling in towns and cities across northern Europe was a by-product of the process of waterfront consolidation, the continual extensions of individual tenements into deeper water necessarily leading to levelling up by neighbours and probable further infilling. The provision of timber revetments not only provided wharves for shipping but also enabled consolidation of made ground upon which warehousing and other port facilities could be built. The Chapel Lane Staith site, east of High Street in Hull, examined part of one tenement where the steep river bank was masked by a revetment and its rear infilling at the end of the 13th century, a second revetment was built in the second quarter of the 14th century and, when this structure was in turn replaced, the stone footings for a large warehouse were erected above both the two early phases.[48]

A consequence of this piecemeal approach was that, over time, the rivers in ports such as Hull became more and more constrained, water needing to be kept in narrower channels. The effect was to require even deeper revetments as the embanked revetted material had to rise to provide security against flooding. The impact upon a flat natural terrain such as that of Hull is immediately visible; public staiths, running at right angles to the River Hull from High Street, slope perceptibly uphill. Another impact was upon hydrology, often with negative effects. In London, the embankment of the great sweeping north bank curve of the Thames led to enhanced erosion on the inside of the bend; 'as the City advanced, so [the southern suburb of] Southwark suffered'.[49]

High Street, Hull originated as Hull Street, a sinuous riverine street following the sinuous course of the River Hull. It is likely that early warehousing was on the west side of this street with wharves to the east. Indeed, mapping of early documentary evidence from the remarkable series of late 13th and 14th-century rentals which survive for the town, show that some property-holders had land on both sides of the street in 1347, their tenements essentially running through the street itself.[50] Other towns betray similar patterns of riverside streets now isolated from the waterfront by development above infilling: King Street and Queen Street in King's Lynn once overlooked the river but now sit more than 100m to the east[51] while in Utrecht documentary evidence suggests that, in the 13th century, tenement plots extended from Steenweg to the haven in the Oude Gracht (the Old Canal) but that subsequently houses were built upon the bank, separating Steenweg from the water.[52]

If such development was, to a large extent, undertaken in a piecemeal manner, there is some evidence from Bergen that the process here may have been more regulated. Settlement in this Norwegian town was regularly devastated by fire, enabling comprehensive re-planning to take place. The extensive area excavated in the wake of the most recent of these disastrous fires in the 1950s, together with more recent observations drawn from excavations at Finnegården 3a and 6a,[53] has enabled an understanding of the particular topography of the Vågen harbour to be established. Rather than extension into deep water occurring at all points along the frontage, it seems rather as if a large embayment was removed by a succession of waterfront encroachments to the effect that a uniform harbour frontage was created by about 1248. Within the harbour area, the process was aided by lines of double tenements, separated by passageways,[54] a pattern which survives within the extant structures of the Bryggen quarter but which did not exist elsewhere in the town.

The pattern of the tenements of Bergen is echoed to some extent by the distinctive street plan of Great Yarmouth where three principal north-to-south streets are crossed by over 130 narrow alleyways (the Yarmouth 'Rows'). Damaged by bombing in the Second World War and even more so by post-war development, the pattern is most clearly seen in Faden's plan of 1797.[55] Great Yarmouth is known to be built upon a sand spit which formed in the (geologically) very recent past. Indeed, in the Roman period, the area was open to the sea as part of a great estuary. The sinuous arrangement of the main streets has long indicated that they may have been associated with successive alignments of the river frontage which housed—and still houses—the port but archaeological evidence confirming this has proved elusive. Indeed, such limited excavation as there has been has suggested that, as in Bergen and Lübeck, the underlying topography is not as uniform as it may seem. Work at Fuller's Hill in 1974 indicated that, in this low-lying region, the site was well-named, the area forming a low eminence upon which the earliest occupation seems to have been located.[56]

The development of the principal streets south of Fuller's Hill and, more particularly, the establishment of the Rows thus remains unclear (although probable progressive infilling eastward can be inferred by the survival of the lower storey of a 12th-century, barrel-vaulted stone house at right-angles to the Yare off Howard Street, some 150m from the river and almost certainly mercantile in origin—above, p. 36[57]). Excavation in Great Yarmouth remains a difficult and expensive exercise, much of the subsoil consisting of light sands which intersperse occupation levels, often at considerable depth (four metres or more). Accordingly, an innovative archaeological programme in 2005 not only explored the series of extant historic maps of the town but also sought to provide a deposit map of the historic walled area from data extracted from excavations and boreholes. The information was computerised on a geographical information system (GIS) to construct a broad, dated, stratigraphic map of the town with which it is possible to postulate urban development (Figure 5.8).[58]

Another east coast English town where archaeological work has done much to explain topographic development is Newcastle-upon-Tyne. Here the steep slopes of the north bank of the river (crowned by the construction of a new castle in the 12th century which gives the location its name) were indented by narrow inlets for the outflow of two streams, Lort Burn and Pandon Burn.[59] Work at Queen Street in 1984–5 demonstrated that the riverbank below the hillside was consolidated with a retaining wall in the 13th century to which a stone-faced pier was added, followed by a second similar structure. Infilling then took place between the piers, enabling the creation of Queen Street parallel to the river and Fenwick's Entry and Broad Garth leading southward towards the Tyne. A southern limit to the infilling was not discovered as it lay beyond the boundary of the excavation, but it seems likely that, by the 14th century, infilling had progressed as far as Quayside (still extant) which then formed a common quay between the two burns as opposed to more private quays upstream off The Close. In the opinion of the excavators, the overall effect was to replicate the urban topography of Bergen, creating narrow lanes between long tenements. It also, like Bergen, straightened the waterfront and provided a more cohesive, public facility.[60]

Manipulation of the natural topography of a site in order to improve port facilities was not limited to embankment, revetting, infilling and occasional deliberate levelling. Where necessary, docks themselves were constructed as has been identified by archaeological survey at Hedon in east Yorkshire. Here a network of watercourses, common features in low-lying Holderness (which was mainly marshland prior to medieval drainage), was extended both to defend the planned town of Hedon and to provide extensions to a haven south of the town. A new haven known as Burstwick Old and New Fleets was established to the east, probably in the late 13th or early 14th century.[61] The Fleets were described as having widths of 18 and 20 feet (2.4m and 6m) respectively in a survey of 1367 with depths of six and ten feet (1.8m and 3m).[62] West of the town, a further probable haven, infilled in 1951, was known as Fore Bank. The sites of the havens, visible from the air at that time, have been much obscured by subsequent modern development.

Other examples of docks are known. Excavation off King Street in Norwich uncovered a well-built brick wall for a small dock at right-angles to the river, complete with two rubbing posts or fenders to

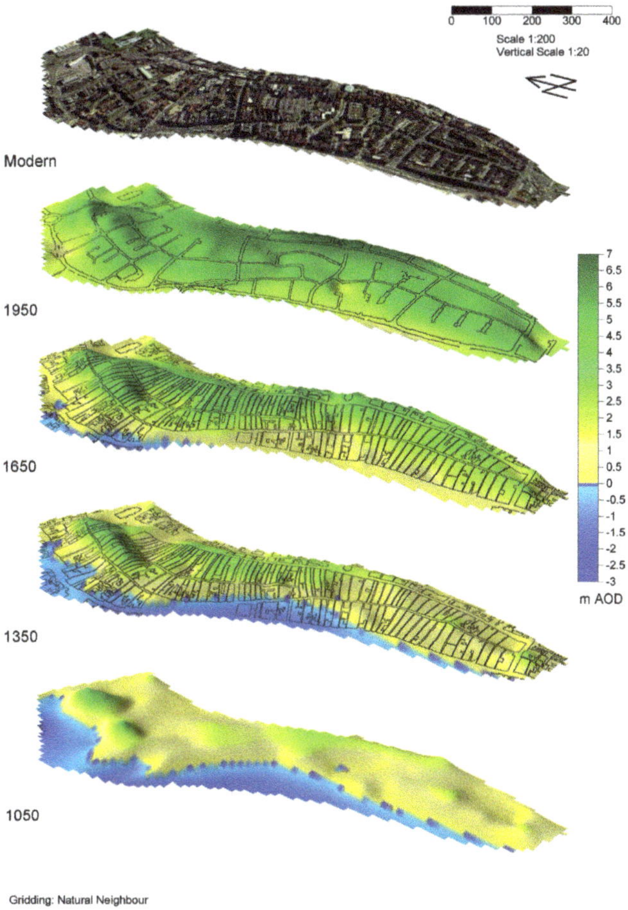

Figure 5.8 Conjectural development of Great Yarmouth (Norfolk Historic Environment Service).

prevent damage to any vessels berthed there as well as a mooring post. The quayside wall had been built above an earlier timber revetment, both structures regularising the northern edge of an inlet from the river.[63] In London, excavation at the site of Baynard's Castle in 1972 uncovered part of a stone-walled dock, again with rubbing posts.[64] Stone foundations for quays have been located at the previously lost hanseatic port of Notow (probably a Germanisation of Nautøy) at Avaldsnes, Karmøy in western Norway, a facility discovered underwater and surveyed in 2000.[65] In Oslo, timber caissons were excavated in 1971 and 1992; these formed a large construction of spruce and pine held in place by vertical piles driven into the seabed around 1300.[66]

Docks were not restricted to towns. Other institutions also required them, particularly at isolated locations such as rural monasteries. A good example is that of St Benet's Abbey, an Anglo-Saxon foundation destroyed by Viking attack and probably re-founded by Cnut *c.* 1020. It stood on an island within the River Bure in eastern Norfolk, one of a series of rivers flowing eastward to the North Sea at Great Yarmouth. Access even today can be difficult by land and the monastery must always have relied primarily upon water transport for its communications with the wider world. Little survives of the monastic fabric but a possible dock is extant as a water- and reed-filled basin immediately outside the only substantial ruins, those of the gatehouse. Very obvious in air photographs, the site has also been surveyed as part of a comprehensive survey of the surviving earthworks (Figure 5.9).[67]

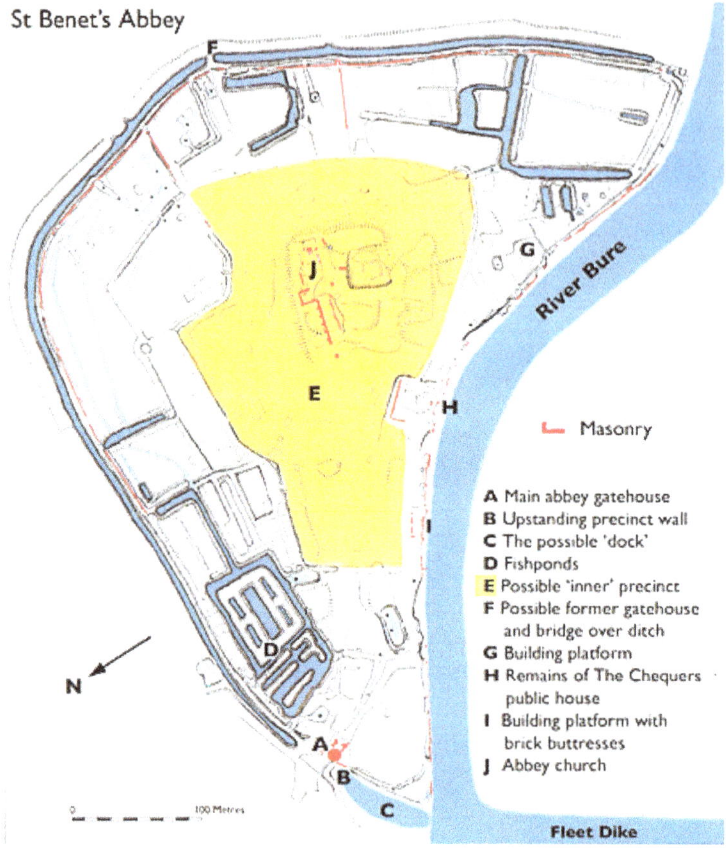

Figure 5.9 St Benet's Abbey, Norfolk–earthwork survey detail showing possible dock (Sue White: Norfolk Archaeological Trust).

Adjustment of waterways themselves to assist commercial development is known from a number of locations. At Beverley, in east Yorkshire, the Beck links the town to the River Hull. It was probably canalised in the 12th century, traditionally at the behest of Archbishop Thurston of York (1119–1140). Beckside developed as a small port with goods being landed at Grovehill (probably from the Old Scandinavian *gróf* 'stream, hollow, the hollow which makes a stream for itself'[68]) throughout the Middle Ages.[69] Across the North Sea such manipulation was carried on to a much greater extent in Bruges. The development of the complex of canals, together with infilled watercourses, is well-illustrated by De Witte.[70]

In some locations, natural changes in river flow or incursions from the sea either led to loss of port functions or severe impediment to trade. Duisburg in Germany ceased to operate as a port when both the courses of the Rhine and Ruhr either dried up or moved. By the late 14th century, its harbour had largely ceased to exist and indeed, by the 16th century, only small lighters could be used, examples of such craft being berthed in the sad remnant of the harbour (known as *Dickelsbach*) are depicted on a town plan produced by Johannes Corputius in 1566.[71] A customs post was established at Ruhrort at the newly-formed junction of the Rhine and the Ruhr rivers by 1371 and it was only from here, in the post-medieval period, that greater Duisburg was to regain its status as a major inland port. Kampen in the Netherlands, a thriving port with between 10 and 12,000 inhabitants in the 14th century, suffered from increasing sedimentation in the later Middle Ages. Attempts here to block up waterways and control the Ijssel river were in vain as were earlier frantic attempts to reopen a channel at the lost port of

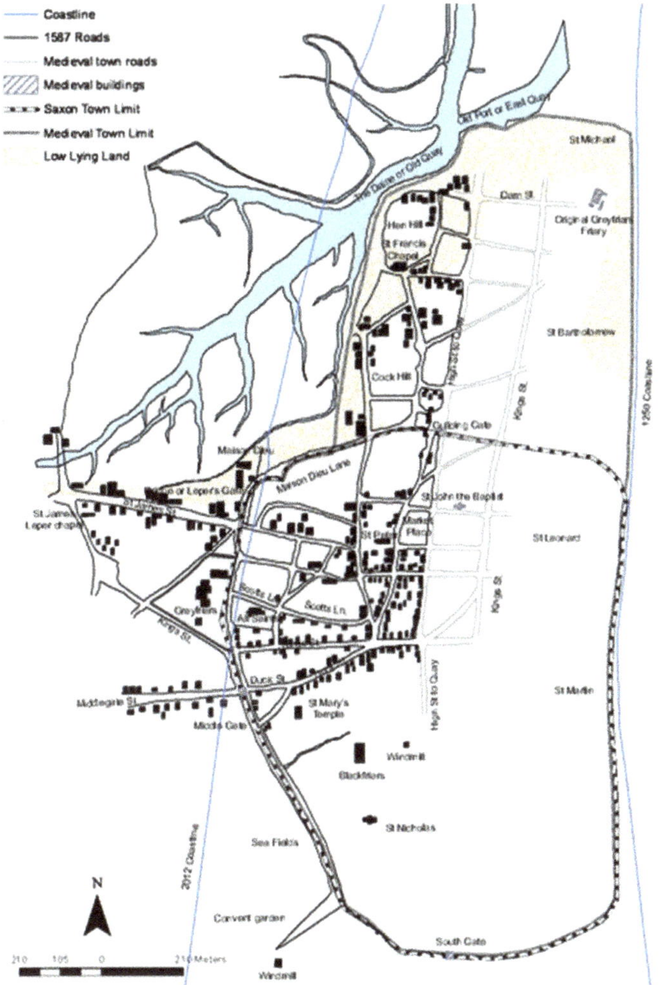

Figure 5.10 Reconstruction of the lost medieval port and town of Dunwich, Suffolk (Southampton University).

Dunwich where, in 1250, the southward movement of a spit blocked entry to the haven.[72] The channel was re-opened on this occasion but ultimately not only the haven but the town itself were both lost to the sea. North of Dunwich, Great Yarmouth suffered similarly with access to the harbour being blocked on a number of occasions, necessitating utilisation of new approaches to the sea.[73]

Dunwich is an example of a port where archaeological research—archival, terrestrial and underwater—can, by utilising a range of techniques, not only explore any vestiges of the medieval town but also undertake such work as 'hind-casting', seeking to plot the eroded coastline back to *c.* 1000 AD using Coastal Change Analysis (CCA) and Bathymetric Change Analysis (BCA). Assessment of the complex data has now enabled a reconstruction of the probable limits of medieval Dunwich which can be seen to have been a significant town, some1.8 sq km in area (Figure 5.10). With justifiable pride the summary report of the work concludes that the historical change analysis undertaken has not only enabled reconstruction of the medieval coastline but also that 'Uncertainty in the locations is low in model terms'. Further, it has been possible 'to conclude that all the major ruins identified on the seabed went through a similar process of abandonment, partial or complete demolition, progressive collapse down a cliff, and progressive passage through the beach and inner sand bank until exposure in the trough between the inner and

Figure 5.11 Rabot fortified sluice, Ghent (Brian Ayers).

Dunwich sand banks'. The available archaeological evidence, both terrestrial and submarine, has now been mapped.[74]

Some of the best evidence for medieval attempts–and indeed success–at controlling water flow has been seen in excavations at Rotterdam. Here the ingress of seawater at high tide along the courses of the Rotte and Schie rivers were controlled by dams, that at Rotterdam (the Middeldam) dating to around 1270. The dams had to work in concert with the protective dikes and had to allow the discharge of inland water. This was effected through sluices, archaeological investigation of two early examples uncovering simple but effective wooden structures consisting of a vertical tube within which hung a sluice gate on a pivot. The sluice closed with incoming water pressure forcing the gate against the sill while, at low tide, diminishing seawater pressure coupled with outward flowing river water pressure opened the gate once more.[75] The Middeldam was some 400m in length of which about 40m has been excavated.

The canal towns of the Low Countries also needed sluices to control water levels within the canals themselves. One such, the Oudezijds Kolk, survives in Amsterdam. 'Kolk' can mean 'sluice' in Dutch and was part of a system of such constructions which allowed river water to refresh and replenish the canals as well as controlling the flow of water. Some sluices were fortified; an example is the extant Rabot sluice across the Lieve canal in Ghent (Figure 5.11). More minor control of water, where smaller watercourses brought effluent and mud that they could discharge into the haven, was effected by the construction of cisterns (which then had to be cleaned). One such existed next to the river Wensum on King Street in Norwich by 1496 at the latest, at the outflow of a minor stream or *cockey* next to St Clement's church. Cleansing of cisterns was presumably profitable; this one was farmed out in that year, the successful individual selling the sewage.[76] Disposal of effluent was clearly a major problem; in London, the matter of butchers' offal was solved in 1393 and 1402 by the construction of 'a place or pier' where 'waste could be stored ... ready for disposal away from the shoreline by boat at ebb tide'.[77]

Dams, sluices, cisterns and piers ameliorated situations even if long-term coastal and riverine change could not be averted. It was, however, also possible to exploit natural features. At Hartlepool, on the northern edge of County Durham, a bay protected by a headland was improved in the 12th century by the construction of a stone-walled dock. Excavations at Southgate in 1981–1982 uncovered evidence for this dock, dating it to c. 1213. Timber posts and planks protecting shipping from damage against the dock walls were also located. The facility was modified in the mid 13th century by construction of a further wall which may acted as a breakwater and again in the later 13th or early 14th century when a substantial wharf was added above the earlier structure.[78] Even so, it would seem that the dock was only ever deep enough for small vessels, perhaps primarily functioning for local and coasting trade rather than international commerce (a supposition supported by the lack of European imported pottery in Hartlepool).

Port facilities

The creation and sustaining of a port required more than appropriate wharfage. Effective use and control of a port necessitated a wide range of other facilities, either provided privately or corporately. At a basic level, the development of larger shipping meant that harbour-side cranes were often needed to simplify the problems of loading and unloading. Manuscript illustrations of such cranes survive such as that shown lifting a tun of wine in a 15th-century representation of the port of Hamburg[79] or the cranes clearly mounted above piles in use on the River Hull in the 16th-century Cottonian plan of the town.[80] The most famous such illustrations are those showing the great tread-wheel crane of Bruges (such as that of about 1525 attributed to Simon Bening).[81] Appropriately this crane stood at the head of Kraanrei ('crane canal') which is now infilled but the location of the crane itself is called Kraanplein. Demolished in the 18th century a slightly smaller replica of the crane was recently built and temporarily erected nearby. The 14th-century crane at Lüneburg was reconstructed in 1797 after a flood but otherwise survives. Following destruction in the Second World War, the 15th-century great crane in Gdańsk was rebuilt (this last was used for raising the masts of ships).[82]

The Hull cranes were probably erected upon private staiths or wharves but two examples of public cranes are the 'jebbets' or 'jibbets' attached to a small tower associated with the weigh-house and the weigh-house crane itself, all shown on a late 16th-century plan.[83] The 'jibbets' were probably used for lifting relatively light loads, the crane for heavier material. The weigh-house in Hull (above, p. 103) shared its space with offices for the customs, regulation and taxing of goods within ports being an important activity for the state. It is interesting in a Hull context that both the weigh-house and the customs office are so far upstream; their location implies that more appropriate locations, close to the mouth of the river and the entry into the haven, had been taken by private individuals prior to the imposition of regulatory procedures in the town.

The weigh-house in Hull is lost but others survive elsewhere. Unfortunately, such survivors do not necessarily include an alleged and celebrated example from Southampton. Here, a building dating from the 13th century and now a severely-damaged ruin following bombing in the Second World War, is known as the Weigh House. Despite this, archaeological survey work found that there was 'no structural evidence to support or refute the contention that this can be identified as the building formerly used to house the weigh-beam' [for weighing wool].[84] In Bruges, however, the weigh-house (the *Tolhuis*) survives and is, as might be expected, a rather grand structure dating to 1477 with three access archways. It stands next to the slightly earlier porters' lodge (*Pijndersloge*) of 1470, the label stops of its doorway being carvings which depict workmen carrying loads (Figure 5.12).

Ghent is another Flemish city with exceptional survival of medieval mercantile public buildings. At Graslei 10 next to the River Leie stands the *Korenstapelhuis*, a storehouse dating from 13th century. Built originally as a large family house in late Romanesque style (latrines at two levels survive at the rear of the structure), it was converted for the storage of grain, Ghent holding the monopoly for the distribution of imported grain (generally from Artois in northern France) throughout Flanders. It stands close

Figure 5.12 Detail of label stop on the doorway of the 15th-century Porters' Lodge, Bruges (Brian Ayers).

to the *Korenmetershuis* or Corn Measurers' Hall, a building at Graslei 12–14 and on a trepezoidal plan. Its façade dates to 1698 but the building is otherwise entirely medieval in construction. Grain was measured here, presumably in tubs similar to the bronze example, manufactured in 1281 by Gillis van Sint-Pieters of Ghent, which is now in the city's Bijlokemuseum.[85]

Weigh-houses served the useful functions of both providing a public check on goods and enabling the imposition of appropriate taxes. The surviving *Stadtwaage* in Langenstraße, Bremen dates from the 1580s (it was badly damaged in 1944 and restored in the late 1950s) but a weigh-house is recorded in the city in 1330 and was in Langenstraße by 1440. Such buildings were especially common in the ports of the Low Countries where numerous, usually post-medieval, examples survive. The 1596 weigh-house building in Leeuwarden, for instance, stands some 30 metres west of an earlier building mentioned in 1486 but which itself must have been in existence for some considerable time.[86] Some extant weigh-houses were created out of medieval buildings; thus the weigh-house or *Waag* in Alkmaar utilised part of the *H. Geestgasthuis* or hospital of the Holy Ghost dating from the 14th century while, in the 16th century, the Amsterdam *Waag* was established in the Sint Anthoniespoort, the former city gate constructed in 1488. Within the rural Netherlands, weigh-houses performed a particular function. Dijkman has tabulated their numbers *c.* 1400 from documentary references in north Holland where she suggests that the development of the economy was such that, in enabling rural locations to gain direct access to international networks, it also necessitated the provision of weigh-houses for control of the commodity market in dairy products.[87]

Prestige goods as well as quotidian requirements of grain and dairy products necessitated measured control, none more so than textiles, the trade in which was a major factor in the economies of countries around the North Sea. Public cloth halls for assessment as well as storage of cloth survive in a number of locations. The most famous, that in Ypres (Ieper) in Flanders is now a replica, having been almost totally destroyed in the First World War but rebuilt thanks to detailed plans and drawings made by the town architect Jules Coomans before 1914.[88] A surviving example is the *Lakenhalle* in Ghent, begun in 1425 to plans prepared by the architect Simon van Assche with work stopping in 1441 when only a little over half-completed, the ambitions of Ghent too great for a cloth trade by now in decline. The English textile city of Norwich had its cloth *seld*, a hall where cloth was sealed and where regulation in the 16th century extended to the differing measures to be used for 'Flemyshe' material and by 'the English people', and where the manner in which cloth should be folded was dictated so 'that the clothes may the more speedily be measured and searched'.[89]

Material culture in forms other than excavated archaeological evidence or surviving buildings can yield information about such structures. Customs- and toll-houses were buildings that were indicative of a town's status and thus could–and did–appear on displays of corporate identity. A *tolhuys* (with a tower) is known from 1273 in Dordrecht for this very reason; it was built 'in the middle of the town at the crossing of the borders of its four quarters, the tower's dominance of both the physical and the economic urban scene is demonstrated by its prominent visibility on a triptych (*c.* 1490) dedicated to the life of St Elisabeth' [now in the Rijksmuseum Amsterdam]. The tower became a visual symbol of legal activity and appears on a 15th-century Dordrecht seal inscribed *sigillum oppidanorum in durdrehct* but had collapsed by 1574 when the town map was published by Braun and Hogenburg.[90]

Effective regulation also meant control of shipping, particularly at night. This could be best achieved by closing the haven as was possible at river ports such as Norwich and York in England. Boom towers still survive either side of the River Wensum in Norwich, linked to the line of the city wall. A chain of Spanish iron was stretched across the river between the towers in order to impede any unlicensed river traffic.[91] In York, a similar chain spanned the river between the extant 14th-century Barker and Lendal towers. This secured the Ouse within central York from illicit upstream traffic; downstream, another chain extended from the surviving, if fragmentary, Davy Tower across to the demolished Crane Tower, the latter tower so-called because of its proximity to the common crane.[92] Other chains in Yorkshire towns are known. Hartlepool's harbour was defended by two substantial towers which were designed to take a chain between them and for which 18th-century illustrations survive;[93] in Hull, a chain across the entrance to the haven may have existed by about 1380 (and was upgraded in 1541 under Henry VIII);[94] and place-name evidence in Hedon to a meadow called 'Chain Close' identifies Fore Bank as a lost haven (above p. 73).

It is interesting to note, however, that such harbour chains are solely an English phenomenon within the North Sea zone. Other examples existed on the French Atlantic Coast (notably at La Rochelle) and also in the Mediterranean (at locations such as Pisa–the chains here symbolically removed by Genoa after success in the battle of Le Meloria in 1284—and Constantinople—across the Golden Horn). However, none seem to have been utilised in ports in Flanders or North Sea-facing Germany. The question has to be asked why? The answer is perhaps found, at least in part, by the differing security needs of an essentially-unified country on an island, privileged behind its defensive moat, and continental sites subject to potentially rapid and devastating attack. Most continental ports protected themselves by constructing a wall between their harbour and the town itself, a drastic solution largely avoided in England (although there were defences on the slope above the harbour at New Winchelsea from the late 13th century [95]) until implemented in Southampton following the disastrous French raid of 1338.[96]

Within the haven itself, a variety of facilities were needed for ships and those who used them, evidence for which can be located by excavation. Stairs up from the foreshore, dating from before 1440, were identified for three different tenements at Trig Lane in London. They consisted of a parallel stair where a platform was laid against the frontage, presumably supporting a stair descending parallel to the wharf; a tangential stair which would have stood at right-angles to the frontage; and a jetty stair which consisted of a planked walkway extending at right-angles in front of the wharf before descending to the foreshore. The archaeological identification of three tenements confirmed the documentary evidence which suggested three properties occupied by separate tenants.[97]

Work at Trig Lane also uncovered evidence for a possible late 14th-century water tank.[98] A larger and later tank dating to about 1480 was excavated at Oyster Street, Portsmouth, a port with access to the

North Sea *via* the English channel, in 1970. This cistern, originally 25ft (8m) in depth, was constructed of timber set into a pit 20ft (6.5m) deep and, when intact, would have held over 11,500 gallons (52,280 litres) of fresh water, presumably for victualing ships.[99]

In those areas where tidal range was particularly great, the fall of water level might impede the unloading of shipping. This was certainly recognised as a problem in Hull where a platform for shipping to rest upon was excavated at Chapel Lane Staith.[100] Such platforms were a long-lived element within the haven; a report by James Oldham, a civil engineer, in 1845 noted that

> ' It has been and still is a custom for persons occupying wharfs and warehouses ... to construct ... embankments of stonework to form what they call "docks", being berths for vessels to lie upon or in, when discharging of or taking in cargoes. They are made by forming a bank of stones along the edge or margin of the stream or channel at low water ... of rough masses of chalk and other stones ...'.[101]

Not all rivers had the tidal range of Hull. In Norwich, the River Wensum is barely tidal and, by the 15th century, most vessels would have consisted of river traffic rather than seagoing ships, shallow-drafted vessels such as the forerunners of the post-medieval East Anglian keel and wherry. Nevertheless, quayside facilities were still required and access to them needed to be assured. Public staithes reached the waterfront from the main river-port street of King Street but private wharves also needed to be linked to mercantile properties at the street frontage. Comprehensive excavation at the rear of the surviving late-medieval Dragon Hall revealed that, in the second quarter of the 15th century, several tenements and a common lane were amalgamated together, the lane closed at the street end and its truncated length to the river converted into a private internal link for the merchant and his goods.[102]

Norwich and locations such as Dragon Hall were not alone in using river craft for the transport and handling of merchandise. The River Wensum is a relatively small and meandering watercourse, most suitable for such craft which carried goods transhipped from deeper seagoing vessels berthed at the estuarine port of Great Yarmouth. In a similar fashion, river craft would have used the Witham from the port of Boston up to Lincoln and the estuarine port of King's Lynn served inland counties of England via the river systems flowing through the Fens. On the continent, rivers were important conduits inland to major ports such as Deventer in the Netherlands. Seagoing craft could use the large River Rhine to get well into inland areas but smaller rivers had their uses as well. Göttingen, deep within Lower Saxony, lies on the small Leine river upstream of Hanover but the Leine connects with the Weser and was of sufficient draught and width to enable Göttingen to function as a hanseatic river-port.

Nevertheless, the main ports could have problems of communication when seeking to transship goods either to or from inland locations. As an example, the salt industry of Lüneburg in northern Germany was a critical factor in the development of Lübeck's mercantile influence. The distribution of salt via Lübeck to destinations such as the hanseatic *kontor* of Bergen was a fundamental necessity for the trade in fish which otherwise had to be dried as stockfish. However this was not the only commercial outlet for salt; Lübeck merchants could, and did, argue that there was demand for Lüneburg salt 'in all the countries with which the Lübeck merchant trades'. Unfortunately, transporting the salt from Lüneburg was difficult and largely dependent upon the *Alte Salzstraße* or Old Salt Road, an overland route utilising largely unmade tracks. This was a traditional route for such transport even before Lübeck was founded, merchants using it to reach Alt Lübeck (now an earthwork adjacent to the River Trave north of Lübeck itself—above, p. 15).[103] Matters improved dramatically in the late 14th century with construction of the *Stecknitzkanal*. This remarkable example of engineering infrastructure was the first 'summit-level' or watershed canal in Europe, crossing a high point between the small Stecknitz river (a tributary of the River Trave) and the Delvenau (a tributary of the Elbe). Completed in 1398, the canal contained 17 wooden locks (of which one, renewed in stone in the 18th century, survives as the *Palmschleuse* at Lauenburg). This 97km long waterway was 7.5m wide but only 0.85m deep. It was traversed by flat-bottomed barges, as many as 1500 a year in the 15th century, bringing salt to Lübeck and returning with goods for the hinterland and onward connection to Hamburg.[104]

The exact nature of the locks on the Stecknitz canal has long been a matter of conjecture. The provision of chamber locks, where water is impounded between two pairs of gates, would have been precocious but not unprecedented. An example of a chamber lock was perhaps built a few years earlier, in 1373, at Vreeswijk near Utrecht in the Netherlands and an even earlier such lock, documented as a *spoje*, may have been installed in 1220–1226 at Spaarndam, also in the Netherlands. However, the topography of the Netherlands and the dual functioning of Dutch canals as elements in the drainage system as well as their self-evident use for transport, meant that it did not necessarily follow that chamber locks were also employed on the Stecknitzkanal.

Recently, a comprehensive review of the Stecknitzkanal evidence has been undertaken. Actual archaeological survey is complicated because much of the medieval canal was recut and significantly enlarged in the 19th century to form part of the Elbe-Trave Canal, destroying much earlier infrastructure in the process. Nevertheless, it was possible to combine such archaeological observation as was possible with a range of other evidence sources—documentary, hydrological, hydraulic function, constructional technique and operational aspects—and to prepare a dynamic flow simulation model, concluding that chamber locks must have existed from the outset. With some pride, the paper's final sentence reads: 'Diese sind unter die ersten nachgewiesenen Kammerschleusen Europas einzuordnen' ('These are classified as the first *proven* [my italics] chamber locks in Europe').[105]

Warehouses, storage and security

Despite the riverine problems noted at Duisburg (above, p. 160), archaeological work here has demonstrated that warehousing continued to be provided even though access to the Rhine was becoming increasingly difficult. Excavations in 1989 uncovered evidence for 12th- and 13th-century harbour buildings beneath Niederstraße. Consisting of long, rectangular warehouses, these buildings were constructed against the massive defensive wall adjacent to the harbour with timber work above stone or brick footings forming their other sides.[106] Duisburg was at the southern end of the salt route and these buildings could have been used for the storage of salt. At the northern end of the route, in Lübeck, great salt warehouses (or Salzspeicher) still stand next to the River Trave. Constructed of brick between 1579 and 1745, it is probable that they were successors to medieval examples within the port. The buildings stand close to the Holstentor and the early bridging point of the River Trave (a bridge is recorded here in 1216); they are thus located at the boundary between the inland and seagoing ports of Lübeck (Figure 5.13).

The salt warehouses of Lübeck were specialist buildings, built specifically for one commodity. The majority of other warehouses were more generally utilitarian and, indeed, before the 15th century at the earliest, waterfront warehousing was rarely within buildings designed exclusively for storage. Rather, quayside structures contained offices, shops and domestic accommodation as well as storage facilities. In consequence, excavated archaeological evidence can prove difficult to interpret and may account for a surprising dearth of buildings reported as warehousing in the academic literature, at least until the later Middle Ages. Even in London, Milne's summary of the extensive excavations on sites associated with the medieval port can only discuss two such discoveries, a 12th-century timber footing for apparently massive—but robbed out—stone buildings (the felling date of the timbers being 1136) and the late 12th-century aisled hall, some 18 metres in length, of German merchants from Cologne (the site subsequently become that of the hanseatic Steelyard, the *Kontor* in London–above pp. 125–126).[107]

A good example of a mercantile complex which incorporated warehousing is that established at the above-mentioned location of Dragon Hall in Norwich (p. 166) in 1427 by a cloth merchant (and politician) named Robert Toppes.[108] Its warehouse, while forming its focal point, was also more than a place to store goods. A two-storey structure, it was designed to be seen and visited, its architecture reflecting the wealth and position of its owner. As an example, on the upper floor, a carved open-work dragon, complete with its original paint, survives within a spandrel of the crown-post roof. If, as seems likely, this image was originally paired with a carving of St George, the ensemble would form a none-too-subtle reminder of the status of Toppes as a member of the Guild of St George, synonymous with the oligarchy

Figure 5.13 Inland port and salt warehouses in Lübeck (Brian Ayers).

which ran the city corporation. This upper hall, almost certainly used as a selling hall for Toppes' cloth, was flanked by a domestic hall at right-angles to the street and further buildings to the north and within the rear tenement area.

The ground-floor river frontage of the main warehouse at Dragon Hall consists of a covered arcade, open to the river but providing shelter from the elements. It is an arrangement that not only enabled goods to be placed under cover rapidly, prior to more considered storage within the warehouse, but is one that is known both from other extant examples and from manuscript illustrations, such as that for the 15th-century port of Hamburg mentioned above (p. 103). Schofield has noted that Wyngaerde's 1544 illustration of Billingsgate in London shows 'four establishments ... [with] open arcading on the ground floor of the western upstream ranges. ... These arcaded ranges must have served the same functions as open-sided market halls elsewhere in medieval towns: temporary storage of bales or crates, and space for examination of goods and bartering'.[109]

The complex at Dragon Hall illustrates well the interdependence of storage, commerce and domestic accommodation within structures located at the waterfront. Its arcaded range is paralleled in Norfolk in a brick-built structure, Hampton Court in King's Lynn. This too dates from the 15th century and was clearly part of a merchant's complex arranged around three sides of a courtyard. Its now blocked brick-arched arcade almost certainly fronted on to a wharf, below a modern lawn (Figure 5.14).[110] A further possible medieval warehouse survives in Lynn, a building known as Marriott's warehouse which stands parallel to the river on South Quay. While the bulk of the present structure probably dates to *c.* 1580, some elements appear to be 14th-century. The structure was erected upon a small island within the estuary of the River Ouse, in advance of most buildings behind properties fronting on to Queen Street. Parker's assessment of the building includes the observation that 'High tide must have surrounded the building; floods washed frequently at its walls ... the series of arched openings which still survive in the ground floor of the north gable end ...were perhaps put there to reduce the danger of structural damage

Figure 5.14 King's Lynn–Hampton Court warehouse arcade (Brian Ayers).

from floods by allowing the water to be taken through the building in a special channel which has since disappeared.[111] This building surely was solely used as a warehouse rather than also providing accommodation.

Riverside warehousing was essentially used for goods in transit as clearly shown by the salt warehouses of Lübeck. Goods less likely to be shipped onward rapidly would often be stored away from the waterfront, as evidenced by the large mercantile buildings of the greater hanseatic ports, Lübeck again being the exemplar. Here numerous buildings, on occasion dating from the 12th century as surviving on the west side of Kleine Burgstraße, combined the functions of commerce and domesticity within a single structure.

Storage in merchants' houses

Work by Bereich Archäologie in Lübeck over the last 30 years has entailed examination of a range of buildings as well as excavation of demolished structures. It is now clear that, by the 13th century, the commercial success of the town had led to the development of building types which ensured a mixture of domestic and commercial functions while maximising the use of a constricted site. Early work by Erdmann,[112] in which he sought to establish a framework for the study of the buildings of the town, has been followed by more detailed typological analysis. Excavated evidence suggests that, while the first urban structures were built of wood, buildings were nevertheless often of several storeys with space for storage as well as domestic apartments.[113] Subsequently stone and then, increasingly and almost ubiquitously, brick structures were erected.

The most common house form in Lübeck from the mid 13th century was the *Dielenhaus* (see also Chapter 4) but it was preceded by a building type of considerable importance, the *Saalgeschlosshaus*. This structure, characterised by narrow tenement plots with the house gable end-on to the street and/or wharf, has been recorded at a number of locations, one of the most significant being that at Alfstraße 38

Figure 5.15 Dielenhäuser in Alfstraße, Lübeck in 1910 (Bereich für Archäologie Lübeck).

which has been dated dendrochronologically to 'around 1216'. The building here was erected above the site of a timber building of 'about 1195' with a half-cellar or undercroft.[114]

Erdmann cites *Saalgeschlosshäuser* from Lübeck locations such as Mengstraße 62, Koberg 2, Königstraße 9 and Große Petersgrube 17 but the type is known from a number of towns around the North Sea and the Baltic. Examples are recorded from Deventer in the Netherlands where a partially-surviving building on the market square was identified, originally more than 15.5 metres in length and dating from the 13th century;[115] beneath the Rathaus in Stade on the lower Elbe where the remains of a 13th-century *Saalgeschlosshaus* have been identified;[116] and on Ossenreyerstraße 52/Heilgeiststraße 22/23 in Stralsund.[117] Not all *Saalgeschlosshäuser* are necessarily associated with maritime trade; examples have also been identified at inland riverine sites such as Göttingen [118] and Einbeck,[119] indicating that the type was a useful structure for a variety of merchants.

The exceptional preservation of the built historic environment in Lübeck in particular has enabled detailed study of buildings such as *Dielenhäuser*, assisted by documentary research (Figure 5.15). A good extant example of such a building is that at Fleischhauerstraße 79, recently restored and with the oldest parts dating from 1293 (although the stepped-gable façade is late 16th-century). In common with other such buildings, the room on the ground floor is exceptionally high with the first floor above relatively low in comparison. Above that are storage lofts and, uniquely surviving here, an internal winch for moving goods within the building.

The evolution of the typical brick-built *Dielenhaus* from earlier timber structures has also been explored in Lübeck through excavation, as at Dr. Julius Leber Straße 34 and 36. Here, timber buildings of mid 13th-century date were fronted by a brick façade before the end of the 1200s and replaced entirely by many-storeyed brick buildings no later than the beginning of the 14th century. Lübeck suffered disastrous fires in 1251 and 1276, leading to strict regulations thereafter, seeking building with fireproof brick.[120] Research further afield indicates that the *Dielenhaus* form originated in Westphalia and was disseminated to the Baltic region, being particularly suited to mercantile communities; the buildings were set at right-angles to the street, thus maximising opportunity for street frontage occupation, they contained a hall (the *Diele*) and they had provision for large quantities of storage space. As noted above (p. 116) examples can be cited from Stade, Uelzen and Lüneburg amongst other locations.[121]

Many *Dielenhäuser* had cellars, often with *Nischen* or side-chambers roofed with shallow barrel vaults, increasing their storage capacity further. The amount of storage space was exceptional; calculations for Lübeck show that the average size of the lower floor of a *Dielenhaus* was some 160 square metres, enough for 16 *last* or 32 tons of grain. Assuming 350kg of grain per person per year, the likely storage capacity on ground floors alone within medieval Lübeck was sufficient to hold grain to feed some 45,000 people. This excluded the storage space of lofts and cellars and of those storage houses which were often constructed behind the *Dielenhaus* itself. This clear over-provision for the needs of the urban population (perhaps some 20,000 people) probably indicates the importance of the grain trade to the city.[122]

Moving bulk goods within buildings such as Dielenhäuser was obviously problematic. Occasionally evidence survives for mechanisms that facilitated such activity as at Fleischhauerstraße 79 in Lübeck. At Marktplatz 15 in Einbeck, a mid 16th-century house still contains a winch wheel and windlass for the lifting of goods to the upper floors (Figure 5.16).[123] In Göttingen, at Johannisstraße 6, the evidence is less overt but still clear for a similar arrangement: wooden sockets survive for the anchoring of a winch wheel in the attic of the building.[124]

The brick buildings of Lübeck and other north German towns are paralleled in Antwerp where a similar dearth of building stone led to the construction of houses utilising brick. Initially, however, archaeological analysis of mercantile structures here suggests that while the earliest buildings dating to the 13th century had brick foundations and side walls, they retained timber façades. Full brick construction with brick gables only began in the 15th century, an example being the splendid building for German merchants which survives on Oude Koornmarkt, complete with a brick-vaulted cellar. The exact function of this building is difficult to determine but recent archaeological examination of another house on the Koolkaai during conservation works has uncovered a late 15th-century interior complete with a cellar accessible from the exterior. This is interpreted as a storage area, quite probably for fish, with trade taking place on the ground floor. The building is not large with only one room on both the ground and first floors although it is possible that the second floor was divided into smaller rooms and also used for storage. The structure as a whole is now regarded as typical of the type of house 'inhabited by the average merchant' in Antwerp.[125]

The lack of stone merchants' houses in Antwerp contrasts sharply with Ghent, only some 50km upstream; while no medieval stone houses have been identified in Antwerp, over 200 (not necessarily all mercantile) are recorded in Ghent. Here major buildings, such as the 15th-century Grote Moor and the Zwarte Moor at Hoogpoort 60 and 62, survive as grand examples of mercantile power, with recent buildings' research enabling understanding of earlier structures. One such is the Hof van Ryhove at Onderstraat 20–22, owned by the international textile merchant Simon de Rijke in 1371 but shown to have a roof dating from the 13th century. Indeed, the quality of the houses in Ghent has led to it being termed 'middeleeuws Manhattan' or the medieval Manhattan, not because of soaring towers but because of the mercantile wealth displayed in the buildings.[126]

Scale, locations and evidence of mercantile activity

Archaeological evidence for commercial activity and interchange is thus readily visible in the form of the built environment, its below-ground footprint where buildings have been demolished, and in the

Figure 5.16 Einbeck, winch in Marktplatz 15 (Photo: Andreas Heege, Zug, Switzerland).

form of artefacts (and occasionally ecofacts) but use of these physical survivals will not be effective if they are merely employed as illustrations to the arguments of economic historians. As an example of such traditional interaction, the movement of bulk goods can be characterised as heavily influenced by the 'pull' exercised by the newly-created urban markets of northern Europe or, conversely, by the 'push' of economic developments further east (such as colonisation of the eastern Baltic and the increased availability of raw materials created thereby) when explored through the available documentation. As an aside, it has been somewhat sardonically noted that these push-pull readings 'are more likely to be reflections of changes in the supply of historical resource material rather than of the actual development of medieval trade'.[127] The grain known to have moved through Lübeck, and for which it has been shown ample storage was available, is an example of a bulk commodity but the existence of grain stores only confirms historical observations rather than helping to provide new concepts of the economic imperatives behind commercial activity.

Imaginative use of archaeological evidence, however, can enable more profound approaches. Verhaeghe has provided one such with regard to the use of ceramics, pointing out that growing awareness of the medieval pottery trade, its diversity and distribution, 'may very well reflect the growing complexity of social and economic systems and behaviour of those times'.[128] Archaeology cannot compete with historical sources when documents speak of trade in hides, fat or wool. However, detailed study of physically-resilient commodities such as pottery can suggest much about the mechanics of trade and thereby by inference about the likely organisation of such trade, structures not necessarily self-evident from the available documentation.

As an example, something of the likely distribution network for exports of German beer, noted above as a major bulk commodity (p. 81) and one documented in production centres such as Bremen, Hamburg and Rostock,[129] can perhaps be gleaned from analysis of the provenance of beer barrels. These utilitarian vessels, which could carry fish as easily as beer when engaged for primary purposes, had varied secondary functions, including frequent re-use to line cesspits. Accordingly, they have been recovered from anaerobic deposits in a number of German towns with dendrochronological analysis of their timbers indicating timber sources in the eastern Baltic and Sweden, suggestive of fish exports (probably herring) to Germany but also indicating likely areas of timber exploitation and trade routes thereafter. Conversely, trade eastwards of German commodities is indicated by the bases of barrels and other wooden objects located in Novgorod, bearing the inscribed marks of western European merchants.[130]

Such analysis of material discoveries means that archaeology has great potential for a significant contribution to the understanding of the mechanics of trade within the wider North Sea region. A further example concerns perhaps the most important of all commercial trades in terms of their revenue (certainly from an English perspective) which were those conducted in wool and textiles. Considerable historical research has been undertaken into the economic impact of these activities, drawing upon customs accounts and the like, for both an understanding of the importance of individual ports and for assessments of the overall importance of wool and cloth exports to national economies (an example of the former being the seminal paper by Carus-Wilson and of the latter the work of Lloyd[131]). One archaeological approach to gloss such research concerns the examination of cloth seals.

These (usually lead) accessories were attached to bolts and bales of cloth to signify their place of origin and their quality. The distribution of these seals clearly provides an indicator of the extent of the trade, such objects being found on sites across northern Europe. Thus a seal from Tournai dating to the 14th century has been found in Greifswald on the Baltic and another, slightly later, in Novgorod in Russia.[132] While such discoveries are not necessarily surprising given known historical transactions, study of cloth seals nevertheless reveals commercial nuances invisible in the documentation. An example is linen production in the small Belgian town of Diest. Documentation of this in historic sources seem to have been subsumed under references to the nearby centre of Leuven (Louvain) through which the products of Diest would have passed on their way to markets as diverse as London, Meols in Cheshire and 's-Hertogenbosch in the Netherlands (all of which are locations of finds of Diest cloth seals). Similarly, while documentary evidence records over 4000 English cloth finishers settled in Antwerp in the early 16th century–individuals presumably fulling, shearing and dyeing English cloths passing through the town–the almost total lack of any archaeological evidence for such activity is extremely puzzling. Despite the documentation, therefore, the conclusion has to be drawn that in Antwerp 'the majority of the [English] goods with their labels presumably just [passed] through to consumers in Germany and Central Europe', contrary to the impression gained from the documents (see also below, p.182).[133]

Archaeological evidence is particularly good for providing information both for those parts of the medieval period when documentation is lacking (such as the 11th and 12th centuries) or those parts of northern Europe where written commercial records can be sparse. Novgorod in Russia brings together both conditions. The anaerobic deposits here are especially noted for preserving textiles and analysis of some 462 samples of woollen cloth has demonstrated that between the 10th and 12th centuries, English woollen cloth was 'widespread' in the town. This is early evidence for the export of English cloth when much traditional historic assessment concentrates upon raw wool exports, traded to cloth-makers on the continent.

The largest customers for English wool were the makers of Flemish cloth, a highly-prized commodity in the 12th and 13th centuries. Flemish cloth traders visited the great fairs in Champagne, France, located at places such as Bar-sur-Aube (where an arcaded galley within which merchants could meet still survives),

Lagny, Provins (the fair taking place on a great open space outside the church of St Ayoul) and Troyes. The main customers were Italian but Germans also bought cloth there, paying in silver from newly-discovered mines in the area of Freiburg. Coinage struck at Provins and Troyes in the late 12th and early 13th centuries took the form of silver deniers or *provinois*; these coins were exported in large numbers to Italy. Many of them were inscribed with a distinctive weaving comb upon them. Paul Arthur has noted such coins have been found 'in many locales in Italy, reaching as far south as the Terra d'Otranto' and perhaps representing 'the far-reaching importance of the great wool fair of Champagne'.[134]

The international troy weight for weighing commodities was developed from the 'Troyes' standard established at the Champagne fairs; Spufford observes, possibly wryly, that it is significant that money seemed to flow south to Italy but that weight standards moved north.[135] However, 'coinage provinces' were established in the north; standardised silver coins were introduced from 1379 by six hanseatic towns–Lübeck, Hamburg, Lüneburg, Rostock, Stralsund and Wismar—once an agreed political authority was in place.[136] These towns formed a 'Stadtrechtsfamilie of town laws and statutes, in this case Lübisches Recht which was applied to most of the Baltic towns. It clearly extended to Hamburg of the North Sea zone but interestingly not to Bremen which fostered 'Bremisches Recht'.

Arthur explores an archaeological approach to the study of fairs, noting the difficulties that such transitory sites present for archaeological study. 'Trace archaeology' is the most that can normally be expected of the temporary booths and stalls which would be set up although there is perhaps potential for concentrated metal-detector survey of small rural fair sites where concentrations of objects could be anticipated (as noted on numerous metal-detector websites). Fairs are documented across northern Europe and some of them were major events; the herring fair at Great Yarmouth was active from at least the 13th century and was held on the great market place which still exists. The Yarmouth burgess Thomas Damet writing in the late 16th century stated it as being filled with 'great numbers of the fishermen of Fraunce, Flaunders and of Holland, Zealand and all the lowe countries yerelie, from the feaste of Sainte Michaell the Archangell, untylle the feaste of Sainte Martine, about the takinge, sellinge and buyenge of herringes'.[137]

Locating archaeological evidence for the Great Yarmouth fair would be exceptionally difficult as is generally the case for the great herring fair held on Skåne (Scania), east of the Øresund in what is now southern Sweden (above, p. 87). Here, initially at Skanör in the 13th century and then, in the 1300s, at Falsterbo, important fairs were held between August and October. Archaeological excavation at Falsterbo has, however, revealed traces of clay floors which have been interpreted as remnants of temporary storehouses measuring some 6.m by 1.8m in size.[138] The original name of the settlement was Falsterbothe meaning 'the Falster huts for fishermen', a good description of the ephemeral structures. The site was sufficiently important for royal buildings to be erected in order to monitor and control the trading activity, Falsterbohus castle surviving as earthworks which were excavated in 1934–35 by Ragnar Blomqvist.

Fairs in Scandinavia seem, in some instances, to have preceded the establishment of towns. The town of Ystad in southern Sweden appears from archaeological work to have had a fair or seasonal market as early as the 8th century while Aalborg on Limfjord in Denmark was probably preceded by a trading site at Bejsebakken which is now on the outskirts of the modern town.[139] The sites of fairs can often be explored by careful topographical analysis. An example is the Newport Green fair of Lincoln, immediately north of the walled medieval city. Here a survey by J. S. Padley about 1840 detailed properties and parish boundaries in the area, revealing 'the long, cigar-shaped market place' used for the site of the fair which gained a charter in 1330 and was known for its sale of Lincoln cloth.[140]

As well as fairs, trade also relied upon a network of local markets. The proliferation of these, particularly in England, is something which has long been noted by economic historians. Mapping the growth has been shown in a number of ways; for Norfolk, Dymond locates markets with red and black dots, each dot linked to the earliest documentary reference of the market but the black dots indicating those markets out of use by the 17th century (Figure 5.17).[141] In Suffolk, Scarfe has illustrated urban growth

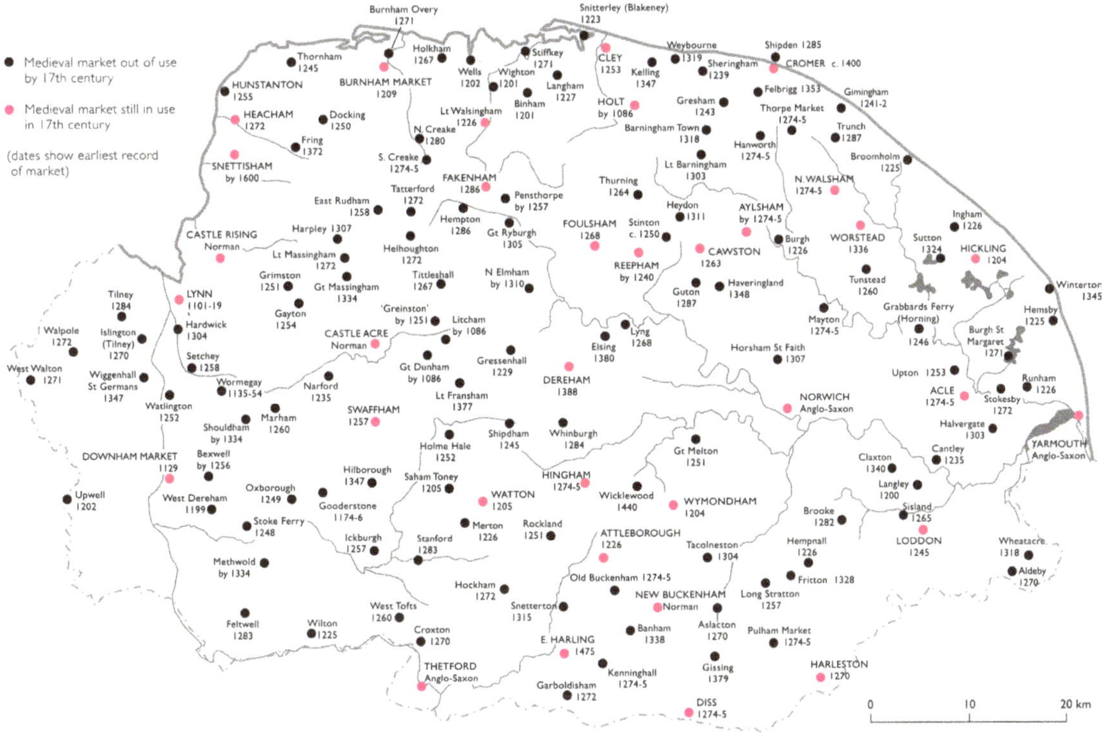

Figure 5.17 Norfolk, medieval markets (David Dymond and Trevor Ashwin).

including markets for the periods before 1100, between 1100 and 1350, and after 1350 (nearly all creations being in the 12th, 13th and early 14th centuries).[142] In the Lincolnshire historical atlas, markets and fairs are presented on the same map, ambitiously seeking to depict relationships between the two types, those that were failures, and relative decline or growth.[143] All three counties show a great number of locations where mercantile activity was possible.

One approach to observing probable mercantile movement through archaeological material concerns the recording of personal seal matrices, usually discovered through metal-detecting. In Norfolk such matrices have been published annually since 1998 by Steven Ashley and Andrew Rogerson and, while the objects are often difficult to date closely, a significant corpus is now available. One recent discovery from Costessey just west of Norwich is inscribed * S' · ThOME : BRVN · DE IERNEMVTE and was the personal seal of Thomas Brown of Yarmouth. It depicts two probable merchants in conversation beneath a merchant's mark (Figure 5.18).[144] Other discoveries indicate the range of likely contacts between Norfolk and the North Sea world, not all of them necessarily mercantile. One such that seems to have served as a seal matrix for a commercial individual is that of Henry le Vigneron, decorated with a woman's head and breasts as well as a vine and probably French. Other likely merchants who seem to have lost their personal matrices were Terry John of Holland (probably German or Dutch) and Werner Wernerson (Flemish, German or Scandinavian). Plotting the incidence of 'alien' matrices is fraught with difficulty as almost all the objects have been recovered from plough-soil without any contextual information to suggest the cause of deposition but, perhaps unsurprisingly, the find-spots generally appear to group close to river valleys linking to the sea—the Yare, the Waveney, the Glaven and the Nar.

A further archaeological approach towards the study of mercantile activity, that of examination of official weights, is also being enhanced by the results of metal-detecting. Weights used on steelyard balances of measurement are well-known (several examples have been catalogued and illustrated from

Figure 5.18 Personal seal matrix of Thomas Brown of Yarmouth (Steven Ashley: Norfolk Historic Environment Service).

London [145]) but control of the accuracy of such balances can also be surmised from the discovery of weights with armorial decoration. Some four-fifths of the examples recovered from London bear the image of a double-headed eagle and it is is tempting, but probably incorrect, to ascribe these as reflecting hanse control (a fine example of a copper-alloy steelyard weight bearing four shields—the arms of England and the double-headed eagle alternating—was found at Catton, outside Norwich in the 19th century). A weight with three single-headed eagles recently discovered in Norfolk may possibly have hanseatic links although it could also bear the arms of Richard of Cornwall (Figure 5.19). A manifestation of national control is perhaps implied by another Norfolk discovery, a flat pan weight cast in the shape of a shield and bearing an heraldic wyvern. Found in 2002, it can be dated to the late 12th century and is therefore both very early and unparalleled for such an object. It implies use by a noble, sheriff or commissioner of the crown regulating weights 'on a local, hundred or county basis, in the name of the king'.[146] Archaeological discovery here helpfully provides the earliest evidence for such royal control.

The Norfolk heraldic weight is unlikely to have been a standard Troy ounce (above, p. 174), being both underweight and too early. However, this 'Troy' measurement, like the silver deniers, was of great influence with the hanse which, as with coinage, introduced its own standards. Scale balances and weights were specially made in Nuremberg. 'Norms for weights and measures were ... agreed upon collectively. This was one of the tools for cutting individual traders' transaction costs (they did not have to carry out checks themselves) and thus make it profitable for them to join the hanseatic network'.[147] As an example of such standardisation, even in the far north on Faroe local measures were replaced by the Hamburg *ell* as the principal unit of measurement, a rod or *stikka* for this length being preserved in the National Museum of Faroe Islands.[148]

Archaeological research therefore continues to contribute to an understanding of commercial interaction, not only through broadening awareness of the legacy of material culture [149] but also by helping

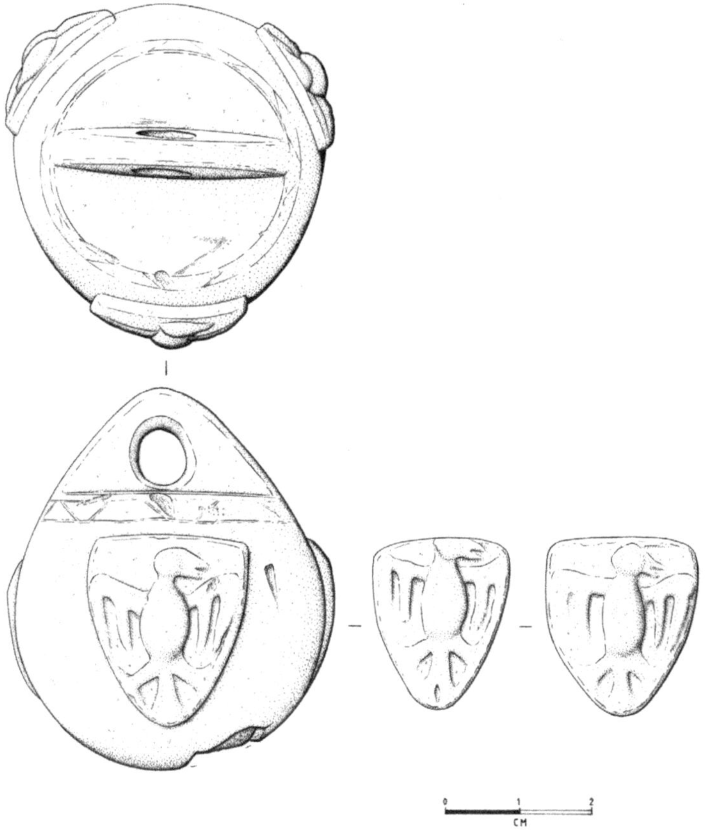

Figure 5.19 Armorial weight with single-headed eagle (Steven Ashley: Norfolk Historic Environment Service).

to shift perceptions of the penetration of commercial and other values across the North Sea world. Developments in theoretical archaeology have sought to envisage artefacts as 'cultural carriers' or *Kulturträger* (see above, p. 105), objects which carry meaning for societies; it has been noted that 'with the widespread distribution of artefacts produced in the core of the Hanseatic League, *Hanseatic* became a particular way of life [for commodity consumers], whether acquired by intention or not'.[150] However, such observations come with caveats; numerous scholars have noted the problems presented by the differing forms of trade, particularly within the area of the Hanseatic League. Trading patterns could be bilateral, multilateral, triangular or the result of indirect or illicit contacts. A recent wreck discovery illustrates the point. A 'bulk carrier' dating to the mid-15th century has been located off Skaftö, on the western (North Sea) coast of Sweden. Analysis of the timbers of the ship indicate that she was likely to have been built in Poland (the hull elements include wood from Gdańsk/Pomerania, northeastern Poland and 'the region of the Baltic coast') while her cargo included copper ingots from central Europe, lime almost certainly from the island of Gotland in the Baltic, and planks, variously from southeastern and northern Poland.[151] Whether she was sailing to a single port-of-call or to several is, of course, unknown but it seems likely that she had already visited at least two locations in order to take on her cargo. Awareness of Verhaeghe's warnings about the 'complexity of social and economic systems and behaviour' remains very important.

The mercantile 'world view'

It is perhaps appropriate to conclude a chapter on the impact of commerce in the medieval North Sea world by consideration of the archaeological evidence for its impact upon the perception, and self-perception, of the practitioners of such commerce themselves: the great medieval merchants. One such impact was obviously social and political; commercial economic success led in many cases to enhanced social status and local, or even regional and national, political power. The symbolic spandrel carving of a dragon in the house of cloth merchant Robert Toppes has been mentioned above (pp. 167–168), visibly emblazoning his status as a member of the guild of St George and thus of the ruling oligarchy of his city. Merchants had their own marks which were used to denote and identify both properties and goods. These marks are found throughout northern Europe, on houses, within seal matrices and, as has been seen, as graffiti such as those of the hanseatic merchants in Scania (above, p. 87). Some merchants practically used their mark as an heraldic device; the brass of Richard Byll for instance, a merchant and alderman of Hull who died in 1451, survives within the church of Holy Trinity, Hull. It depicts Byll, arms held together in prayer, next to his wife Margaret who is also praying, and with his mark housed within a shield (Figure 5.20). Other merchants used more subtle signifiers; Simon Seman, a vintner and a member of the Vinters' Company in London, died in 1433 and was buried and commemorated in St Mary's church, Barton-upon-Humber (across the Humber estuary from Hull). His brass depicts him in his merchant's gown, his feet resting on two wine casks.[152]

The public face of the mercantile class could also be enhanced by group promotion, the membership of guilds and the expression of guild rights, together with the establishment of guildhalls, all enhancing the importance of the merchant class. Such promotion could be further demonstrated by group statements as seen, for instance, in altars dedicated by mercantile organisations. The *Schonenfahrer* altar of merchants trading from Lübeck to Scania in what is now southern Sweden was placed in the

Figure 5.20 Brass of Richard Byll and his wife Margaret with his merchant's mark (copyright unknown).

Marienkirche in Lübeck and now survives in the St Annen Museum there. The altarpiece depicts St John the Baptist using a Rhenish stoneware vessel as a water container to baptise Christ,[153] thus combining piety with a reminder to the viewer, through the illustration of an everyday jug, of the commercial commodities underpinning such artistic largesse (John the Baptist was a patron saint of the *Schonenfahrer*). The Lübeck *Bergenfahrer*, trading with Norway, also had an altar in the church (housed in the *Bergenfahrerkapelle*) but this was largely destroyed by bombing in 1942. In Hamburg, the *Englandfahrer* paid for an altarpiece in the Johanniskirche which included a scene from the life of St Thomas Becket. The choice of saint by these Hamburg merchants was apposite; images of Becket had been adopted by English merchants whose seal matrix (of 'the English merchants in Flanders, Brabant, Holland and Zeeland' and now in the British Museum) depicts the saint standing in a ship.[154]

It was noted above (p. 96) that, in Boston, the numbers of mercantile grave slabs in the church of St Botolph indicated a commercial grouping of individuals 'bound by a communion of trade'. Such group identity, a 'mercantile bonding', is also suggested for the appearance of later medieval churches across northern Europe as commemorative slabs accumulated. 'A merchant travelling between Boston, King's Lynn, Bruges, Lübeck, Stralsund, Toruń, Riga, Tallinn and Visby, cannot fail to have seen these groups of monuments ... and been sensitive of the wider link between them all'.[155]

Such evidence of elite group commemoration (and perhaps also of piety) linked to commerce and travel can also be seen in acts of individual commemorative piety by affluent merchants. Documentary evidence has often been used to illustrate this, such as the 15th-century will of the above-mentioned Robert Toppes of Norwich who not only made bequests to every parish church in Norwich (no mean feat when there were nearly 60 such at the time) but, as noted above (p. 122), he also paid for window glass in the greatest of those churches (St Peter Mancroft), much of it still extant. Toppes is depicted in this glass, kneeling with both his wives (probably), the surviving one of whom subsequently became involved in litigation which may mean that the bequest to all the parish churches was not fulfilled.[156]

Toppes was perhaps mixing self-promotion with piety when he made his expensive gift of glass. A similar but even more dramatic mixture can perhaps be seen with the church embellishment funded by a merchant who died a generation after Toppes. John Barton was a wool merchant who was buried in Holme church on the banks of the River Trent in Nottinghamshire in 1491. A fabulously wealthy man, he had made money through the Calais staple where he had been mayor. Based in Hull in the 1450s, his move to Holme may have been a business decision, perhaps fostered by proximity to his estates but with continuing commercial links via the Trent to the Humber estuary. He built a great house (now lost but perhaps similar to the surviving house of Great Ponton in nearby Lincolnshire) within which was recorded the inscription ' I thank God, and ever shall, the sheep hath payd for all'. In the 1480s his largesse doubled the size of the Holme parish church of St Giles, creating a new south aisle and Lady Chapel as well as a two-storey porch. He himself was buried within the new south arcade, his remarkable tomb surmounted by effigies of himself and his wife Isabella while, beneath, was placed a further effigy depicting his cadaver in a state of decay. The position of the burial meant that his surviving family, seated in their stalls which he had also provided (and which also survive), could view the elevation of the host during the Mass across and above his tomb.

The church building contains at least 150 references to Barton in glass or sculpture. The latter includes a sculpted tun and bar upon which the feet of his effigy rest and which thereby form his rebus. Outside, a frieze above the porch entrance has shields which hold his coat of arms (acquired unilaterally rather than bestowed) and those of the Calais staple.[157] Here was self-promotion, chutzpah even, and piety on a grand scale.

Elsewhere, the success and piety of such men is often less overt in material terms but still visible: the de la Pole family, Hull merchants who rose to become Earls of Suffolk, had an extensive trading network, especially along the English North Sea coast and it is only fitting therefore that Michael de la Pole should have been a patron of Cley-next-the-Sea church, his largesse commemorated by an heraldic shield on the porch. He also implemented his father William's intention and founded a Carthusian priory outside the walls of Hull (destroyed in 1538 but its almshouse hospital survived until the Civil War in the 17th century) which, re-founded, exists today as the Hull Charterhouse. The family subsequently established themselves at Wingfield in Suffolk where a successor, John, 2nd Duke of Suffolk, has a monument in the church and the remains of a castle nearby.

A recent study of hanseatic merchant memorials notes a significant difference between those to English merchants and those on the continent. In England, there tended to be an emphasis upon the trade of the merchant (John Barton is a obvious example where his wool interests are clear) whereas continental memorials often emphasise commercial links (a Münster merchant was commemorated in 15th-century Tallinn as were mercantile links with Cologne). The distribution of memorials is interesting too; on the continent German merchants seem to have been commemorated exclusively in the towns where they had commercial interests whereas in England, apart from notable urban centres such as King's Lynn and Boston (the German merchant Wissel Smalenburgh—above, p. 147—was commemorated both in an English urban centre and as a merchant from Münster), Flemish or Flemish-style monuments are more widely distributed [158] (as in the damaged example in the village church of Gressenhall, Norfolk depicting the 'choice specimen' of an unknown male figure in civilian dress and a woman wearing 'a tight-sleeved kirtle and long *cote* [a loose-fitting robe] reaching to her feet'.[159]

Not all commercial players were successful. An example of a bankrupt is Colard de Marke, operating as a moneylender in Bruges in 1368–1369. His business failing, his ledger was confiscated by the City of Bruges and still survives. Many thrived, however; another account book, that of Henry Tooley , 'Great Tooley' of Ipswich, also still exists, dating from the end of the Middle Ages in the 1530s.[160] Tooley died in 1551 and was buried in the church of St Mary Quay, Ipswich; his tomb and brass can still be seen. Tooley is known to have traded south to Bordeaux and Spain as well as north to Iceland. Tangible evidence of this extensive commercial range is now confined to the surviving account book.

Some twenty years earlier in 1530, and 70km to the north, one Robert Jannys, a merchant of Norwich, died 'as rich as the city of Rochester'. His will left £350 to the poor including '4d each to the blind lame and sore with bedridden in the city and at every gate about Norwich' but he also bequeathed to posterity a physical impression of his commercial and cosmopolitan outlook. He was buried beneath an ornate painted terracotta tomb which survives in the church of St George Colegate in his city. This is the earliest known Renaissance monument in East Anglia, probably manufactured locally by Flemish artisans but using Italian designs.[161] By his commission Jannys ensured that, in death, he expressed both piety and modernity while the nature of the work can be seen to personify the commercial reach and contacts made possible by the North Sea.

— 6 —

The 16th Century: A New World

Physical expression of an association with modernity, as exemplified by the tomb-chest of Robert Jannys, can be found elsewhere in eastern England at the beginning of the 16th century. Decorative terracotta has been located at Westhorpe Hall in Suffolk (the country home of the Brandon family, Dukes of Suffolk), at Layer Marney in Essex, and at East Barsham Hall in Norfolk, all locations with close access to the continent. In London, recent excavations at Brandon House, the Duke of Suffolk's palace in Southwark, have revealed elaborate terracotta detailing from the remodelling of the building between 1518 and 1522. Some 310 pieces of terracotta include a profile head of a girl with plaits, laurel leaves and garlands, and 'rather chubby cherubs'. Terracotta decoration was used even more extensively across the North Sea on the continent and antecedents to the decorative devices at Brandon House can be found in Germany.[1]

Such developments imply that the north European world was indeed changing rapidly at the beginning of the 16th century and the period is sometimes called the 'age of transition', that is moving from the medieval period into the early modern era—just as the Old World was beginning to discover the New World. It is tempting to view the feudal Middle Ages drawing to a close, to be replaced by a nascent capitalism presaging modernity. Frans Verhaeghe cautions against this perception as an over-simplification, arguing that examination of material culture will often show that what appear to have been radical new developments in the 1500s were actually the results of a long period of transformation. He cites the technological changes in ceramics and glassware as examples but also reflects upon the urban environment and how static in broad terms much infrastructure remained well into the post-medieval period. Somewhat to Verhaeghe's own surprise he concludes that it was not his intention to emphasise 'the very strong links with earlier medieval situations and phenomena ... developments in the period 1400 to 1600 and even later appear to have strong and long medieval roots'—but notes that these must be acknowledged alongside those fundamental changes that can be observed (such as increased commodification, expanding trade networks, more sophisticated economic approaches, and architectural transformations).[2]

Trans-North Sea contact in the early 16th century

One strong link which remained unbroken at the beginning of the 1500s (despite occasional political interference) was that of contact across the North Sea. It is clear from the evidence of material culture, both in terms of portable artefacts and of stylistic developments, that interaction between continental Europe and the British Isles was as significant as in earlier centuries. However, the parameters of such contact seems to have broadened. The Jannys tomb-chest and other terracotta works are good examples.

The ultimate source for nearly all terracotta designs was Italy and indeed Italian examples of terracotta exist at Hampton Court outside London, fashioned by Italian craftsman who are known to have been employed in the first quarter of the 16th century by Cardinal Wolsey. There had obviously been contact with Italy in the past (excavations in Hull and Beverley, for instance, have produced fragments of Italian goblets and *cristallo* beakers dating to the 13th and 14th centuries) but such evidence is acknowledged as occasional with most direct late medieval trade with Italy confined to southern ports such as Sandwich, Southampton and London.[3] The Hull material had probably been imported via the Low Countries and it was from this direction that renewed Italian influence was felt increasingly in the 16th century.

Here, in the southern Netherlands and Flanders, the impact of Italy was not only on design but also on technological innovation. For example, Italian immigrants to Antwerp in early 1500s introduced majolica production; archaeological evidence for a majolica manufacturing site was uncovered in 2005 which, although it seems to have operated into the 17th century, may have been in existence from the 1530s given the discovery of a majolica tile fragment which can be associated with the workshop of one Guido Andries who is known to have been working in that decade.[4] *Façon de Venise* glass and faience were also made in the city, Antwerp becoming known for its production of such luxury items.[5] The city was indeed rapidly developing as a major metropolis; it had supplanted Bruges, which was in terminal decline as an entrepôt, and was now of particular importance for the textile trade. English cloth was imported to Antwerp for onward export to Germany and beyond, but it was purchased by Italian merchants as well. High-quality local Flemish cloth was also produced; 16th-century cloth seals, although a rare find, have been located in Antwerp such as examples from a well in Hoogstraat.

However, there are currently two archaeological problems regarding the textile trade in Antwerp. The first concerns evidence for English involvement as finds of cloth seals are negligible (in contrast to London where it is considered that Thameside discoveries of seals in large numbers derive mainly from riverside dyers' workshops), and it is claimed that as many as 4000 English cloth-workers settled in Antwerp region in the early 16th century. These artisans were presumably fulling, shearing and dyeing cloth there. The lack of English cloth seals might be explained by Flemish control of the finished products but there is a second problem concerning an apparent archaeological absence of industrial premises for such cloth-working. The answer may be that Antwerp acted more as a market for cloth, an entrepôt rather than a production centre. Why then did it need so many English cloth-workers? Both Germans and Italians were offered special privileges in Antwerp, the Germans obtaining the large cellared building know as *de Cluyse* in 1468 (it still stands at Oude Koornmarkt 26—Figure 6.1).[6]

Antwerp and the Low Countries in general obviously also found markets across the North Sea. Majolica was exported to England, some of it clearly designed specifically for the English customer. An intact vessel embellished with the royal arms of England and dating to *c.* 1500 was excavated from the moat of the Tower of London in 1938. Chemical analysis has shown that this vessel was made in northern Italy and presumably traded to England via the Low Countries.[7] Stove-tiles also crossed the North Sea; fragments of polychrome tin-glazed stove-tile were found in excavations on the site of the abbey of St Mary Graces in London, the largest piece of which was part of an Adoration of the Magi scene depicting Balthasar holding his pot of myrrh.[8] In this instance chemical analysis indicated that the earthenware body of the tile had been made in Antwerp.

There is both historical and archaeological evidence that trading of such artefacts was increasingly undertaken by specialised dealers and merchants. A good example concerns a property in the port of Bergen-op-Zoom in the Netherlands. Documentary evidence from *c.* 1518–1550, records occupants here as Jan-Peterss and Cornelius de Kanneman ('Kanneman' perhaps denoting a pottery dealer). Excavation of a refuse pit within the property uncovered large amounts of Cologne stonewares 'including mugs and jugs with applied botanical relief and *Pinten* (straight-sided tankards) with figurative relief, but, in terms of numbers, [the deposit] was dominated by plain Raeren-type mugs, jugs and chamber pots'.[9] The context and quantity of the finds together with the documentary evidence strongly implies specialised trading in ceramics, England being a likely market.

Figure 6.1 de Cluyse, the house of German merchants in Antwerp (© Stephan Dewickere).

Affluent consumers in England were themselves perhaps becoming selective; analysis of the pottery recovered from Baconsthorpe Castle in Norfolk showed a very high percentage of imported wares at the beginning of the 16th century, dominated by German stonewares but also with some majolica. Commenting on the assemblage, John Hurst noted that the Cologne jugs included rare decorative forms and that 'taken with the unusual maiolica there seems to have been a definite attempt to obtain unusual types, which would not normally be found in a typical household of the period'. Baconsthorpe was an aristocratic establishment belonging to Sir John Hotham and the pottery may therefore 'simply be due to Sir John's desire to impress and be different' but the ceramics indicate that exotic varieties were available to those who could afford them.[10] Within the Netherlands, specialisation of the products of the ceramics business itself has been observed through archaeological material with the stoneware market in Amsterdam being divided between imports from Cologne, Frechen, Raeren/Aachen, Siegburg and Langerwehe.[11]

Painted window glass was imported to England too and, if not the glass itself, individual craftsmen either visited England in order to work with local glassmakers or their ideas were transmitted and adopted. Assessment of surviving panels of glass in the church of St Andrew, Norwich, illustrating Old Testament themes and dated to *c.* 1515–*c.* 1525, 'are in the fully realistic Franco-Flemish mode'.[12] Outwell St Clement church in the Fens of eastern England retains fragments of Magi stained glass, including a full-length figure of Balthasar (in a similar pose to the tile fragment from London, clasping his pot of myrrh), which was clearly influenced by German glass of the immediate pre-Reformation period, even if it was perhaps made in an otherwise unknown King's Lynn workshop. This might explain 'the rather provincial style, but also the Continental influence which must have pervaded this Hanseatic port and is perceptible in the glass' (as expressed cautiously by the Corpus Vitrearum Medii Aevi).[13]

Further north, Dutch window forms are strongly suspected of being the influences behind the tracery in the ruined Dominican church at St Andrews in Scotland. As strikingly, the north chapel of the same church, built after 1516, has a laterally-directed polygonal apse, very similar to examples at Zaltbommel St Michael and Leiden St Peter in the Netherlands while the west window of King's College chapel in Aberdeen bears similarities to 's-Hertogenbosch cathedral amongst other Low Countries' examples.[14] It follows that an understanding of developments at the beginning of the 16th century in architectural style as well as in technological progress and stylistic change need to be explored in the Low Countries. Examples of such work can be seen at Wijk bin Durrstede where, after 1517, the Bishop of Utrecht's residence was provided with classical paintings by the artist Jan Gossaert (known as Mabuse) who had studied in Rome and in Utrecht itself, the first city in the Northern Netherlands [to develop] a classical language in its commissions for sculpture and architecture' (this included converting three medieval houses into a town hall after 1546).[15]

The surviving doorframe from the Utrecht town hall is a piece of neo-classical art illustrating the migration northwards of ideas of renaissance taste. Such ideas crossed the North Sea too but, at a more common level, the importance of the sea as as a trading route for resources and everyday commodities remained the most critical of factors. At Perth in Scotland, continued contact with the Baltic can be demonstrated through dendrochronological and dendro-provenancing analysis of eight carved oak panels now in Perth Museum. These panels contain openwork tracery and were clearly designed for liturgical use but it seems likely that, in this instance, although the raw material was of eastern Baltic origin, the actual carving is likely to have been undertaken either in Scotland or elsewhere in Britain.[16]

Material culture also provides a reminder that the Reformation proceeded at different rates in different locations. In Scotland, for instance, the Catholic king James V maintained traditional contacts with France and, in his building programme at Falkland Palace for example, incorporated continental Renaissance ideas and designs in his alterations which were completed in 1541. These included decorative sandstone roundels of French and Italian inspiration, probably carved by a French master named Nicholas Roy. Recently surveyed and conserved, recording has included 'structure-from-motion' photogrammetry which enables the roundels to be viewed in 3D on the computer screen.[17]

Just as Renaissance decorative ideas could be imported, so too could devotional or theological ones, incorporated in the production of and trade in everyday commodities. In Hull, a Beauvais Yellow medallion jug with applied 'pressoir mystique' motif was found at Blanket Row. The 'mystic wine press' emblem was a symbolic reference to the Mystery of the Sacrament at Easter and was in common use in Germany and France in the 15th and 16th centuries. The jug from Hull is the first published example of such a Beauvais jug in Britain but it nevertheless 'provides eloquent material testimony to the climate of devotional piety, which may have obtained amongst parts of the town's population on the Eve of the Reformation'.[18]

The Blanket Row find was from a domestic context as was a similar find suggestive of devotional piety, the St John the Baptist terracotta plaque found in fire deposits of 1507 in Pottergate, Norwich (above, p. 118). This latter discovery hints at a particular devotion to the Baptist within that city; five medieval churches in Norwich were dedicated to St John, four of these to St John the Baptist and only one to the Evangelist. The Pottergate discovery was from a house within St Gregory's parish, the neighbouring parish of St John the Baptist Maddermarket. This Maddermarket church also shared a parish boundary with that of the greatest of the city churches, St Peter Mancroft, which itself had a chapel dedicated to St John the Baptist. Elsewhere in the city, repair work at the church of St Martin-at-Oak following damage in the Second World War uncovered fragments of an alabaster panel from an altarpiece depicting the beheading of St John the Baptist. It had been smashed but what survives shows the wall of John's prison with the saint kneeling at its entrance wearing his camel-hair coat; the identifying head of the camel and its hoof can be seen attached (Figure 6.2).[19]

Figure 6.2 Alabaster fragments from an altarpiece dedicated to St John the Baptist, St Martin-at-Oak, Norwich (Sandy Heslop).

The excavation of a waste pit in the Dutch town of Deventer in 2004 produced two pipeclay figures which can also be interpreted as illustrating lay piety. One of the figurines is badly damaged and probably depicted St George; the other was almost intact (although it was mounted on a pedestal above niches which also contained figures and of which little survives) and is an image of St Anne, the Virgin Mary and the infant Christ (Figure 6.3). The cult of St Anne became increasingly popular during the 15th and into the 16th century. As the mother of the Virgin, she was associated with marriage, fertility, pregnancy and family, inspiring particular devotion amongst women. In the case of the Deventer discovery, the documentary evidence for the property in question (29 Lange Bisschopsraat) is especially good. It was purchased by one Richard Pafraet, a printer, in 1480 (he was already living there). Pafraet had been born in Cologne and he was joined by another German, Alexander Hegius, in 1479. Hegius in turn was in contact with the humanist scholar Rudolf Agricola who visited Deventer in 1484 in which year Pafraet printed Agricola's poem *Anna Mater* about St Anne. It is known that four of Pafraet's daughters entered a convent, emphasising the likely piety of the family. The excavator concludes that the dating of the figurine 'from a closed context, 1475–1515, roughly coincides with the presence of Alexander Hegius and the Pafraet family (1480–1500) in the house ...[and to] propose either ... as owners of the statue of St Anne would be an attractive hypothesis'.[20]

Lay piety with regard to St Anne can be seen on a stove-tile of late 15th-century date excavated in Lübeck which, in common with the Deventer figurine, also depicts the Virgin and the infant Christ.[21] Study of St Anne has formed a significant part of recent research into the relationship of women and religion in late medieval Norwich. Carole Hill has shown how veneration of the saint was important throughout the city despite most physical evidence having been removed from Norwich churches.[22] It was noted above, however (p. 111), that one high-quality image has survived with St Anne represented in the mid-15th-century stained glass in St Peter Mancroft church. Here the church is documented as having once contained an altar frontal with an image of St Anne and the Virgin as well as a banner of St Anne and at least two copes embroidered with her image.

Figure 6.3 Figurine image of St Anne, the Virgin and Christ child from Deventer (Michiel Bartels).

Archaeology can therefore illustrate lay piety on both sides of the North Sea but it is also capable of illustrating how far such ideas, and indeed 'counter-cultural' ideas, permeated through society. The growth in finds from metal-detectorists has led to a corresponding increase in the numbers found of small metallic badges and other objects. These are not necessarily all pilgrim badges or similar; indeed many of them depict singularly earthy, sexual subjects. A study of such artefacts recovered in the Netherlands has demonstrated how ideas of religiosity and of 'the world turned upside down' can be found on cheap secular badges and portable artefacts, with parallels in surviving 'high' art. Thus a bone knife handle depicting Eve incised on one side and St Barbara on the other can be viewed in a similar manner to a miniature showing a variation of the Fall of Man with Eve and the Virgin Mary (woman characterised as both causing suffering and bringing mercy). The elite and the more common people shared a similar iconography.[23]

There was clearly a trade associated with piety. A similar panel in English alabaster to the Baptist panel from Norwich survives intact in the Marienkirche in Gdańsk.[24] This item was most probably exported through King's Lynn at the end of the 15th century. Imports to King's Lynn continued as well in the 16th century, evidenced by plain Dutch earthenwares and stonewares from Siegburg and Langerwehe.[25] Such imports were also reaching Norwich where German stove tiles of the early 1500s are known. Indeed, the fire deposit of 1507 in that city 'provides the earliest archaeologically reliable date for the use of tile-stoves in an urban context in the country'.[26] Gaimster has argued for an ethnic dimension to explain some of the imports to England at this time, noting that imported stonewares and Dutch-type slipped red ware into both Southwark and Norwich 'during the period around 1500 corresponds to a consumer pattern heavily influenced by immigrant taste'. This is as may be although his later joint paper exploring English households at this period unfortunately undermines the thesis with a misunderstanding of the Norwich evidence; the statement that 'the Stranger [that is Dutch- and Walloon-speaking immigrant] community numbered 6,000 out of a total population of 16,000 at the beginning of the 16th century' misquotes the reference by antedating the influx of Strangers to that city by almost three-quarters of a century.[27]

That immigrants were resident in England in the early 1500s is, of course, known both from documentary evidence and, famously in the 1530s, from Holbein's portraits of German merchants of the Steelyard in London. Investigation of those has not only led to the provision of short biographies (where possible) and details of trading contacts associated with the various sitters but also suggested a link between Holbein and Mabuse (above, p. 184) whose portrait of a banker dated to *c.* 1530 may have influenced the style of Holbein's most famous Steelyard portrait, that of Georg Gisze of 1532.[28] John Cherry, in an overview survey of administrative and personal seals, notes that this portrait shows the merchant opening a letter with an ivory-handled seal on the table. He construes this to be an indication of the increasingly bureaucratic nature of business in the 16th century, although one could argue that the growing evidence for personal seals earlier in the medieval period, often at a relatively low level within society as evidenced by metal-detector finds over the last two decades, would suggest that while bureaucracy may have become more organised in the 1500s it was certainly not an innovation.[29]

Dyer maintains 'the traditional medieval economy' retained an important role in England in 1520. However, he is also careful to observe that one should not 'dismiss as resistant to change a period which saw the invention, introduction or much wider dissemination of brick buildings, paper mills, drinking glasses, guns, gunpowder, the printing press ... as well as blast furnaces, deep mining, beer brewing and carvel-built, three-masted lateen rigged ships'.[30] Many of these innovations were carried to England, no doubt some of them on carvel-built three-masted ships. Indeed the Walloon method of refining pig iron was one of the earliest forms of blast furnace process and was brought to England early in the 16th century (probably about 1525; the technology had reached Germany a century earlier), having been pioneered in Wallonia (modern Belgium).[31]

Commercial contacts across northern Europe helped to maintain the flow of fashion regarding domestic items as much as they assisted technological innovations. Willemsen has recently published an assessment of two collections of decorated leather and base-metal mounts dating from the 14th to 16th centuries and now in Leiden Museum. Although these objects derived primarily from Dordrecht and Zeeland in the Netherlands, she nevertheless felt able to claim that 'the most notable aspect of this material may well be that it is relatively similar not only within the region studied here, but in France, Germany and England as well ... a certain shared way of expressing identity ...'. Significantly, she noted that the mass-produced base-metal artefacts in the Dutch collections (using the term 'bling-bling') showed much similarity in style and imagery to more expensive items in gold and silver known elsewhere; 'the relationship between cheap and rich jewellery and decoration is somewhat more complex than authors on jewellery state'.[32]

Ideas and the Reformation

It is possible therefore to demonstrate how objects of everyday functionality such as ceramics, dress accessory artefacts of decoration, blast furnace technological innovations, concepts of taste as shown by painted glass, and religious concepts encapsulated in devotional imagery, all contributed to a common cultural flow across northern Europe in the early years of the 16th century. Indeed, Holbein's paintings of London Steelyard merchants, often with letters from or to German destinations as part of their milieu, stress the inter-connectedness of the period. However, just as these traditional contacts were facilitated by ease of access across the North Sea, so too were new ideas able to find assistance in dissemination. Foremost amongst such ideas were those associated with the Protestant Reformation.

Figure 6.4 Bishop Stewart's pulpit of 1532 to 1545, formerly in St Machar's cathedral and now in King's College chapel, Aberdeen (Creative Commons Attribution 4.0 International).

Material culture illustrates, sometimes fairly subtly, support for the new ideology. Stove-tiles, common in Germany where Lutheranism in particular achieved great sway from the 1520s onward, can communicate this. Tiles were produced with portrait busts of prominent Protestant princes in the second quarter of the 16th century and exported to the Baltic and to England. They included medallion portraits of the Lutheran Landgrave Philip I and his wife Christine, and of Johann Friedrich, Elector of Saxony, and his wife Sybille of Cleves. The portraits were based on medals and woodcuts and were widely distributed, 'secular personality cults more suited to the new confessional and sectarian loyalties of the Baltic mercantile communities'. Portrait tile moulds found with wasters in Lübeck have proved to be matrix-identical to moulds and tiles in Stockholm and Riga.[33]

Medallion-style portraits on oak panelling seems also to have originated in Germany and were certainly in use in England and Scotland by the early 16th century. These pre-Reformation artefacts often depicted secular heads rather than religious ones with even those in an ecclesiastical context being doctrinally neutral; a pulpit of 1532 to 1545 that was formerly in St Machar's cathedral in Aberdeen is one such example (Figure 6.4). Another is a curious mixture of portraits on panelling now in the Norwich Cathedral vestry. Detailed consideration of the figures and inscriptions on this panelling has led Susan Hedge to conclude that originally the portraits consisted of pairings of the Nine Worthies and the Power of Women *topoi* or motifs. She notes that they might seem an odd commission by Bishop Rugge, the likely patron, although the iconography was uncontroversial which, in the 1530s, was perhaps wise. She further observes that 'Lutheran heads do not seem to appear in the panelling installed by the upper classes of England and Scotland', again no doubt displaying caution in a volatile period.[34]

As well as helping to disseminate imagery of proponents and supporters of the Protestant movement, material culture can also provide examples of increasing criticism of the church prior to the Reformation. A surprising example of this can be seen in the cathedral at Lund in southern Sweden where four panels were designed by the architect in 1514 for a well-head. One of these depicts a fat monk accompanied by the text 'Many give others good advice, but don't follow it themselves'. To be fair, the same panel depicts a secular woman so it seems that the admonishment was directed at both the clergy and the laity.[35]

In Denmark, study of the survival of wall painting imagery and other iconography in Danish churches notes the generally non-destructive nature of the Reformation in that country with the somewhat surprising assertion that, once account is taken of size and population, 'the Lutheran Nordic countries today probably house more historical Catholic imagery than any other European country'. In seeking to substantiate that statement an examination of late medieval Danish wall paintings is interpreted as depicting 'secularized popular belief', the result of a reformation or 'reinterpretation' within Danish religious belief 'by the lower orders of society' in the century preceding the actual Reformation. It is possible that there was greater secular control of church decoration (some late medieval wall paintings have inscriptions in the vernacular, not Latin, for instance) which led to a greater sense of public 'ownership' of the buildings so that the imposition of the Reformation, while 'official' and top-down, was actually largely enacted by a populace with a pre-existing reforming tradition.[36]

Occasional archaeological discoveries can also hint at continuing loyalty to traditional imagery after the Reformation. A recently-published example concerns a polychrome dish of Palissy-type ware which was manufactured in the Saintonge region of southern France. This dates from *c.* 1550 to *c.* 1650 and was found in a pit associated with a probable 18th-century building in Norwich. The base of the dish depicts an image of St John the Evangelist, writing his gospel and observed by his emblem, an eagle. It is considered likely that the dish was a treasured family item through several generations before its eventual breakage and subsequent disposal.[37]

The impact of the Reformation

The classic image of the material impact of the Reformation is that of the destruction of monasteries. Such actions took place in most of the countries around the North Sea albeit at differing times, at different rates, and to a range of scale, not all of which can be rehearsed here. Archaeological contributions to understanding of the processes involved, however, can cast particular light upon how monastic institutions had been developing in the decades preceding the Reformation, to what extent they had contributed to the societies within which they were set, what happened to monastic fabric, and how their sites were used subsequently. A methodological approach to some of these areas of enquiry was set out in a useful paper by Richard K. Morris where, *inter alia*, he detailed results that could be obtained from careful examination of individual worked stones, exploring evidence for how demolition was undertaken, any patterns of movement around the monastic site once material had been removed from the standing fabric, and differentiation of 16th-century material from earlier stone (this last to correct an historic bias whereby careful study of early fabric has often been undertaken at the expense of understanding the latest structure).[38]

In the same volume, Maurice Howard charts the often-surprisingly rapid reuse of monastic sites, notably in urban areas where the large complexes could be readily adapted, partially-demolished and adapted, or completely removed and redeveloped. He cites the examples of the Blackfriars in Newcastle which the city corporation acquired in 1544 and where the cloisters were leased out to craft companies in 1552. In consequence, although the friary church has gone, elements of the claustral buildings and the 16th-century alterations remain.[39] An even earlier acquisition was that of the Blackfriars in Norwich in 1540 by the city corporation there which sought the complex in order to create a common hall for the city from the great church (which therefore survives) and adapted the other buildings to a range of uses.

Howard makes the point that 'the broadest picture of the reconsideration of monastic adaptation ... can be provided by the examination of a whole town, looking not just at one site but at the entire monastic legacy'.[40] Norwich is a good example for exploring both this overall impact of the closure of monastic institutions and the particulars about subsequent reuse, partly because of the number of religious establishments in the early 16th-century city and partly because of the variety of recent research. Thus, the great Benedictine monastery around the cathedral ceased to exist but the cathedral church itself survived under a reformed administration which permitted married clergy. As a consequence, Roberta Gilchrist has demonstrated how the monastic buildings were subdivided to form more private, domesticated dwelling places for married inhabitants with families, rather than the celibate quarters that had been needed previously.[41] The 13th-century Great Hall of the Bishop's Palace was demolished in the 1550s, it being documented that the city authorities took timbers from the building to repair the Great Hospital;[42] this latter building survives as do the reused timbers which were not cut down and thus enable the scale of the Great Hall to be determined.[43]

Archaeological study of medieval monastic buildings lost at the Reformation can therefore produce illuminating evidence. In Ribe in Denmark, it is now clear from excavation and survey work there that, prior to the Reformation, monastic building activity was at its greatest in the three-quarters of a century after 1450.[44] A further example concerns the chapel nave roof of Jesus College, Cambridge which, in 2007, was re-leaded, the opportunity being taken for recording by the Cambridge Archaeological Unit. It was discovered that the mid-18th century king post truss roof utilised much re-used timber from an early 16th-century roof (dateable to 1510–1511), sufficient elements surviving from the original roof to enable the form of the original principal rafter and purlin roof to be suggested.[45]

Utilisation of fabric and fittings, in whole or in part, can be seen elsewhere. In Norwich the Dominican Friary or Blackfriars, mentioned above, was one of four large friary sites in the city; the other three were demolished but have been partially excavated. Much material from the Franciscan friary was sold (some of it to the city corporation to repair the Blackfriars); here the evidence for destruction includes the melting of metal for reuse as well as the probable salvaging of an ornate doorway by the leaseholder of the site, John Bassingham, for use on his own house (the doorway was subsequently inserted into the Guildhall where it survives—Figure 6.5) while window glass seems to have been salvaged and sold.[46] At the Augustinian friary, excavated in 2015, careful preliminary observation of worked stone (as enjoined by Morris) suggests the possibility that an exotic marble shaft might just be associated with the *Scala Celi*, a sacred staircase in imitation of that at St John Lateran in Rome, a feature known to have attracted many pilgrims. Tracery fragments from windows at the friary have parallels with windows of surviving churches in the city, implying both an architectural interdependence (as noted above, p. 138) and probable emulation by patrons of the churches.[47]

The Reformation impacted upon towns across the North Sea region, to varying degrees depending upon local circumstances. An overarching summary of research has been provided by a recent volume in the Lübeck *Stadtarchäologie im Hanseraum* series. Deventer in the Netherlands serves as a good example. Here the Meester Geerts house, a late medieval community of sisters, was taken over by the city council and became dwellings, a mint and a guildhall. The Rijke Frater house was used for the storage of grain and subsequently a military academy. The Arme Frater house was turned into a workhouse, the Buiskens house (another community of women, founded 1401–1402) became a majolica workshop, and the 'Olde Convent' beguinage an orphanage.[48]

Such reuse of monastic institutions or their spaces can be interpreted through the mechanism of archaeological methodologies. Increasingly, such methodologies are investigating the Reformation's impact on the manner in which society viewed the changing landscape and how people approached changing policies with regard to religious artefacts and iconography. However, in order to achieve effective interpretation it is important to note that the Reformation occurred within an increasingly literate society. Perrin has noted 'a surge in the use of text as a technology of power to reorder the material world' in the 16th century,[49] and that therefore incorporation of archaeological research with textual research is necessary. This ensures a contextual understanding, one that can explore strategies of power, social relationships and changing approaches to religious identity.

Figure 6.5 Doorway formerly in the Franciscan friary now set within the south wall of Norwich Guildhall (Brian Ayers).

As an example to illustrate her point, Perring discusses Reformation changes at York Minster Close. Here she studied images of St William unearthed in the 19th century, considering them in concert with an awareness of Henry VIII's 1541 injunction for the removal of shrines which housed such images. Examination showed that the statues had been carefully defaced with a small chisel and then equally carefully dismantled and buried. Thus, rather than wanton destruction in the 16th century, there appears to have been compliance with the letter if not the spirit of the law.

Archaeological research into the economic and social impact of monastic closures and adaptations is in its infancy although steps are being taken to widen understanding. Monasticism was an international movement but one where application in northern Europe could be adapted to local conditions (the siting of friaries, accommodating themselves to densely-occupied pre-existing towns, is a good instance of this). In a similar manner, dissolution and closure varied from country-to-country and even within countries (the abbey of St Benet's in Broadland, Norfolk was never dissolved for instance although it was closed by the end of the 1540s). St Benet's was linked with the cathedral priory in Norwich and, as here, the relationship of urban centres with their rural hinterlands clearly underwent profound change with

Figure 6.6 Excavations by the University of Sheffield at Thornton Abbey, Lincolnshire, 2015 (Brian Ayers).

the closure of urban monastic institutions which held large rural estates or rural monasteries which serviced urban ones. Alterations in patterns of consumption are but one area where examination of the Reformation period through archaeological research could prove fruitful. Detailed exploration of particular sites, such as the five year programme of topographical survey, geophysical work and excavation by the University of Sheffield at Thornton Abbey, an Augustinian foundation in Lincolnshire, can be particularly enlightening; work here has explored the rather ill-fated construction of a major house within the post-Dissolution estate (Figure 6.6).[50]

Dissolution and associated iconoclasm caused a severe dislocation between the Catholic and Reformation worlds in England and Scotland. In consequence, despite rare survivals of medieval memorials from English monasteries and churches (such as that of Henry FitzRoy, the illegitimate son of Henry VIII, which was moved from Thetford Priory to Framlingham Church where it now remains), there is little material evidence offering a direct illustration of the religious transition. In contrast, across the North Sea, the relative lack of iconoclastic fervour in Denmark, allied to survival of post-Reformation material, offers much for archaeological study. Examination of 16th-century grave-slabs, for instance, has enabled a greater understanding of the transition from a Catholic world to a Protestant one. Perhaps unsurprisingly, although a clear Protestant ethic can be seen to emerge in terms of the use of symbols and text on grave-slabs of this period, this memorial form illustrates an innate conservatism so that older iconography persists, only being replaced slowly by the new beliefs. Research has been able also to detect a difference in the pace of change between mercantile areas (and trading towns in particular) and locations which can be designated 'bishop-towns' such as Roskilde. The commercial towns were obviously early points of contact with reforming ideas being inscribed on grave-slabs from the 1530s.[51]

A different form of commemoration concerns that of civic portraiture and civic identity. In England, prior to the Reformation, there had been a tradition of commemoration of benefactors, usually paid for by the benefactor him- or herself, in stained glass. Images of individuals, often with their families, would accompany windows in churches and, occasionally, in locations such as guildhalls. Examples are extant in Norwich where both Thomas Elys and Robert Toppes, prominent city merchants, are depicted in the glass of the church of St Peter Mancroft (above, p. 179). After the Reformation, with the destruction of much glass, the production of portraits on board or canvas became more common, either as private commissions subsequently donated to the public (or at least semi-public) domain such as guildhalls, or as civic commissions of commemoration. Referring to the process in Norwich where two rich former mayors, Robert Jannys and Augustine Steward, had commissioned glass, Tittler notes that both men were posthumously commemorated in panel portraits paid for by the city—the 'commissions mark the transition from personal acts of pious benefaction and invocations for prayer ... to civic and secular commemoration ..'. The portrait series extant in Norwich, 'the largest and most remarkable ... of early civic portraits of any English town or city' marked, at least in part, the refurbishment of the Guildhall (Tittler 2007, 24–25 and 50). Artefacts of representation therefore moved from the spiritual sphere to a more temporal one in the light of changes brought by the Reformation.

As data is accumulated therefore, the potential for exploring the greater changes of the 16th century is considerable. In doing so, however, it can also take account of the significance of smaller changes. For instance, John Cherry's overview of official and private seals in England in the 15th and 16th centuries noted how organisations adapted these objects following the Reformation. He cited the example of the hospital of St Stephen in Norwich which had been subject to the Priory of Horsham St Faith before the Dissolution. Subsequently, however, its seal was modified to show a crowned rose which 'appears like a great stone ready to crush the saint and the inscription announces in English *This seael belonge to the hospetal of saint stevens in Norwich*', an emphatic visual and written expression of the new order.[52]

An age of change

The 16th century was not only a period of change for religious institutions. The assets and capital released by the closure and sequestration of resources had a direct impact upon the environment and investment in that environment. In Sweden, Thomasson suggests that a change in the patterns of ownership and use within towns can be observed as a result of the Reformation. He is particularly concerned to explore the impact of gentrification on the landscape taking Malmö as a case study. He argues that economic and cultural capital was fixed in towns and that the phenomenon (viewed globally in modern times) of poor areas being refurbished by the affluent middle classes can be observed in late medieval/ early modern urban centres. Archaeological testing of such refurbishment is undertaken by exploring both land use and buildings themselves. In Malmö it has proved possible to establish that most late medieval settlement along the main street, Adelgatan ('Old Street'), was characterised by prominent architecture: churches and brick-walled houses with cellars. Documentary evidence for the town shows that, until the 16th century, every known mayor, councillor and bailiff,except for two individuals, lived on this street. The large buildings are clearly visible on Braun and Hogenberg's plan of 1594.

Following the Reformation, however, the pattern began to change. All church resources, except those of the main church, were expropriated by the town council and invested in a new great market and town hall, located south of Adelgaten. A different pattern of movement emerged, providing competition to Adelgaten itself. One of the streets which became important was Södergaten ('South Street'), leading to a gate clearly depicted in 1594 and, from the mid 16th century, mayors and others began to settle on this street, occupying sites formally used by artisans. A late 17th-century building commission in 1692 suggests that the process was by then well-advanced; Södergaten was largely occupied by two storey buildings but the adjacent streets held one storey cottages.

The form of buildings belonging to the affluent gentry of Malmö changed as both style and resource opportunities themselves changed. Thus, in the early 16th century, large ornate houses were timber-framed; by the end of the century, such buildings were fashioned in brick or stone. Thomasson concludes that, within the urban core, development of the streets was not speculative but rather a result of investment in order to retain and demonstrate importance. The location of the buildings was essentially dictated by corporate considerations as the main gentrified blocks were adjacent to the important public spaces. Malmö's townscape became an expression of the preferred social organisation of an urban elite.[53]

Thomasson has supplemented his deductions with detailed analysis of a building which stood on plot 395 on Södergaten and known as the Lembke house. The house was erected in the 16th century and was constructed of timber which was then for the most part plastered. Thomasson's work was made more difficult in that the house was demolished at the end of the 19th century, although selected elements of its timbers were salvaged and subsequently used in a reconstruction of a 'burgher's house' now on display in the grounds of the Museum of Cultural History in Lund. However, detailed drawings were made before demolition including depictions of intricately-decorated timber consoles. Consideration of the iconography upon these is instructive.

Representations of Justitia and Temperamenta, two of the Virtues, are construed as indicative of construction of the house during a period of 'reformative thoughts' although they were complemented by more Catholic iconography such as scenes of purgatory. This iconographic mixture in turn reflects the positioning of the building and its complex as established by archaeological excavation. The property stood immediately adjacent to and above the former Hospital of St George but construction avoided building upon the newly-closed hospital cemetery. Indeed, care was taken to ensure the cemetery was decently covered with earth at the time of the building of the house and that the structure's footprint was outside the graveyard, positioned sufficiently accurately so that the gateway to the inner yard was located exactly above that to the former churchyard. Layout and construction in the post-Reformation period therefore illustrated a sensitivity to the pre-existing milieu.[54]

The Lembke building was a large house although, being constructed of wood, not necessarily in the forefront of building technology in the 16th century when brick houses were certainly becoming more common. However, timber remained the norm across much of northern Europe, even if a shortage of wood led to increasing use of timber-framing as a constructional technique. Recent excavations at Odense in Denmark have explored three such structures of 14th- and 15th-century date which it was discovered had burnt down in the same fire event, probably around 1500. Examination of their location and internal arrangements indicated possible medieval reorganisation of tenement plots as well as a conservatism in domestic taste; one house contained in-built benches for which evidence normally suggests an absence after *c.* 1200, never mind survival as a fitting for a further 300 years. The buildings were probably similar in form, if smaller, than a surviving frame building of 1547 known as Ejler Rønnows Gård which now stands in the Møntergården museum complex in Odense to which it was moved from Nørregade in the city centre in 1939.[55]

Archaeological research also has the potential for studying greater change than urban morphology. In an interesting paper, Atzbach has argued that archaeological evidence can be used alongside that of biology to indicate changes within wider society as a result of climate change. Examining the foraminifera and stable isotopes of marine fauna in Skagerrak sediments, he notes firstly that *Uvagerina mediterranea* thrives in warm sea water and is therefore an indicator of warmer water temperatures in the North Sea region between 1150 and 1450. Thereafter, however, it is known that, from the 15th century onward, the climate of Europe steadily worsened. leading to a period called the 'Little Ice Age'. Sixteenth-century paintings by artists such as Pieter Breughel the Younger often depict snow scenes and frost fairs took place in the 17th century on frozen rivers such as the Thames. People in northern Europe adapted to this deterioration in a number of ways, including adaptation of their houses illustrated by 'the spread of the tile stove, the modification of the size of windows and of the fireplace during the post-medieval period could be seen as an answer to a colder climate'.[56]

One of the greatest changes to overtake the North Sea world at the end of the Middle Ages concerned the design of ships and particularly the move away from clinker-built construction to carvel-built vessels (that is from overlapping planks where the body of the ship was constructed first, to one of flush planks added after the building of the frame). Documentary evidence from the Netherlands suggests that carvel construction was already known as early as 1459 in Holland and Zeeland although clinker-built vessels were clearly still made. Carvel ships were being illustrated by the 16th century; STAM (the town museum of Ghent), has a relief of 1531 showing a 'karveel'. The relief once decorated the guild house *van de Schippers* on the Graslei in Ghent. It depicts rigging, an anchor and stern- and fore-castles.

Exploration of carvel innovation is complicated by the surprisingly few shipwrecks which are known to date to the period 1450 to 1600. However, recent study of an early 17th-century vessel in the Netherlands and its likely predecessors has enabled some conclusions to be drawn about ship development, notably making a distinction between 'flush-planked' ships and carvel ones. The former seem to have been characterised by the the so-called 'watership', a craft which was used primarily, although not exclusively in inland waterways, and was equipped with a well within which live fish could be transported. The use of flush planking reduced the likelihood of the fish being harmed in transit. These vessels were essentially built in a similar manner to clinker ships, that is with the body being created before insertion of the frame. The 17th-century example (wreck VAL7) from the IJ river near Amsterdam was a later version of this type of craft, an intermediary between traditional clinker-built vessels and fully-formed carvel shipping.[57]

This book opened with a consideration of the role of fish and, in particular, new and exciting techniques in the study of fish remains for increasing an understanding of how society around the North Sea was both developing and organising its resource management at the end of the 11th century. It is appropriate therefore, as the text draws to a conclusion, to reflect that changes in the technology of shipping in the 16th century increased the ability of fishermen and fish merchants to service growing markets. Not only were ships carrying live fish to retail outlets but it is known that trawlers were fishing the Zuider Zee from about 1520.[58] There is even evidence for the processing of fish on board; archaeozoological work subsequent to excavation of a 16th-century vessel at Biddinghuizen in the Netherlands in 1992 was able to examine the skeletal remains of thousands of herring. These had been located packed into 17 barrels with clear evidence for gutting of the fish, a possible indication of proto-industrialisation.[59]

Such study illustrates well the inter-disciplinary nature of archaeological research. Adoption of inter-disciplinary approaches is particularly pertinent for examination of the North Sea world because of the range of environments present and the extent of human activities which took place within those environments. The maritime world alone is varied, between the saline North Sea and the brackish Baltic Sea, with differing preservation of archaeological material ensuing from immersion in their waters, to maritime areas which are no longer maritime, such as recently-reclaimed polders in the Netherlands. The volatility of the coastline itself provides opportunities to archaeologists, often requiring a rapid response from them as sites are revealed or threatened by erosion or inundation. More considered study is also possible as with programmes of coastal protection such as 'managed retreat'. Potential evidence can be gleaned of past actions when steps were taken to consolidate marginal land for settlement, agriculture and commerce.

Managing the historic environment

Whether as a result of rapid response or proactive consideration of opportunities, such archaeological approaches are examples of effective management of the historic environment within the North Sea region. Such work is not confined to coastal and rural areas. Urban locations present particular problems, not least because of the difficulties that can arise within a dynamic economic context. Many towns and cities now possess broad-ranging published resources upon which to draw in order to assist positive management. In England these extend from early urban assessments as provided for the port of Boston (and supplemented in 2015 by a new publication)[60] to comprehensive overviews such as that for Lincoln.[61] Much other information for single sites is often unpublished, languishing in so-called grey literature, access to which varies from place-to-place although online access is being improved continuously through the centralised database provided by Archaeology Data Services (ADS) at the University of York.[62]

Similar archives of unpublished data exist across the North Sea although here too attempts are made to provide access, as at Ghent where regular summaries are published both in hard copy and online.[63] Groups of towns have also been examined, as in the Netherlands where a relatively small project was initiated in 1975 exploring four towns within which redevelopment was imminent (Nijmegen, Tiel, Deventer and Dordrecht).[64] The hinterlands of towns have not been ignored[65] and surveys of rural landscapes, such as that for fields in East Anglia, have been undertaken.[66]

Management of the historic terrestrial landscape is also now being complemented by a growing awareness of the potential of the submarine landscape. While much recent research and its public profile has concentrated upon the increase in understanding of the drowned prehistoric extent of 'Doggerland', there is also considerable research into both medieval submerged landscapes and medieval features within submarine contexts. An example is spatial analysis of shipwrecks within the province of Flevoland, a reclaimed part of the former Zuiderzee and an area claimed as 'the largest ship graveyard on land in the world'. Some 430 shipwrecks have been located, their sites mapped using the geographical information system ArcGis. Assessment has noted differing densities of shipwrecks and is using historical, geographical, geophysical and archaeological sources to explore links between the historic cultural landscape and the natural environment.[67]

Shipwrecks enable specialist research, often of materials unavailable through terrestrial archaeology. As well as dendrochronological examination of timber, for instance, attention is being given increasingly to more ephemeral evidence from wrecks such as surface treatment of timbers and caulking. The use of gas chromatography-mass spectrometry and the application of a scanning electron microscope (SEM) to provide chemical and biological analysis of tars and caulks has recently been reported for three Scandinavian vessels dating from the 13th to 17th centuries. The results revealed much heat-altered pine tar as well as birch bark tar. The latter had not previously been observed within Scandinavian boat-building.[68]

Such specialist scientific research has been noted elsewhere in this volume. The use of Mitochondrial DNA (mtDNA) for analysis of human skeletal remains is providing increasing information for certain individuals (most recently the excavated remains of King Richard III in England) but, more particularly, for increasing understanding of populations and their movements in the past. Continuing improvements in geophysical survey through applications which include magnetometry, earth resistance, ground penetrating radar (GPR) and electric resistivity tomography (ERT) are ensuring much greater understanding of archaeological landscapes and the potential of features within them. In this respect the application of LiDAR (Light Detection and Ranging) which uses a pulsed laser from an aircraft to measure variable distances on the earth is of significance. The technique provides results which give detailed topographical information of great use to archaeologists: minor changes in relief which are otherwise obscured can indicate the presence of historic features. 'Invisible' palaeochannels within the fenland area of the Witham valley in Lincolnshire have been mapped using this technique.[69] Within ceramics' studies, traditional work in the North Sea region is hampered by the main pottery sources being 'located in areas with similar geological histories: tertiary or quaternary strata, in which flint, chalk, quartz and mica are predominant rocks and minerals'. However, the use of neutron activation analysis (NAA) irradiates crushed samples and measures radioactive decay. Together with inductively coupled plasma spectroscopy (ICPS), which vaporises samples to measure composition through the emitted light spectrum, it becomes possible to isolate fabrics much more closely.[70]

Concluding review

Archaeological research within the North Sea region thus has a developing range of scientific applications and analytical techniques available to explore landscapes, individual sites, artefacts, ecofacts and people themselves. The breadth of material examined across northern Europe over the last 40 years in particular has been enormous, much of it barely touched upon by this volume and much missing altogether (the importance of castle studies, for instance, is a major lacuna in the foregoing). This is perhaps inevitable in a volume which has not sought to provide a comprehensive overview of archaeological work, much less to place this work within a coherent assessment of historical cause and effect. Nevertheless, the above synthesis does provide scope for observations on some of the implications of completed and ongoing research and thus suggest some areas within which future research might develop.

Firstly, all the work summarised above has taken place within an historical context which has been much debated and which continues to be embellished and modified. An example of such embellishment and modification is the debate over the so-called 'Pirenne thesis' deriving from the innovative work of Henri Pirenne who, *inter alia*, explored the origins of towns and, in particular, the relationship of Europe to the Islamic world. The flow of capital was central to Pirenne's arguments, much of which he saw as a flow from south to north, influencing the development of northern economies.[71] Archaeologists are often slow to recognise that they can contribute to such discussions, either by providing information which is supportive or by exploring likely mechanisms and networks. With regard to Pirenne's ideas, archaeological work within the North Sea region suggests a largely sophisticated and interconnected trading system which, through major towns such as Bruges, linked to the great fairs of France and the merchants of Italy, as well as distributing goods to an extensive hinterland. Parts of that hinterland, however, were much less sophisticated, perhaps relying less upon coinage and the flow of bullion and more upon exchange of commodities: the presence of hoards in medieval Scotland and Scandinavia implies as much.[72]

A second and perhaps unusual archaeological consideration is that of an appreciation of political contexts within the medieval North Sea region. Assessment of the transmission of ideas and commodities is often difficult without consideration of such matters. Thus French influence upon English architectural development is usually accepted as obvious given the Norman Conquest of England. However, the hesitant use of innovative technologies such as stove-tiles in England can perhaps in part be attributed to particular political circumstances: this essentially German technology relies upon friable material which is easily broken in transit. Shipment therefore seems to have been avoided wherever possible, the technological process itself being exported successfully to locations such as southern Sweden or the Baltic States, both with significant—and often self-governing—German enclaves. Such independence of action available to German merchants and entrepreneurs was not possible in England where the country, centralised relatively early, controlled the influence of aliens and even waged war against German mercantile interests (as occurred in the mid-15th century). On the other hand, Anglo-Scottish political antipathy for much of the medieval period might be taken to imply a lack of trade between the two countries but work in Aberdeen has shown that this was not the case, coastal trade southward flourishing from the 12th century onward.[73]

A third, more local, political consideration is that of an understanding of the importance of collective action. Historically, within the medieval North Sea, this has frequently taken the form of assessments of the influence of the Hanseatic League and of how a fluctuating group of German towns and their merchants sought to impose their collective will at various times and in various locations.[74] An important archaeological contribution to the understanding of day-to-day political action has been the provision of an increased awareness of the sophistication of both public and private institutions within their communities. This is particularly evident in urban settings where infrastructural development can be seen either as a result of corporate endeavour (as at Große Petersgrube in Lübeck) or of private initiative (as at Trig Lane in London) but also in rural areas (such as evidence provided by increasingly sophisticated exploration of medieval land management in the Flemish coastal zone).

If the above are all areas where archaeology can be viewed as having some direct influence upon essentially historical paradigms, there are others where the discipline is making considerable advances as well as fashioning answers to research questions which have been formulated by itself. It has been noted above how scientific applications are transforming the informative potential of archaeological material. The archaeological obsession with data collection, careful cataloguing and archiving has been vindicated through the advent and application of such sophisticated scientific techniques. Nobody in the 1970s and 1980s, when undertaking sieving for fishbone on excavations in London, York and

Antwerp, could have foreseen the innovative analysis and assessments that would be undertaken on the recovered assemblages in the early 21st century. Not only has astonishing new information been revealed (e.g. above, p. 87) but the ability to reach an improved understanding of aspects of the North European medieval economy, such as network distribution, is considerable.

A further archaeological contribution has been that of an understanding of commodity usage and of how coastal and mercantile communities frequently imitated the status of more elite households. The ceramics located at the fishing village of Walraversijde illustrate contact with an extensive trading network while the mercantile assemblages of ports such as Hull indicate contact with sophisticated ideas and innovative technologies. Survey also brings awareness of the resources exploited and the disposable income that was available to certain individuals; an example is the elaborate Wulflamhaus in Stralsund, a mercantile dwelling constructed in deliberate imitation of the grandeur of the nearby Rathaus.[75]

Lifestyle itself is evident from archaeology. Changes in lifestyle can be explored throughout medieval society, many such changes often bringing a sophistication that can be traced to the influence of networks of exchange across the North Sea. Thus East Anglian cloth and rabbit fur hats were prized in the ports of the Baltic just as Norwegian shist, Swedish iron ore, German lava stones and Dutch ceramics found their way to England. English and German pottery formed much of the everyday ceramic usage of medieval Norway. The addition of hops to ale provided beer, a commodity which travelled much more easily. Knowledge of the brewing process itself travelled and can be traced by the ecofacts located in the often-anaerobic conditions of coastal archaeological deposits.

The mechanisms of trade led to technological innovation, a developing understanding of which is another archaeological contribution to study of the medieval period. The adoption of deep water craft capable of bulk transportation across the North and Baltic Seas transformed economies, ensuring a movement away from high-value specialist and therefore elite goods to low-value bulk goods of more widespread application within society. The increasing sophistication of shipping, charted through archaeological discovery and assessment, was complemented by the increasing sophistication of infrastructure requirements at ports and the topographical impact upon ports themselves.

Archaeological contributions to awareness of the socio-economic control and influence exerted by groups through resource utilisation, landscape organisation, settlement activity, and commodity exchange enable insights into probable power relationships. The resources required by growing towns entailed acquisition from both immediate and distant hinterlands, exchanges being effected through commercial procedures and capital often controlled within towns. Rural estates, frequently under the control of institutional landlords, organised resources for maximum exploitative benefit both for their own communities and for broader markets. The workings of the market gave plenty of scope for the development of lucrative business for middlemen. The North Sea wine trade with south-western France ensured significant assemblages of Saintonge ceramics in ports such as Hull and Great Yarmouth.[76]

Finally, it is the relationship between diversity and interconnectedness that is perhaps the greatest contribution of archaeology to study of the North Sea region. It is a large region, encompassing rugged uplands and tundra in the far north and flat coastal lowlands in the south. It produces natural resources which range from reindeer antler to rabbit fur and from timber to wool. Its geology encompasses iron ore-bearing rocks to clays for ceramics and even silt sands for use as ballast. It has deep estuarine inlets, shallow sandy beaches, good natural harbours, fens, marshes, forests and food resources of fish, fowl, animal and grain. Much of the raw material that was sourced, transported, transmuted into artefacts and traded is, at best, mentioned only in passing in documentation. Archaeology enables this material to be recovered, its provenance determined, its movements recorded, its utilisation observed, and its impact assessed. The archaeologists who work on the material are fortunate to study a region that is historically well-documented as well as socially and economically dynamic. It is a maritime region where the seas bind communities together rather than dividing them; contemporary archaeological research and its results are thus timely reminders of the importance of the European interconnectedness that is provided by the North Sea.

End Notes

Introduction

1. Jordan 2004, 4.
2. Fairclough 2012, 76
3. Van de Noort 2011, 23
4. Gilchrist 2012; Stamper 2013.
5. Gerrard 2003, 217ff.
6. Austin and Alcock 1990.
7. Thomasson 2004a, 187–210.
8. Carelli 2001.
9. Roslund 2009, 181–190.
10. Galloway 2012.
11. Milne 2003; Ayers 1979; Sarfatij 1999.
12. De Witte 2008.
13. Oosthuizen 2012.
14. Ahrens 1981; Bayley 1996, Mays 1997.
15. Harnow *et al.* 2012.
16. Bates and Liddiard 2013.
17. Williamson 2013, 44–45.
18. Liddiard 2013, 6–7.
19. Bailey 1988, 15.
20. Ansorge 2005, 96 and fig. 3.
21. Mehler 2014, 3209–3210.
22. Gläser (ed.) 1997 and succeeding volumes.
23. Graham-Campbell 2007; Carver and Klápště 2011.
24. Carver and Klápště 2011, 15.
25. Liddiard 2013, 14.
26. Roesdahl 2010, 285–287.
27. Herteig 1968, 77.

Chapter 1

1. Barrett *et al.* 2011, 1516–1524.
2. Tait 1936; Pirenne 1952; Ennen 1953.
3. Reynolds 1977.
4. Barley 1977; Schofield and Vince 2003.
5. Perring 2002; Giles and Dyer 2005; Dyer and Lilley 2012.
6. Barrett *et al.* 2011, 1522.
7. Verhulst 1999, 114.
8. Van de Noort 2011, 54.
9. Brown 1984, 1.67; Palliser 2000, 753 and 755.
10. Harden 1978, 9.
11. Gillett and MacMahon 1980, 2; Evans 2000a, 200.
12. Bowler, D. P. 2004, 21 and Appendix 1.
13. For York–Hall 1996; Lincoln–Hill 1948 and Jones 2004; Norwich–Ayers 2009; London–Schofield 2011.
14. De Witte 1997, 77–78.
15. Ryckaert 2002, 59.
16. Feveile 2006, 65–91.
17. Kieffer-Olsen, J. 2004, 543.
18. Herteig 1985, 69ff.
19. Myrvoll 1987, 100–109.
20. Sinbæk 2011, 305.
21. Heidinga 1984.
22. Besteman 1990, 96ff, 112 and figs. 3 and 15. , 112 and fig. 15.
23. Darby 1974, 4 in fn 4.
24. Silvester 1985, 109.
25. Crowson *et al.* 2000, 225–230.
26. Williamson 2003, 115 and fig. 40.
27. George 1992, 87–88.
28. Silvester 1991, 93 and 107–108.
29. Hinman and Popescu 2012, 83.
30. Everson and Stocker 2011, 293–295.
31. Rose 1982, 38–39 and fig. 14.
32. Cushion and Davison 2003, 151 and fig. 98.
33. Pestell 2004, 104 and fig. 23.
34. Bos 1990, 124.
35. Van der Linden 1955.
36. Vos and Gerrets 2005, 69–73 and figs. 9 and 10. See also map on http://www.zeeinzicht.nl/vleet/index.php?id=4888&template=template-vleeteng&language=2&item=Westergo.
37. Siegmüller 2010a and 2010b.
38. Busch 2006, 195–197.
39. Loveluck and Tys 2006, 160ff.
40. Øye 2009, 45.
41. Silvester 1988, 146–149.
42. Goodall 2011, 84 and fig. 43.
43. Kent 2002, 374; Butler 1984, 46.

44. Creighton 2002, 104–105.
45. Janssen 1990, 228–229 and figs. 7 and 10.
46. Trimpe Berger 1973; plan illustrated in Janssen 1990, fig. 4.
47. De Witte 2010, 102 and fig.6.
48. Först 2010, 256–258 and figs. 2 and 4.
49. Fehring 1991, 102.
50. Neugebauer 1964/65, 144–145 and fig 6; 179 and fig. 24.
51. Creighton 2002, 140.
52. Brown 1984, 1.116b.
53. Shepherd Popescu 2009, 275.
54. Heslop 1994.
55. Pirenne 1952, 74ff; Verhulst 1999, 116.
56. Curtis 2013, un-numbered.
57. Verhulst 1999, 75–79, map 5 and 116–117.
58. De Groote 2010, 252ff.
59. Mus 1996, 43.
60. Verhulst 1999, 108.
61. Buurman 1999, 286–287.
62. Verhulst 1996, 35.
63. Verhulst 1996, 38.
64. Oksanen 2012, 180.
65. Williamson 2003, 125 and 132–135.
66. Adams 2005.
67. Hyermind *et al.* (eds) 1998, 327; Iversen *et al.* (eds) 2005, 550.
68. Albarella 2005, 144.
69. Grimm 2006, 56 and fig 6; 52.
70. Silvester 1988, 40.
71. Beresford and St Joseph 1979, 263–264 and fig 111B.
72. Murphy 2009, 39.
73. Leenders 2004, 108.
74. Murphy 1987, fig.93.
75. Spoerry 2005, 91.
76. Van Neer and Ervynck 2006, 97–98.
77. Dyer 2002, 64.
78. Adams 2008, 139.
79. Walton Rogers unpublished.
80. Nilsson 1976, 228.
81. Von Brandt 1970.
82. Riddler 2006, 171–180.
83. MacGregor 1978, 48.
84. MacGregor 1991, 356.
85. Berge 2009, 123.
86. Goodburn 1992, 125.
87. Eckstein and Wrobel 2007, 8–9.
88. Atkin 1991.

89. Goodall 2011, *passim*; Steane 2001, 22ff.
90. Heslop 194; Drury 1982; Impey 2008.
91. Shepherd Popescu 2009.
92. Creighton 2002.
93. Liddiard 2000; Coad and Streeten 1982.
94. Fehring 1991, fig. 36.
95. Fries and Heine 2008, 78–83 and figs 5 to 10; Tschan 2002, 103.
96. Delbanco and Jansen 2013, 67 and fig.1.
97. Schweitzer and Frey 2013, 94 and figs. 2 and 3.
98. Gilchrist 2005, 143–144.
99. Liddiard 2005, 46–51.
100. Tschan 2002, 117.
101. Phillips 1985, 108 and plates 84–86; plates 46–52.
102. Ashley *et al.* 2009, 28–32.
103. Stocker and Everson 1990, 84ff and figs. 26 and 27.
104. Ayers 2009, 82.
105. Herrman 2004, 336.
106. Stirland 1985, 56.
107. Budd *et al.* 2004, 139.
108. Kosiba *et al.* 2007, 408.
109. Price 2012, 6.
110. Töpf and Hoelzel 2005, 280–282.
111. Töpf 2009, 253.
112. Dunning 1933; Dunning 1968.
113. Hurst 1974, 221–255.
114. Gaimster and Redknap 1992.
115. Hodges 2012.
116. Verhoeven1990, 276–277.
117. Verhaeghe 1999, 155.
118. Hodges 1995, 105.
119. Felgenhauer-Schmiedt 2007, 225.
120. Sindbæk 2012, 30.
121. Jankuhn 1976; Schietzel 2014; Various 1969–2007; Herteig 1975; Various 1985 onward; Hansen 2005; Van Es and Verwers 1980; Vince 1990; Schofield 2011; Hall 1994.
122. Various 1981–1990; Feveile 2006; Hjermind *et al.* 1998; Iversen *et al.* 2005.
123. Kermode 2000, 442, table 18.1.
124. Ilkjaer 2001.
125. Schofield and Vince 2003, fig. 1.12.
126. Wickham 2005, 822; Hodges 2012, 12.
127. Dallas 1993, 58–75.
128. Hall *et al.* 2007, 639ff.
129. Murray 2010, 127.
130. Hinton 2014, 384.
131. Beresford and St Joseph 1979, 215–217.
132. Conzen 1968.
133. Lilley 1999, 18.

134. Schofield and Steuer 2007, 145; Rieger 2010, 87ff.
135. Wade 1993, 148.
136. Groothedde 2001, fig. 4c; Spitzers 2001, 201 and fig. 6a; Arndt and Ströbl 2005, 36ff and fig. 6; Thiemann, 2001, 459; Skov 2001, fig. 3b and 3c.
137. Tesch 2001, 728–730 and figs. 4, 5 and 8.
138. Molaug 2010, 143 and fig. 7.
139. Ayers 1987, 18, 166 and plate VII.
140. Roesdahl 1982, 47–49; Milne 2003, 56; Harrison 2004, 102 and 104.
141. Hodges 2012, 15–16.
142. Morris 1989, 141.
143. Blair 2005, 392; Ayers 1985; Beazley and Ayers 2001; Roberts 1982.
144. Ahrens 181, 501–531 and fig. on p. 525.
145. Sawyer and Sawyer 1993, 110; Kjellström and Wikström 2007, 3–4.
146. Anders Reisnert,
147. pers. comm. http://www.nottingham.ac.uk/archaeology/research/projects/current/stavnsager.aspx (accessed on 24th October 2013).
148. Jeppesen 2005, 56–57.
149. Ayers 1985; Ahrens 1994.
150. Stephen Heywood, pers. comm.
151. Heywood 2013, 268.
152. Spoerry 2008, 1; Spoerry 2005, 99.
153. Stocker and Vince 1997.
154. Taylor 2010, 163.
155. Stocker and Everson 2006, 92.
156. Milne 1997, 102; White 1988, 18–25 and 71–73; Gilmour and Stocker 1986, 16 and 20.
157. Gilchrist 2012, 201.
158. Meier 2007, 427 fig.15.4; Lynnerup 2007, 429.

Chapter 2

1. Loveluck 2013, 365.
2. Van Eenhooge 2001, 122ff.
3. Harris 1994, 44.
4. Harris 1994, 125, fig. 68 and 295ff.
5. Rieger 2014, 42-3.
6. Jones *et al.* 2003, fig. 9.55.
7. Loveluck 2013, fig. 34.
8. Van Eenhooge 2001, 124; Bischop 2005, 67–68.
9. Fehring 1991, 204.
10. Rech 2001, 377ff; Barbry *et al.* n.d.; Caune 2001, 558ff.
11. Rötting 2001, fig 7; Rieger 2010, 29 -35 and figs. 5 and 6.
12. Parker 1971, 89.
13. Norfolk Historic Environment Record 6161
14. Ayers and Smith 1992, 338–350.
15. Rutledge 2002, 105-107.
16. Rieger 2014, 46–47.

17. Haneca *et al.* 2009, 99–133.
18. Gläser 2001, *passim.*
19. Goodburn 1992, 106–130.
20. Schofield 35, 229–232 and fig. 264.
21. Stocker 1991.
22. Stocker 1991, fig. 37.
23. Creighton and Barry 2012, 67–68 and 71–72.
24. Tys 2010, 289–301.
25. Marshall 2002, 30.
26. Steane 2001, 75.
27. Christie 1966, 49; Keller and Schia 1994.
28. Steane 2001, 60–65 and 142.
29. Stocker and Everson 2006, fig 3.43; David Stocker, *pers. comm.*; Stocker and Dixon forthcoming.
30. Shapland 2013, 220.
31. Larsson 2002; Hårdh 2010.
32. Carelli 1997, 434.
33. Faulkner 1974, 340–344.
34. Coad and Streeten 1982, 138–301.
35. Kermode 2000, table 18.1.
36. Platt 1976, fig. 4 (after Scarfe)
37. Stcanc 2001, 194.
38. Loveluck 2013, 330 and 356.
39. De Groot 1997, 102–104.
40. Hoekstra 1996, 205–207.
41. Ayers 2002, 73; Rutledge 1982.
42. Rosser 2000, 343–344.
43. Barrowclough 2010, 32–33; 43.
44. Creighton and Heigham 2005, 166 and 211.
45. Finch 2002, 107.
46. Verhulst 1999, 115.
47. De Biève 2012, 320–321 and fig. 2.
48. Creighton and Higham 2005, 166. Zeune 2000, 40.
49. Ayers 2010, 42.
50. Birk Hansen 2010, 825.
51. Thomasson 1997, 702.
52. Anders Reisnert, *pers. comm.*
63. Reisnert 2004, 465.
64. Gaimster 2014, 64–65.
55. Øye 1997, 443.
56. Hansen 2005.
57. Øye 2004, 518 and 522.
58. Risvaag and Christophersen 2004, 91.
59. Molaug 2007, 1.
60. Creighton and Barry 2012, 75.
61. Ingle and Saunders 2011, 109; Clarke 2003, 77.

62. Rogerson and Ashley 2003, 353.
63. McDonagh 2003.
64. Wrathmell 20012, 230–232.
65. Stoepker 1990, 206 and fig. 5.
66. Bult 1987, 24.
67. Tys 1997, 157–158 and fig. 1.
68. Tys 2010, 297.
69. Kristiansen, M. S. 1996, 47–52 and fig. 3.
70. Svensson *et al.* 2008, 74
71. Donkin 1960, 142–165.
72. Fenwick 2000, 184.
73. Evans *et al.* 2012, 17.
74. Platt 1969, 93 and 91.
75. Loveluck 2013, 299–300.
76. Waites 1980, 116.
77. Childs 2001, 29.
78. Moorhouse 1983, 53.
79. Bond 2004, 340
80. Hudson and Tingey 1910, lx.
81. 'Mapping medieval monastic wetland management'. *Past Horizons*. April 28, 2013, from http://www.pasthorizonspr.com/index.php/archives/04/2013/mapping-medieval-monastic-wetland-management accessed on 9th September 2014.
82. Deforce *et al.* 2006, 141–153; Jongepier *et al.* 2011, 77 and 79–80.
83. Lambert *et al.* 1952; Beresford and St Joseph 1979, 270.
84. Hoffman 2014, 237.
85. Lenders 1986, 161–168.
86. Hoffman 2014, fig. 4.2.
87. Williamson 2003, 81–82.
88. Renes 2010, 58 and fig. 11.
89. Loe Hjelle 2007, 167–171.
90. Williamson 2012, 233.
91. http://www.nottingham.ac.uk/archaeology/research/projects/current/leffinge.aspx accessed on 29th October 2014.
92. Ervynck *et al.* 2013, 153–162.
93. Sawyer and Sawyer 1993, 111; Carelli 2001, 388.
94. Kastholm 2011, 28–31.
95. Carver 2011, 472–464.
96. Long 1975, 14–15.
97. Rodwell 1981, fig. 50; Blair and Pyrah (eds.) 1996, fig. 1.7.
98. Richards 1990, 3 and 88.
99. De la Riestra 1999, 193–195.
100. Hoffman 2014, 231
101. Loveluck 2013, 348.
102. Abrahamse and Kosian 2013, 119; 120–124.
103. Barrett (ed.) 2012, 280–282.

104. Haneka *et al.* 2005, 262; https://onderzoeksbalans.onroerenderfgoed.be/book/export/html/2416 for dendrochronological dates of the St John hospital timbers–accessed on 27th April 2015.
105. Crone n.d., 1–2.
106. Mills and Crone 2012, 20.
107. Simpson 2014, 242–246.
108. Simpson 2014, 235 and 239–242.
109. Crone 2000, 212.
110. Andersson 2001, 372.
111. Hinton 2000; Blair 2000.
112. Schofield and Vince 2003; Gläser 1997.
113. Aston and Bond 1976.
114. Lilley 2002, 138–177.
115. Evans 2000, 193–200.
116. O'Brien *et al.* 1988, 154ff.
117. Ayers 2009, 105–110.
118. Emery 2007, 65.
119. Information from site visit and discussion with Andy Shelley, August 2015.
120. Stones (ed.) 1989, fig. 42.
121. Jantzen 2013, 54–55.
122. Magnusson Staaf 2014, 567.
123. Gilchrist 2009, 388.
124. Carelli 2001; Thomasson 1997.
125. Gläser 1999, 2001, 2004, 2006, 2010 and 2014.
126. Gläser 2008.
127. Rieger 2014, 47 and fig. 18.
128. Dobat 2008, 33 and 43.
129. http://www.ribe-domkirke.dk/upload/pdf/Lindegaarden-web_100.pdf (accessed on 7th October 2013).
130. Schofield and Vince 2003, 129.
131. Hansen and Sørensen 1980.
132. Abrahamse and Koslan 2013, 123.
133. Carmiggelt 1999, 53–65.
134. Schofield 2011, figs. 2.9 and 2.6.
135. Watson *et al.* 2001, 88–89 and fig.54.
136. McCombie 2009, 108.
137. Skov 2004, 552.
138. de Witte 2004, 107–108.
139. Schäfer 2004, 268, 273 and fig. 9.
140. Anund 2004, 449.
141. Harder 2012, 128–129 and figs. 14 to 16.
142. Rawcliffe 2013, 127.
143. Cessford 2015, 63.
144. Gläser 2004, *passim*; Moloney and Coleman 1997, 776; Biermann and Schenk 2014, 71 and fig. 2.
145. Spoerry 2005, 96.
146. Bailey 1995, 3; Ekwall 1960, 284.
147. Oosthuizen 1993, 34.
148. Crumlin-Pedersen 2010, 116.

149. Robinson and Aaby 1994, 182.
150. Spoerry *et al.* 2008, 190–202.
151. Spoerry 2005, 100–101; Spoerry 2008, 24.
152. Vince 2002, 139.
153. Jones, Stocker and Vince 2003, 242.
154. Bailey 2007, 94; Cessford *et al.* 2006, 11–13.
155. Moloney and Coleman 1997, 778.
156. Kock 2004, 3–6.
157. Hall 2012, 45–53.
158. Aliaga-Kelly and Proudfoot 1995, 68–69.
159. Kelly 1983, 24–25.
160. http://www.mola.org.uk/blog/three-quays-update; abstract of paper at 13th International Symposium on Boat and Ship Technology, Amserdam 2012 http://european-maritime-heritage.org/docs/conferences/ISBSA13%20Program.pdf (both accessed on 13th November 2015).
161. Perry *et al.* 2010, 115.
162. Spencer 1992, 143.
163. De Groote *et al.* 1995/1996, 128.
164. Dyer 2003, 88, 98 and 102, table 1.
165. Daniels 2010, 209–210 and table 7.14.
166. Brandt 1985, 99–105.
167. Hoffman 2014, 167–168.
168. Heidinga and van Regteren Altena (eds.) 1989, 25–27.
169. Holm 2002, 51–52.
170. Hinman and Popescu 2012, 21 and plate 5B.
171. Silvester 1988, 163 and fig. 115.
172. Rogerson 1975, 131 and 159–160.
173. 'The Climate of Late Medieval England: Reconstruction and Impacts'. Lecture by Kathleen Pribyl, Climate Research Unit University of East Anglia, and University of Bern, Switzerland at Norwich Castle Museum, 2 November 2013. http://www.nnas.info/sites/default/files/downloads/NNASLecture021113Pribyl.pdf (accessed on 10th January 2015).
174. Connell *et al.* 2012.
175. Perry *et al.* 2010, 119–120.
176. Hinman and Popescu 2012, 4.
177. Ufkes *et al.* 1999.

Chapter 3

1. Crowther 1992, 51–54.
2. http://www.lancewadplan.org/Workshop/Cross%20section/3.3%20Pellworm Nordstrand/3.3%20CS_Pellworm-Nordstrand.htm (accessed on 26th October 2014).
3. German *Terra X* ZDF TV programme–http://www.zdf.de/ZDFmediathek/beitrag/video/1220602/Atlantis-der-Nordsee#/beitrag/video/1220602/Atlantis-der-Nordsee (accessed on 7th January 2015).
4. Meier 2012, 154
5. http://corporate.vattenfall.com/news-and-media/news/2014/lost-underwater-city-discovered-at-vattenfall-wind-farm-site/ (accessed on 26th October 2014).
6. Information from David Evans, Humber Archaeology.
7. Evans 2004, 52, fig. 1.
8. Hayfield and Slater 1984, 5; 86; Slater 1985, 23–41.

9. Parker 1978, 247.
10. Lamb 1991, 18; 16.
11. Van Marrewijk *et al.* 2001, 48.
12. Spufford 2002, 59; 98–99.
13. Kermode 1991, 480.
14. Spufford 1963, 127.
15. Marsden 2013, 546.
16. Mayhew 1975, 36.
17. Mayhew 1975, 37.
18. Dennison and Stones 1997, 63–64.
19. Murray 1982, 182.
20. Kermode 1998, 332, 338 and 340.
21. Amor 2011, 129.
22. Evans 1999, 65–66; fig.3.
23. Verhaeghe 1999, 142–143.
24. Verhaeghe 1999, 144.
25. Moorhouse 1983.
26. Ring 2011, 12 and fig. 11.
27. Mührenberg 1999a, 620.
28. Auer and Maarleveld (eds.) 2013, 25–28.
29. Rammo 2012, 125–146; De Witte 1999a, 171.
30. Egan 2012, 21.
31. Hall 1999, 116.
32. Ayers and Murphy 1983, 55
33. Sutton 1989, 213.
34. Egan 2012, 19–21 and fig. 1.
35. Maik 2009, 113–116.
36. Clarke and Carter 1977, 374–376.m
37. Pedersen 2009, 139–148 and fig. 7.5.
38. Hudson and Tingey 1910, 209–212.
39. Dunn 2004, 224–225.
40. Sutermeister 2002, 133.
41. Evans and Tomlinson 1992, 282–286.
42. Dahl 2009, 122–138; figs. 6.2 and 6.6.
43. Walton 1991, 338.
44. Dransart *et al.* 2012, 3–142.
45. Gläser 1999.
46. Mührenberg 1999a, 620–621.
47. Ayers 1999, 27; Spufford 2002, 319.
48. Steven Ashley, *pers. comm.*
49. Pluskowski 2013, 153.
50. Bailey 1988.
51. Rębkowski 2006, 451.
52. Hall 2006, 98.
53. Pluskowski 2013, 155.

54. British Library, MS Royal 2. B. VII.
55. Mason 2010, 16, 21–23 .
56. Mason 2009, 5.
57. Mason 2010s, passim.
58. Bailey 1988, 4.
59. Bailey 1988, 12–13.
60. Gras 1918, 527–553.
61. Dunn 2004, 220.
62. Pluskowski 2013, 161.
63. Ayers and Murphy 1983, 42.
64. Bartels 2006, 143–147.
65. http://www.thehistoryblog.com/archives/24314 (accessed on 13th January 2015).
66. *Pers. Comm.* Matthias Benjamins in lecture at European Association of Archaeologists conference, Lyon, 2004.
67. Spufford 2002, 295.
68. Teuber 2006, 54 and fig. 2.
69. Heege 2002, 309 and fig. 662.
70. Först 2006, 206; Rech 2004, 253.
71. Mulsow 2006, 293 and fig. 8, Paner 2006, 425–426.
72. Latałowa *et al.* 2007, 48 and 58.
73. Viklund 2007, 125.
74. Spufford 2002, 295)
75. Armstrong and Ayers 1987, 51 and fig 35, phase 5iii.
76. Teuber 2006, 55, fig.4.
77. Gaimster 1997, 51 and 164; Beckmann 1974, 183–189 and fig. 2.
78. Kühne 2014, 1–2.
79. Kermode 1998, 177–179; Allison 1969, 86–89.
80. Stean 1985, 277.
81. Carus-Wilson 1962–63, 189.
82. Pecci *et al.* 2013, 109–115.
83. Alsleben 2007, 29–30 and table 6.
84. Livarda 2011, 159.
85. Armstrong and Ayers 1987, 255 and plate 36.
86. Kermode 1998, 180.
87. Livarda 2011, 159.
88. Windeatt 1985, 127.
89. Locker 1987, 114–117.
90. Slavin 2012, 170.
91. Van Neer and Ervynck 2006, 97–99.
92. Schietecatte and Sealy 2006, 73–74.
93. Mays 1997, 561–567.
94. Curtis-Summers *et al.* 2014, 21–43.
95. Barrett and Richards 2007, 249–271.
96. Barrett *et al.* 2008, 858.
97. Agnarsdóttir 2013, 203 and 208.
98. Jahnke 2009, 170ff.

99. Gaimster 1999, 61 and fig. 1.
100. Svensson *et al.* 2008, 70–71; figs 2 and 3.
101. Bolander 2014, 193.
102. M. Steineke, 2015. 'To Travel to Øresund and Elsewhere ...'–poster at the Conference of the European Association of Archaeologists, Glasgow, September 2015 and abstract within EAA2015 Abstracts volume, 127.
103. Turner 2013, 71ff.
104. Yoder 2010, 2232–2235.
105. Polet and Katzenberg 2003.
106. Müldner and Richards 2005, 45–46.
107. Anders Reisnert, *pers. comm.*
108. Rawcliffe 2013, 234–235.
109. Schofield 2011, 205.
110. http://www.crossrail.co.uk/news/articles/new-research-shows-crossrails-charterhouse-skeletons-were-black-death-victims–accessed on 18th January 2015.
111. Schuenemann *et al.* 2011, E746–E752.
112. Carver and Klápště (eds.) 2011, 496.
113. Pringle 2007, 45–49.
114. Schofield 2011, 204.
115. DeWitte 2014, 99.
116. Gilchrist 2012, 219.
117. Gilchrist and Sloane 2005, 41–42 and fig. 21; 194.
118. Kowaleski 2014, 593–594.
119. Beresford 1954, 162.
120. Meier 2012, 241.
121. Bos 1990, 127.
122. Wade-Martins 1980, 87–89.
123. Pribyl *et al.* 2012, 393–412.
124. Hoffmann 2014, 332.
125. Schreg 2014, 104ff.
126. Creighton and Barry 2012, 64 and fig. 5.1.
127. http://maps.nls.uk/view/108520509 (accessed on 9th December 2015).
128. Lewis and Pringle 2002, 11.
129. Soens 2013, 230–232.
130. Tys 2006, 27.
131. Eden 1980, 348–350.
132. http://www.access.arch.cam.ac.uk/reports/norfolk/wiveton/2008 (accessed on 25th January 2015).
133 . http://www.medieval-g135raffiti.co.uk/index.htm (accessed on 25th January 2015).
134. Freeman 2012, 148–149 and fig. 8.1.
135. Cameron 1979, 153–164.
136. Cameron 1986, 331–351.
137. Cockerham 2012, 90–92.
138. Cockerham 2014, 402–403.
139. Caption to display of the Macclesfield Psalter in the Fitzwilliam Museum,Cambridge.
140 . King 2013, 94–95.
141. Jennings and Rogerson 1994, 117–118.
142. Walker 2012, 115.

143. Dunning 1968, 38–39; Long 1975, 21.
144. http://www.lodosemuseum.se/en/Vastarvet---natural-and-cultural-heritage-in-West-Sweden/Subsites/Lodose-museum/Exhibitions/Exhibitions-visningssida/?btid=episerver_71361 (accessed on 9th December 2014).
145. Barron 1998, 19.
146. De Witte 2014a, 273–281.
147. Sarfatij 1990, 109.
148. King 2013, 97.
149. Heywood 1989, 231, plate IV and Stephen Heywood, *pers. comm.*
150. Allison 1969,76; Eddy 1993, 45ff; Brooks 1939, 151–174.
151. Armstrong and Ayers 1987, 28, 38–39, 266 and plates 7 and 8.
152. Lee 2011, 55–58 and 173.
153. Armstrong and Ayers 1987, 42–43, 49–50 and fig. 32.
154. Allison 1969, 412; Evans 2010,48–56; Creighton and Higham 2005, 135.
155. Ayers and Evans 2001, 42–46.
156. Evans 2010, 55 and fig. 2.
157. Andrews 2008, 60 and 66; Ayers *et al.* 1988.
158. Andrews 2008, 68ff.
159. Ayers 2009, 94 and 116.
160. Rutledge 2010, 68.
161. Hoare *et al.* 2002, 91–105.
162. W. DeClercq, *pers. comm.*-paper delivered at the European Association of1 Archaeologists conference, Glasgow 2015 and abstract within EAA2015 Abstracts volume, 86.
163. Ansorge *et al.* 2011, 161–173.
164. Groothedde 2010, 177–179 and figs. 11, 12 and 14.
165. Drury and Pratt 1975.
166. Van Roooijen and Hoekstra 1996, 209–215.
167. Laleman 2008, 170–174.
168. Debone 2008, 189–196.
169. Hoekstra 1996, 202–203 and plate XXIIIB.
170. Lehouck 2008, 217.
171. Giles and Clark 2011, 230–233.
172. Allison 1969, 434.
173. Meier 2006, 120.
174. Milne 2014, 46–47; Schofield 1981, 104.
175. Rieger 2014, 39–49.
176. Spitzers 2001, 207–209 and fig. 14.
177. Reisnert 2001, 681–684 and fig. 6.
178. Smith and Carter 1983, 10 and fig. 11.
179. Tvauri 2009, 53.
180. Atzbach 2013, 244.
181. Betty Arndt, *pers. comm.*
182. Gaimster 2014, 64–65.
183. Verhaeghe 1999, 156.
184. Gaimster 2014, 64–65.
185. Rębkowski 1999, 406 and figs. 1 and 2.

186. Nawrolska 1999, 375.
187. Gaimster 2014, 66–67.
188. Mehler 2009, 104–105.
189. Kruip 2011, 420–423.
190. Wallis 2009, 478-82 and fig. 9.
191. Clarke and Carter 1977, 78–82 and fig. 35; Parker 1971, 38.
192. Gilchrist 2008, 130 and fig.2.
193. Nagel 2005, 381–384.
194. Bischop 2011, 55.
195. Gilchrist and Sloane 2008, 98.
196. Milne 1997, 4.
197. Roberts and Atkin 1982, 11–29.
198. Rütz 2005, 376–378.
199. Rech 2004, 50–53.
200. Magilton 1980.
201. Heege 2002, 144- 145.
202. Stirland 2009.
203. Rodwell 1981, 107–122.
204. Bell *et al.* 1985.
205. Stocker 2012, 240–262.
206. Champion 2012, 68–72.
207. Fawcett 1996, 175.
208. Morris 1989.
209. Stoepker 1990, 206–210.
210. Stocker and Everson 2009, 1–15.
211. Silvester 1988, 172.
212. Spooner 2008, 170–185.
213. Emery 2007, 139–143.
214. Caption in 'Making Colour' exhibition at the National Gallery 2014.
215. Gilchrist 2012, 73.

Chapter 4

1. Gilchrist and Oliva 1993; Gilchrist 1994; Gilchrist 1999, x.
2. Gilchrist 2012, 24.
3. Hill 2010, 168.
4. Ring 2014, 395–398; Bitter 2014, 119–127.
5. Simons 2001, 143.
6. Information from lecture by Thomas Coomans (University of Leuven) to the Society of Antiquaries of London in 2013.
7. Bergmans 2008, 235–246 and figs. 7.24 to 7.40.
8. Tanner 1984, 65.
9. King 2006, 6.3.2.
10. Gilchrist and Oliva 1993, 97–99.
11. Gilchrist and Sloane 2005, 72; Skov 2012, 593 and fig.5.
12. Møller 2000, 87.

13. Planer 2012, 325–329.
14. Mellor 2014, 77–86 and figs 5.2 and 5.3.
15. Reisnert 2012, 460–461 and fig. 9.
16. Ayers 2012, 32
17. Gilchrist and Sloane 2005, 68.
18. Penny-Mason and Gowland 2014.
19. Smith 2014, 62.
20. Smith 2014, 63–66.
21. Skov 2012, fig. 8.
22. Ayers 2012, fig. 2.
23. Atkin 1991
24. Meier 2012, 132–133.
25. Thijssen 1999, 181–187.
26. Mührenberg 2001, 843–852.
27. Rech 2004, 133 – 5
28. Klück 1999, 131–141.
29. Bitter 1999, 11–29.
30. Boekwijt 1999, 37–51.
31. Van de Waard 1999, 229–248.
32. Norfolk Historic Environment Record–http://www.heritage.norfolk.gov.uk/record-details?MNF19461 (accessed 28th April 2014).
33. Smith and Carter 1983, 6 -7.
34. Quiney 2003, 150; Whittingham 1984, 39–40 and plates II and VII.
35. Quiney 2003, 149–150.
36. Schofield 1994, 76–79.
37. Gaimster 1993a, 168
38. Evans and Carter 1985, 84.
39. Quiney 2003, 185.
40. Whittingham 1984, 47–50 and plate VI.
41. Hewett 1969, 119–121 and fig. 46.
42. Edward Martin, *pers.comm.* within lecture available online–http://www.letheringhamlodge.com/lecture-letheringham-lodge-a-tudor-wonder/ (accessed 27th April 2015).
43. Wrathmell (ed.) 2012, 341 and plate 36; Wrathmell in Hayfield 1988, 106.
44. Pieters 2006, 51–53.
45. Schietecatte and Sealy 2006, 72–74; Pieters 2006, 48.
46. Pieters 2006, 48–49.
47. Pieters and Verhaeghe 2006–2008, 114.
48. De Groote 2005, 42.
49. Dyer 2012, 336.
50. Gaimster 2011, 347.
51. Gaimster 2014,71; Gaimster 1999, 66.
52. Jansen 2008, 66.
53. Gaimster 2012, 69.
54. Atzbach 2013, 250.
55. Hjermind 2006, 630–633 and figs 10 and 18.
56. Ayers 2015, 15.

57. Ayers 2006, 35–36 and fig. 5; Emery 2007, 73–74.
58. Emery 2007, 122 - 125 and fig. 3.18.
59. Hill 2010, 49.
60. King 2006, 4 , fig. 43 and plates 12a, 12b and 12f; Ayers 2008, 36.
61. Munro 2009, 2–9.
62. Kirjavainen 2009, 96.
63. Gläser (ed.) 2006, 226, 530–531 and *passim*
64. Information from David Adams.
65. Hall 2006, 99–100.
66. Clarke forthcoming.
67. King 2013, 105.
68. King 2006, 138.
69. Rhodes 1982, 57–73.
70. Dyer 2000b, 282–286; Kermode 2000, 453.
71. Stirland 2009.
72. Ayers 2009, 117–118.
73. Vermeersch 2000, 74–77.
74. Monckton 2012, 47.
75. Jansen 2008, 66–82.
76. Parker 1971, 113ff and fig. 26.
77. Schofield 1984, 1119–120 and fig. 97; Jansen 2008, fig. 6.
78. Schlauch 1957, 116.
79. Salter and Higgins 2000, 1.
80. Janssen and Nijhof 2010, 132.
81. Dyer 2000, 227–229.
82. https://www.academia.edu/4659065/The_Zwinproject_-_Medieval_Bruges_and_its_outer_ports._A_landscape_archaeological_contribution_to_the_Zwin-debate (accessed on 12th June 2015).
83. Spitzers 2004, 119.
84. Larsson 2009, 176–177.
85. Rawcliffe 2013, 144.
86. Shiels and Campbell 2011, 75–79 and figs 3.5 and 3.8.
87. Saunders 1985, 118.
88. Gläser (ed.) 2010, *passim.*
89. http://www.copenhagen.dk/en/excavations/at_the_metro_stations/kongens_nytorv1/ accessed on 19th June 2015.
90. Host-Madsen *et al.* 2010, 848–852.
91. Høst-Madsen 2014, 369–371 and figs. 6–8.
92. Gralow 2010, 306–308 and fig. 13.
93. Możejko 2014, 67–68 and figs. 1A and 1B.
94. Ossowski 2014, 281.
95. Zwick 2010, 62–71.
96. Zwick 2012, 286
97. Ortlam 1996, 31.
98. Hutchinson 1994, 142.
99. Evans 1999, 76 and fig. 5.
100. Johnson 1988, 107, 110 and fig 2; Johnson 1998, 76 and figs. 1–5.

101. C. Thomsen, *pers. comm.*-paper delivered at European Association of Archaeologists conference, Glasgow 2015.
102. Hutchinson 1994, 44.
103. Adams 2013, 79–86.
104. Krüger 2005, 85.
105. Simpson 2008, 53–65 and figs 2 and 4.
106. De Witte, 2014b, 102.
107. Arndt 2014, 153–155 and figs. 6 to 10.
108. Evans 2014, 57 and 60.
109. Ose 2014, 516.
110. Roberts *et al.* 2013, 273–285.
111. Evans 2014, 56; Evans 2002, 22.
112. Emery 2007, 238.
113. Møller 2000, 67.
114. Gläser (ed.) 2014.
115. Bitter 2014, 119–129 and figs. 5, 9, 11 and 14.
116. Lauritsen 2014, 686–694 and fig. 7.
117. Schneider 2014, 413–422
118. Evans 2014, 53 and fig. 7.
119. On-site observation by the writer.
120. Emery 2007, 75–79, figs. 3.19 to 3.20 and plates 3.14 to 3.18.
121. Gralow 2014, 233 and fig. 6.
122. Widerström 2014, 605 and fig.12.
123. Babington and Stewart 1997, 1.
124. Kjaer and Morgensen 2000, 14 and 31.
125. King 1996, 216–225.
126. Fawcett 1996a, 176–177.
127. Sekules 1996, 205.
128. Fawcett 1996b, 221.
129. Sany Heslop, *pers. comm.*
130. Finch 2004, 66 and 68.
131. http://norwichmedievalchurches.org.
132. Hourihane 2012, 185.
133. Marks and Williamson (eds.) 2003, 452, cat. 344.
134. Ohm *et al.* (eds.) 2006, 365 and fig. 286.
135. Childs 1986, 91 and 110; Cheetham 2005, 47–48, 61.
136. Cameron 1974, 230–231.
137. Blair and Blair 1991, 94.
138. Oman 1930, 120, fn1.
139. Cameron 1974, 231.
140. Oman 1930, 141–143.
141. Cronne and Gallagher 2008, 247–255.
142. Cronne and Mills 2002, 792.
143. Cattermole and Cotton 1983, 258; Heslop, *pers. comm.*
144. Ayers 2014, 42.
145. Slavin 2012.

146. Hillier and Hanson 1984; Johnson 1993, 30.
147. Giles 2000, 3–4.
148. McNeil 2003, 143.
149. Schofield 1994, 92–93 and figs. 100–101.
150. Ayers 2005, 68 - 82.
151. Obrink, M. *pers. comm.* in paper entitled 'City Planning as a Reflection of Cultural Norms' at the Conference of the European Association of Archaeologists, Glasgow–September 2015.
152. Thomasson 2004b, 165–189.
153. Boysen 2013, 77–88.
154. Igel 2013, 23–30.
155. Platz 2013, 67–76.
156. Gärtner 2013, 177–188.
157. King 2009, 471.
158. King 2015, 353.
159. Willemsen 2015, 1–36 and fig. 32.
160. Tittler 2007, 129–134.
161. Green 2015–paper delivered at the 21st Annual Conference of the European Association of Archaeologists in Glasgow and Abstract on p.145 of Conference Abstracts book.
162. Naum 2013, 388–396.
163. Pacey 2007, 311–323 and figs. 2–4 and 6.
164. Hardwick 2011, 70–71 and fig. 13.
165. Pacey 2007, 317.
166. Cheetham 2005,
167. Evans 1999, 79.
168. Hall 1999, 117.
169. De Witte 1999, 173–174; 178. Enrique or Henry III died in 1406; he was also called Henry the Sufferer or Henry the Sick.
170. Bjerregaard and Lauridsen 2014, 264 and figs. 2, 5, 7 and 8
171. Graßmann 1980, 165–166. The item is illustrated as fig. 8 in Mührenberg 1999b, 268.
172. Hoffmann 2014, 357.
173. Lewin 2010, 268.
174. www.tiergartentunnel.de accessed on 27th February 2014.
175. Brown and Pluskowski 2011, 1965.
176. Latałowa *et al.* 2007, 52 and 57–59.
177. Abrahamse and Kosian 2013, 126–127.
178. Hoffmann 2004, 26–28.
179. van Damm 2001, 42.
180. Jongepier *et al.* 2011, 90.
181. Abrahamse and Kosian 2013, 126
182. Slive 2005, 106, cat. 31.
183. Danbury and Scott 2015, 185–190 and figs. 22–23.

Chapter 5

1. Krüger 2005, 81 and fig 1.
2. Hudson and Tingey 1910, lxxviii.
3. Schofield 1994, 198.

4. Hall 1999, 114.
5. De Witte 1999a, 171.
6. Gillett and MacMahon 1980, 19.
7. Kermode 1998, 169.
8. Cockerham 2012, 79 and fig. 5.6.
9. Campbell 1990, 116.
10. Mead 1972.
11. Vandewalle 2002, 48–49.
12. Ayers 1999, 29.
13. Kowaleski 2000, 493.
14. Vandewalle 2002,10–11.
15. Barron 2000, 401.
16. Spofforth 2002, 16.
17. Olsen and Crumlin-Pedersen 1968.
18. Crumlin-Pedersen 1997.
19. Bill *et al.* 1998.
20. Unger 1980, 138.
21. Ellmers 1979.
22. Haneka and Daly 2013, 96–97.
23. http://kamper-kogge.nl/wrak_ijssel_kogge_kampen/index.php (accessed on 13th June 2015).
24. Crumlin-Pedersen 1985, 88.
25. Rech 2004, 327.
26. Unger 1980, 136.
27. Bärenfänger and Ellmers 1999, fig 1 and 2.
28. Flatman 2011, 357.
29. Clarke and Carter 1977, 1.
30. Brown 1984, 1.67.
31. Dyer 2000a, 755.
32. Lloyd 1977, 12.
33. Milne and Hobley 1981; Herteig 1985; Good *et al.* 1991; Bill and Clausen 1999.
34. Herteig 1981, 83-4 and fig. 86.
35. Parker 1965.
36. Sarfatij 1981.
37. Ayers 1979.
38. Milne 2003, 135–146.
39. Milne and Milne 1982, 14–42.
40. Steedman *et al.* 1992, 137–138.
41. Jondell 1981, 125–128.
42. Baart *et al.* 1977, 58 and fig. 42.
43. Rech 2004, 105.
44. Gläser 1999, 79–82.
45. Erdmann 1980, 87 – 90; figs. 65 and 65; Gläser 2009, 59–64.
46. Gläser 1999, 84.
47. Lüdecke 2003, 26–27; Busch 1997, fig. 4.
48. Ayers 1979.

49. Milne 2003, 20.
50. Horrox 1978, map and gazetteer.
51. Clarke and Carter, fig.191.
52. De Groot and Hoekstra 1985, 110.
53. Myrvoll 1991, 150ff.
54. Herteig 1975, fig. 31.
55. http://www.gtyarmouth.co.uk/html/map_1797.htm (accessed on 12th November 2013).
56. Rogerson 1976, 131–245.
57. Ayers and Smith 1992, 338–350.
58. http://www.heritage.norfolk.gov.uk/record?tnf382 (accessed on 13th November 2013).
59. O'Brien *et al.* 1988, fig. 2.
60. O'Brien *et al.* 1988, 155–159.
61. Beresford and St Joseph 1958, fig. 93–the haven is visible near the right hand margin.
62. Slater 1985, 39.
63. Percival 2004, 15–16.
64. Milne 2003, 143, fig. 70.
65. Elvestad 2002; http://en.vikingkings.com/PortalDefault.aspx?portalID=116&activeTabID=851&parentActiveTabID=848 (accessed on 30th October 2013).
66. Molaug 1999, 169–170.
67. Cushion and Davison 2003, fig. 98 and plate XXXIII.
68. Smith 1937, 198.
69. Miller *et al.* 1982, 18–19 and 31.
70. De Witte 1999b, 137ff and fig. 4.
71. Krause 2003, 32–33.
72. Parker 1978, 87.
73. Ecclestone and Ecclestone 1959, 92ff and fig. on p.93.
74. http://www.dunwich.org.uk/resources/documents/dunwich_12_report.pdf, 126–128 (accessed on 13th November 2013).
75. Reinders 1999, 133–134.
76. Hudson 1889, 7.
77. Rawcliffe 2013, 201.
78. Young 1987; Daniels 1991, 45 – 7 and figs. 6.2 and 6.3.
79. Evans 1966, 201.
80. De Boer 1973, plate x.
81. Vermeesch 2002, 77.
82. Schofield and Vince 2003, fig. 2.20.
83. Allison 1969, 435.
84. Platt and Coleman-Smith 1975, 78.
85. Barbry *et al.* n.d., 10–12.
86. Kunst 1999, 82–83.
87. Dijkman 2011, 347; 387–388.
88. Dendooven and Dewilde n.d., 14–15.
89. Hudson and Tingey 1910, 146.
90. de Biève 2012, 317–318; fig. 1.
91. Ayers 2009, 91.
92. RCHME 1972, 90; 106; 108; 158.

93. Daniels 2010, 57 and figs. 3.15 and 3.16.
94. Allison 1969, 412.
95. Martin 2004, fig. 5.2.
96. Platt 1973, 113–114.
97. Milne and Milne 1982, 45 and 63; a reconstruction drawing showing all three stairs is given in fig. 47.
98. Milne and Milne 1982, fig. 28.
99. Moorhouse 1971, 204 and plate XA.
100. Ayers 1979, 18 and figs 7 and 8.
101. Wood 1845, 53.
102. Shelley 2005.
103. Ulf Stammitz, *pers comm.* at DGAMN colloquium, Lübeck 2013.
104. Dollinger 1964, 150–151 and 226; Hammel-Kiesow 1997, 82–83.
105. Wellbrock 2009, 258; McNeil 1990, 490.
106. Krause 1999, 116 and fig.7.
107. Milne 2003, 75–78.
108. Shelley 2005.
109. Schofield 1981, 31.
110. Parker 1971, 40 and fig. 8.
111. Parker 1971, 114 and plate 29.
112. Erdman 1983.
113. Gläser 2001, fig. 12.
114. Gläser 2001, 298 and fig. 26 for typology of building types.
115. Spitzers 2001, 207.
116. Lüdecke 2001, 334 and fig.9.
117. Schneider 2001, 441 and fig. 15.
118. Arndt 2001, fig. 14.
119. Heege 2002, 35 and 171.
120. Schalies 2012, 117–121.
121. Gläser 2001, *passim.*
122. Hammel-Kiesow 2002, 63–65.
123. Heege 2002, 187.
124. Arndt 2001, 235 and fig. 2.
125. Veeckman 2001, 148ff and fig. 9.
126. Capiteyn *et al.* 2007, 21, Barbry *et al.* n.d., 3, 26, 40 and 41.
127. Hybel 2002, xvi.
128. Verhaeghe 1999, 161.
129. Unger 2002, 114–115.
130. Rybina 1992, 199.
131. Carus-Wilson 1962-3; Lloyd 1977.
132. Biermann 2005, fig. 1; Rybina 1992, 203 and fig. VI.3.
133. Egan 2010, 57, 61 and 63.
134. Arthur 2000, 420, fn 2.
135. Spufford 2002, 146.
136. Postan *et al.* 1987, 839.
137. Palmer 1847.

138. Information from http://www.ts.skane.se/fakta/skaanemarknaden (accessed on 20th January 2014).
139. Sawyer and Sawyer 1993, 150.
140. Jones, Stocker and Vince 2003, 227 and fig. 9.64.
141. Dymond 2005, 76–77.
142. Platt 1976, 24.
143. Ambler 2001, 55.
144. Rogerson and Ashley 2010, 117, no. 45.
145. London Museum 1940, 171–174 and plate XXXVIII.
146. Ashley 2008, 93–99.
147. Wubs-Mrozewicz 2013, 11.
148. Mehler 2009, fig.1.
149. De Groote *et al.* 2010.
150. Mehler 2009, 91.
151. von Arbin 2 2009, 67–74.
152. Freeman, 2012, fig.8.2.
153. Gaimster 2014, 69.
154. Rogers 2014, 210–212.
155. Cockerham 2014, 410.
156. King 2006, cxxiii; Hill 2014, 126 fn 46.
157. Information from lecture by Allan Barton, Norwich 2014.
158. Cockerham 2014, 408–409.
159. Greenhill 1965, 424–425.
160. Webb 1962, plate opposite p.5.
161. Rolfe 2013 unpublished.

Chapter 6

1. Smith and Watson 2014, 90–132.
2. Verhaeghe 1997, 25–44.
3. Evans 1999, 79–80.
4. Veeckman 2010, 186 and fig. 19.
5. Veeckman 1999, 127–130 and fig. 3.
6. Egan 2012, 61: Veeckman 1999, 123 ff.
7. Gaimster and Nenk 1997, 176 and fig. 13.2.
8. Gaimster 2003, 125–126 and fig. 1.
9. Gaimster 1997, 56 and figs. 3.9 to 3.12.
10. Hurst 2002, 47.
11. Gaimster 1997, 55.
12. King 2006, clvi.
13. http://www.cvma.ac.uk/publications/digital/norfolk/sites/outwell/history.html (accessed on 6th November 2015).
14. Fawcett 1996, 177–180 and plate XVIIIc.
15. De Biève 1996a, 263–265 and plate XLIIc.
16. Hall 2005, 220 and fig. 11.6.
17. http://www.archaeologists.net/sites/default/files/SG%20CIFA%20Newsletter%20August%2015.pdf and https://sketchfab.com/models/bda6a969b98a42189f925f0197c8ac18 (both accessed on 16th November 2015).

18. Lee 2003, 70–71, fig. 29 no. 4 and plate 10.
19. Hildburgh 1955, 110.
20. Bartels 2010, 21ff.
21. Gaimster 2007, 51, fig. 6.
22. Hill 2010, 17ff.
23. Ostcamp 2009, 107–125 and figs. 5 and 6.
24. Cheetham 1984, 118.
25. Clarke and Carter 1977, 270–273 and 279–281.
26. Gaimster 1993b, 257.
27. Gaimster 1993b, 251; Gaimster and Nenk 1997, 172; Margeson 1993, 236.
28. Holman 1980, 141.
29. Cherry 1997, 260.
30. Dyer 2002, 328.
31. Awty 2007, 790–792.
32. Willemsen 2012, 200; 187.
33. Gaimster 2007, 52–53 and fig. 7.
34. Hedge 2012, 320–327.
35. Staaf 2014, 570 and fig. 10.
36. Bolvig 2003, 84–93.
37. Goffin in Shepherd-Popescu 2009, 843 and fig. 10.13.
38. Morris 2003, 248.
39. Howard 2003, 229.
40. Howard 2003, 230.
41. Gilchrist 2005, 259.
42. Carole Rawcliffe, *pers. comm.*
43. Sandy Heslop, *pers. comm.*
44. Søvsø 2014, 732.
45. http://www.riven-oak.appspot.com/medieval.html#5 accessed on 16th November 2014.
46. Emery 2007, 94–97 and 111.
47. Sandy Heslop, *pers. comm.*; Fawcett 1996b, 221.
48. Vermeulen and Mittendorff 2014, 137–140.
49. Perring 2013, 188.
50. http://www.thorntonabbeyproject.com/#!historical-background/c1ozl (accessed on 5110th November 2015).
51. Staecker 2003, 432.
52. Cherry 1997, 257.
53. Joakim Thomasson, *pers. comm.* in paper delivered at the European Association of Archaeologists conference in Lyon 2004.
54. Thomasson 2004, 177–183.
55. Thaastrup-Leth 2014, 223–230.
56. Atzbach 2013, 250–251.
57. Verweij *et al.* 2012, 85–88.
58. Verweij *et al.* 2012, 81–82.
59. Lauwerier and Laarman 2008, 135–142.
60. Harden 1978; Minnis and Carmichael 2015.
61. Jones *et al.* 2003.

62. http://archaeologydataservice.ac.uk (accessed on 21st December 2015).
63. Anon 2011; http://www.archeoweb.gent.be (accessed on 9th August 2013).
64. Sarfatij 1997.
65. Perrin 2002.
66. Martin and Satchell 2008.
67. Abstract for conference paper by Yftinus van Popta of the University of Groningen, The Netherlands given at the 13th International Symposium on Boat and Ship Archaeology held in Amsterdam in 2012. http://european-maritime-heritage.org/docs/conferences/ISBSA13%20Program.pdf (accessed on 11th November 2015).
68. Abstract for conference paper by Laura White of the Institute of Nautical Archaeology, Texas A&M University, USA given at the 13th International Symposium on Boat and Ship Archaeology held in Amsterdam in 2012. http://european-maritime-heritage.org/docs/conferences/ISBSA13%20Program.pdf (accessed on 11th November 2015).
69. Jones (ed.) 2010, 18 and fig. 22.
70. Vince 2002, 130.
71. Pirenne 1952, 221–224.
72. I am grateful for discussions with Richard Hodges and Jenny Kermode for the ideas in this paragraph.
73. Cameron and Stones (eds.) 2001, 309.
74. Dollinger 1964, 62ff.
75. Möller 2008, 300 and fig. 3.
76. Evans 1999, 76–78.

Bibliography

Abrahamse, J. E. and Kosian, M. 2013. 'A metropolitan countryside: Peatland reclamation and the birth of a world city'. *Landscapes* 14.2, 117–140.

Adams, D. 2005. 'An archaeological evaluation at 17–27 Fishergate, Norwich, Norfolk'. *Norfolk Archaeological Unit Report* No. 1062 (unpublished).

———. 2008. 'An archaeological excavation at the former Bussey's Garage, Palace Street, Norwich'. *Norfolk Archaeological Unit Report* No. 1376 (unpublished).

Adams, J. 2013. *A Maritime Archaeology of Ships: Innovation and Social Change in Medieval and Early Modern Europe*. Oxford.

Agnarsdóttir, A. 2013. 'Iceland's 'English Century' and East Anglia's North Sea World'. In Bates and Liddiard (eds.), 204–216.

Ahrens, C. 1981. *Frühe Holzkirchen im Nördlichen Europa*. Hamburg.

———. 1994. 'Om "Stavkirkeproblemet",' *Foreningen Til Norske Fortidsminnesmerkers Bevaring*, 37–50

Albarella, U. 2005. 'Meat production and consumption in town and country'. In Giles and Dyers (eds.), 131–148.

Aliaga-Kelly, C. and Proudfoot, E. 1995. 'Floor tiles in medieval and post-medieval Scotland'. *Medieval Ceramics* 19: 67–75.

Allison, K. J. (ed.) 1969. *Victoria County History: Yorkshire East Riding*, I. London.

Als Hansen, B. and Sørensen, M. A. 1980. 'Bistrup teglværk. Arkæologiske undersøgelser af en middelalderlig teglværkstomt ved Roskilde'. *Hikuin* 6: 221–264.

Alsleben, A. 2007. 'Food consumption in the Hanseatic towns of Germany'. In Karg (ed.), 13–37.

Ambler, R. W. 2001. 'Markets and fairs, 1086–1792'. In Bennett and Bennett (eds.), 54–55.

Amor, N. R. 2011, *Late Medieval Ipswich: Trade and Industry* (Woodbridge).

Andersson, H. 2011. 'The development of Medieval towns'. In Carver and Klápště (eds.), 370–375.

Andersson, H. *et al.* (eds.) 1997. 'Visions of the past: Trends and traditions in Swedish medieval archaeology'. *Lund Studies in Medieval Archaeology* 19.

Andrews, D. 2008. 'The influence of Low Countries on Medieval brick building in eastern England'. In Coomans and van Royen (eds.), 53- 72.

Anon 2011. *Archeologisch onderzoek in Gent 2002-2011*. Ghent.

Ansorge, J. 2005. 'Siegelstempel und Siegel im archäologischen Fundgut'. In Jöns *et al.* 2005, 95–98.

Ansorge, J. *et al.* 2011. 'Cogs, sand and beer–a paleontological analysis of medieval ballast sand in the harbour of Wismar (Southwestern Baltic Sea Coast, Germany)'. In Bork *et al.* (eds.), 161–173.

Anund, J. 2004. 'Interaction, convention and regulation infrastructures in medieval Uppsala'. In Gläser (ed.), 437–454.

Armstrong, P. and Ayers, B. 1987. *Excavations in High Street and Blackfriargate*. Hull Old Town Report Series 5. East Riding Archaeologist 8.

Arndt, B. 2001. 'Archäologische Aspekte zum Hausbau in Göttingen'. In Gläser (ed.), 233–250.

———. 2014. 'Klöster und klösterliche Anlagen in Göttingen'. In Gläser (ed.), 149–165.

Arndt, B. and Ströbel, A. 2005. *Vom Dorf... gutingi ... zur Stadt*. Göttingen.

Ashley, S. 2008. 'A Wyvern on a twelfth-century armorial weight from Norfolk'. *The Coat of Arms* 3rd ser. 4, no. 216, 93–99.

Ashley, S. *et al.* 2009. 'Rhineland lava in Norfolk Churches'. *Church Archaeology* 13: 27–33.

Ashwin, T. and Davison, A. (eds.) 2005. *An Historical Atlas of Norfolk*. Chichester.

Astill, G. 2000. 'Archaeology and late-medieval urban decline'. In Slater (ed.), 214–234.

Aston, M. and Bond, J. 1976. *The Landscape of Towns*. London.

Atherton, I. *et al.* (eds.) 1996. *Norwich Cathedral: Church, City and Diocese 1096-1996*. London.

Atkin, M. 1991. 'Medieval clay-walled building in Norwich'. *Norfolk Archaeology* 41: 171–185.

———. 'Excavations on the bottling plant, Westwick Street (Site 159N)'. In Atkin and Evans (eds.), 115–153.

Atkin, M. W. *et al.* (eds.) 1985. 'Excavations in Norwich 1971–1978, Part II'. *East Anglian Archaeology* 26.

Atkin, M. W. and Evans, D. H. (eds.) 2002. 'Excavations in Norwich 1971–1978, Part III'. *East Anglian Archaeology* 100.

Atzbach, R. 2013. 'The house, the stove and the climate change'. *Zeitschrift für Archäologie des Mittelalters* 41: 241–256.

Auer, J. and Maarleveld, T (eds.) 2013. *Skjernøysund Wreck 3: Fieldwork Report 2011*. Esbjerg Maritime Archaeology Reports 5.

Austin, D. and Alcock, L. (eds.) 1990. *From the Baltic to the Black Sea: Studies in Medieval Archaeology*. London.

Awty, B. 2007. 'The development and dissemination of the Walloon method of ironworking'. *Technology and Culture* 48(4): 783–803.

Ayán Vila. X. M. 2003 *et al.* (eds.). *Archaeotecture: Archaeology of Architecture*. British Archaeological Reports International Series 1175.

Ayers, B. 1979. *Excavations at Chapel Lane Staith 1978: Hull Old Town Report Series No. 3*. East Riding Archaeologist 5.

———. 1985. 'Excavations within the North-East Bailey of Norwich Castle, 1979'. *East Anglian Archaeology* 28.

———. 1987. 'Excavations at St. Martin-at-Palace Plain, Norwich, 1981'. *East Anglian Archaeology* 37.

———. 1999. Archaeological evidence for trade in Norwich from the 12th to the 17th centuries'. In Gläser (ed.), 25–35

———. 2002. 'Recent archaeological research into secular Romanesque buildings in Norfolk'. In Pitte and Ayers (eds.), 69–76.

———. 2005. Understanding the urban environment: Archaeological approaches to medieval Norwich, in Harper-Bill (ed.), 68–82.

———. 2006. 'Craft industry in Norwich from the 12th to the 18th century'. In Gläser (ed.), 27–46.

———. 2008. 'Lifestyle! Luxury in medieval Norwich'. In Gläser (ed.), 29–42.

———. 2009. *Norwich: Archaeology of a Fine City*. Stroud.

———. 2010. 'The fortifications of medieval and early modern Norwich'. In Gläser (ed.), 29–46.

———. 2012. 'Infancy and adolescence, education and recreation in medieval and early post-medieval Norwich'. In Gläser (ed.), 25–38.

———. 2014. 'Monastic institutions in medieval Norwich'. In Gläser (ed.), 25–46.

———. 2015. 'The development of an urban landscape: Recent research in medieval Norwich'. In Heslop and Lunnon (eds.), 1–22.

Ayers, B. and Murphy, P. 1983. 'A Waterfront Excavation at Whitefriars Street Car Park, Norwich, 1979'. *East Anglian Archaeology* 17: 1–60.

Ayers, B. and Smith, R. 1992. 'Twelfth- and fifteenth-century undercrofts at Howard Street, Great Yarmouth'. *Norfolk Archaeology* 41(3): 338–350.

Ayers, B. *et al.* 1988. 'The Cow Tower, Norwich: A detailed survey and partial reinterpretation'. *Medieval Archaeology* 32: 184–207.

Baart, J. *et al.* 1977. *Opgravingen in Amsterdam*. Amsterdam.

Babington, C. and Stewart, S. 1997. *Wall Painting Condition Audit, Greyfriars Cloister, Great Yarmouth, Norfolk*. English Heritage Ancient Monuments laboratory Report 23/97.

Badham, S. and Cockerham, P. 2012. *The beste and fayrest of al Lincolnshire': The Church of St Botolph, Boston, Lincolnshire, and its Medieval Monuments'*. British Archaeological Reports British Series 554.

Bailey, M. 1988. 'The rabbit and the medieval East Anglian economy'. *Agricultural History Review* 36: 1–20.

Bailey, M. 1995. 'The prior and convent of Ely and their management of the manor of Lakenheath in the fourteenth century'. In Franklin and Harper-Bill (eds.), 1–20.

Bailey, M. 2007. *Medieval Suffolk*. Woodbridge.

Barbry, N. *et al.* n.d. *Middeleeuws Manhatten: Rijkdom in Gentse Stenen*. Ghent.

Bärenfänger R. and Ellmers D. 1999. 'Der Backstein und das Schiff'. *Archäologie in Niedersachsen* 2: 124 – 126.

Barley, M. W. (ed.). *European Towns: Their Archaeology and Early History*. London.

Barrett, J. H. (ed.) 2012. *Being an Islander: Production and Identity at Quoygrew, Orkney, AD 900–1600*. Cambridge.

Barrett, J. H. *et al.* 2008. 'Detecting the medieval cod trade: a new method and first results'. *Journal of Archaeological Science* 35(4): 850–861.

Barrett, J. H. *et al.* 2011. 'Interpreting the expansion of sea fishing in medieval Europe using stable isotope analysis of archaeological cod bones'. *Journal of Archaeological Science* 38(7): 1516–1524.

Barrett, J. H. and Richards, M. P. 2007. 'Identity, gender, religion and economy: new isotope and radiocarbon evidence for marine resource intensification in early historic Orkney, Scotland, UK'. *European Journal of* Archaeology 7(3): 249–271.

Barron, C. 1998. 'Introduction: England and the Low Countries 1327–1477'. In Barron and Saul (eds.), 1–21.

———. 2000. 'London 1300–1540'. In Palliser (ed.), 395–440.

Barron, C. and Saul, N. (eds.) 1998. *England and the Low Countries in the Late Middle Ages*. Stroud (paperback edition).

Barron, C. and Sutton, A. (eds.) 2014. 'The medieval merchant'. *Harlaxton Medieval Studies* XXIV. Donnington.

Barrowclough, D. A. 2010. 'Expanding the horizons of island archaeology: Islandscapes imaginary and real, Ely: the case of the dry island'. *Shima: The International Journal of Research into Island Cultures* 4(1): 27–46.

Bartels, M. 2006. 'Hansebier aus Deventer. Der räumliche Niederschlag einer Veränderung bei der Herstellung eines handwerklichen Produkts'. In Gläser (ed.), 135–155.

———. 2010. 'Admiration in clay, devotion on paper. Archaeology, context and interpretation of an *Anna Selbdritt* statuette (1475–1515) from the Hanseatic town of Deventer, the Netherlands, in the context of early Renaissance poetry by Rudolf Agricola and book printing by Richard Pafraet'. In De Groote *et al.* (eds.), 21–30.

Bates, D. and Liddiard, R. (eds.) 2013. *East Anglia and its North Sea World in the Middle Ages*. Woodbridge.

Bayley, J. 1996. 'Innovation in later medieval urban metalworking'. *Historical Metallurgy* 30(2): 67–71.

Beazley, O. and Ayers, B. 2001. 'Two Medieval Churches in Norfolk'. *East Anglian Archaeology* 96.

Beckmann, B. 1974. 'The main types of the first four production periods of Siegburg pottery'. In Evison *et al.* (eds.), 183–220.

Bell, R. D. *et al.* 1985. *Wharram, a Study of Settlement on the Yorkshire Wolds: Wharram Percy, the Church of St Martin*. Society for Medieval Archaeology Monograph Series 11.

Bennett, S. and Bennett, N. (eds.) 2001. *An Historical Atlas of Lincolnshire*. Chichester.

Beresford, M. W. 1954. *The Lost Villages of England*. London.

Beresford, M. W. and St Joseph, J. K. S. 1979. *Medieval England: An Aerial Survey*. Cambridge (second edition).

Berge, R. 2009. 'Archaeological discoveries of charcoal pits in the close hinterland of medieval Trondheim: Perspectives on charcoal production in central Norway before and after the turn of the 1st millennium AD'. *Vitark* 7: 110–132.

Berggren, L. *et al.* (eds.) 2002. *Cogs, Cargoes, and Commerce: Maritime Bulk Trade in Northern Europe 1150-1400*. Toronto.

Bergmans, A. 2008. 'De muurschilderingen van de begijnhofkerk: functie, betekenis en context'. In Coomans and Bergmans (eds.), 231–259.

Besteman, J. C. 1990. 'North Holland AD 400–1200: Turning tide or tide turned?' In Besteman *et al.* (eds.) 1990, 91–120

Besteman, J. C. *et al.* (eds.) 1990. *Medieval Archaeology in the Netherlands*. Assen.

Biermann, F. 2005. 'Chinesische Seide und Oostburger Gewebe–Spätmittelaltlicher Tuchhandel in Mecklenburg-Vorpommern'. In Jöns *et al.* (eds.), 107–110.

Biermann, F. and Schenk, T. 2014. 'Neue Einsichren zur Gründung der Stadt Freyenstein'. *Mitteilungen der Deutschen Gesellschaft für* Archäologie *des Mittelalters und der Neuzeit* 27: 69–76.

Bill, J. *et al.* (1998), 'Roskildeskibene'. *Nationalmuseets Arbejdsmark.*

Bill, J. and Clausen, B. L. (eds.) 1999. 'Maritime topography and the medieval town'. *National Museum Studies in Archaeology & History* 4. Copenhagen.

Birk Hansen, P. 2010. 'Nestved–a city without city wall'. In Gläser (ed.), 825–835.

Bischop, D. 2005. 'Die Steinkammern am Fluß–Vorberichte über die Ausgrabungen auf dem Grundstück Hotel Überfluss'. *Bremer Archäologische Blätter*, Neue Folge 6: (1/4): 67–78.

Bischop, D. 2011. 'Die Frohe Botschaft aus der Kloake'. *Mitteilungen der Deutschen Gesellschaft für Archäologie des Mittelalters und der Neuzeit* 23: 51–62.

Bitter, P. 1999. 'Bewoningsgeschiedenis aan de hand van verschillende bronnen. Een onderzoek in Alkmaar'. *Rotterdam Papers* 10: 11–29.

Bitter, P. 2014. 'Beguines, friars and nuns in medieval Alkmaar'. In Gläser (ed.), 117–131.

Bjerregaard, M. and Lauridsen, M. 2014. 'Et middelalderligt saltkar fra Odense'. *KUML-Årbog for Jysk Arkaeologisk Selskab*, 245–264.

Blair, C. and Blair, J. 1991 . 'Copper alloys'. In Blair and Ramsay (eds.), 81–106.

Blair, J. 2000. 'Small towns 600–1270'. In Palliser (ed.), 245–270.

———. 2005. *The Church in Anglo-Saxon Society*. Oxford.

Blair, J. and Pyrah, C. (eds.) 1996. 'Church archaeology: Research directions for the future'. Council for British Archaeology Research Report 104.

Blair, J. and Ramsay, N. (eds.) 1991. *English Medieval Industries*. London.

Boekwijt, H. W. 1999. 'Bouwhistorie en archeologie in 's-Hertogenbosch. Raakpunten in het huizenonderzoek van de middeleeuwse stad. *Rotterdam Papers* 10: 37–51.

Bolander, A. 2014. 'Smoke houses and entrepreneurship in two rural villages of medieval Scania, Örja and Skegrie'. In Svart Kristiansen and Giles (eds.), 185 -194.

Bolvig, A. 2003. 'Reformation of what? Whose and which Reformation is exposed in Danish wall-paintings?'. In Gaimster and Gilchrist (eds.), 84–93.

Bond, C. J. 2004. *Monastic Landscapes*. Stroud.

Bork, H. -R. *et al.* (eds.) 2011. *Umweltarchäologie-Naturkatastrophen und Umweltwandel im archäologischen Befund*. Tagungen des Landesmuseums für Vorgeschichte Halle (Saale) 6.

Bos, J. M. 1990. 'The bog area of North Holland after AD 1000: Crises and opportunities'. In Besteman *et al.* (eds.), 121–132.

Bowler, D. P. 2004. *Perth: The Archaeology and Development of a Scottish Burgh*. Perth.

Boysen, E. 2013. 'Soziale Interpretation einer Doppelkloake aus Lüneburg: Versuch einer Modellentwicklung'. *Mitteilungen der Deutschen Gesellschaft für die Archäologie des Mittelalters und der Neuzeit* 25: 77–88.

Brandt, K. 1985. 'Medieval harbour settlements in the marshland between Ems and Weser, Northwestern Germany'. In Herteig (ed.), 99–105.

Brisbane, M. (ed.) 1992. *The Archaeology of Novgorod, Russia.* Society for Medieval Archaeology Monograph Series 13.

Brooks, F W, 1939. 'A medieval brick-yard at Hull'. *Journal of the British Archaeological Association* (Ser 3) 4: 151–174.

Brown, A. and Pluskowski, A. 2011. 'Detecting the environmental impact of the Baltic Crusades on a late-medieval (13th–15th century) frontier landscape: Palynological analysis from Malbork Castle and hinterland, Northern Poland'. *Journal of Archaeological Science* 38: 1957–1966.

Brown, P. 1984. *Domesday Book: Norfolk.* Chichester.

Bruce-Mitford, R. (ed.) 1975. *Recent Archaeological Excavations in Europe.* London.

Budd *et al.* 2004. 'Investigating population movement by stable isotope analysis: A report from Britain'. *Antiquity* 78: 127–141.

Buko, A. and McCarthy, M. (eds.) 2010. *Making a Medieval Town: Patterns of Early Medieval Urbanization.* Warsaw.

Bult, E. J. 1987. 'Moated sites in their economical and social context in Delfland'. *Château Gaillard* 13: 21–40.

Busch, M 2006. 'The Danish coastal landscape, fishery and transport 1050–1700'. In Pieters *et al.* (eds.), 195–206.

Busch, R. 1997. 'Stadtarchäologie in Hamburg–Eine Bilanz im Jahre 1995'. In Gläser (ed.), 171–180.

Butler, R. 1984. 'Skipsea Brough'. *Archaeological Journal* 141: 45–46.

Buurman, J. 1999. 'Plant remains from an early medieval site at Schagen, the Netherlands'. In Sarfatij *et al.* (eds.), 279–290.

Cameron, A. S. and Stones, J. A. (eds.) 2001. *Aberdeen: An In-Depth View of the City's Past.* Society of Antiquaries of Scotland Monograph 19.

Cameron, H. K. 1974. 'Technical aspects of medieval monumental brasses'. *Archaeological Journal* 131: 217–237.

———. 1979. 'The fourteenth-century Flemish brasses at King's Lynn'. *Archaeological Journal* 136: 151–172.

———. 1986. 'Flemish brasses of the fourteenth century in Northern Germany and their use by merchants of the Hanse'. *Archaeological Journal* 143: 331–351.

Campbell, M. 1991. 'Gold, silver and precious stones'. In Blair and Ramsay (eds.), 107–166.

Capiteyn, A. *et al.* (eds.) 2007. *Historische Atlas van Gent: Een visie op verleden en toekomst.* Amsterdam.

Carelli, P. 1997. ''The past and future of archaeology in Lund'. In Gläser (ed.), 429–439.

———. 2001, *en kapitalistisk anda: Kulturella förändringar i 1100-talets Danmark.* Unpublished PhD thesis. University of Lund.

Carmiggelt, A.1999. 'Het nut van contradicties. Archeologisch en historisch onderzoek naar het ontstaan van de middeleeuwse stad Rotterdam'. *Rotterdam Papers* 10: 53–65.

Carus-Wilson, E. 1962-3. 'The medieval trade of the ports of the Wash'. *Medieval Archaeology* 6/7: 182–201.

Carver, M. 'How churches change: St Colman's, Portmahomack, Scotland 1100–1580'. In Carver and Klápště (eds.), 472–475.

Carver, M. and Klápště, J. (eds.) 2011. *The Archaeology of Medieval Europe Vol. 2–Twelfth to Sixteenth Centuries.* Aarhus.

Cattermole, P. and Cotton, S. 1983. 'Medieval parish building in Norfolk'. *Norfolk Archaeology* 38(3): 235–279.

Caune, A. 2001. 'Typen des Wohnhäuser Rigas im 12. bis 14. Jahrhundert aufgrund der archäologischen Ausgrabungen'. In Gläser (ed.), 551–568

Cessford, C. *et al.* 2006. *Between Broad Street and the Great Ouse: Waterfront Archaeology in Ely.* East Anglian Archaeology 122.

Cessford, C. 2015. 'The St. John's Hospital cemetery and environs, Cambridge: Contextualizing the medieval urban dead'. *Archaeological Journal* 172(1): 52–120.

Champion, M. 2012. Architectural inscriptions: New discoveries in East Anglia'. *Church Archaeology* 16: 65–80.

Cheetham, F. 2005. *English Medieval Alabasters*. Woodbridge.

Cherry, J. 1997. 'Seals and heraldry, 1400–1600: Public policy and private post'. In Gaimster and Stamper (eds.), 251–263.

Childs, W. (ed.) 1986. *The Customs Accounts of Hull 1453–1490*. Yorkshire Archaeological Society Record Series 144.

Childs, W. 2001. 'Mercantile Scarborough'. In Crouch and Pearson (eds.), 15–31.

Christie, H. 1966. 'Old Oslo'. *Medieval Archaeology* 10: 45–58.

Christie, N. and Stamper, P. (eds.) 2012. *Medieval Rural Settlement: Britain and Ireland, AD 800–1600*. Oxford.

Clarke, H. and Carter, A 1977. *Excavations in King's Lynn 1963–1970*. Society for Medieval Archaeology Monograph Series 7.

Clarke, R. 2003. 'A Medieval Moated Site and Windmill: Excavations at Boreham Airfield, Essex 1996'. *East Anglian Archaeology* Occasional Paper 11.

———. forthcoming. 'Norwich Whitefriars: Medieval Friary and Baptist Burial Ground. Excavations at Jarrold's Printing Works, Norwich 2002–03'. *East Anglian Archaeology*.

Coad, J. G. and Streeten, A. D. F. 1982. 'Excavations at Castle Acre Castle, Norfolk, 1972–77': Country house and castle of the Norman Earls of Surrey'. *Archaeological Journal* 139: 138–301.

Cockerham, P. 2012. 'Incised slab commissions in fourteenth century Boston'. In Badham and Cockerham (eds.), 74–99.

———. 2014. 'Hanseatic merchant memorials: Individual monuments or collective 'memoria'?'. In Barron and Sutton (eds.), 392–413.

Coomans, T. and Bergmans, A. (eds.) 2008. *Het Sint-Agnesbegijnhof van Sint-Truiden: het hof, de kerk, de muurschilderingen*. Brussels.

Coomans, T. and van Royen, H. (eds.) 2008. *Medieval Brick Architecture in Flanders and Northern Europe: The Question of the Cistercian Origin*. Novi Monasterii 7.

Connell, B. *et al.* 2012. *A Bioarchaeological Study of Medieval Burials on the Site of St Mary Spital: Excavation at Spitalfields Market, London E1, 1991–2007*. MOLA Monograph 60.

Conzen, M.R.G. 1968. 'The use of town plans in the study of urban history'. In Dyos, 113–130.

Cotton, J. *et al.* (eds.) 2014. *'Hidden Histories and Records of Antiquity': Essays on Saxon and Medieval London*. London and Middlesex Archaeological Society Special Paper 17.

Cowan, E. J. and Henderson, L. (eds.) 2011. *A History of Everyday life in Medieval Scotland, 1000 to 1600*. Edinburgh.

Creighton, O. 2002. *Castles and Landscapes: Power, Community and Fortification in Medieval England*. London.

Creighton, O. and Barry, T. 2012. 'Seigneurial and elite sites in the medieval landscape'. In Christie and Stamper (eds.), 63–80.

Creighton, O. and Higham, R. 2005. *Medieval Town Walls: An Archaeology and Social History of Urban Defence*. Stroud.

Crone, A. 2000. 'Native tree-ring chronologies from some Scottish medieval burghs'. *Medieval Archaeology* 44: 201–216.

Crone, A. n.d. *Wood Use in the Medieval Scottish Burgh: Timber Supply and Building Design*. Tayside and Fife Archaeological Committee.

Crone, A. and Fawcett, R. 1998. 'Dendrochronology, documents and the timber trade: New evidence for the building history of Stirling Castle, Scotland'. *Medieval Archaeology* 42: 68–87.

Crone, A. and Gallagher, D. 2009. 'The late-medieval roof over the Great Hall in Edinburgh castle'. *Medieval Archaeology* 52: 231–260.

Crone, A. and Mills, C. M. 2002. 'Seeing the wood *and* the trees: Dendrochronological studies in Scotland'. *Antiquity* 76: 788–794.

Crouch, D. and Pearson, T. (eds.) 2001. *Medieval Scarborough: Studies in Trade and Civic Life*. Yorkshire Archaeological Society Occasional Paper 1.

Crowson, A. *et al.* (eds.) 2000. *Fenland Management Project Excavations 1991–1995*. Lincolnshire Archaeology and Heritage Reports Series No.3

Crowther, P. 1992. 'Ravenser and Ravenser Odd: The early history of Spurn'. *Spurn Wildlife* 2: 51–54.

Crumlin-Pedersen, O. 1985, 'Cargo ships of northern Europe AD 800–1300. In Herteig (ed.), 83–98.

———. 1997. *Viking-Age Ships and Ship-building in Hedeby/Haithabu and Schleswig*. Schleswig and Roskilde.

———. 2010. *Archaeology and the Sea in Scandinavia and Britain*. Roskilde.

Curtis, D. 2013, 'Medieval land reclamation: The creation of new societies and their environmental problems. Comparing Holland and the Po Valley, c. 800–c.1500'. Paper delivered at *Rural History* conference, Bern in August 2013: http://www.ruralhistory2013.org/papers/11.1.3._Curtis.pdf (accessed on 20th August 2013).

Curtis-Summers, S. *et al.* 2014. 'Stable isotope evidence for dietary contrast between Pictish and medieval populations at Portmahomack, Scotland'. *Medieval Archaeology* 58: 21–43.

Cushion, B. and Davison, A. 2003. 'Earthworks of Norfolk'. *East Anglian Archaeology* 104.

Dahl, C. L. 2009. '*Mengiad klæthe* and *tweskifte klædher*. Marbled, patterned and parti-coloured clothing in medeival Scandinavia. In Pedersen and Nosch (eds.), 122–138.

Dallas, C. 1993. 'Excavations in Thetford by B. K. Davison between 1964 and 1970'. *East Anglian Archaeology* 62.

Dallas, C. and Sherlock, D. 2002. 'Baconsthorpe Castle, Excavations and Finds, 1951–1972.' *East Anglian Archaeology* 102.

Damm, A. (ed.) 2005. *Viking Aros*. Moesgård.

Danbury, E. A. and Scott, K. A. 2015. 'The plea rolls of the court of Common Pleas: An unused source for the art and history of later medieval England, 1422–1509'. *Antiquaries Journal* 95: 157–210.

Daniels, R. 1991. 'Medieval Hartlepool: Evidence of and from the waterfront'. In Good *et al*, 43–50.

———. 2010. *Hartlepool: An Archaeology of the Medieval Town*. Tees Archaeology Monograph Series 4.

Darby, H. C. 1974. *The Medieval Fenland*. Newton Abbot

De Biève, E. (ed.) 1996. *Utrecht: Britain and the Continent-Archaeology, Art And Architecture*. British Archaeological Association Conference Transactions 18.

De Biève, E. 1996a. 'Of gods and shepherds: Utrecht, Rome and London'. In De Biève (ed.), 262–269.

———. 2012. 'Sealed architecture: City seals, architecture and urban identity in the northern Netherlands, 1200–1700'. In Franklin, J. *et al.* (eds.), 315–332.

De Boer, G. 1973. 'The two earliest maps of Hull'. *Post-Medieval Archaeology* 7: 79–87.

Debone, V. 2008. 'Bouwen met baksteen in het Kortrijkse en het Oudenaardse tides de middeleeuwen'. In Coomans and van Royen (eds.), 185–202.

Deforce, K. et *al.* 2006. 'Archeobotanisch bewijs voor ontginning en lange-afstandtransport van turf in Vlaanderen rond 1200 AD: heropgegraven even unit de abdij van Ename (Oudenaarde, prov. Oost-Vlaanderen). *Relicta* 1: 141–153.

De Groot, H. L. 1997. 'Utrecht: Archaeology in transition?'. In Gläser (ed.), 95–109.

De Groot, H. L. and Hoekstra, T. J. 1985. 'The moving river, the 12th-century riverfront in the north of the city of Utrecht'. In Herteig (ed.), 106–111.

De Groote, K. *et al.* 1995/1996. 'Middeleeuwse sporen op de Grote Markt en het fabrieksterrein *'t Haantje* te Aalst (Oost-Vlaanderen). Een kleine bijdrage tot de ontwikkelingsgeschiedenis van de stad'. *Archeologie in Vlaanderen* 5: 111–130.

De Groote, K. 2005. 'The use of ceramics in late medieval and early modern monasteries: Data from three sites in East Flanders (Belgium). *Medieval Ceramics* 29: 31–43.

De Groote, K. 2010, 'The contribution of archaeological sources to the research of the formation of towns. The example of Aalst, a border town in the county of Flanders'. In de Groote *et al.* (eds.), 249–266.

De Groote, K. *et al.* (eds.) 2010. *Exchanging Medieval Material Culture: Studies on Archaeology and History Presented to Frans Verhaeghe*. Brussels.

De la Riestra, P. 1999. 'Gothic Architecture of the "German Lands"'. In Toman (ed.), 190–235.

Delbanco, J-E. and Jansen, M. 2013. 'Die Iburg: Residenz der Osnabrücker Bischöfe'. *Archäologie in Niedersachsen* 16: 67–70.

Dendooven, D. and Dewilde, J. n.d. *The Reconstruction of Ieper*. Flanders.

Dennison, E. P. and Stones, J. 1997. *Historic Aberdeen: the archaeological implications of development*. Scottish Burgh Survey. Historic Scotland.

Dewilde, M. *et al.* (eds.) 1996. *Ypres and the Medieval Cloth Industry in Flanders: Archaeological and Historical Contributions*. Asse-Zellik.

DeWitte S. N. 2014. 'The anthropology of plague: Insights from bioarchaeological analyses of epidemic cemeteries'. In Green (ed.), 97–123.

De Witte, H. 1997. 'State, tasks and outlook for archaeology in Brugge'. In Gläser 1997, 75–86.

———. 1999a, 'Archaeological indications for trade in Brugge from the 12th to the 17th centuries'. In Gläser (ed.), 169–181.

———. 1999b. 'The maritime topography of medieval Bruges'. In Bill and Clausen, 137–144.

———. 2004. 'Some notes on the infrastructure of Brugge, with the emphasis on the water supply'. In Gläser (ed.), 107–115.

———. 2008. 'Lifestyle! Luxury in medieval Bruges. The value of the archaeological contribution'. In Gläser (ed.), 105–120.

———. 2010. 'The city fortifications of Bruges: A short survey'. In Gläser (ed.), 99–110.

———. 2014a. 'Grabmalerei im spätmittelalterlichen Brügge'. In Falk *et al.* (eds.), 273–281.

———. 2014b. 'Bruges, city of monasteries: Archaeological, monumental and historical evidence'. In Gläser (ed.), 91–104.

Dijkman, J. 2011. *Shaping Medieval Markets: The Organisation of Commodity Markets in Holland, c. 1200 to c. 1450*. Leiden.

Dobat, A. S. 2008. 'Danevirke revisited: An investigation into military and socio-political organisation in south Scan dinavia (*c* AD 700–1100). *Medieval Archaeology* 52, 27–67.

Dollinger, P. 1964. *The German Hansa*. London.

Donkin, R. A. 1960. 'Settlement and depopulation on cistercian estates during the twelfth and thirteenth centuries, especially in Yorkshire'. *Bulletin of the Institute of Historical Research* 33(88): 142–165.

Dransart, P. Z.. *et al.* 2012. *Perth High Street Archaeological Excavation 1975–1977: The Textiles and the Leather*. Perth.

Drury, P. J. 1982. 'Aspects of the origins and early development of Colchester Castle'. *Archaeological Journal* 139: 302–409.

Drury, P. J. and Platt, G. D. 1975. 'A Late 13th and Early 14th- Century Tile Factory at Danbury, Essex'. *Medieval Archaeology* 19: 92–164.

Dunn, P. 2004. ''Trade'. In Rawcliffe and Wilson (eds.), 213–234.

Dunning, G. 1933. 'Inventory of medieval polychrome ware found in England and Scotland'. *Archaeologia* 83: 126–134.

———. 1968. 'The trade in medieval pottery around the North Sea'. *Rotterdam Papers* I: 35–58.

Dyer, A. 2000a. 'Ranking Lists of English medieval towns'. In Palliser (ed.), 747–770.

———. 2000b. ''Urban decline' in England, 1377–1525'. In Slater (ed.), 266–288.

Dyer, C. 2002. *Making A Living in the Middle Ages: The People of Britain 850–1520*. New Haven and London.

———. 2003. 'The archaeology of medieval small towns'. *Medieval Archaeology* 47: 85–114.

———. 2012. 'The late medieval village of Wharram Percy: Living and consuming'. In Wrathmell (ed.), 327–340.

Dyer, C. and Lilley, K. 2012. 'Town and countryside: Relationships and resemblances'. In Christie and Stamper 2012, 81–98.

Dymond, D. 2005. 'Medieval and later markets'. In Ashwin and Davison (eds.), 76–77.

Dyos, H.J. (ed.) 1968. *The Study of Urban History*. London.

Ecclestone, A. W. and Ecclestone, J. L. 1959. *The Rise of Great Yarmouth*. Great Yarmouth.

Eckstein, D. and Wrobel, S. 2007. 'Dendrochronological proof of origin of historic timber–retrospect and perspectives'. In Haneca *et al.* (eds.), 8–20.

Eden, P. 1980. 'The estuary of the Glaven'. *Archaeological Journal* 137: 348–350.

Eddy, M. 1993. 'Excavation of the medieval gaol of Hull and adjacent structures (Site QU76)'. *East Riding Archaeologist* 4: 45–54. (Hull Old Town Report Series 2).

Egan, G. 2010. 'Medieval and later trade in textiles between Belgium and England. The picture from some finds of cloth seals'. In De Groot *et al.* (eds.), 55–66.

———. 2012. 'Archaeological evidence for textile finishing in London and the cloth trade between England and the Baltic, c. 1200–1800'. In 'Medieval Urban Textiles in Northern Europe'. *Muinasaja Teadus* 22: 17–35. Tartu.

Ekwall, E. 1960. *The Concise Oxford Dictionary of English Place-names*. Oxford.

Ellmers, D. 1979. 'The cog of Bremen and related boats'. In McGrail (ed.), 1–15.

Elvestad, E. 2002. *The Kings' port, the cultural landscape and the North Sea–a story of a maritime centre at Avaldsnes, Rogaland*. Stavanger.

Emery, P. A. 2007. 'Norwich Greyfriars: Pre-conquest Town and Medieval Friary'. *East Anglian Archaeology* 120.

Engberg, N. *et al.* (eds.) 2009. *Archaeology of Medieval Towns in the Baltic and North Sea Area.* Copenhagen.

Ennen, E. 1953. *Frühgeschichte der Europäischen Stadt*. Bonn.

Erdmann, W. 1980. 'Besiedlungs- und Baugeschichte von Lübecks Hafenvierteln im 12. und 13. Jahrhundert'. *Archäologie in Lübeck*, 87–90.

———. 1983. 'Entwicklungstendenzen des Lübecker Hausbaus 1100 bis um 1340–eine Ideenskizze'. *Lübecker Schriften zur Archäologie und Kulturgeschichte* 7: 19–38.

Ervynck, A. et *al.* 2013. 'Leffinge -Oude Werf': the first archaeozoological collection from a *terp* settlement in coastal Flanders'. In Raemaekers *et al.* 153–162.

Evans, D. H. (ed.) 1993. 'Excavations in Hull 1975–76'. Hull Old Town Report Series No. 2. *East Riding Archaeologist* 4.

Evans, D. H. 1999. 'The trade of Hull between 1200 and 1700'. In Gläser (ed.), 59–97.

———. 2000a. 'Archaeology in the modern city of Kingston-upon-Hull, and recent research at Kingswood'. In Van de Noort and Ellis (eds.), 193–216.

———. 2000b. 'Buried with the friars'. *British Archaeology* 53, 18 -23.

———. 2004. 'The infrastructure of Hull between 1275 and 1700'. In Gläser (ed.), 51–73.

———. 2010. 'The fortifications of Hull between 1300 and 1700'. In Gläser (ed.), 47–70.

———. 2014. 'The archaeology of religious houses in Hull'. In Gläser (ed.), 47–62.

Evans, D. H. and Carter, A. 1985. 'Excavations on 31–51 Pottergate (Site 149N)'. In Atkin *et al.* (eds.), 9–85.

Evans, D. H. and Tomlinson, D. G. 1992. *Excavations at 33-35 Eastgate, Beverley 1983-86*. Sheffield Excavation Reports 3.

Evans, J. (ed.) 1966.*The Flowering of the Middle Ages*. London.

Evans, S. *et al.* 2012. *East Riding of Yorkshire, Chalk Lowland and the Hull Valley NMP: Aerial Investigation and Mapping Report*. English Heritage Report Series 39.

Everson, P. and Stocker, D. 2011. *Custodians of Continuity: The Premonstratensian Abbey at Barlings and the Landscape of Ritual*. Lincolnshire Archaeology and Heritage Reports Series No.11

Evison, V. I. *et al.* (eds.) 1974. *Medieval Pottery from Excavations: Studies Presented to Gerald Clough Dunning*. London.

Fairclough, G. 2012. 'Review of Van de Noort, R. *North Sea Archaeologies: A Maritime Biography, 10,000 BC–AD 1500*'. Oxford. *Landscapes* 13(1): 75–76

Falk, A. *et al.* (eds.) 2014. *Lübeck und der Hanseraum: Beiträge zu Archäologie und Kulturgeschichte. Festschrift für Manfred Gläser*. Lübeck.

Faulkner, P. A. 1974. 'Lincoln Old Bishop's Palace'. *Archaeological Journal* 131: 340–344.

Fawcett, R. 1996a. 'Architectural links between Scotland and the Low Countries in the Late Middle Ages'. In de Biève (ed.), 172–182.

———. 1996b. 'The influence of the Gothic parts of the cathedral on church building in Norfolk'. In Atherton *et al*, 210–227.

Fehring, G. 1991. *The Archaeology of Medieval Germany: An Introduction*. London.

Felgenhauer-Schmiedt, S. 2007. 'Continental ceramics'. In Graham-Campbell and Valor (eds.), 224–230.

Fenwick, H. 2000. 'Medieval sites in the Hull valley: Distribution and modelling'. In Van de Noort and Ellis (eds.), 183–191.

Feveile, C. 2006. 'Ribe on the north side of the river, 8th–12th century'. In Feveile, C. 2006, 65–91.

Feveile, C. (ed.) 2006. *Ribe Studier: Det Ældste Ribe. Udgravninger på nordsiden af Ribe Å 1984–2000*, Bind 1.1 & Bind 1.2. Aarhus.

Finch, J. 2002. 'Regionality and medieval landscapes'. In Perrin (ed.), 107–115.

———. 2004. 'The churches'. In Rawcliffe and Wilson (eds.), 49–72.

Flatman, J. 2011. 'Review of Crumlin-Pedersen, O., *Archaeology and the Sea in Scandinavia and Britain: A Personal Account* (Copenhagen 2009)'. *Medieval Archaeology* 55: 357.

Först, E. 2006 'Handwerksnachweise in Hamburg vom 12. bis zum 18. Jahrhundert'. In Gläser (ed.), 199–209.

———. 2010. 'Befestigungen des Mittelalters und der Neuzeit in der Hamburger Innenstadt'. In Gläser (ed.), 255–272.

Fraiture, P. 2011. *Central Panels of the Ghent Altarpiece: Report of Dendrochronological Analysis*. Koninklijk instituut voor het kunstpatrimonium, Brussel (Dossier Dendro. no. P463–P464–P465–P466).

Franklin, J. *et al.* (eds.) 2012. *Architecture and Interpretation: Essays for Eric Fernie*. Woodbridge.

Franklin, M. J. and Harper-Bill, C. (eds.) 1995. *Medieval Ecclesiastical Studies in Honour of Dorothy M. Owen*. Woodbridge.

Freeman, J. 2012. 'Two Lincolnshire merchants: Walter Pescod of Boston and Simon Seman of Barton-on-Humber'. In Badham and Cockerham (eds.), 142–150.

Friedland, K. and Richards, P. (eds.) 2005. *Essays in Hanseatic History: The King's Lynn Symposium 1998*. Dereham.

Fries, J. E. and Heine, H-W 2008. 'Der "Heidenwall" in Oldenburg (Oldb.): Eine Burganlage des 11. Jahrhunderts. Grabungsvorbericht'. *Mitteilungen der Deutschen Gesellschaft für* Archäologie *des Mittelalters und der Neuzeit* 20, 77–86.

Füssell, S. (ed.) 2008. *Civitates Orbis Terrarum. Cities of the World (Georg Braun and Franz Hogenburg)*. Cologne.

Gaimster, D. 1993a. 'Imported stove-tile fragments'. In Margeson, 168–169.

———. 1993b. 'Cross-Channel ceramic trade in the late Middle Ages: Archaeological evidence for the spread of Hanseatic culture to Britain'. In Mührenburg *et al.* (eds.), 251–260.

———. 1997. *German Stoneware, 1200–1900: Archaeology and Cultural History*. London.

———. 1999. 'The Baltic Ceramic Market c. 1200–1600: An Archaeology of the Hanse'. *Fennoscandia archaeolociga* 16: 59–69.

———. 2003. 'Pots, prints and protestantism: Changing mentalities in the urban domestic sphere, *c.* 1480–1580'. In Gaimster and Gilchrist (eds.), 122–144.

———. 2007. 'The Baltic ceramic market 1200–1600: Measuring Hanseatic cultural transfer and resistance'. In Roodenburg (ed.), 30–58.

———. 2011. 'Archaeology of a trade network: The Hanseatic League, 1200–1500 AD'. In Carver and Klápště (eds.), 340–349.

———. 2014. 'The Hanseatic cultural signature: Exploring globalization on the micro-scale in late medieval Northern Europe'. *European Journal of Archaeology* 17(1): 60–81.

Gaimster, D. and Gilchrist, R. (eds.) 2003. *The Archaeology of Reformation 1480–1580*. Society for Post-Medieval Archaeology Monograph 1.

Gaimster, D. and Nenk, B. 1997. 'English households in transition c. 1450–1550: The ceramic evidence'. In Gaimster and Stamper (eds.), 171–195.

Gaimster, D. and Redknap, M (eds.) 1992. *Everyday and Exotic Pottery from Europe: studies in honour of John G. Hurst*. Oxford.

Gaimster, D. and Stamper, P. (eds.) 1997. *The Age of Transition: The Archaeology of English Culture 1400–1600*. Society for Medieval Archaeology Monograph 15.

Galloway, J. A. 2012. 'Metropolitan Food and Fuel Supply in Medieval England: Regional and International Contexts'. In Van Cruyningen and Thoen (eds.), 7–18.

Gardiner, J. (ed.) 1993. 'Flatlands and Wetlands: Current Themes in East Anglian Archaeology'. *East Anglian Archaeology* 50.

Gärtner, T. 2013. 'Pferdehaltung in ländlichen Siedlungen des Mittelalters im sozialhistorischen Kontext'. *Mitteilungen der Deutschen Gesellschaft für die Archäologie des Mittelalters und der Neuzeit* 25: 177–188.

George, M. 1992. *The Land Use, Ecology and Conservation of Broadland*. Chichester.

Gerrard, C. 2003. *Medieval Archaeology: Understanding Traditions and Contemporary Approaches.* London.

Gilchrist, R. 1994. *Gender and Material Culture: The Archaeology of Religious Women*. London.

———. 1999. *Gender and Archaeology: Contesting the Past*. London.

———. 2005. *Norwich Cathedral Close: The Evolution of an English Cathedral Landscape.* Woodbridge.

———. 2008. 'Magic for the dead? The archaeology of magic in later medieval burials'. *Medieval Archaeology* 52: 119–159.

———. 2009. 'Medieval archaeology and theory: A disciplinary leap of faith'. In Gilchrist and Reynolds, 385–408.

———. 2012. *Medieval Life. Archaeology and the Life Course.* Woodbridge.

Gilchrist, R. and Oliva, M. 1993. *Religious Women in Medieval East Anglia*. University of East Anglia, Norwich.

Gilchrist, R. and Reynolds, A. (eds.) 2009. *Reflections: 50 Years of Medieval Archaeology 1957-2007*. Society for Medieval Archaeology Monograph Series 30.

Gilchrist, R. and Sloane, B. 2005. *Requiem. The Medieval Monastic Cemetery in Britain*. London.

Giles, K. 2000. *An Archaeology of Social Identity: Guildhalls in York, c. 1350-1630*. British Archaeological Reports British Series 315.

Giles, K. and Clark, J. 2011. 'St Mary's Guildhall, Boston, Lincolnshire: The archaeology of a medieval 'public' building'. *Medieval Archaeology* 55: 226–256.

Giles, K. and Dyer, C. 2005. 'Town and country in the Middle Ages: Contrasts, contacts and interconnections, 1100–1500'. *Society for Medieval Archaeology Monograph Series* 22.

Gillett, E. and MacMahon, K. A. 1980. *A History of Hull*. Oxford.

Gilmour, B. J. J. and Stocker, D. A. 1986. 'St Mark's Church and cemetery'. *The Archaeology of Lincoln* , Vol. XIII-1, Council for British Archaeology.

Gläser, M. 1999. 'The development of the harbours and market places of Lübeck'. In Bill and Clausen (eds.), 79–86.

———. 2009. 'Mittelalterliche Baulandgewinnung in Lübeck'. *Mitteilungen der Deutschen Gesellschaft für Archäologie des Mittelalters und der Neuzeit* 21, 59–64.

Gläser, M. (ed.) 1997. *Lübecker Kolloquium zur Stadtarchäologie I: Stand, Aufgaben und Perspektiven*. Lübeck.

———. 1999. *Lübecker Kolloquium zur Stadtarchäologie II: Der Handel*. Lübeck.

———. 2001. *Lübecker Kolloquium zur Stadtarchäologie III: Der Hausbau*. Lübeck.

———. 2004. *Lübecker Kolloquium zur Stadtarchäologie IV: Die Infrastruktur*. Lübeck.

———. 2006. *Lübecker Kolloquium zur Stadtarchäologie V: Das Handwerk*. Lübeck.

———. 2008. *Lübecker Kolloquium zur Stadtarchäologie VI: Luxus und Lifestyle*. Lübeck.

———. 2010. *Lübecker Kolloquium zur Stadtarchäologie VII: Die Befestigungen*. Lübeck.

———. 2012. *Lübecker Kolloquium zur Stadtarchäologie VIII: Kindheit un Jugend, Ausbildung und Freizeit*. Lübeck.

———. 2014. *Lübecker Kolloquium zur Stadtarchäologie IX: Die Klöster*. Lübeck.

Good, G. L. *et al.* 1991. *Waterfront Archaeology: Proceedings of the third international conference, Bristol, 1988*. Council for British Archaeology Research Report 74.

Goodall, J. 2011. *The English Castle.* New Haven and London.

Goodburn, D. 1992. 'Woods and woodland: Carpenters and carpentry'. In Milne (ed.), 106–130.

Graham-Campbell, J. and Valor, M. (eds.) 2007. *The Archaeology of Medieval Europe Vol. 1-Eighth to Twelfth Centuries AD.* Aarhus.

Gralow, R. 2010. 'Die Stadtbefestigungen des Mittelalters und der Neuzeit in Wismar im archäologischen Kontext'. In Gläser (ed.), 293–311.

———. 2014. Klösterliche Einrichtungen in Wismar im archäologischen Kontext'. In Gläser 2014, 229–244.

Gras, N.S.B. 1918. *The Early English Customs System*. Cambridge, MA.

Graßmann, A. 1980. 'Ein Wachstafelbuch vom Schranken zu Lübeck'. *Lübecker Schriften zur Archäologie und Kulturgeschichte* 3: 165–166.

Green, M. H. (ed.) 2014. *Pandemic Disease in the Medieval World: Rethinking the Black Death*. The Medieval Globe 1.

Greenhill, F. A. 1965. 'An Incised slab at Gressenhall'. *Norfolk Archaeology* 33(4): 423–426.

Grimm, J. M. 2006. 'Break a leg: Animal health and welfare in medieval Emden, Germany'. *Veterinarija Ir Zootechnika* 41(63): 49–59.

Groothedde, M. 2001. 'Der Hausbau in Zutphen zwischen 850 und 1400'. In Gläser (ed.), 175–195.

Günsenin, N. (ed.) 2012. *Between Continents: Proceedings of the Twelfth Symposium on Boat and Ship Archaeology*. Istanbul.

Hadley, D. M. and Hemer, K. A. (eds.) 2014. *Medieval Childhood : Archaeological Approaches*. Oxford.

Hall, D. 2012. 'Excavations at North Berwick nunnery tile kiln, Old Abbey Road, North Berwick'. *Medieval Ceramics* 33: 45–53.

Hall, D. W. *et al.* 2007. 'The early medieval origin of Perth, Scotland'. *Radiocarbon* 49(2): 639–644.

Hall, M. 2005. 'Burgh Mentalities: A Town-in-the-Country Case Study of Perth, Scotland'. In Giles and Dyer (eds.), 211–228.

Hall, R. A. (ed.) 1978. *Viking Age York and the North*. Council for British Archaeology Research Report 27.

———. 1994. *Viking Age York*. London.

———. 1996. *York*. London

———. 1999. 'The archaeology of medieval trade—observations from York'. In Gläser (ed.), 111–121.

———. 2006. 'York: A medieval centre of craft and production'. In Gläser (ed.), 93–103.

Halle, U. 2004. 'Die Bremer Stadtbefestigungen des Mittelalters und der frühen Neuzeit'. In Gläser (ed.).

Hammel-Kiesow, R. 1997. 'Stecknitzkanal'. *Lexikon des Mittelalters* VIII: 82–83.

Hammel-Kiesow, R. 2002. 'Lübeck and the Baltic trade in bulk goods for the North Sea region 1150–1400'. In Berggren *et al.* (eds.), 53–91.

Haneca, K. *et al.* (eds.) 2005. 'Provenancing Baltic timber from art historical objects: success and limitations'. *Journal of Archaeological Science* 32(2): 261–271.

———. (eds.) 2007. *Tree Rings in Archaeology, Climatology and Ecology*, Vol. 5. Tervuren.

———. 2009. 'De 'houten eeuw' van een Vlaamse stad. Archeologisch onderzoek in Ieper (prov. West-Vlaanderen). *Relicta* 4: 99–133.

Haneca, K. and Daly, A. 2014. 'Tree-Rings, timbers and trees: A dendrochronological survey of the 14th-century cog, Doel 1'. *International Journal of Nautical Archaeology* 43(1): 87–102.

Hansen, G. 2005. *Bergen c 800–c 1700: The Emergence of a Town*. The Bryggen Papers, Main Series No 6.

Harden, G. 1978. *Medieval Boston and its Archaeological Implications*. Sleaford.

Harder, J. 2012. 'Hölzerne Infrastruktur des Mittelalters aus dem sogenannten Gründungsviertel der Hansestadt Lübeck'. *Mitteilungen der Deutschen Gesellschaft für Archäologie des Mittelalters und der Neuzeit* 24: 123–130.

Harnow, H. *et al.* (eds.) 2012. *Across the North Sea: Later Historical Archaeology in Britain and Denmark, c. 1500–2000 AD*. Copenhagen and Odense.

Harper-Bill, C. (ed.) 2005. *Medieval East Anglia*. Woodbridge.

Hårdh, B. 2010. 'Viking Age Uppåkra'. *Uppåkrastudier* 11: 247–316.

Hardwick, P. 2011. *English Medieval Misericords:The Margins of Meaning*. Woodbridge.

Harris, R. 1994. 'The origins and development of English medieval townhouses operating commercially on two storeys'. Unpublished Ph. D thesis, Oxford University.

Harrison, D. 2004. *The Bridges of Medieval England.* Oxford.

Hayfield, C. 1988. 'Cowlam deserted village: A case study of post-medieval village desertion'. *Post-Medieval Archaeology* 22: 21–109.

Hayfield, C. and Slater, T. 1984. *The Medieval Town of Hedon: Excavations 1975–1976.* Hull.

Hedge, S. 2012. 'Virtue and vice in the vestry: Sixteenth-century wall panelling in Norwich Cathedral'. *Norfolk Archaeology* 46(3): 311–330.

Heege, A. 2002. *Einbeck im Mittelalter: Eine archäologisch-historishe Spurensuche.* Oldenburg.

Heidinga, H. A. 1984. 'Indications of severe drought during the 10th century AD from an inland dune area in the central Netherlands'. *Geologie en Mijnbouw* 63: 241–248.

Heidinga, H. A. and van Regteren Altena, H. H. (eds.) 1989. *Medemblik and Monnickendam: Aspects of Medieval Urbanization in Northern Holland.* Amsterdam.

Herrmann, V. 2010. 'Befestigungsanlagen der Duisburger Pfalz und Stadt im Mittelalter'. In Gläser (ed.), 329–341.

Herteig, A. 1968. 'The hansa town of Bergen and its commercial relations, seen in the light of excavations at Bryggen'. *Rotterdam Papers*, 73–79.

———. 1975. 'The excavation of Bryggen, Bergen, Norway'. In Bruce-Mitford (ed.), 65–89.

———. 1981. 'The medieval harbour of Bergen'. In Milne and Hobley (eds.), 80–87

———. 1985. 'Details from the Bergen Medieval Waterfront'. In Herteig (ed.) 1985, 69–78.

Herteig, A. (ed.) 1985. *Conference on Waterfront Archaeology in North European Towns No. 2.* Bergen.

Heslop, T. A. 1994. *Norwich Castle Keep.* Norwich.

Heslop, T. A. and Lunnon, H. (eds.) 2015. 'Norwich: Medieval and Early Modern Art, Architecture and Archaeology'. *British Archaeological Association* Conference Transactions 38.

Hewett, C. 1969. *The Development of Carpentry 1200–1700: An Essex Study.* Newton Abbot.

Heywood, S. 1989. 'The Priory of St. Mary in the Meadow of the Order of Peterstone, Beeston next the Sea, Norfolk'. *Norfolk Archaeology* 40(3): 226–259.

———. 2013. 'Stone Building in Romanesque East Anglia'. In Bates and Liddiard (eds.), 256–269.

Hildburgh, W. L. 1955. 'Three English Medieval Alabaster Tablets of the Embattled Type'. *Connoisseur* 135, 108–110.

Hill, C. 2010. *Women and Religion in Late Medieval Norwich.* Woodbridge.

———. 2014. 'Merchants' wives and widows: Networking in Norwich'. In Barron and Sutton (eds.), 111–126.

Hill, F. 1948. *Medieval Lincoln.* Cambridge.

Hillier, W. and Hanson, J. 1984. *The Social Logic of Space.* Cambridge.

Hines, J. *et al.* (eds.), *Land, Sea and Home.* Society for Medieval Archaeology Monograph Volume 20.

Hinman, M. and Popescu, E. 2012. 'Extraordinary Inundations of the Sea: Excavations at Market Mews, Wisbech, Cambridgeshire'. *East Anglian Archaeology* 142.

Hinton, D. 2000. 'The large towns 600–1300'. In Palliser (ed.), 217–243.

———. 2014. Review of Perry, D. *et al.* 2010. 'Perth High Street archaeological excavation 1975–1977'. *Antiquaries Journal* 94: 383–385.

Hoare, P. G. *et al.* 2002. 'Re-used bedrock ballast in King's Lynn's 'town wall' and the Norfolk port's medieval trading links'. *Medieval Archaeology* 46, 91–105.

Hodges, R. 1995. 'Review Article: Valediction or Vision?'. *Medieval Ceramics* 19: 103–107.

———. 2012. *Dark Age Economics: A New Audit.* London.

Hoekstra, T. J. 1996. 'Medieval and early modern houses in Utrecht'. In de Biève (ed.), 199–208.

Hoffman, R. 2005. 'A brief history of aquatic resource use in medieval Europe'. *Helgoland Marine Research* 59: 22–30.

———. 2014. *An Environmental History of Europe.* Cambridge.

Holm, P. 2002. 'Maritime dependency in Ribe and Aalborg, 1450-1800'. In Starkey and Hahn-Pedersen (eds.), 47–68.

Holman, T. S. 1980. 'Holbein's portraits of the steelyard merchants: An investigation'. *Metropolitan Museum Journal* 14: 139–158.

Horrox, R. 1978. *The Changing Plan of Hull*. Hull.

Høst-Madsen, L. 2015. 'An anchor island and five ships under the opera–a short review of the results of the archaeological excavation in Copenhagen'. In Falk *et al.* (eds.), 367–372.

Høst-Madsen, L. *et al.* 2010. 'The fortification of Copenhagen'. In Gläser (ed.), 845–865.

Hourihane, C. 2012. *The Grove Encyclopedia of Medieval Art*, Vol. 2. Oxford.

Howard, M. 2003. 'Recycling the monastic fabric: Beyond the Act of Dissolution'. In Gaimster and Gilchrist (eds.), 221–234.

Hudson, W. (ed.) 1889. *The Streets and Lanes of Norwich: A memoir by J. Kirkpatrick*. Norwich.

Hudson, W. and Tingey, J.C. 1910. *The Records of the City of Norwich II*. Norwich.

Hurst, J. G. 1974. 'Sixteenth- and seventeenth-century imported pottery from the Saintonge'. In Evison *et al.*, 221–255.

———. 2002. 'Summary of the imported ware'. In Dallas and Sherlock, 47–49.

Hutchinson, G. 1994. *Medieval Ships and Shipping*. Leicester.

Hybel, N. 2002. 'Introduction'. In Berggren *et al.* (eds.), xiii–xii.

Hyermind, J. *et al.* (eds.) 1998. *Viborg Søndersø 1018–1030: Byarkæologiske* undersøgelser 1981 og 1984–85. Viborg.

Hjermind, J. 2006. 'Craftwork in Viborg from 11th to the 18th century'. In Gläser (ed.), 625–639.

Igel, K. 2013. 'Soziale Strukturen im archäologischen Befund? Anmerkungen eines Historikers am Beispiel lübischrechtlicher Städte'. *Mitteilungen der Deutschen Gesellschaft für die Archäologie des Mittelalters und der Neuzeit* 25, 23–30.

Ilkjær, J 2001. *Illerup Ådal-archaeology as a magic mirror*. Moesgård.

Impey, E. 2008. *The White Tower*. Yale.

Ingle, C. and Saunders, H. 2011. 'Aerial Archaeology in Essex: The Role of the National Mapping Programme in Interpreting the Landscape'. *East Anglian Archaeology* 136.

Iversen, M. *et al.* (eds.) 2005. *Viborg Søndersø 1018–1030: Arkæ*ologi og naturvidenskab i et væ*rkstedsområde* fra vikingetid. Viborg.

Jahnke, J. 2009. 'The medieval herring fishery in the western Baltic'. In Sicking and Abreu-Ferreira (eds.), 157–186.

Jankuhn, H. 1976. *Haithabu: Ein Handelsplatz der Wikingerzeit*. Neumünster.

Jansen, V. 2008. 'Trading places: Counting houses and the Hanseatic 'steelyard' in King's Lynn'. In McNeil (ed.), 66–82.

Janssen, H. L. 1990. 'The archaeology of the medieval castle in the Netherlands. Results and prospects for future research'. In Besteman (ed.), 217–264.

Janssen, H. L. and Nijhof, E. 2010. 'Fifteenth-century pottery production in 's-Hertogenbosch. The excavation of two pottery workshops'. In De Groote *et al.* (eds.), 93–136.

Jantzen, C. 2013. *Middelalderbyen Aarhus*. Aarhus.

Jennings, S. and Rogerson, A. 1994. 'The distribution of Grimston Ware in East Anglia and beyond'. In Leah (ed.), 116–119.

Jeppesen, J. 2005. 'Lisbjerg'. In Damm (ed.), 52–61.

Johnson, Mark 1988. 'The medieval and post-medieval port of Filey'. *Yorkshire Archaeological Journal* 70: 73–84.

Johnson, M. 1988. 'A medieval harbour at Flamborough'. *Yorkshire Archaeological Journal* 60: 105–111.

———. 1993. *Housing Culture: Traditional Architecture in an English Landscape*. London.

Jondell, E. 1981. 'Medieval waterfronts in Bergen'. In Herteig (ed.), 125–128.

Jones, D. (ed.) 2010. *The Light Fantastic: Using airborne lidar in archaeological survey*. Swindon.

Jones, M. 2004. *Lincoln: history and guide*. Stroud.

Jones, M., Stocker, D. and Vince, A. 2003. *The City by the Pool: Assessing the archaeology of the city of Lincoln*. Oxford.

Jongepier, I. *et al.* 2011. 'The brown gold: A reappraisal of medieval peat marshes in Northern Flanders (Belgium)'. *Water History* 3: 73–93.

Jöns, H. *et al.* (eds.) 2005, *Archäologie unter dem Straßenpflaster*. Schwerin.

Jordan, P. 2004. *North Sea Saga*. Harlow.

Karg, S. (ed) 2007. *Medieval Food Traditions in Northern Europe*. Copenhagen.

Kastholm, O. T. 2011. 'Six ship graffiti from Himmelev church'. *Maritime Archaeology Newsletter from Denmark* 26, 28–31.

Keller, K-F. and Schia, E. 1994. *The Medieval Town in Oslo*. Oslo.

Kelly, S. 1983. 'The economic topography and structure of Norwich *c.* 1300'. In Priestley (ed.), 13–39.

Kent, G.H. R. (ed.) 2002. *A History of the County of York East Riding: Volume 7-Holderness Wapentake, Middle and North Divisions*. London

Kermode, J. 1991. 'Money and Credit in the fifteenth century: Some lessons from Yorkshire'. *Business History Review* 65: 475–501.

———. 1998. *Medieval Merchants: York, Beverley and Hull in the Later Middle Ages*. Cambridge.

———. 2000. *'The greater towns 1300–1540'*. In Palliser (ed.), 441–465.

Kieffer-Olsen, J. 2004. 'The infrastructure of Ribe'. In Gläser 2004, 543–550.

King, C. 2006. *House and Society in an English Provincial City: The Archaeology of Urban Households in Norwich, 1370-1700*. Unpublished PhD thesis, University of Nottingham.

King, C. 2009. 'The interpretation of urban buildings: power, memory and appropriation in Norwich merchants' houses, c. 1400– 1660' *World Archaeology 41.3, 471–488.*

———. 2015. 'Private lives and public power: Norwich merchants' houses between the 14th and 16th centuries'. In Heslop and Lunnon (eds.), 341–358.

King, D. 1996. 'A glazier from the Bishopric of Utrecht in fifteenth-century Norwich'. In de Biève (ed.), 216–225.

———. 2006. *The Medieval Stained Glass of St Peter Mancroft Norwich*. Oxford

———. 2013. 'Medieval art in Norfolk and on the continent'. In Bates and Liddiard (eds.), 82–118.

Kjellström, A. and Wikström, A. 2007. 'Early medieval cemeteries and living conditions in Sigtuna, Sweden'. *Medieval Europe conference* paper. Paris.

Kirjavainen, H. 2009. 'A Finnish perspective on medieval broadcloth'. In Pedersen and Nosch (eds.), 90–98.

Kjaer, U. and Morgensen, E. S. 2000. *Danish Murals-a World to be Discovered*. København.

Kleingärtner, S. and Zeilinger, G. (eds.) 2012, *Raumbildung durch Netzwerke? Der Ostseeraum zwischen Wikingerzeit und Spätmittelalter aus Archäologischer und Geschichtswissenschaftlicher Perspektive*. Bonn

Klück, B. 1999. 'Met de rug naar de kerk. Utrecht anders bekeken'. *Rotterdam Papers* 10: 131–141.

Kock, J. 2004. 'Medieval pottery kilns in Denmark'. *Medieval Ceramics* 28: 2–17.

Kosiba, S. B. *et al.* 2007. 'Stable isotopes as indicators of change in the food procurement and food preference of Viking Age and Early Christian populations on Gotland (Sweden)'. *Journal of Anthropological Archaeology* 26: 394–411.

Kowaleski, M. 2000. 'Port towns: England and Wales 1300–1540'. In Palliser (ed.), 467–494

———. 2014. 'Medieval people in town and county: New perspectives from demography and bioarchaeology'. *Speculum* 89(3): 573–600.

Krause, G. 1999. 'Duisburg, Lower Rhineland: The harbour and the topography of the town from the Merovingian period to c. 1600'. In Bill and Clausen, 109–118.

———. 2003. 'Duisburg als Handels- und Hafenort im Mittelalter und der frühen Neuzeit'. *Mitteilungen der Deutschen Gesellschaft für Archäologie des Mittelalters und der Neuzeit* 14: 30–42.

Kristiansen, M. S. *Tårnby-A Rural Settlement Through 800 Years on Amager, Denmark*. Ruralia I, Památky archeologické–Supplementum 5. Prague.

Kristiansen, M. S. and Giles, K. (eds.) 2014. *Dwellings, Identities and Homes: European Housing Culture form the Viking Age to the Renaissance*. Højbjerg.

Krüger, K. 2005. 'Church and church business in Hanseatic agencies'. In Friedland and Richards, 80–93. Dereham.

Kruip, M. 2011. 'Pilgrim badges: A case study from the Netherlands'. In Carver and Klápště (eds.), 420–423.

Kühne, C. 2014. 1–2. 'Siegburg stoneware in the economic zone of the German Hanseatic League'. *Medieval Pottery Research Group Newsletter* 78: 1–2.

Kunst, R. (ed.) 1999. *Leeuwarden 750-2000: Hoofdstad van Friesland*. Franeker.

Laleman, M. C. and Stoops, G. 2008. 'Baksteengebruik in Vlaamse Steden: Gent in de middeleeuwen'. In Coomans and van Royen (eds.), 163–183.

Lamb, H. H. 1991. *Historic Storms of the North Sea, British Isles and Northwest Europe*. Cambridge.

Lambert, J. *et al.* 1952. *The Origins of the Broads*. Royal Geographical Society London Research Series 2.

Larsson, L. 2002. 'Uppåkra — research on a central place: Recent excavations and results'. In Hårdh, B. and Larsson, L. (eds.), 'Central places in the migration and the Merovingian periods: Papers from the 52nd Sachsensymposium'. *Uppåkrastudier* 6: 19–30.

Larsson, S. 2009. 'Theoretical and methodological directions in urban archaeology: The case of Lund, Sweden'. In Engberg *et al.* (eds.), 167–179.

Latałowa, M *et al.* 2007. 'Useful plants in medieval archaeobotanical material from the Hanseatic towns of northern Poland (Kołobrzeg, Gdańsk and Elblag). In Karg (ed.), 39–72.

Lauritsen, L. P. 2014. 'Stadtklöster auf Lolland und Falster'. In Gläser (ed.), 683–696.

Lauwerier, R. and Laarman, F. 2008. 'Relics of 16th-century gutted herring from a Dutch vessel'. *Environmental Archaeology* 13(2): 135–142.

Leah, M. 'The Late Saxon and Medieval Pottery Industry of Grimston, Norfolk: Excavations 1962–92'. *East Anglian Archaeology* 64.

Lee, J. 2011. 'Excavations at Blanket Row, Hull, 1997–2003'. *East Riding Archaeologist* 13.

Leenders, K. A. H. W. 1986. 'De Antwerpse Polders in de Middeleeuwen'. *Rotterdam Papers* 5: 161–168.

———. 2004. 'The start of peat digging for salt production in the Zeeland region'. In Lodewijckx (ed.), 107–110.

Lehouck, A. 2008. 'Gebruik en productive van baksteen in de regio Veurne van circa 1200 tot circa 1550'. In Coomans and van Royen (eds.), 203–232.

Lewin, J. 2010. 'Medieval environmental impacts and feedbacks: The lowland floodpalins of England and Wales'. *Geoarchaeology* 25(3): 267–311.

Lewis, J. and Pringle, D. 2002. *Spynie Palace and the Bishops of Moray: History, Architecture and Archaeology*'. Society of Antiquaries of Scotland Monograph Series 21.

Liddiard, R. 2000. *Landscapes of Lordship: Norman Castles and the Countryside in Medieval Norfolk, 1066-1200. British Archaeological Reports* British Series 309.

Liddiard, R. 2005. 'The castle landscapes of Anglo-Norman East Anglia: A regional perspective'. In Harper-Bill (ed.), 33–51.

Liddiard, R. 2013. 'Introduction: The North Sea'. In Bates, D. and Liddiard, R. 2013, 1–14.

Lilley, K. D. 1999. 'Urban landscapes and the cultural politics of territorial control in Anglo-Norman England'. *Landscape Research* 24(1): 5–23.

———. 2002. *Urban Living in the Middle Ages 1000-1450*. Basingstoke.

Livarda, A. 2011. 'Spicing up life in northwestern Europe: Exotic food imports in the Roman and medieval world'. *Vegetation History and Archaeobotany* 20(2): 143–164.

Lloyd, T. H. 1977. *The English Wool Trade in the Middle Ages*. Cambridge.

Locker, A. 1987. ' The fish remains'. In Ayers 1987, 114–117.

Lodewijckx, M (ed.) 2004. *Bruc ealles well. Archaeological essays concerning the peoples of North-West Europe in the first millennium AD*. Leuven.

Loe Hjelle, K. 2007. 'Foreign trade and local production-plant remains from medieval times in Norway'. In Karg (ed.), 161–179.

London Museum. 1940. *Medieval Catalogue.* London (fourth impression 1975).

Long, C. D. 1975. 'Excavations in the medieval city of Trondheim, Norway'. *Medieval Archaeology* 19: 1–32.

Loveluck, C. 2013. *Northwest Europe in the Early Middle Ages, c. AD 600–1150: A Comparative Archaeology.* Cambridge.

Loveluck, C. and Tys, D. 2006. 'Coastal societies, exchange and identity along the Channel and southern North Sea shores of Europe, AD 600–1000'. *Journal of Marine Archaeology* 1: 140–169.

Lüdecke, T. 2003. 'Stade und Hamburg: zur Entwicklung ihrer Hafen- und Stadttopografie im Mittelalter'. *Mitteilungen der Deutschen Gesellschaft für Archäologie des Mittelalters und der Neuzeit* 14: 24–29.

Lynnerup, N. 2007. 'Putting the people in the picture: What physical anthropology can do for archaeology'. In Graham-Campbell and Valor (eds.), 428–429.

MacGregor, A. 1978. 'Industry and commerce in Anglo-Scandinavian York'. In Hall (ed.), 37–57.

———. 1991. 'Antler, bone and horn'. In Blair and Ramsay (eds.), 355–378.

McAvoy, F. 1994. 'Marine salt extraction: The excavation of Salterns at Wainfleet St Mary, Lincolnshire'. *Medieval Archaeology* 38: 134–163.

McCombie, G. 2009. *Newcastle and Gateshead (Pevsner Architectural Guides).* New Haven and London.

McDonagh, B. 2003. 'Church / manor / settlement relationships in the Yorkshire Wolds'. *Medieval Settlement Research Group Annual Report* 18: 16–26.

McGrail, S. (ed.) 1979. *Medieval Ships and Harbours in Northern Europe.* British Archaeological Reports International Series 66.

McNeil, I. (ed.) 1990. *An Encyclopaedia of the History of Technology.* London.

———. 2008. *King's Lynn and the Fens: Medieval Art, Architecture and Archaeology.* British Archaeological Association Conference Transactions 31.

McNeil, R. 2003. 'The archaeology of space'. In Ayán Vila *et al.* (eds.), 143–153.

Magilton, J. R. 1980. *The Church of St Helen-on-the Walls, Aldwark.* Archaeology of York 10.1. Council for British Archaeology.

Magnusson Staaf, B. 2014. 'Monasteries, convents and nunneries in medieval Lund'. In Gläser (ed.), 559–572.

Maik, J. 2009. 'The influence of Hanseatic Trade on textile production in medieval Poland'. In Pedersen and Nosch (eds.), 109–121.

Margeson, S. 1993. 'Norwich Households: Medieval and Post-Medieval Finds from Norwich Survey Excavations 1971–78'. *East Anglian Archaeology* 58.

Marks, R. and Williamson, P. 2003. *Gothic: Art for England 1400–1547.* London.

Marsden, A. 2013. 'Coin finds from Norfolk, 2012'. *Norfolk Archaeology* 46: 542–576.

Marshall, P. 2002. 'The great tower as residence'. In Meirion-Jones (ed.), 27–44.

Mårtensson, A. W. 1976. *Archaeologica Lundensia VII: Uppgrävt förflutet för PKBanken i Lund.* Lund.

Mason, A 2009. *The Archaeology of the Warrens of Thetford Forest.* Forestry Commission.

———. 2010. *The Warrens of Breckland.* Oxborough.

Mayhew, N. 1975. 'The Aberdeen, Upper Kirkgate, hoard of 1886'. *British Numismatic Journal* 44: 33–50.

Mays, S. 1997. 'Carbon stable isotope ratios in medieval and later human skeletons from northern England'. *Journal of Archaeological Science* 24(6): 561–567.

Mead, V. K. 1977. 'Evidence for the Manufacture of Amber Beads in London in 14th – 15th Century'. *Transactions of the London & Middlesex Archaeological Society* 2: 211–214.

Mehler, N. 2009. The perception and interpretation of Hanseatic material culture in the North Atlantic: Problems and suggestions. *Journal of the North Atlantic,* Special Volume 1: 89–108

Mehler, N. 2014. 'Hanse archaeology'. *Springer Encyclopedia of Global Archaeology.* New York, 3209-3219.

Meier, D. 2006. *Seafarers, Merchants and Pirates in the Middle Ages*. Woodbridge.

———. 2012. *Schleswig-Holstein im Hohen und Späten Mittelalter: Landesausbau, Dörfer, Städte*. Heide.

Meier, T. (with Graham-Campbell, J.) 2007. 'Life, death and memory'. In Graham-Campbell and Valor (eds.), 420–449.

Meirion-Jones, G. (ed.) 2002. *The Seigneurial Residence in Western Europe AD c 800-1600*. British Archaeological Reports International Series 1088.

Mellor, M. 2014. 'Seeing the medieval child: Evidence from household and craft'. In Hadley and Hemer (eds.), 75–94.

Miller, K. *et al*. 1982. *Beverley: An Archaeological and Architectural Survey*. London.

Mills, C. and Crone, A. 2012. 'Dendrochronological evidence for Scotland's native timber resources over the last 1000 years'. *Scottish Forestry* 66: 18–33.

Milne, G. (ed.) 1992. *Timber Building Techniques in London c. 900-1400*. London and Middlesex Archaeological Society Special Paper 15.

———. 1997. *St Bride's Church, London: Archaeological research 1952-60 and 1992-5'*. English Heritage Archaeological Report 11.

———. 2003. *The Port of Medieval London*. Stroud.

Milne, G. 2014. 'London's Elizabethan custom house rediscovered: A review of excavations at Wool Quay in 1973'. In Cotton *et al*. (eds.), 44–52.

Milne, G. and Hobley, B (eds.) 1981. *Waterfront Archaeology in Britain and Northern Europe*. Council for British Archaeology Research Report 41.

Milne, G. and Milne, C. 1982. *Medieval Waterfront Development at Trig Lane, London*. London & Middlesex Archaeological Society Special Paper 5.

Minnis J. and Carmichael, K. 2015. *Boston, Lincolnshire: Historic North Sea Port and Market Town*. Swindon.

Molaug, P. 1999. 'King's Quay and Bishop's Quay–the harbour of medieval Oslo'. In Bill and Clausen (eds.), 169–178.

———. 2007. 'Occupying town plots on the early development of habitation in Norwegian medieval towns'. http://medieval-europe-paris-2007.univ-paris1.fr/P.Molaug.pdf (accessed on 7th September 2014)

Molaug, P. 2010. 'Early urbanization in Norway'. In Buko and McCarthy (eds.), 131–150.

Möller, G. 2008. 'Luxus in der mittelalterlich-frühneuzeitlichen Stadt Stralsund: Anmerkungen zum Lebensstil der Bürger'. In Gläser (ed.), 293–310.

Møller, S. B. 2000. *Aalborg gråbrødrekloster*. Aalborg.

Moloney, C. and Coleman, R. 1997. 'The development of a medieval street frontage: the evidence from excavations at 80–86 High Street, Perth'. *Proceedings of the Society of Antiquaries of Scotland* 127: 707–782.

Moorhouse, S. 1971. Post-medieval Britain in 1970'. *Post-Medieval Archaeology* 5: 197–222.

———. 1983. 'Documentary evidence and its potential for understanding the inland movement of medieval pottery'. *Medieval Ceramics* 7: 45–87.

Morris, R. 1989. *Churches in the Landscape*. London (1997 edition).

Morris, R. K. 2003. 'Monastic architecture: Destruction and reconstruction'. In Gaimster and Gilchrist (eds.), 235–251.

Możejko, B. 2014. 'Shipping and maritime trade in Gdańsk at the turn of the 14th century: The maritime and commercial background of the sinking of the copper ship in 1408'. In Ossowski (ed.), 57–74.

Mührenberg, D. 1999a. 'The Lübeck Colloquium 1997–summary'. In Gläser (ed.) 1999, 619–624.

———. 1999b. 'Archäologische Erkenntnisse zum Handel in Lübeck vom 12. bis zum 17. Jahrhundert'. In Gläser (ed.) 1999, 263–292.

———. 2001, ' The Lübeck Colloquium 1999 (Domestic Architecture)–summary'. In Gläser (ed.), 843–852.

Mührenburg, D. *et al*. (eds.) 1993. *Archäologie des Mittelalters und Bauforschung* (Rostock).

Müldner, G. and Richards, M. P. 2005. 'Fast or feast: Reconstructing diet in late medieval England by stable isotopic analysis'. *Journal of Archaeological Science* 32(1): 39–48.

Mulsow, R. 2006. 'Archäologische Nachweise zum mittelalterlichen Handwerk in Rostock'. In Gläser (ed.), 285–302.

Munro, J. 2009. 'Three centuries of luxury textile consumption in the Low Countries and England, 1330–1570: Trends and comparisons of real values of woollen broadcloths (then and now).' In Pedersen and Nosch (eds.), 1–73.

Murphy, P. 1987. 'Plant macrofossils'. In Ayers, 118–126.

———. 2009. *The English Coast: A History and a Prospect*. London

Murray, J. C. 1982. *Excavations in the Medieval Burgh of Aberdeen 1973-81*. Society of Antiquaries of Scotland, monograph series 2. Edinburgh.

Murray, H. 2010. 'The buildings'. In Perry, D *et al., Perth High Street Archaeological Excavation 1975-1977 Fascicule 1 The Excavations at 75-95 High Street and 5-10 Mill Street, Perth*, Perth, 127–198.

Mus, O. 1996. 'L'évolution de la ville d'Ypres depuis l'origine jusqu'à 1400'. In Dewilde *et al.* (eds.), 43–56.

Myrvoll, S. 1987. 'Archaeological investigations in Bergen 1980–1986: Some new aspects on the development of the town'. *Norwegian Archaeological Review* 20(2): 100–109.

———. 1981. 'Vågen and Bergen: The changing waterfront and the structure of the medieval town'. In Good *et al.*, 150–161.

Nagel, K. 2005. '"...*umme salicheit miner zele* ..."-Wallfahrten und Wallfahrtsdevotionalien in den Städten Mecklenburg-Vorpommerns'. In Jöns *et al.* (eds.), 381–384.

Naum, M. 2013. 'Premodern translocals: German merchant diaspora between Kalmar and northern German towns (1250–1550).' *International Journal of Historical Archaeology* 17(2): 376–400.

Nawrolska, G. 1999. 'Archaeological evidence for trade in Elblag from the 13th to the 17th centuries'. In Gläser (ed.), 373–385.

Neugebauer, W.1964/65. 'Der Burgwall Alt Lübeck. Geschichte, Stand und Aufgaben der Forschung'. *Offa* 21/22: 127–257.

Nilsson, T. 1976. 'Stadsbornas binäringar; jordbruk, jakt och fiske'. In Mårtensson, 223–288.

O'Brien, C. *et al.* 1988. *The Origins of Newcastle Quayside: Excavations at Queen Street and Dog Bank*. Society of Antiquaries of Newcastle-upon-Tyne Monograph Series 3.

Ohm, M. *et al.* (eds.) 2006. *Ferne Welten-Freie Stadt: Dortmund im Mittelalter*. Bielefeld.

Oksanen, E. 2012. 'Economic relations between East Anglia and Flanders in the Anglo-Norman Period'. In Bates and Liddiard (eds.), 174–187.

Olsen, O. and Crumlin-Pedersen, O. 1968. 'The Skuldelev ships (II)'. *Acta Archaeologica* (Copenhagen) 38: 73–174.

Oman, C. 1930. 'Medieval brass lecterns in England'. *Archaeological Journal* 87: 117–149.

Oosthuizen, S. 1993. 'Isleham: A medieval inland port'. *Landscape History* 15: 29–35.

———. 2012. 'Cambridgeshire and the peat fen: Medieval rural settlement and commerce, *c.* AD 900–1300'. In Christie, N. and Stamper, P. 2012, 206–224.

Ortlam, D. 1996. 'Das mittelalterliche Flusssystem der Weser im Bremer Becken. Die Balge–als Hauptstrom der Werra/Weser?' *Der Aufbau* 51: 28–32.

Ose, I. 2014. Mittelalterliche Klöster in Riga im 13.–16. Jahrhundert'. In Gläser (ed.), 509–520.

Ossowski, W. (ed.) 2014. *The Copper Ship: A Medieval Shipwreck and its Cargo*. Gdańsk.

Ossowski, W. 2014. 'The copper ship's cargo'. In Ossowski (ed.), 241–300.

Ostkamp, S. 2009. 'The world upside down. Secular badges and the iconography of the Late Medieval Period: Ordinary pins with multiple meanings'. *Journal of Archaeology in the Low Countries* 1(2): 107–125.

Øye, I. 1997. 'State, tasks and outlook for archaeology in Bergen'. In Gläser (ed.), 441–454

Øye, I. 2004. 'The infrastructure of Bergen in the Middle Ages and Early Modern Period to c. 1700'. In Gläser (ed.), 513–529

———. 2009. 'Settlement patterns and field systems in medieval Norway'. *Landscape History* 30(2): 37–54.

Palliser, D. (ed.) 2000. *The Cambridge Urban History of Britain: Volume 1, 600-1540*. Cambridge.

Parker, H. 1965. 'A medieval wharf in Thoresby College courtyard, King's Lynn'. *Medieval Archaeology* 9: 94–104.

Parker, R. 1978. *Men of Dunwich: The Story of a Vanished Town*. London.

Parker, V. 1971. *The Making of King's Lynn*. London and Chichester.

Parsons, D. (ed.) 1990. *Stone: Quarrying and Building in England AD 43–1525*. Chichester.

Pecci, A. *et al.* 2013, 'Identifying wine markers in ceramics and plasters using gas chromatography–mass spectrometry. Experimental and archaeological materials'. *Journal of Archaeological Science* 40(1): 109–115.

Pedersen, K. V. 2009. 'Archaeological Evidence of multi-coloured cloth and clothing'. In Pedersen and Nosch (eds.), 139–151.

Pedersen, K. V. and Nosch, M-L. B. (eds.) 2009. *The Medieval Broadcloth: Changing Trends in Fashions, Manufacturing and Consumption*. Oxford.

Penny-Mason, B. J. and Gowland, R. L. 2014. 'The children of the Reformation: Childhood palaeoepidemiology in Britain, AD 1000–1700'. *Medieval Archaeology* 58: 162–194.

Perbellini, G. 2000 (ed.). *The Town Walls in the Middle Ages: Les Enceintes Urbaines au Moyen Âge*. The Hague

Percival, J. W. 2004. 'An archaeological evaluation south of Read's Flour Mill'. *Norfolk Archaeological Unit Report* No. 902 (unpublished).

Perring, D. (ed.) 2002. *Town and Country in England: Frameworks for Archaeological Research*. Council for British Archaeology Research Report 134.

Perring, S. M. 2013. 'Reformation of the English cathedral landscape: Negotiating change in York Minster close *c.* 1500–1642'. *World Archaeology* 45(1): 186–205.

Perry, D. *et al.* 2010. *Perth High Street Archaeological Excavation 1975–1977: The excavations at 75–95 High Street and 5–10 Mill Street, Perth*. Perth.

Pestell, T. 2004. *Landscapes of Monastic Foundation: The Establishment of Religious Houses in East Anglia, c. 650–1200*. Woodbridge.

Phillips, D. 1985. *Excavations at York Minster Volume II*. Royal Commission on the Historical Monuments of England. London.

Pieters, M. 2006. 'The archaeology of fishery, trade and piracy: The material environment of Walraversijde and other late medieval and early modern fishing communities along the southern North Sea'. In Pieters *et al.* (eds.), 41–61.

Pieters, M. and Verhaeghe, F. 2006–2008. 'Medieval fishing communities in coastal Flanders, Belgium, and western Mediterranean commodities'. *Medieval Ceramics* 30: 103–118.

Pieters, M. *et al.* (eds.) 2006. *Fishery, Trade and Piracy: Fishermen and Fishermen's Settlements in and around the North Sea Area in the Middle Ages and Later*. Brussels.

Pirenne, H. 1952. *Medieval Cities: Their Origins and the Revival of Trade*. Princeton.

Pitte, D. and Ayers, B. (eds.) 2002. *La Maison Médiévale en Normandie et en Angleterre/The Medieval House in Normandy and England*. Rouen.

Planer, H. 2006. 'Crafts in Gdańsk from the 12th to 17th century'. In Gläser (ed.), 417–435.

Planer, H. 2012. 'Infancy and adolescence, education and recreation'. In Gläser (ed.), 321–333.

Platt, C. 1969. *The Monastic Grange in Medieval England*. London.

———. 1976. *The English Medieval Town*. London.

Platt, C. and Coleman-Smith, R. 1975. *Excavations in Medieval Southampton 1953–1969*. Leicester.

Platz, K. T. 2013. 'Ordenshaus oder Universitätsgebäude? Zur sozialen Interpretation archäologischer Befunde in Duisburg am Beispiel aktueller Grabungen in der Altstadt'. *Mitteilungen der Deutschen Gesellschaft für die Archäologie des Mittelalters und der Neuzeit* 25: 67–76.

Pluskowski, A. 2013. 'The castle and the warren: Medieval East Anglian fur culture in context'. In Bates and Liddiard (eds.), 152–173.

Polet, C. and Katzenberg, M. A. 2003. 'Reconstruction of the diet in a mediaeval monastic community from the coast of Belgium'. *Journal of Archaeological Science* 30(5): 525–533.

Pribyl, K. *et al.* 2012. 'Reconstructing medieval April-June mean temperatures in East Anglia, 1256–1431'. *Climate Change* 113: 393–412.

Price, T. D. *et al.* 2012. 'Sebbersund: isotopes and mobility in an 11th–12th c. AD Danish churchyard'. *Journal of Archaeological Science* 39(12): 3714–3720.

Priestley, U. (ed.) 1983. *Men of Property: An analysis of the Norwich enrolled deeds 1285-1311.* Norwich.

Pringle, H. 2007. 'Medieval DNA, modern medicine'. *Archaeology* 60(6): 45–49.

Quiney, A. 2003. *Town Houses of Medieval Britain.* New Haven and London.

Raemaekers, D. *et al.* (eds.) 2013. *A Bouquet of Archaeozoological Studies. Essays in Honour of Wietske Prummel.* Groningen.

Rammo, R. 2012. 'Fragments of clothing from medieval Tartu (Estonia): Archaeological sources'. In 'Medieval Urban Textiles in Northern Europe'. *Muinasaja Teadus* 22: 125–146. Tartu.

Ratilainen, T. *et al.* (eds.) 2014. *Fresh Approaches to the Brick Production and Use in the Middle Ages.* British Archaeological Reports International Series 2611.

Rawcliffe, C. 2013. *Urban Bodies: Communal Health in Late Medieval English Towns and Cities.* Woodbridge.

RCHME 1972. *An Inventory of the Historical Monuments in the City of York Volume II The Defences.* London.

Rębkowski, M. 1999. 'Archäologische Erkenntnisse zum Handel in Kohlberg (Kołobrzeg) vom 13. bis zum 15. Jahrhundert'. In Gläser (ed.), 403–414.

———. 2006. 'Remarks on handicraft in medieval Kołobrzeg'. In Gläser (ed.), 449–457.

Rech, M. 2001. 'Zum Hausbau im mittelaltlichen Bremen'. In Gläser (ed.), 377–385

———. 2004. *Gefundene Vergangenheit—Archäologie des Mittelalters in Bremen.* Bremen.

Reinders, R. 1999. 'Medieval water routes and harbour sites in the Netherlands'. In Bill and Clausen, 119–136.

Reisnert, A. 2001. 'Houses and yards in Malmö during the Medieval Period and Renaissance'. In Gläser (ed.), 677–701.

———. 2004. 'Infrastructure in Malmö during the Medieval Period and early Renaissance'. In Gläser (ed.), 465–476.

Renes, H. 2010. 'Grainlands. The landscape of open fields in a European perspective'. *Landscape History* 31(2): 37–70.

Reynolds, S. 1977. *An Introduction to the History of English Medieval Towns.* Oxford.

Rhodes, M. 182. 'A pair of fifteenth-century spectacle frames from the City of London'. *Antiquaries Journal* 62(1): 57–73.

Richards, P. 1990. *King's Lynn.* Chichester.

Riddler, I. 2006. 'Early Medieval fishing implements of bone and antler. In Pieters *et al.* (eds.), 171–180.

Rieger, D. 2010. '*platea finalis*: Forschungen zur Braunschweiger Altstadt im Mittelalter'. *Beiträge zur Archäologie in Niedersachsen* 15.

———. 2014. 'The use of early bricks in secular architecture of the 12th and early 13th century in Lübeck'. In Ratilainen *et al.* (eds.), 39–49.

Ring, E. 1999. 'Archäologische Belege für den Handel in Lüneburg'. In Gläser (ed.), 323–329.

———. 2006. 'Handwerk in Lüneburg vom Mittelalter bis zur frühen Neuzeit—der archäologische Nachweis'. In Gläser (ed.), 315–330.

———. 2011. 'Zwei Jahrzehnte Stadtarchäologie in Lüneburg–ein Rückblick'. *Denkmalplege in Lüneburg* 2011: 7–16. Lüneburg.

———. 2014. 'Klöster in Lüneburg–historische, bauhistorische und archäologische Forschungen'. In Gläser (ed.), 385–399.

Risvaag, J. A. and Christophersen, A. 2004. 'Early Medieval coinage and urban development: A Norwegian experience'. In Hines *et al.* (eds.), 75–91.

Roberts, C. A. *et al.* 2013. 'Isotopic tracing of the impact of mobility on infectious disease: The origin of people with treponematosis buried in Hull, England, in the late Medieval Period'. *American Journal of Physical Anthropology* 150: 273–285.

Roberts, J. P. (with Atkin, M.) 1982. 'St Benedict's Church'. In Carter, A. (ed.), 'Excavations in Norwich 1971–1978, Part I'. *East Anglian Archaeology* 15: 11–29.

Robinson, D. and Aaby, B. 1994. 'Pollen and plant macro fossil analyses from the Gedesby ship–a medieval shipwreck from Falster, Denmark'. *Vegetation History and Archaeobotany* 3: 167–182.

Rodwell, W. 1981. *The Archaeology of the English Church*. London.

Roesdahl, E. 192. *Viking Age Denmark*. London.

———. 2010. 'Danish sponsors, English lead, Vikings, and roof for the church of Sainte Geneviève in Paris'. In De Groote *et al.*, 285–287.

Rogers, N. 2014. 'Trading saints: Cults associated with mercantile activity'. In Barron and Sutton (eds.), 208–2220.

Rogerson, A. 1976. 'Excavations at Fuller's Hill, Great Yarmouth'. *East Anglian Archaeology* 2: 131–245.

Rogerson, A. and Ashley, S. 2003. 'Medieval seal matrices from Norfolk, 2002'. *Norfolk Archaeology* 44: 348–353.

Rolfe, M. 2013. *Conservation Report on the Terracotta Monument to Robert Jannys in the Church of St George's Colegate, Norwich*. Unpublished.

Roodenburg, H. (ed.) 2007. *Cultural Exchange in Early Modern Europe IV: Forging European Identities 1400–1700*. Cambridge.

Rose, E. 1982. 'A Linear Earthwork at Horning'. *East Anglian Archaeology* 14: 35–39.

Roslund, M. 2009. 'Transcending borders: Social identity as a factor in the Middle Ages and in Medieval archaeology'. In Engberg *et al*, 181–190.

Rosser, G. 2000. 'Urban culture and the Church 1300–1540'. In Palliser (ed.), 335–369.

Rötting, H. 2001. 'Zu Hausbau und Grundstücksbebauung in der hochmittelalterlichen Altstadt von Braunschweig'. In Gläser (ed.), 403–420.

Rutledge, E. 2002. 'The early stone house in Norwich: The documentary evidence'. In Pitte and Ayers, 100–110.

Rutledge, E. and Rutledge, P. 1982. 'King's Lynn and Great Yarmouth, two thirteenth century surveys'. *Norfolk Archaeology* 37: 92–115.

Rutledge, P. 2010. 'Great Yarmouth's settlement pattern'. *Norfolk Archaeology* 46(1): 63–70.

Rütz, T. 2005. 'Die Jakobikirche in Rostock'. In Jöns *et al.* (eds.), 375–380.

Rybina, E. A. 1992. 'Trade links of Novgorod established through archaeological data'. In Brisbane (ed.), 193–205.

Ryckaert, M. 2002, 'Geography and Genesis'. In Vermeersch, V. (ed.), 58–61.

Sarfatij, H. 1981. 'Dordrecht: The late medieval waterfront at the Poortzijde'. In Milne and Hobley (eds.), 77–79.

Sarfatij, H. 1990. *Verborgen Steden: Statsarcheologie in Nederland*. Amsterdam.

Sarfatij, H. 1997. 'Vier Städte in einem Projekt. Das Forschungsprojekt "Urbanisierung im Flußgebiet während des Mittelalters" (Niederlande)'. In Gläser (ed.), 111–121.

Sarfatij, H. 1999. 'Tiel und Dordrecht. Archäologie und Handel in zwei Städten im niederländischen Rheingebiet (10. bis 17. Jahrhundert)'. In Gläser (ed.), 183–200.

Sarfatij *et al.* (eds.) 1999. *In Discussion with the Past: Archaeological studies presented to W. A. van Es*. Amersfoort.

Saunders, A. D. 1985. 'The Cow Tower, Norwich: An East Anglian Bastille?'. *Medieval Archaeology* 29: 109–119.

Sawyer, B. and Sawyer, P. 1993. *Medieval Scandinavia*. Minneapolis and London.

Schäfer, H. 2004. 'Öffentliche Bautätigkeiten und Einrichtungen in Greifswald unter besonderer Berücksichtigung der archäologischen Quellen des 13. bis 15. Jahrhunderts'. In Gläser (ed.), 263–274.

Schalies, I. 2012. 'Gebäude und topographische Strukturen im hoch- und spätmittelalterlichen Lübeck Ergebnisse stadtarchäologischer Untersuchungen'. *Mitteilungen der Deutschen Gesellschaft für Archäologie des Mittelalters und der Neuzeit* 24: 111–122.

Schietecatte, L. and Sealy, J. 2006. 'Fish in a medieval fishing village along the North Sea: What do the isotopes say?' In Pieters *et al.* (eds.), 63–80.

Schietzel, K. 2014. *Spurensuche Haithabu: Dokumentation und Chronik 1963–2013*. Neumünster/Hamburg.

Schlauch, M. 1957. 'A sixteenth-century English satirical tale about Gdańsk'. *Kwartalnik Neofilologiczny* 4: 95–120.

Schneider, M. 2014. 'Archäologie in monastischen Einrichtungen der Hansestadt Lübeck'. In Gläser (ed.), 401–428.

Schofield, J. 1981. 'Medieval waterfront buildings in the City of London'. In Milne and Hobley (eds.), 24–31.

———. 1984. *The Building of London from the Conquest to the Great Fire*. London.

———. 1994. *Medieval London Houses*. New Haven and London.

———. 2011. *London 1100–1600: The Archaeology of a Capital City*. Sheffield.

Schofield, J. and Steuer, H. 2007. 'Urban settlement'. In Graham-Campbell and Valor (eds.), 111–153.

Schofield, J. and Vince, A. 2003. *Medieval Towns* (revised edition). London.

Schreg, R. 2014. 'Ecological approaches in medieval rural archaeology'. *European Journal of Archaeology* 17(1): 83–119.

Schuenemann, V. J. *et al.* 2011. 'Targeted enrichment of ancient pathogens yielding the pPCP1 plasmid of *Yersinia pestis* from victims of the Black Death'. *Proceedings of the National Academy of Sciences of the United States of America* 108.38, E746–E752.

Schweitzer, C. and Frey, C. 2013. 'Bischof Bernward von Hildesheims Burg in Wahrenholz'. *Archäologie in Niedersachsen* 16: 92–94.

Sekules, V.1996. 'The Gothic sculpture'. In Atherton *et al.*, 197–209.

Shapland, M. 2013. *Buildings of Secular and Religious Lordship: Anglo-Saxon Tower-Nave Churches*. Unpublished Ph D. thesis, University College London.

Shelley A. 2005. 'Dragon Hall, King Street, Norwich: Excavation and Survey of a Late Medieval Merchant's Trading Complex'. *East Anglian Archaeology* 112.

Shepherd Popescu, E. (ed.) 2009. 'Norwich Castle: Excavations and Historical Survey, 1987–98 Part I: Anglo-Saxon to c. 1345'. *East Anglian Archaeology* 132.

Shiels, J. and Campbell, S. 2011. 'Sacred and banal: The discovery of everyday material culture'. In Cowan and Henderson, 67–88.

Sicking, L. and Abreu-Ferreira, D. (eds.) 2009. *Beyond the Catch: Fisheries of the North Atlantic, the North Sea and the Baltic 900–1850*. Leiden.

Siegmüller, A. 2010a. *Die Ausgrabungen auf der frühmittelalterlichen Wurt Hessens in Wilhelmshaven: Siedlungs- und Wirtschaftsweise in der Marsch*. Rahden.

———. 2010b. 'Waschtag vor der Wollernte: Eine frühmittelalterliche Anlage zur Schafwäsche auf der Wurt Hessens'. *Archäologie in Niedersachsen* 13: 67–70.

Silvester , R. J. 1985. 'West Walton: The Development of a Siltland Parish'. *Norfolk Archaeology* 39: 101–117.

———. 1988. 'The Fenland Project Number 3: Marshland and the Nar Valley, Norfolk'. *East Anglian Archaeology* 45.

———. 1991. 'The Fenland Project Number 4: The Wissey Embayment and the Fen Causeway, Norfolk'. *East Anglian Archaeology* 52.

Simons, W. 2001. *Cities of Ladies: Beguine Communities in the Medieval Low Countries, 1200–1565*. Philadelphia.

Simpson, G. 2008. 'The pine standard chest in St Margaret's Church, King's Lynn, and the social and economic significance of the type'. In McNeill (ed.), 53–65.

Sindbæk, S. M. 2011. 'Trade and exchange. Part 2: Northern Europe'. In Graham-Campbell and Valor 2011, 302–312

———. 2012. 'Viking disruptions or growing integration? Contextualising communication networks in the 10th century North Sea'. In Kleingärtner and Zeilinger (eds.), 19–38

Skov, H. 2001. 'House types in Aarhus, Denmark, *c.* 900–1600 AD'. In Gläser (ed.), 819–832.

———. 2004. 'The infrastructure in Aarhus between 900 and 1600 AD'. In Gläser (ed.), 551–566.

———. 2012. 'Infancy and adolescence, education and recreation in Aarhus from 800 to 1700'. In Gläser (ed.), 591–603.

Slater, T. R. 1985. *'Medieval New Town and Port: A Plan-Analysis of Hedon, East Yorkshire'.* Yorkshire Archaeological Journal 57: 23–41.

Slater, T. R. (ed.). 2000. *Towns in Decline AD100–1600*. Aldershot.

Slater, T. R. and Higgins, J. P. P. 2000.'What is urban decline: Desolation, decay and destruction, or an opportunity?'. In Slater (ed.), 1–22.

Slavin, P. 2012. *Bread and Ale for the Brethren: The Provisioning of Norwich Cathedral Priory 1260–1536*. Hertfordshire.

Slive, S. 2005. *Jacob van Ruisdael: Master of Landscape*. London.

Smith, A. H. 1937. 'The place-names of the East Riding of Yorkshire and York'. *English Place-Name Society*, vol XIV.

Smith, R. and Carter, A. 1983. 'Function and site: Aspects of Norwich buildings before 1700'. *Vernacular Architecture* 14: 5–18.

Smith, S. V. 2014. 'The spaces of Late Medieval peasant childhood: Children and social reproduction'. In Hadley and Hemer (eds.), 57–74.

Smith, T. P. and Watson, B. 2014. 'Suffolk Place, Southwark, London: A Tudor palace and its terracotta architectural decoration'. *Post-Medieval Archaeology* 48(1): 90–132.

Soens, T. 2013. 'Flood security in the Medieval and Modern North Sea Area: A question of entitlement?'. *Environment and History* 19: 209–232.

Søvsø, M. 2014. 'The monastic institutions of Ribe'. In Gläser (ed.), 717–734.

Spencer, B. 1992. 'Objects of lead alloy'. In Evans and Tomlinson (eds.), 143–147.

Spitzers, T. 2001. 'Archaeological data on domestic architecture in Deventer from the 9th to the 15th Centuries'. In Gläser (ed.), 197–211.

———. 2004. 'Archaeological evidence and models on waste-disposal and the infrastructure of Deventer'. In Gläser (ed.), 117–136.

Spoerry, P. 2005. 'Town and country in the Medieval Fenland'. In Giles and Dyer (eds.), 85–110.

———. 2008. 'Ely Wares'. *East Anglian Archaeology* 122.

Spoerry, P. *et al.* 2008. 'Ramsey Abbey, Cambridgeshire: Excavations at the site of a fenland monastery'. *Medieval Archaeology* 52: 171–210.

Spooner, J. 2008. 'The fourteenth-century wall-paintings at Castle Acre Priory and Greyfriars, Great Yarmouth'. In McNeill (ed.), 170–185.

Spufford, P. 1963. 'Continental coins in late medieval England'. *British Numismatic Journal* 32: 127–139.

———. 2002. *Power and Profit: The Merchant in Medieval Europe*. London.

Staaf, B. M. 2014. 'Monasteries, convents and nunneries in medieval Lund'. In Gläser (ed.), 559–572.

Staecker, J. 2003. 'A Protestant *Habitus*: 16th-century Danish graveslabs as an expression of changes in belief'. In Gaimster and Gilchrist (eds.), 415–436.

Stamper, P. 2013. 'Review of Gilchrist, R. *Medieval Life: Archaeology and the Life Course.*' In *British Archaeology* (March/April 2013), 56.

Starkey, D. J. and Hahn-Pedersen, M. (eds.) 2002. *Concentration and Dependency. The Role of Maritime Activities in North Sea Communities, 1299-1999*. Esbjerg

Steane, J. M. 1985. *The Archaeology of Medieval England and Wales*. London.

———. 2001. *The Archaeology of Power*. Stroud.

Steedman, K. *et al.* 1992. *Aspects of Saxo-Norman London III: The Bridgehead and Billingsgate to 1200*. London & Middlesex Archaeological Society Special Paper 14

Stirland, A 1985. 'The human bones'. In Ayers, 49–57

———. 2009. 'Criminals and Paupers: The Graveyard of St Margaret in combusto Fybriggate, Norwich'. *East Anglian Archaeology* 129.

Stocker, D. 1991. 'St Mary's Guildhall, Lincoln: The survey and excavation of a Medieval building complex'. *The Archaeology of Lincoln, XII-1*. Council for British Archaeology.

Stocker, D. 2012. 'A new understanding of the church fabric'. In Wrathmell (ed.), 240–262.

Stocker, D. and Dixon, P. forthcoming. *Lincoln before St Hugh*.

Stocker, D. and Everson, P. 1990. 'Rubbish recycled: A study of the re-use of stone in Lincolnshire'. In Parsons (ed.), 101.

———. 2006. *Summoning St Michael: Early Romanesque Towers in Lincolnshire*. Oxford.

———. 2009. 'The Witham Valley: A landscape with monasteries?'. *Church Archaeology* 13: 1–15.

Stocker, D. and Vince, A. 1997. 'The early Norman castle at Lincoln and a re-evaluation of the original west tower of Lincoln Cathedral'. *Medieval Archaeology* 41: 223–233.

Stoepker, H. 1990. 'Church archaeology in the Netherlands. Problems, prospects, proposals'. In Besteman *et al.* (eds.), 199–218.

Stones, J. A. (ed.) 1989. *Three Scottish Carmelite Friaries: Excavations at Aberdeen, Linlithgow and Perth 1980-1986*. Society of Antiquaries of Scotland Monograph Series 6.

Sutermeister, H. 2002. 'The documentary evidence'. In Atkin and Evans (eds.), 133–134.

Sutton, A. 1989. 'The early linen and worsted industry of Norfolk and the evolution of the London Mercers' Company. *Norfolk Archaeology* 40: 201–225.

Svart Kristiansen, M. and Giles, K. (eds.) 2014. *Dwellings, Identities and Homes: European Housing Culture from the Viking Age to the Renaissance*. Jutland Archaeological Society 14, Højbjerg.

Svensson, E. *et al.* 2008. 'Medieval rural archaeology in Sweden: An introduction to the field and presentation of two recently excavated sites'. *Medieval Settlement Research Group* 23: 69–74.

Tait, J. 1936. *The Medieval English Borough*. Manchester.

Tanner, N. P. 1984. *The Church in Late Medieval Norwich 1370 - 1532*. Toronto.

Taylor, D. 2010. 'The early west front of Lincoln Cathedral'. *Archaeological Journal* 167: 134–164.

Tesch, S. 2001. 'Houses, town yards, and town planning in Late Viking Age and Medieval Sigtuna, Sweden'. In Gläser (ed.), 723–741.

Teuber, S. 2006. '"...9 mark vor 1 vath Embekesch bers"'. *Archäologie in Niedersachsen* 9: 53–58.

Thaastrup-Leth, A. K. 2014. 'Burned-down timber-framed houses in medieval Odense, Denmark'. In Kristiansen and Giles (eds.), 223–230.

Thiemann, B. 2001. 'Bauformen des Hochmittelalters in Soest'. In Gläser (ed.), 455–472.

Thijssen, J.R.A.M. 1999. 'Begijnhuizen op de Hessenberg te Nijmegen. Ontwikkelingen aan de rand van de middeleeuwse stad'. *Rotterdam Papers* 10: 181–187.

Thomasson, J. 1997. 'Private life made public: One aspect of the emergence of burghers in medieval Denmark'. In Andersson *et al.* (eds.), 697–728.

———. 2004a. 'A feudal way to gentrify? The modern concept of gentrification versus changes in the social topography of a medieval and early modern town'. *Current Swedish Archaeology* 12: 187–210.

Thomasson, J. 2004b. 'Out of the past. The biography of a 16th-century burgher house and the making of society'. *Archaeological Dialogues* 11(2): 165–189.

Tittler, R. 2007. *The face of the city: Civic portraiture and civic identity in early modern England*. Manchester.

Toman, R. (ed.) 1999. *The Art of Gothic*. Cologne.

Töpf, A. 2009. 'DNA Analysis'. In Shepherd Popescu (ed.), 248–253.

Töpf, A. L. and Hoelzel, A. R. 2005. 'A Romani mitochondrial haplotype in England 500 years before their recorded arrival in Britain'. *Biological Letters* 1: 280–282

Trimpe Berger, J. A. 1973. 'Oost-Souburg, Province of Zeeland: A preliminary report on the excavation of the site of an ancient fortress (1969–1971). *Berichten Rijksdienst voor het Oudheidkundig Bodemonderzoek* 23: 355–365.

Tschan F. J. (trans.) 2002. *History of the Archbishops of Hamburg-Bremen: Adam of Bremen*. New York.

Turner, Sara A. 2013. 'Dietary reconstruction in medieval Holbæk, Denmark using dental microwear and macrowear, isotopic analyses, and dental caries'. *Thesis, Georgia State University*. http://scholarworks.gsu.edu/anthro_theses/74.

Tvauri, A. 2009. 'Late medieval hypocausts with heat storage in Estonia'. *Baltic Journal of Art History*, 49–78.

Tys, D. 1997. 'Landscape and settlement: The development of a medieval village along the Flemish coast'. *Rural Settlements in Medieval Europe-Papers of the 'Medieval Europe Brugge 1997' Conference*, vol. 6, 157–167.

———. 2006. 'Walraversijde, another kettle of fish? Dynamics and identity of a late medieval coastal settlement in a proto-capitalistic landscape'. In Pieters *et al.* (eds.), 19–40.

———. 2010. 'Medieval moated sites in coastal Flanders: the impact of social groups on the formation of the landscape in relation to the early estates of the Count of Flanders'. In de Groote *et al.* (eds.), 289–301.

Ufkes, A. *et al.* 1999. 'Een archeologisch onderzoek aan de Eewal te Leeuwarden'. *ARC-Publicaties* 27. Groningen.

Unger, R. W. (ed.) 1980. *The Ship in the Medieval Economy 600-1600*. London and Montreal.

Unger, R. W. 2002. 'Beer: A new bulk good of international trade'. In Berggren *et al.*, 113-127.

Van Cruyningen, P. and Thoen, E. (eds.) 2012. *Food Supply, Demand and Trade: Aspects of the Economic Relationship Between Town and Countryside (Middle Ages-19th century)*. Turnhout.

Van Damm, P. J. E. M. 2001. 'Sinking peat bogs: Environmental change in Holland, 1350–1550'. *Environmental History* 6(1): 32–45.

Van der Linden, H. 1955. *De cope: bijdrage tot de rechtsgeschiedenis van de openlegging der Hollands- Utrechtse laagvlakte*. Assen

Van de Noort, R. 2011. *North Sea Archaeologies: A Maritime Biography, 10,000 BC–AD 1500*. Oxford.

Van de Noort, R. and Ellis, S. (eds.) 2000. *Wetland Heritage of the Hull Valley: An Archaeological Survey*. Hull.

Van de Waard, F. 1999. 'Kelders in Groningen'. *Rotterdam Papers* 10: 229–248.

Vandewalle, A. 2002. *Bruges, Crossroads of European Cultures*. Brugge.

Van Es, W. A. and Verwers, W. J. H. 1980. *Excavations at Dorestad*. Amersfoort.

Van Eenhooge, D. 2001. 'The archaeological study of buildings and town history in Bruges: Domestic architecture in the period 1200–1350'. In Gläser (ed.), 121–141.

Van Marrewijk, D. *et al.* 2001. *Waddenland: Het landschap en cultureel erfgoed in de Waddenzeeregio*. Leeuwarden.

Van Neer, W. and Ervynck, A. 2006. 'The zoological reconstruction of the development of the exploitation of the sea: A *statis quaestionis* for Flanders'. In Pieters *et al.* (eds.), 95–103.

Van Roooijen, C. and Hoekstra, T. 1996. In De Biève (ed.), Utrecht between Pleshey Castle (Essex) and the Hasker Convent (Friesland): The origin and distribution of late thirteenth- and early fourteenth-century decorated floor tiles in the Netherlands', 209–215.

Various 1969–2007. *Berichte über die* Ausgrabungen *in Haithabu*. Neumünster.

Various 1981–1990. *Ribe Excavations 1970-1976*. Esbjerg.

Various 1985 onward. *The Bryggen Papers*. Bergen

Veeckman, J. 1999. 'Trade in Antwerp from the 12th to the 17th centuries: Archaeological data in a historical context'. In Gläser (ed.), 123–137.

———. 2001. 'Domestic Architecture in high and late medieval Antwerp (Belgium)'. In Gläser (ed.), 143–157.

———. 2010. 'Sherds from a church. Majolica production waste from the Augustinian friary in Antwerp'. In De Groot *et al.* (eds.), 177–188.

Verhaeghe, F. 1997. 'The archaeology of transition: A continental view'. In Gaimster and Stamper (eds.), 25–44.

———. 1999. 'Trade in ceramics in the North Sea region, 12th to 15th centuries: A methodological problem and a few pointers'. In Gläser (ed.), 139–167.

Verhoeven, A. 1990. 'Ceramic and economics in the Low Countries AD 1000–1300'. In Besteman *et al.* (eds.), 265–281.

Verhulst, A. 1996. 'Sheep-breeding and wool production in pre-thirteenth century Flanders and their contribution to the rise of Ypres, Ghent and Bruges as centres of the textile industry'. In Dewilde *et al.* (eds.), 33–42.

Verhulst, A. 1999. *The Rise of Cities in North-West Europe*. Cambridge.

Vermeersch, V. (ed.) 2002, *Bruges*. Antwerp

Vermeulen, B. and Mittendorff, E. 2014. 'Convents and houses of the Devotio Moderna in Deventer'. In Gläser (ed.), 133–147.

Verweij, J. *et al.* 2012. 'Continuity and change in Dutch shipbuilding in the early modern period. The case of VAL7 and the watership in general'. *Journal of Archaeology in the Low Countries* 4(1): 65–93.

Viklund, K. 2007. 'Sweden and the Hanse–archaeobotanical aspects of changes in farming, gardening and dietary habits in medieval times in Sweden'. In Karg (ed.), 119–135.

Vince, A. 1990. *Saxon London: An Archaeological Investigation*. London.

———. 2002. 'The use of pottery to chart trade routes in the North Sea and Baltic Sea areas'. In Berggren *et al.* (eds.), 128–142.

Von Arbin, S. 2009. 'A 15th-century bulk carrier, wrecked off Skaftö western Sweden. In Günsenin (ed.), 67–74.

Von Brandt, A. 1970. *Netzwerk aus Haithabu, Ausgrabungen in Haithabu, 4: Das Archäologische Fundmaterial, I (1963-1964)*. Neumünster, 69–73.

Vos, P. C. and Gerrets, D. A. 2005. 'Archaeology: A major tool in the reconstruction of the coastal evolution of Westergo (northern Netherlands)'. *Quaternary International* 133/134: 61–75.

Wade, K. 1993. 'The urbanisation of East Anglia: The Ipswich perspective'. In Gardiner (ed.), 144–151.

Wade-Martins, P. 1980. 'Village Sites in Launditch Hundred'. *East Anglian Archaeology* 10.

Waites, B. 1980. 'Monasteries and the wool trade in North and East Yorkshire during the 13th and 14th Centuries'. *Yorkshire Archaeological Journal* 52: 111–121.

Walker, H. 2012. 'Hedingham Ware: A Medieval Pottery Industry in North Essex; Its Production and Distribution'. *East Anglian Archaeology* 148.

Wallis, H. 2009. 'Excavations at Cinema City, Norwich, 2003–06: Late Saxon and Medieval Occupation', *Norfolk Archaeology* 45, 478-82.

Walton, P. 1991. 'Textiles'. In Blair and Ramsay (eds.), 319–354.

Walton Rogers, P. unpublished. 'Textiles, Cordage and Hair from Spurriergate, York,YORYM 2000.548'. TRA Report to MAP Archaeological Consultancy, 12 June 2006

Watson, B. *et al.* 2001. *London Bridge: 2000 Years of a River Crossing*. Museum of London Archaeology Service Monograph 8.

Webb, J. 1962. *Great Tooley of Ipswich*. Suffolk Records Society.

Wellbrock, K. 2009. 'Wasserwirtschaftliche Untersuchungen an der historischen Stecknitzfahrt. Nachweis einer Kammerschleuse für das Ende des 14. Jh. anhand eines dynamischen Abflussmodells'. *Schriften der Deutschen Wasserhistorischen Gesellschaft* 13: 197–259.

White, W. 1988. *Skeletal Remains from the Cemetery of St Nicholas Shambles*. London and Middlesex Archaeological Society Special Paper 9.

Whittingham, A. B. 1984. The White Swan Inn, St Peter's Street, Norwich'. *Norfolk Archaeology* 39(1): 38–50.

Wickham, C. 2005. *Framing the Middle Ages*. Oxford.

Widerström, P. 2014. ''Monasteries and friaries in Visby'. In Gläser (ed.), 595–611.

Willemsen, A. 2012. ''Man is a sack of muck girded with silver': Metal decoration on Late-medieval leather belts and purses from the Netherlands'. *Medieval Archaeology* 56: 171–202.

———. 2015. 'The Geoff Egan Memorial Lecture 2013. Taking up the glove: finds, uses and meanings of gloves, mittens and gauntlets in western Europe, *c.* AD 1300–1700'. *Post-Medieval Archaeology* 49(1): 1–36.

Williamson, T. 2003. *Shaping Medieval Landscapes: Settlement, Society, Environment*. Macclesfield.

———. 2012. *Environment, Society and Landscape in Early Medieval England*. Woodbridge.

———. 2013. 'East Anglia's character and the 'North Sea World''. In Bates and Liddiard (eds.) 2013, 44–62.

Windeatt, B. (trans.) 1985. *The Book of Margery Kempe*. Harmondsworth.

Wood, T. 1845. *Tidal Harbours Commission*. Hull.

Wrathmell, S. (ed.) 2012. *A History of Wharram Percy and its Neighbours*. York University Archaeological Publications 15.

Wubs-Mrozewicz, J. 2013. 'The Hanse in medieval and early modern Europe: An introduction'. In Wubs-Mrozewicz, J. and Jenks, S. (eds.), *The Hanse and Late Medieval Europe*. Leiden/Boston, 1–35

Yoder, C. 2010. 'Diet in medieval Denmark: A regional and temporal comparison'. *Journal of Archaeological Science* 37(9): 2224–2236.

Young, G. A. B. 1987. 'Excavations at Southgate, Hartlepool, Cleveland, 1981–82. *Durham Archaeological Journal* 3: 15–55.

Zeune, J. 2000. 'German town walls: Functionalism and symbolism'. In Perbellini, G. (ed.), 39–42.

Zwick, D. 2010. 'Neues vom 'Beluga Schiff'-ein Bremer Klinkerwrack aus dem 15. Jahrhundert'. *Nachrichtenblatt Arbeitskreis Unterwasserarchä*ologie 16: 62-71.

Zwick, D. 2012. 'Variationen in der mittelaltlichen Schiffbautechnik anhand von Wrackfunden in Bremen'. *Mitteilungen der Deutschen Gesellschaft für Archäologie des Mittelalters und der Neuzeit* 24: 283–298.

Subject Index

Numbers in *italic* denote pages with illustrations.

Placename Index

Places shown on the maps on pages xviii - xx are in **bold** font.

Numbers in *italic* denote pages with illustrations.

Þingeyrar in Iceland is filed as Thingeyrar.

C

H

M

www.ingramcontent.com/pod-product-compliance
Ingram Content Group UK Ltd.
Pitfield, Milton Keynes, MK11 3LW, UK
UKHW061957041026
15591UKWH00016B/1051

9 781781 797228